Advances in Spatial Science

Titles in the Series

Börje Johansson · Charlie Karlsson
Roger Stough (Editors)

The Emerging Digital Economy

Entrepreneurship, Clusters, and Policy

With 36 Figures
and 41 Tables

 Springer

Professor Börje Johansson
Professor Charlie Karlsson

Jonkoping International Business School
P. O. Box 1026
551 11 Jonkoping
Sweden

borje.johansson@ihh.hj.se
charlie.karlsson@jibs.hj.se

Professor Roger Stough

George Mason University
School of Public Policy
4400 University Dr.
MS 2C9
Fairfax, VA 22030
USA
rstough@gmu.edu

Cataloging-in-Publication Data
Library of Congress Control Number: 2006928860

ISBN-10 3-540-34487-X   Springer Berlin Heidelberg New York
ISBN-13 978-3-540-34487-2   Springer Berlin Heidelberg New York

Springer is a part of Springer Science+Business Media
springeronline.com

© Springer-Verlag Berlin Heidelberg 2006
Printed in Germany

Cover design: Erich Kirchner

SPIN 11753230   Printed on acid-free paper – 88/3153 – 5 4 3 2 1 0

Acknowledgements

The editors thank Ms. Emilia Istrate, George Mason University, for her long an laborious effort to work with the publisher to ensure that almost all if not all wordings, footnotes, references, and typos were eliminated in this final version. Further, she questioned us over and over on the content of various figures and charts and also on construction of various parts of the prose. In short, she is due considerable recognition for working to provide a clean manuscript. Ms. Irene Johansson, University West, Sweden collected and ensured all manuscripts were in reasonable shape for a formal peer review. She worked with the authors to obtain first and second drafts so that an initial review could be performed. Others not mentioned here are due considerable thanks for the support they provided during and before the conference that produced the chapters of this book.

Preface

The contributions forming the different chapters in this book were first presented and discussed at the fifth Uddevalla Symposium which was held in June 2002 at Uddevalla, Sweden. The symposium's theme was "Innovation, Entrepreneurship, Regional Development and Public Policy in the Emerging Digital Economy" and the chapters forming this book were selected from the papers presented at this symposium. All chapters have been peer refereed and refined after the symposium.

The University West (former the University of Trollhättan/Uddevalla), Department of Economics and Informatics arranged the symposium in co-operation with Jönköping International Business School, Sweden and the School of Public Policy at George Mason University, USA. The University West hosted the symposium.

The symposium was in part sponsored by the municipality of Uddevalla, Sweden and the European Union Interreg IIIA Sweden-Norway program. We thank them for their generous sponsorship. Financial support by VINNOVA – The Swedish Agency for Innovation Systems – is also acknowledged.

Jönköping, Sweden and Fairfax, VA, USA
March, 2006

Börje Johansson
Jönköping International
Business School
Professor of Economics

Charlie Karlsson
Jönköping International
Business School
Professor of Economics

Roger R Stough
George Mason University
NOVA Endowed Chair and
Professor of Public Policy

Contents

1 Entrepreneurship, Clusters and Policy in the Emerging Digital Economy

Börje Johansson[1], Charlie Karlsson[1], and Roger R. Stough[2]

[1] Jönköping International Business School, Jönköping University
[2] School of Public Policy, George Mason University

1.1 Introduction

The rapid developments in information and communication technologies (ICTs) and the increased use of ICTs motivate the vision of an evolving digital economy. ICTs are composed of a wide range of product and service technologies including computer hardware, software and services and a host of telecommunications functions that include wire or wireline, and wireless, satellite products and services. The rapid diffusion of ICTs has produced important changes in how goods and services are produced, the nature of the goods and services produced, and the means by which goods and services are brought to the market and distributed to customers. During the last decade this evolving digital economy has been the pre-eminent driver of structural change and economic growth at both the national and the regional level in the developed, industrialised economies. However, there are substantial differences among countries and regions as regards their role in the development of ICTs and their propensity to adopt and apply ICTs applications in various sectors and activities. Hence, countries and regions differ markedly in how far they have come on the road to the digital economy.

The emerging digital economy has attracted much interest in recent years and various authors have used different concepts to characterise the new developments. Besides the digital economy we also find in the literature concepts such as e-economy (Cohen et al. 2000) and information economy[1]. In the more popular debate it also has been nicknamed "the new economy" (Castells 1996, p.66). The unexpected economic strength of in particular the US economy in the late 1990s stimulated much discussion about the 'new economy', and what the emergence of

---

[1] The "information economy" is defined as an economy in which information assets play a major role in the economy, and a large share of the labour force is employed in ICT based occupations (Cohen et al. 2002). The ICT driven developments in recent decades have also been labelled as the "information revolution" or the "information age" (Castells 1996; Friedrichs 1989).

a 'new economy' implied for the sustainability of the economic expansion in future years. According to Weinstein (1997) the 'new economy' has the following attributes:

- An economy that grows without apparent threat of recession.
- An economy that continues to expand without a pickup in inflation.
- An economy constantly restructuring itself for greater efficiency and productivity.
- An economy replenishing and revitalizing itself through new technology and capital investment.
- An economy that functions without excessive debt, either public or private.
- An economy that maintains a balanced budget.
- An economy that is increasingly globalized and export driven.

It was even assumed that with good macroeconomic management, the 'new economy' could grow virtually without interruption for the foreseeable future (Weinstein 1997). It is important to stress that the 'new economy' discussion has been inconclusive, partly because the term 'new economy' means different things to different people. Some definitions of the 'new economy' embrace a very broad notion, which in principle implies that the fundamental economic concepts that guided economic policy in the past have become irrelevant in an age of global competition and rapid technological change. Others have a more narrow focus stressing the role of ICTs in acceleration of the economy's trend in rate of output and productivity growth.

It is important to stress that not all economists sang the 'new economy' song. Krugman (1997) accused the 'new economy' advocates for a lack of historical perspective. Also the media contained warnings. Shepard (1997, p. 38) explained, for example, what the 'new economy is not': "It does not mean that inflation is dead. It does not mean we'll never have another recession or that the business cycle is extinct. It does not mean the stock market is destined to … rise forever, …" Stiroh (1999) pointed out that current evidence suggests that it was still too early to tell if a 'new economy' had truly emerged in the US.

The positive expectations in the late 1990s about what the 'new economy' would bring resembles very much what was taught at universities in the 1960s during the heyday of Keynesian economics. At that time students learned that business cycles could be relegated to economic history since politicians with the help of economists know how to fine-tune the economy.

Today in the year 2006 we know that the thoughts expressed in the late 1990s were as wrong as those of the 1960s. However, even if the 'new economy' did not fulfil all its promises, the developed economies are still following a road that will lead to the establishment of what rightfully should be termed a digital economy (cf. Brynjolfsson and Kahin 2000). We argue that the concept 'new economy' should be used as a rather broad concept including, not only the emerging digital economy, but also the deregulation, the globalisation, etc. of economies that have taken place in recent decades. We claim in this connection that the term 'new economy' is too broad and can carry (and has carried) anything anybody wants to put into it[2].

We use the term 'digital economy' referring specifically to the recent and still largely unrealised transformation of all sectors of the economy by the general spread of ICTs. It must be admitted that there exists no clear and unambiguous agreement on the definition of ICTs or what sectors should be termed ICT sectors, which has been generally accepted (Schwartz 1990; Malecki 1991; Graham and Marvin 1996). At face value, ICTs are a collection of technologies and applications, which enable electronic processing, storing, retrieval, and transfer of data to a wide variety of users or clients. ICTs are currently characterised by (Cohen et al. 2002):

- very dynamic technological changes, with rapid penetration and adoption rates,
- decreasing costs for new equipment and features;
- a rapidly increasing range of applications and penetration in many realms of professional and personal life;
- an intertwined institutional market place, with the private sector acting in a decreasingly regulated environment;
- a production and services package dependent on a range of qualities of skilled human resources, and
- a convergence of technologies.

In our view, the emerging digital economy is driven by the development and diffusion of modern ICTs. In its broadest conceptualisation this emergence of a digital economy can be viewed as an evolutionary process whereby the economy and all its sectors are being transformed by the rapid development, adoption and use of ICTs innovations. In this respect ICTs functions as a new generic general-purpose technology, which impacts society both broadly and deeply by giving rise to a wide array of new products, production processes and services (Bryjolfsson and Kahin 2000; Mowery and Simcoe 2002). Carlsson (2003) takes this idea one step further arguing that ICTs, which involve among other things a combination of digitalisation and the Internet, seem to have much broader applicability than previous general-purpose technologies. It not only affects all manufacturing industries but also, and even more so, all different service industries which account for an increasing and dominating share of the economy in developed economies. Furthermore, it has given rise to new industries within both the manufacturing sector and the service sector. However, one should observe that it is a common feature of new general-purpose technologies that it takes a long time before they are implemented (including organisational changes) and used in such a way that they could develop their abilities to the fullest (David 1991).

It is unquestionable that the effects of the development, spread and use of ICTs go much further than changing the industrial composition of industrialised economies. ICTs are playing an increasing role in economic growth, capital investments

---

[2] One interesting exception is the rather narrow definition of the new economy provided by New Economy Handbook (Jones 2003), relatively close to our conceptualisation of the new economy.

and other aspects of the macro-economy (Brynjolfsson and Kahin 2000). The emergence of new goods and services as well as changes in the characteristics of old goods and services due to ICTs, including the ways goods and services are distributed lead to changes in market structures and competitive conditions affecting not least entrepreneurs and SMEs. The adoption of ICTs allows for a reduction of transaction costs and leads possibly to more efficient markets (Malone et al.1987; Lee and Clark 1997). In addition the digital economy is changing the labour market by generating new ICTs occupations and at the same time changing the skill requirements for non-ICT jobs. Due to the structural changes generated by ICTs employment has been increasing in some sectors, while declining in others. As ICTs are routinely deployed in organisations to re-engineer processes, gain new strategic advantages, or network across organisational boundaries it changes both the internal organisation of organisations and the relationships between co-operating organisations (OECD 2002).

At the same time as we can observe that ICTs are stimulating the birth of new goods and services, new industries, new occupations, etc. we can also observe tendencies of technology-related industry convergence (Dosi 1988; Rosenberg 1963; Sahal 1985) in the emerging digital economy. There are today numerous claims that industries like telecommunications, computing and entertainment are converging and one day might evolve into one huge multimedia industry (Collis et al. 1997; The Economist 2000). This convergence of the telecommunications, media and information technology sectors might even have been increasing in recent years with the emergence of the Internet and with the increasing capability of existing networks to carry both telecommunications and broadcasting services (Knieps 2003). Developments in digital technologies and software are creating large innovative technological potential for the production, distribution and consumption of information services. Convergence, characterised as the ability of different network platforms to carry essentially similar kinds of services, may have very different faces: telecommunications operators may offer audio-visual programming over their networks; broadcasters may provide data services over their networks, cable operators may provide a range of telecommunication services, etc.

The Internet as the prime driver of convergence is integrating traditional isolated computer networks; it is providing an alternative means of offering telecommunication services (e.g. Internet telephony) and it is also becoming a significant instrument for broadcasting services. Moreover, technological convergence makes possible innovative services, which combine product characteristics from the traditionally distinct branches of telecommunications, information technology and the media, thereby enlarging the scope of voice, data, multimedia and audio-visual services. Not least is the mobile phone in focus as a receiver of many of these innovative services. However, as Stieglitz (2003) remarks there are different types of industry convergence, which have to be distinguished because they differ in their underlying patterns of industry dynamics. One important reason for such differences is that government intervention and regulation has very different traditions in the media, the information technology and telecommunications sectors as well as in different counties. The media industry has traditionally been attributed a function as the bearer of social, cultural and ethical values within society.

Whereas, for example, newspapers have been mainly unregulated in democratic countries, radio and TV broadcasting has been traditionally regulated to some extent and in several countries for considerable time been national monopolies. In a similar manner the telecommunications sector has been a national monopoly in many countries. The computer and information technology sector, on the other hand, developed in an unregulated manner under general competition laws. Naturally, these differences in legal frameworks have influenced the various patterns of industry dynamics as well the general convergence patterns. In recent decades both the telecommunications sector and the radio and TV broadcasting sector have been deregulated in most democratic countries opening up possibilities for new patterns of industry dynamics as well as general convergence patterns.

Information and communication technologies (ICTs) have, in essence, destabilised the near equilibrium conditions of an earlier time and contributed to conditions of greater disequilibrium. Thus one major implication of ICTs is they have created prime conditions for entrepreneurial discovery and action. But while the emerging digital economy is a genuine source and generator of new business models and new wealth, it is also undermining old business models and threatening and even destroying investments and jobs in certain established businesses. This implies that there are strong motives to study various aspects of the digital economy, since ICTs continue to penetrate the developed economies also after the burst of the ICTs stimulated stock market bubble. The economic research issues raised by the emerging digital economy are as we have mentioned above very diverse ranging from the internal organisation of firms to macroeconomic performance.

Since the use of ICTs enables major reductions in geographical transaction costs by reducing spatial information frictions (Flamm 1999; Sichel 1997), the spatial consequences of the emerging digital economy also becomes a major research issue (Johansson and Karlsson 2001; Stough et al. 2002). The emerging digital economy makes trade and commerce less local, more inter-regional, and, especially, more global, in line with a long-term trend toward market liberalisation and reduced trade barriers. The Internet plays a central role in this process but Internet markets have some specificities of strong importance. Since the Internet is essentially a network activity, it can be associated with network externalities and very strong increasing returns, which substantially influences demand. The extent of network externalities, however, is likely to be change substantially when variations in the size of markets and their nature are introduced. If network suppliers are commercially rational, the law of diminishing returns implies that the most valuable connections will be made first with centres of lesser value being added subsequently or not at all (Button and Taylor 2001). What furthermore complicates the situation is that Internet markets are far from perfect on the supply-side, due to among other things the decreasing cost nature of providing information goods (Varian 1999). Information goods have high fixed production costs but marginal distribution costs close to zero (de Fontenay 2000). In such markets in the absence of regulations supply concentration is needed to secure supply. The solution is to work via market segmentation in the form of "versioning" (Shapiro and Varian 1999) instead of supplying a homogenous product. Versioning is important because it involves price discrimination and, thereby, a mechanism for potentially recovering outlays when there are decreasing costs. However, price discrimination is only possible if a supplier has a degree of monopoly power in the market. Furthermore, many on-line markets are advertising- and technology-intensive, creating tendencies towards growing concentration (Daripa and Kapur 2001). Contrary to what is often assumed, price search may often be imperfect and firms can dampen price competition by introducing product heterogeneity and switching costs. This implies that the claim that e-commerce has created a more competitive environment by encouraging the entry of new on-line firms at its best is only partly true.

However, the growth of e-commerce will also have other implications. It will certainly change the way economic actors work and interact. It will also affect the structure of value chains but their impact on value chains can be expected to vary widely between sectors as a function of sector-specific characteristics (Desruelle and Burgelman 2002). Changing value chains will also have locational implications since the use of e-commerce will make it easier for firms to use suppliers with a more distant location.

The emerging digital economy also has other dramatic impacts on the factors that influence industrial location. In most advanced economies an ever increasing share of economic inputs and outputs is in the form of ICTs and knowledge (Bristow 2003). As a result, the traditional determinants of industrial location – access to raw materials, transportation networks, customers, low costs, and a large pool of labour – are becoming less and less important. Instead, locational choice is increasingly becoming determined by access to particular skills, technology and knowledge, as well as to entrepreneurial talent and venture capital. In addition, these processes are in their infancy – this impact will continue to grow and to do so rapidly. Although there is now a substantial body of literature on the spatial consequences of the increased use of ICTs in the economy, much of it is inconclusive. One reason is that the context has been rapidly changing not least due to the success of the Internet and e-commerce. Thus, the spatial consequences of the emerging digital economy are a major theme in this book.

In the 1980s and early 1990s, some cyber prophets and technological optimists predicted that the emergence of the digital economy would kill distance and make urban regions superfluous (Cairncross 1997; Knoke 1996; Naisbitt 1995; Negroponte 1995; Toffler 1980) and at the same time eliminating the scale disadvantages of smaller and more peripheral regions. The basic idea was that the spread of the use of ICTs has the potential to replace face-to-face activities that formerly occurred in central locations, which would strongly reduce or even eliminate agglomeration economies and hence make economic activities totally 'foot-loose'. At the beginning of the 21st century, however, it has become clear that this picture is at least single-sided. New technologies are likely to remain grounded in existing urban regions, which imply that these regions will keep their locational attractiveness. There is also increasing evidence that the digital revolution actually reinforces the position of leading urban regions (Castells 1989, 1996; Hall 1998; Wheeler et al. 2000). Ogawa (2000) shows, for example, that ICTs development may not necessarily encourage the dispersion of economic activities due to the network effects and the technology effects of ICTs infrastructure supply. Cities are a means of reducing the fixed travel costs involved in face-to-face interactions. Even if in principle improvements in ICTs could eliminate the demand for face-to-face interactions and make cities obsolete, empirical results point in the direction that telecommunications is mainly a complement to face-to-face interactions (Gaspar and Glaeser 1998).

Leading urban regions are concentrations of knowledge – human resources, universities and R&D institutes – and knowledge constitutes the principal 'input' in the digital economy. Leading urban regions are also leading centres of innovation but also host newly propulsive and emergent economic growth sectors such as tourism and cultural industries. Leading urban regions are growing in importance as places where information is created and interpreted. The shift towards growing reliance on tele-mediated information, electronic transactions, and financial flows, as well as the continuing importance of fashion, art, the media, dance, consumption, leisure, research, collective consumption, travel, tourism, education, and governance place a premium on reflexivity, interpretation and innovation – the key assets of large urban regions (Storper 1996). In this context it should be observed, as the discussion above showed, that the provision of network infrastructures would vary substantially between different locations making only certain locations viable for communication intensive organisations. Thus, it should be no surprise that the majority of the firms in the Internet industry is concentrated in key metropolitan regions (Bristow 2003; Zook 2002) and that the same general pattern prevails for both the so-called Internet 'backbones' in the United States (Malecki and Gorman 2001) and the multimedia industry. Interestingly, Zook (2000) shows that there over time seems to be a stronger connection between Internet content and information-intensive industries than between Internet content and the industries providing the computer and telecommunications technology necessary for the Internet to operate.

Even if these different agglomerations may interact digitally over long distances, their existence does not suggest a geography of dispersion or that the industries in question should be indifferent to distance or proximity (Leamer and Storper 2001). On the contrary, these industries are heavily concentrated in existing large agglomerations, thereby al least in the short run reinforcing existing patterns of uneven development. Furthermore, the developments within ICTs in recent decades have brought about a new pattern of competition for income growth between urban regions (Alles et al. 1994; Graham 1999). Actually, it has been maintained that ICTs are and will be an important policy tool for urban regions to attract activities at a worldwide scale (Goddard 1995; Graham 1992). At the same time is must be recognised that analyses of existing success cases have revealed that the successful outcome has only in part been a result of designed and implemented policies (Saxenian 1983). Several other factors, including chance, appear to have crucial effects as well. Therefore, it is important to bear in mind that public ICTs policy[3] may have limited effects given among other things that it has to

---

[3] Public ICTs policy can be defined as any public-sector action taken to advance the development of ICT or to promote their use by constituents for the benefit of society.

be designed and implemented in competition with other public policies. However, one should also remember that ICTs are a young field and that ICTs policy-making is still in its infancy. Information and communication technologies (ICTs) policy-making is also suffering from the knowledge gap in the current understanding of what impacts ICTs and the interrelationships between ICTs and transportation have on urban regions (Cohen et al. 2002).

However, over time we expect ICTs to affect generally industrial patterns of concentration and convergence. Concentration is the tendency of an industry to cluster geographically, while convergence is the tendency of an industry to become more uniformly distributed geographically, i.e. less concentrated over time. Kolko (2002) found that information technology intensive industries exhibit slower convergence than other industries. This is certainly an interesting result in particular since so many regions look upon such industries as the major sources of future jobs. The results also indicate that clusters of information technology intensive industries persist not because they are technology-intensive per se, but because they tend to rely on high-skilled labour. Furthermore, a new-firm birth analysis suggests that information technology reduces the need for firms to locate near their clients, which may slow the convergence of service industries. Since convergence reduces the long-run efficacy of place-based economic policies, public policies that attract low-skill support functions for information technology intensive industries confer only short-term benefits in exchange of potentially large upfront costs (Kolko 2002).

The growing penetration and popular adoption of ICTs have given rise to wide and diverse expectations and policies geared to affect economic and social systems, not least in terms of their spatial configuration. A clear example is the popular belief in the net substitution for travel. There have been a lot of expectations concerning ICTs and, in particular, the opportunity to telecommute would have substantial effects on traffic congestion (Boghani et al. 1991; Garrison and Deakin 1988; Salomon and Mokhtarian 1997). Virtual offices at home, at 'village' sites or on-board busses and trains were supposed at a massive scale to substitute car travel to work. However, these expectations cannot at present be supported by hard data (Salomon 1998). Perhaps this is not very surprising, since ICTs are far from being a perfect substitute for the car. The nature of virtual access is very different compared with the nature of physical access. Nijkamp and Salomon (1989) also argue that over time the total of all forms of communication has increased due to higher real incomes, higher car ownership rates and socio-economic life-styles that encourage greater levels of interpersonal contacts. High growth rates in the service sector and the information industries have also resulted in a greater inherent emphasis on face-to-face communication and the development of interpersonal relationships during work hours. The increased frequency of meetings 'after work' in pubs and bars seems to confirm this increased importance of face-to-face meetings.

At the same time we can observe how the use of ICTs makes work at distance a reality as well as the location of information-handling activities, such as call centres, in peripheral regions. These potentials of ICTs have to be combined with systematic observations showing that rural and remote communities tend to lag behind urban ones with regard to ICTs infrastructure, services and human resources (Ramirez 2001). Telecommunication investments are perceived as strategic tools for economic development in rural areas (Bryden and Sproull 1998; Richardson and Gillespie 1996; Ullman et al. 1996) but their reach into rural and remote areas is limited by weak demand, partly as a direct result of their sparse populations and limited economic activities.

Hence, it is obvious that the emerging digital economy has a potential to re-shape intra-regional as well as inter-regional activity patterns (Karlsson and Klaesson 2002). However, even if considerable research has been conducted on the spatial implications of ICTs, it remains inherently difficult to assess the social and economic impact of ICTs on regional and local development. Certainly, there is a substantial amount of evidence on the possible impact of ICTs on 'physical space' based on technical engineering characteristics of these technologies. But as Luc Soete remarks in Chap. 2 the acknowledgement and recognition of such characteristics represent of course nothing more than the listing of the various enabling technical factors. By addressing them he of course does not imply any kind of technological determinism, rather he emphasises that ICTs, from the perspective of possible spatial impacts, represent a radical set of new technologies, despite the many, increasingly popular claims to the contrary. He stresses that, contrary to other previous radical technological breakthroughs, ICTs appear, in particular, to be characterised by its use flexibility. As a consequence, there is much more 'malleability' in the impact of ICTs on physical space. Soete claims that this malleability is extreme. It ranges from a relatively straightforward diffusion process of ICTs (foremost as a set of complementary technologies reinforcing existing regional and local development trends including many forms of reorganisation of existing production and distribution activities), to much more radical, 'creative destruction' diffusion process whereby ICTs act as substitution technologies challenging and in some cases even replacing existing regional trends. These developments provide a complex picture of the possible impacts of ICTs on physical space that cannot be easily summarised.

It has been the intention of the editors of this book to add to the complex picture of the possible impacts of ICTs with a special focus on spatial impacts and at the same time hopefully, in some instances, making the picture more comprehensible. The rest of the contributions presented in this book highlight three important aspects of the emerging digital economy:

- Clusters, innovation and entrepreneurship
- Location and dynamics of ICT industries
- Telecommunications and policy

In the last chapter of the book (Chap. 15), the editors summarize the main findings of the studies and provide suggestions for future research.

1.2 Clusters, Innovation and Entrepreneurship

Innovation through the creation, diffusion and use of knowledge has become a central driver of economic growth. However, the determinants of innovation performance have changed in the globalizing knowledge economy, partly as a result of recent developments in ICTs. Innovations result from increasingly complex interactions among individuals, enterprises and different kinds of knowledge institutions. However, important elements of the process of innovation tend to be regional, rather than national or international. These trends are probably most important in science-based and high technology industries such as ICT industries. This means that innovation activities are localised and that they tend to cluster in regions offering favourable conditions for innovation. Thus, emerging regional innovation networks create new forms of learning and knowledge production (Fischer 2003; Florida 1995). They generate and cumulate knowledge that can be exchanged with and spillover to other actors. One important aspect of these localised clusters of knowledge production is that such knowledge flows can be exploited by third-party economic agents, i.e. entrepreneurs. Hence, the relevant focus is on economic agents confronted with new knowledge or new combinations of old knowledge and their decisions of whether and how to act upon that knowledge (Audretsch 1995). Such a focus is at the heart of modern entrepreneurship research (Shane and Venkataraman 2000).

In the first chapter in Section A (Chap. 3) Karen R. Polenske hypothesises that two types of economies of scale can enhance regional economic growth. The first type is the well-known agglomeration economies. The second is dispersion economies, a concept introduced by Polenske (2001). She argues that if some firms group in urban areas partially because of agglomeration economies, there is also a need to present some explanation for why other firms do not locate there. Polenske's explanation is that these firms enjoy dispersion economies. Although an analyst can measure both agglomeration and dispersion economies by looking at the average cost curves of the firms, Polenske claims that the factors underlying these two types of scale economies differ. She discusses how analysts can use dispersion economies as an explanation of the role that the development of ICTs plays in regional development. She also explores factors creating agglomeration and dispersion economies and the formation of world-class information and communication technologies and practices, regardless of size and type of industry, by examining (i) industrial clusters, industrial complexes, industrial districts, growth poles and inter-firm networks; (ii) learning regions, (iii) innovations; and (iv) supply chains.

The second chapter in Sect. A (Chap.4) by Martin Andersson and Charlie Karlsson starts with the assertion that continuous product and process innovations are prerequisites for sustainable competitiveness of both nations and regions. How such innovations are created and how successful innovation processes can be initiated are therefore extremely important questions. In recent years, it has been recognized that innovations are localised. They are now believed to be the result of ongoing and prolonged collaboration and interaction between firms and a variety of actors in environments that have been termed regional innovation systems. The actors in the regional innovation systems include customers, producers, subcontractors, consultants, governmental institutions, research institutes, universities, etc. The authors establish that most of the research on regional innovation systems has focused on high-tech clusters (with a preference for ICT clusters) in large metropolitan regions well equipped with a broad spectrum of all kinds of actors who behave strategically in the innovation process. Much less interest has been devoted to regional innovation systems in small and medium-sized regions that are less diversified as regards strategic actors in the innovation process. The purpose of the chapter is to provide a critical state-of-the-art overview of current research on regional innovation systems in small and medium-sized regions. In particular, the authors focus on what should be meant by a regional innovation system in this context and the possibilities of identifying regional innovation systems that are typical for different types of industrial clusters and regions. Regional innovation policies in small and medium-sized regions are also discussed in the chapter.

The following chapter (Chap.5) by Christian Friis, Charlie Karlsson and Thomas Paulsson starts from the ongoing debate about whether there has been a structural shift in the rich industrialised countries during the last two-three decades, from a dependency on large firms and routinized production towards a new economy characterised by small firms and flexible production. Whatever the outcome of this debate, it has certainly renewed the interest in the economics of entrepreneurship. The aim of this chapter is to make a critical survey of the theoretical treatment of the relationship between entrepreneurship and economic growth and recent empirical research in the field. The authors observe that there is little consensus about how to define entrepreneurship. In the context of economics the concept encompasses innovation, creative destruction, acceptance of uncertainty and exploitation of disequilibria. In the survey entrepreneurship is assumed to affect economic growth through three economic instruments: innovation, competition and firm start-ups. In the empirical studies of this debate there is a dispute regarding the importance of small firms in net job creation. Competition appears to correlate positively with both employment levels and total factor productivity growth. Finally, with the caveat of sectoral differences, small firms produce a large share of the total number of innovations. Furthermore, they appear to innovate in less explored fields of technology, thus opening up new fields for potential growth. The authors make the interesting observation that theoretical approaches to entrepreneurship are biased towards innovative activities, whereas the empirical studies are biased towards start-ups.

In the last chapter in Section A (Chap.6) Roger R. Stough presents a Cluster Analytical methodology utilizing location quotient analysis and industry sector relative growth rates to identify propulsive clusters and apply it to the nine sub-state economic regions of the Commonwealth of Virginia, USA. The analyses identify emergent and fast growing clusters of industries in each of the economic regions. Three of the regions focus group meetings with industry representatives were designed and conducted to identify ways to broaden and deepen the understanding of development paths tied to the propulsive clusters of industries. These meetings were also used to identify hard and soft technology infrastructure investments that would extend the development and expansion of the propulsive sectors. The final part of the chapter assesses the strength and weaknesses of the methodology used, the viability of the recommendations for technology infrastructure investments, and the portability of the methodology.

1.3 Location and Dynamics of ICT Industries

Many observers show that the development, production, and application of ICTs infrastructure, hardware and software occur first and foremost in or near urbanised economic core regions (Alles et al. 1994; Graham and Marvin 1996; Quah 2001; Shields et al. 1993; Schmand et al. 1990). Many urban regions in the US and Europe host a large ICTs sector that has grown rapidly during the 1990s (van Winden 1990). However, the location of industries normally changes over time. Thus, it is relevant to ask how the digital economy in general, and ICT industries, in particular, develops in space across the system of functional regions both within a country and internationally. An important purpose of the theory of spatial industrial dynamics is to explain why the economic milieu of a functional region can be advantageous for certain sets of economic activities and less advantageous for others, and why economic activities diffuse and/or relocate between functional regions. What are the conditions for diffusion/relocation to occur? What are the driving forces behind diffusion/relocation? What are the mechanisms of diffusion/relocation? What industries are diffusing/relocating? What geographical patterns do the diffusion/relocation processes follow? What does the interaction pattern between functional regions of different size look like?

In the first chapter in Section B (Chap.7) Börje Johansson analyses the existence of spatial clusters of ICT industries in Sweden. A sectoral cluster is here defined as an interaction phenomenon that generates positive externalities for firms that belong to the sector and that are localised in the same region. Several categories of cluster economies are discussed and two of these are the focus of a study of the ICTs sector across 81 functional regions in Sweden. The ICTs sector is subdivided into a fine structure of sub-sectors or industries. A basic assumption made is that when such industries localise in the same functional region, cluster economies can develop, and these economies form an attractor for further localisation. The author examines how the location of each of these different sub-sectors is influenced by ICTs localisation and urbanisation economies. The empirical study is a static analysis of location patterns and indicates that location patterns are influenced by urbanisation rather than localisation economies. The analysis contributes to the problem of how to identify the existence of and to indicate the strength of a sectoral cluster, and to determine which industries can be classified as members of the cluster.

Johan Klaesson and Lars Pettersson maintain in their chapter (Chap.8) that the provision of ICT services is an essential attribute of the consumption milieu that affects regional attractiveness. Thus, population migration as well as firm localisation can be attributed to differences in the urban economic milieu. The authors focus on how locally 'trapped' conditions are tied to the size of the local market. In larger markets one should expect to find a higher degree of diversity and more competitors on the supply side. In their analysis the authors investigate the relation between the presence of a number of ICT services with respect to market size in Swedish municipalities. Market size is measured in terms of accessibility to aggregate income. The empirical analysis is based on considerations of the probability distribution and employs a logit model. The authors also reflect on dynamic changes of the probability distributions. In this context the situation in 1999 is also compared with the situation in 1993.

The chapter by Martin Andersson and Johan Klaesson (Chap.9) provides an explanation of regional growth patterns in the Swedish economy. Using an accessibility-based hierarchy of municipalities they relate growth to intra-municipal, intra-regional and inter-regional accessibility. The authors explore the growth in (i) population, (ii) employment, and (iii) commuting patterns. These variables are perceived as being dependent on a municipality's location in the hierarchy. The purpose of the analysis is to reveal systematic regularities in growth performance. Having established the overall pattern of change, the authors relate this pattern to the ICT service sector performance. In this manner, they examine whether these service sectors and all other sectors in the economy are governed by one and the same process or not. The study is based on data describing the growth in Swedish municipalities between 1993 and 1999. The time period is chosen to capture how the Swedish aggregate growth after the economic crisis in the early 1990s was allocated across municipalities. One of the major differences found between the general growth pattern and that of the ICT service sectors was that the factors that are important to employment growth in the ICT service sectors are more local.

1.4 Telecommunications and Policy

The emergence of the digital economy is intimately connected with the emergence of new telecommunications networks and infrastructures, where the traditional copper and coaxial cable links are increasingly being supplemented or replaced by optic fibre, wireless, microwave and highly efficient satellite systems. While telecommunications were an integrated part of the industrial economy, it has become a major dynamic part of the digital economy. The main reason is that deregulation in the US the EU and elsewhere has stimulated competition and technological dynamics in this field. Moreover, privatisation of incumbent operators has further contributed to innovation dynamics since private telecom operators which face declining telecommunication prices in a more competitive environment naturally try to raise revenues by product innovations and new services (Welfens and Jungmittag 2003).

The strong association between telecommunications and the emergence of the digital economy has generated expectations that investing in telecommunications infrastructures has a positive effect on economic growth. However, the casual relationship between telecommunications investments and economic growth is not clear. Telecommunications investments could bring about economic growth, or economic growth could bring about increased investments in telecommunications but most probably the relationship is reciprocal over a period of time (Gillespie and Cornford 1996). Whatever the casual relationship, it seems obvious that variations in the capacity and the quality of telecommunications infrastructures are exerting a growing influence on corporate decision making about the location of activities. Thus, the spatial patterns of investments in telecommunications infrastructure are likely to influence the patterns of spatial centralisation and decentralisation in the economy. Traditionally the telecommunications sector has been strongly regulated in most countries. Even if the sector in recent years has been deregulated in many countries a significant amount of regulation still prevails. The strategic role of the telecommunications infrastructure to the emergence of the digital economy and the still significant role played by political decision making make telecommunications and policy a very important research area for national economic development.

Edward J. Malecki in the first chapter in Section C (Chap.10) makes an attempt to synthesize the new realities of cities and the new urban geographies that have appeared during the past decade or two. Recent research at both the interurban scale of city systems and at the intra-urban scale of the individual metropolis makes claims that new trends, patterns, and processes are operating. Both scales of analysis are focal points of this chapter, centred around aspects of technology and its effects on cities. The chapter begins with a survey of 'the new geography' and the technological, social, and political factors that have created it. Next, the chapter turns to the urban hierarchy and the largest urban regions, or world cities, in particular. In both the new geography and the evolving world city hierarchy, there appears to be winners and losers. The chapter then focuses on the 'new economy' and its effects on cities. The shape of the post-modern metropolis is analysed with attention paid to 'edge cities' and the poly-nuclear urban form increasingly found throughout the world. The chapter ends with an assessment of 'splintered urbanism', the trend toward social, economic, and spatial bifurcation of urban spaces.

In the second chapter in Section C (Chap.11) Mustafa Dinc, Kingsley E. Haynes and Serdar Yilmaz argue that telecommunications technology investments have a direct positive impact on the competitiveness of firms, particularly in the service-related sectors. These developments may also generate a cumulative direct effect on the overall economy of states and regions. The authors examine the impacts of telecommunications infrastructure on output growth in the co-terminus US states. Their findings suggest that not every state receives the full benefits from its own telecommunications infrastructure investments. A state-by-state econometric analysis shows the variation in return to telecommunications investments across states. This variation may be due to inefficient utilization of telecommunications infrastructure as a factor of production. Data Envelopment Analysis confirms that the states accruing significantly positive benefits are those where businesses use the telecommunications infrastructure efficiently.

Peter L. Stenberg in his chapter (Chap.12) observes that communication and information technology has undergone a rapid evolution over the last decade. The diffusion of the new technology, however, has been uneven across geographical space over time. In addition, the rapid diffusion of the Internet into households and businesses has led to many new economic policy and technology myths and realities. One operating assumption in the policy debate is that the Internet plays an increasingly significant economic role in the market place. Using industry data, this chapter examines the communication and information issues of technology diffusion, economic returns to investment, economic policy, and technological feasibility as they pertain to rural communities. It is argued that the market is functioning, but rural areas, vis-á-vis urban areas, have an economic disadvantage when it comes to obtaining the full set of communication and information technology. Newer technology may yet overcome this disadvantage, but the analysis shows that policy will likely remain a key element.

As in many other countries Sweden has recently allocated licences to the third generation (3G) of wireless telecommunication technology. However, in contrast to many other countries that used auctions, a so-called 'beauty contest' was used to distribute the rights. The underlying motivation was that by using criteria other than price in the allocation of rights it would be to the advantage of both consumers and producers and would speed up infrastructure investments. Considering that the choice was between two ways of allocating scarce resources – the use of the radio spectrum – economists should have something to contribute. Surprisingly enough the theoretical underpinnings for the use of a 'beauty contest' seem to be lacking in the economics literature, while the same literature has a lot to offer concerning auctions. The purpose of the chapter by Per-Olof Bjuggren (Chap.13) is to evaluate 'beauty contests' compared to auctions as a means of allocating scarce resources. The basic question in this chapter is if a 'beauty contest' like the Swedish one really is rewarding 'beauty' or whether it is better for a firm to be a 'beast' to get a 3G license?

The last chapter of Section C (Chap.14) is written by Robert J. Stimson. This chapter focuses on the digital divide and is a review of socio-economic and spatial distributional issues of ICTs and implications for regional strategy. The author observes that regional development patterns vary widely across the space economy. While innovations in ICTs theoretically permit widespread socio-economic access to, and spatial diffusion in the location of those goods and services, the reality is that spatial concentration of these activities and of access to their benefits is often the outcome, creating a 'digital divide' for both people and places. This chapter provides an overview of recent literature addressing these outcomes, including a discussion of implications for policy and regulation and for regional development.

References

Alles P, Esparza A, Lucas S (1994) Telecommunications and the large city – small city divide: evidence from Indiana cities. Professional Geographer 46: 307-316

Audretsch D (1995) Innovation and industry evolution. MIT Press, Cambridge, MA

Boghani A, Kimble E, Spencer E (1991) Can telecommunications help solve America's transportation problems? Arthur D. Little, Cambridge, MA

Bristow G (2003) The Implications of the new economy for industrial location. In Jones DC (ed) New economy handbook. Academic Press, London, pp 269-287

Bryden J, Sproull A (1998) Information and communication technology and rural economic development: the adoption and impact of telematics use by small and medium-sized enterprises. In United States Department of Agriculture (USDA) Economic Research Service (ed) Telecommunications in Rural Areas. Proceedings of a Workshop, USDA, Washington, DC, pp 37-46

Brynjolfsson E, Kahin B (2000) Introduction. In Brynjolfsson E, Kahin B (eds) Understanding the digital economy. Data, tools, and research. MIT Press, Cambridge, MA, pp 1-10

Button K, Taylor S (2001) Towards an economics of the Internet and e-commerce. In Leinbach TR, Brunn SD (eds) Worlds of e-commerce: economic, geographical and social dimensions. Wiley, Chichester, pp 27-43

Cairncross F (1997) The death of distance. Harvard Business School Press, Boston, MA

Carlsson B (2003) The new economy: what is new and what is not? In Christensen JF, Maskell P (eds) The industrial dynamics of the new digital economy. Edward Elgar, Cheltenham, pp 13-32

Castells M (1989) The informational city. Information technology, economic restructuring and the urban-regional process. Basil Blackwell, Oxford

Castells M (1996) The rise of the network society. The information age: economy, society and culture. Vol 1, Blackwell, Oxford

Cohen G, Salomon I, Nijkamp P (2002) Information-communications technologies (ICT) and transport: does knowledge underpin policy?. Telecommunications Policy 26: 31-52

Cohen SS, De Long JB, Zysman J (2000) Tools for thought: what is new and important about the 'e-economy'?. Berkeley International Roundtable on the International Economy (BRIE) Working Paper 138, University of California, Berkeley

Collis DJ, Bane PW, Bradley SP (1997) Winners and losers: industry structure in the converging world of telecommunications, computing and entertainment. In Joffie DB (ed) Competing in the age of digital convergence. Harvard Business School Press, Boston, pp 159-199

Daripa A, Kapur S (2001) Pricing on the Internet. Oxford Review of Economic Policy 17: 202-216

David PA (1991) Computer and dynamo: the modern productivity paradox in a distant mirror. In OECD (1991) Technology and productivity: the challenge for economic policy. OECD, Paris, pp 315-348

De Fontenay E (2000) The digital economy: how digital goods are reshaping the rules of commerce. Communications & Strategies 40: 179-192

Desruelle P, Burgelman J-C (2002) The impact of e-commerce: a prospective look at changing value chains in selected areas. Communications and Strategies 42: 331-349

Dosi G (1988) Sources, procedures and microeconomic effects of innovation. Journal of Economic Literature 36: 1126-1171

The Economist (2000) The great convergence gamble. The Economist 357, pp 67-68

Fischer MM (2003) The new economy and networking. In Jones DC (ed) New economy handbook. Academic Press, London, pp 343-367

Flamm K (1999) Digital convergence? The set-top box and the network computer. In Eisenach JA, Lenard TM (eds) Competition, innovation and the Microsoft monopoly: antitrust in the digital market place. Kluwer Academic Publishers, Boston, pp 255-290

Florida R (1995) Toward the learning region. Futures 27: 527-536

Friedrichs J (1989) The information revolution and urban life. Journal of Urban Affairs 11: 327-337

Garrison W, Deakin E (1988) Travel, work and telecommunications: a long view of the electronic revolution and its potential impacts. Transportation Research 22A: 2246-2390

Gaspar J, Glaeser EL (1998) Information technology and the future of cities. Journal of Urban Economics 43: 136-156

Gillespie A, Cornford J (1996) Telecommunication infrastructures and regional development. In Dutton WH (ed) Information and communication technologies. Visions and realities. Oxford University Press, Oxford, pp 335-351

Goddard JB (1995) Information and communication technologies, corporate hierarchies and urban hierarchies in the new Europe. In Broychie J, Batty M, Blakely E, Hall P, Newton P (eds) Cities in competition: productive and sustainable cities for the 21st century. Longman, Harlow, pp 127-138

Graham S (1992) Electronic infrastructures in the city: some emerging municipal policy roles in the UK. Urban Studies 29: 755-781

Graham S (1999) Global grids of glass-on global cities, telecommunications and planetary networks. Urban Studies 36: 929-949

Graham S, Marvin S (1996) Telecommunications and the city: electronic spaces, urban places. Routledge, New York

Hall P (1998) Cities in civilization. Culture, innovation and urban order. Weinfield and Nicholson, London

Johansson B, Karlsson C (2001) Geographical transaction costs and specialisation opportunities of small and medium-sized regions: scale economies and market extension. In Johansson B, Karlsson C, Stough RR (eds) Theories of endogenous regional growth. Lessons for regional policies. Springer, Berlin Heidelberg New York, pp 150-180

Jones DC (2003) (ed) The new economy handbook. Academic Press, London

Karlsson C, Klaesson J (2002) The spatial industrial dynamics of the ICT sector in Sweden. In Acs ZJ, de Groot HLF, Nijkamp P (eds) The emergence of the knowledge economy. A regional perspective. Springer, Berlin Heidelberg New York, pp 243-275

Knieps G (2003) Competition in telecommunications and Internet services: a dynamic perspective. In Barfiled CE, Heiduk G, Welfens PJJ (eds) Internet, economic growth and globalisation. Perspectives on the new economy in Europe, Japan and the US. Springer, Berlin Heidelberg New York, pp 217-227

Knoke K (1996) Bold new world: the essential road map to the twenty-first century. Kodansha, New York

Kolko J (2002) Silicon mountains, silicon molehills: geographic concentration and convergence of Internet industries in the US. Information Economics and Policy 14: 211-232

Krugman P (1997) Requiem for the new economy. Millennial optimism confronts reality. Fortune: November 10

Leamer E, Storper M (2001) The economic geography of the Internet. Journal of International Business Studies 32: 641-665

Lee HG, Clark T (1997) Market process reengineering through electronic market systems: opportunities and challenges. Journal of Management Information Systems 13: 13-30

Malecki EJ (1991) Technology and economic development. Longman, New York

Malecki EJ, Gorman SP (2001) Maybe the death of distance, but not the end of geography: the Internet as a network. In: Leinbach TR, Brunn SD (eds) Worlds of e-commerce: economic, geographical and social dimensions. Wiley, Chichester, pp 87-105

Malone T, Yates J, Benjamín R (1987) Electronic markets and hierarchies. Communication of the ACM 30: 484-497

Mowery DC, Simcoe T (2002) Is the Internet a US invention? – An economic and technological history of computer networking. Research Policy 31: 1369-87

Naisbitt R (1995) The global paradox. Avon Books, New York

Negroponte N (1995) Being digital. Vintage Books, New York

Nijkamp P, Salomon I (1989) The future spatial impacts of telecommunications. Transportation Planning and Technology 13: 275-287

Organisation for Economic Co-operation and Development (OECD) (2002) Measuring the information economy. The ICT sector. In: OECD Proceedings Science & Information Technology, vol 2002, no 14, pp 35-69

Ogawa H (2000) Spatial impact of information technology development. The Annals of Regional Science 34: 537-551

Polenske KR (2001) Competitive advantage of regional internal and external supply chains. In Lahr M, Miller RE (eds) Essays in honor of Benjamin H. Stevens. Elsevier Publishers, Amsterdam, pp 259-284

Quah D (2001) ICT clusters in development: theory and evidence. European Investment Bank (EIB) Papers 6: 85-100

Ramirez R (2001) A model for rural and remote information and communication technologies: a Canadian exploration. Telecommunications Policy 25: 315-330

Richardson R, Gillespie A (1996) Advanced communications and employment creation in rural and peripheral regions: a case study of the Highlands and Islands of Scotland. The Annals of Regional Science 30: 91-110

Rosenberg N (1963) Technological change in the machine tool industry, 1840-1910. The Journal of Economic History 23: 414-446

Sahal D (1985) Technological guideposts and innovation avenues. Research Policy 14: 61-82

Salomon I (1998) Technological change and social forecasting: the case of telecommuting as a travel substitute. Transportation Research Part C 6: 17-45

Salomon I, Mokhtarian P (1997) Why don't you telecommute? Access 10: 27-29, University of California Transport Center

Saxenian A (1983) The urban contradictions of Silicon Valley. International Journal of Urban and Regional Research 7: 237-261

Schmand, J, Williams FH, Wilson R (1990) The new urban infrastructure: cities and telecommunications. Praeger Publishers, New York

Schwartz GG (1990) Telecommunications and economic development policy. Economic Development Quarterly 4: 83-91

Shane S, Venkataraman A (2000) The promise of entrepreneurship as a field of research. Academy of Management Review 25: 217-226

Shapiro C, Varian HR (1999) Information rules. a strategic guide to the network economy. Harvard Business School Press, Boston, MA

Shepard SB (1997) The new economy: what it really means. Business Week 3553: 38-41

Shields P, Dervin B, Richter C, Soller R (1993) Who needs 'POTS-Plus' services? A comparison of residential user needs along the rural-urban continuum. Telecommunications Policy 17: 563-587

Sichel DE (1997) The computer revolution. An economic perspective. Brookings Institution Press, Washington, DC

Stieglitz N (2003) Digital dynamics and types of industry convergence: the evolution of the handheld computers market. In Christensen JF, Maskell P (eds) The industrial dynamics of the new digital economy. Edward Elgar, Cheltenham, pp 179-208

Stiroh K (1999) Is there a new economy? Challenge 42: 82-101

Storper M (1996) The world of the city: local relations in the global economy. School of Public Policy and Social Research, University of California, Los Angeles

Stough RR, Kulkarni R, Paelinck J (2002) ICT and knowledge challenges for entrepreneurs in regional economic development. In Acs ZJ, de Groot HLF, Nijkamp P (eds) The emergence of the knowledge economy. A regional perspective. Springer, Berlin Heidelberg New York, pp 195-214

Toffler A (1980) The third wave. Bamtam Books, New York

Ullman D, Willliams S, Emal J (1996) Using technology to stimulate rural economic development: Nebraska's community internet navigator program. Economic Development Review 14: 14-15

Van Winden W (2000) Three ICT clusters compared. Paper presented at the 40th Congress of the European Regional Science Association, 29 August- 1 September, Barcelona

Varian HL (1999) Market structure in the network age. Paper prepared for Understanding the Digital Economy Conference, May 25-26, 1999, Department of Commerce, Washington, DC. Available at http://www.sims.berkeley.edu/%7Ehal/Papers/doc/doc.pdf

Weinstein BL (1997) Welcome to the new economy. Perspectives 12: 1-4

Wheeler JO, Aoyama Y, Warf B (2000) Cities in the telecommunications age. The fracturing of geography, Routledge, New York

Zook M (2000) The web of production: the economic geography of commercial Internet content production in the United States. Environment and Planning A 32: 411-426

Zook M (2002) Ground capital: venture financing and the geography of the Internet industry, 1994-2000. Journal of Economic Geography 2: 151-177

2 Information and Communication Technologies and the New Regional Economy

Luc Soete

Maastricht Economic Research Institute on Innovation and Technology, Maastricht University

2.1 Introduction

While it remains difficult to assess the social and economic impact of Information and Communication Technologies (ICTs) on regional and local development, there is nevertheless a substantial amount of evidence on the possible impact of ICTs on 'physical space' based on the technical, 'engineering' characteristics of these technologies. As in the case of other technologies, the acknowledgement and recognition of such characteristics represent of course nothing more than the listing of the various technical 'enabling' factors. By addressing them in a first section we hence do not imply any kind of technological determinism, rather we want to emphasize the consequences that ICTs represents from the perspective of the possible physical impact, despite the many, increasingly popular claims to the contrary, a radical sets of 'new' technologies. Contrary to other, previous radical technological breakthroughs, ICTs appears, however, characterized by its flexibility in use. There is hence much more 'malleability' in the impact of ICTs on physical space. This malleability is extreme. It ranges form a relatively straightforward diffusion process of ICTs as foremost a set of complementary technologies reinforcing existing regional and local developments trends including many forms of reorganisation of existing production and distribution activities, to a much more radical, 'creative destruction' diffusion process whereby ICTs act in first instance as substitution technologies challenging and in some cases even replacing existing regional development trends. It is to these latter issues that we turn in a second section. We conclude with some general observations. Issues in this chapter are also reflected from alternative perspectives in Chaps. 8, 10 and 14.

2.2 Information and Communication Technologies– a Breakthrough Technology?

The impact of ICTs – it is customary in Europe to speak of information *and* communication technologies – on the economy, and society in general, is founded on a number of technological breakthroughs that seem to be historically unique. It remains, of course, difficult to give a fair, historical estimation of 'new' technological breakthroughs. To many scientists and technologists, the breakthroughs in the area of nuclear know-how and technology in the 1940s and 1950s represented an almost inexhaustible new source of energy. Only few of these promises eventually came true; worse still, the cost of storing non-degradable nuclear waste draws heavily on citizen's future well-being. A substantial dose of scepticism seems to be justified when scientists and technologists refer to 'radical' new technologies and use them to distil future scenarios, whether these are put in a positive or in a negative light.

In a certain sense, it is the task of an economist to confront technologists with the numerous social, economic and societal factors that are related to the diffusion of new technology, no matter how radical the technology may be perceived by the business community and policy makers, scientists and technologists. However, from the perspective of its social, economic, and organisational implications and broader societal embedding, the current cluster of ICTs represents a potentially radical technological and organisational transformation[1]. It might even be argued that every single introduction of new ICTs equipment in an organisation represents an innovation. However, before discussing these organisational features, we first review in this first section some of the more technical aspects of ICTs. The cluster of what is currently described as 'new ICTs' is based on a broad range of continuous, sometimes radical, converging technological breakthroughs that, when viewed as a group, appear to be historically unique in terms of speed and worldwide impact.

First, there is the dramatic technological improvement in the capacity of semiconductors, which led to a gigantic increase in the capacities and speed of computers to store and process data. Using what is called Moore's Law, these improvements were described in 1965 as a logarithmic increase in the processing capacity of computer chips. This law still seems to apply 35 years after its formulation. This trajectory of continuous technological improvement has been described in depth and analysed by a great many economists since the 1980s (see for example Katz and Phillips 1982; Dosi 1984), so in fact there is not much 'new' to it. Nevertheless, the process of technological improvement in semiconductors in

---

[1] See, among others, Freeman and Soete (1994) for an overview. Groot and De Grip (1991) and Autor et al. (2000) study the impact of ICTs in two large banks in the Netherlands and the United States, respectively. They find that the introduction of ICTs has led to a lot of organisational changes. Lindbeck and Snower (2000) give a theoretical explanation as to how the organisation of production has shifted from a Taylorist-based to a more 'holistic' production method, in which teamwork, job rotation, the integration of tasks, and learning through job rotation are essential ingredients.

particular has gained momentum with Intel's invention of the microprocessor in 1971. Triplett (1996) mentions a price reduction with a factor of 3,000 during the 1974-1994 period. In other words, the continuous technological improvements over the past 25 years combined with the individualisation of computer use thanks to personal computers has led to the ever-increasing diffusion of IT applications throughout the various sectors of the economy. Thus, IT – and the computer in particular – has made its entry in the numerous economic analyses as a 'general purpose' technology (Bresnahan and Trajtenberg 1995), the diffusion of which is accompanied by a great many organisational mismatches and tensions (Freeman and Perez 1988; David 1991)[2].

Secondly, there is the tendency to miniaturise IT. I put this forward as a clear, separate second trend, because the impact of IT miniaturisation has been essential to the physical integration of electronic functions in existing (and new) equipment, and has made this equipment itself more handy and efficient in use. Previously it was impossible to apply a lot of the old IT equipment in both electromechanical capital and consumption goods, simply because it would have taken up too much space. Apart from the development of the miniaturisation of IT equipment new, user-friendly products as illustrated in the case of the computer by the development of mainframe to mini-computer, PCs, laptops and palms, offer the possibility to include electronic intelligence in practically any existing mechanical apparatus. Thus, IT equipment further increases the efficiency of existing products, whether they are instruments, machines, or household appliances. Miniaturisation also leads to a lower use of energy[3]. Ultimately, the possibilities for ever-increasing miniaturisation open the avenue to nanotechnology, i.e., the production of electronic material at sub-micron level that can interact with tiny matter and cells, including live cells. As yet, the latter developments are clearly in their early stages and subject to research in a lot of countries. Nevertheless, these mainly technologically driven developments towards further miniaturisation are important, because they show that the technological trajectory within the IT sector is far from completed and that the application areas of the technology expand further to other areas and sectors. In other words, IT is not just limited to the Internet.

Third, there are the almost equally radical technological improvements in the area of telecommunication. The developments in the field of optical fibres allow for the transmission of digital signals without noticeable loss of energy. Combined

---

[2] Helpman (1998) provides a good overview of such technological changes. Harris (1998) studies the Internet as a 'general purpose' technology, focusing on the Internet as a communication network. His main findings are that the introduction of a communication network increases the 'virtual' mobility of both services and labour, resulting in an increase of the wage premium for high-skilled employees.

[3] The intensive use and large-scale diffusion of their widespread presence, for example computers, can of course, undo this energy benefit per appliance. Undoubtedly, the share of energy use in the Netherlands will rise because of the increasing use of computers. According to calculations in the United States, the production and use of computers are responsible for 295 billion kilowatt-hour, about eight percent of the total American demand for electricity.

with the trend towards miniaturising IT equipment described above – the 'routers' and networks stations – and the strong expansion of the bandwidth of communication channels, this allows for the development of a communication network infrastructure in which information and communication goods can be supplied at minimal variable cost. Communicating with someone nearby or with someone on the far side of the globe will be virtually the same. Thus, the concept of "death of distance" (Cairncross 1998) is not as farfetched as it may seem. It is mainly from this perspective that the technological developments in the area of communication technology differ from other, previous breakthroughs in the area of network technology, such as electricity. Apart from being dependent on the much higher capital costs of the various 'network stations', an electricity network is also dependent on energy loss over its own network. In other words, distance continued to be an important cost factor in such previous networks. The way ICTs is different from such geographical impact is discussed in the next section.

Fourth, there are the specific developments in the area of mobile communication. In a certain sense, mobile communication represents the ultimate form of reachability. Physical access to the infrastructure of the network is no longer necessary, but can be effectively communicated from any place. Naturally, the antenna infrastructure continues to be a major cost factor, but once again, this is not in proportion to the physical network costs of, for example, the distribution of electricity. As to the rest, the fixed network cost is formed by the property of a piece of 'space'. Hence, mobile communication implies more than the end of physical distance; it might be described as 'any place, any time, anywhere; information and communication are in the air'. It goes without saying that this additional dimension of communication, reachability, explains the originally unexpected boom in mobile telephone communication in the 1990s. This area, too, is still in its initial stages of further technological development.

Finally, there are the developments in the field of supporting technology, such as software and other communication standards, in particular the Internet protocols (for example WWW), and mobile communication standards (such as GSM, WAP and UMTS). Software development have appeared to be essential not only in the development of new information goods such as content, they have also shown to be particularly important in the improvement of the use of the physical communication infrastructure. ASDL, for example, allowed for the better and more efficient use of the old copper telephone lines. On the other hand, the different layers of open Internet protocols are crucial to the development of new information goods and Internet trade in general. Thus, the possibilities of communication expand further and further and the tradability of services strongly increases due to new software development and internationally accepted information and communication standards. The public availability of the Internet standards is really at the basis of the 'new' Internet network advantages, such as B2B (business-to-business), which is the reason why these are far more important than the 'old' closed EDI standards. Thanks to these open international standards, it is now possible to achieve network advantages worldwide, independent of close local interactions.

In brief, what is historically unique in terms of technological developments in the area of ICTs, is, in a certain sense, the historically long, unremitting technological improvement in various sub-areas, and on the other hand, the exceptional technological spillovers and convergence between the various ICTs areas. As to what the implications are for regional development, ICTs appears first and foremost a cluster of technologies, which appear flexible in use. While hence the phenomenon of 'death of distance' might lead to new possibilities for regional development in peripheral areas and for the decentralisation of economic activities to such areas particularly those dealing with information handling and exchange, they might also lead to the opposite trend: a further concentration of activities in existing growth centres. This malleability in use of ICTs raises hence many questions about alternative uses of ICTs and their regional impact, which we discuss next.

2.3 The Impact of ICTs on Physical Space

At the outset, it seems useful to discuss the physical space impact of ICTs from the perspective of the impact of ICTs on production, distribution and consumption. The discussion with respect to the regional concentration of the production of ICTs equipment and/or the impact of ICTs on the concentration of industrial production activities is at the centre of a number of other chapters in this book (Chaps. 3 and 7). It is to some extent the bread and butter of regional studies in this area. Undoubtedly the concentration of such activities in some regions and not in others has been a core variable in explaining differences between regional growth. It falls broadly speaking within the long Marshallian tradition of local agglomeration economics, leading to the further concentration of industrial and service activities as a result of formal and informal network effects. Despite the 'death of distance' feature associated with ICTs – with information being so to say 'in the air' – physical agglomeration effects are still likely to dominate because of the need of physical contact. Here we will not further develop on this literature; the focus will rather be on the impact of ICTs on distribution and consumption, the two areas which have received less attention and are, certainly when viewed from a regional and local urban planning perspective, important activities in which both economic agents and citizens are involved. We first turn to ICTs and distribution.

2.3.1 Information and Communication Technologies and Distribution

As already mentioned in Sect. 2.2, through better monitoring with the help of ICTs, a better, faster, timelier flow of goods and persons to their place of destination can in principle be realised. ICT is in this sense first and foremost a complementary technology to existing distribution and transportation systems. While the term e-commerce seems to imply a process of substitution of physical commerce,

ICTs is rather likely to increase the efficiency of the distribution and transport delivery systems through reduction in transaction costs and better usage of transport infrastructure whether by ship, rail road or air transport. Substitution might occur but rather *between* different, alternative transport infrastructure systems.

Many authors have pointed to a trend towards the customisation of transportation and distribution of goods. Just like in the case of mass-customisation, one might expect that ICTs will here too ultimately lead to 'transport-customisation'. Depending on the individual time pressures the client is confronted with, an alternative transport system will be selected. This does not hold only for the transport of goods but also for the transport of persons.

The use of ICTs so as to increase the efficiency and the rate of return of existing infrastructural space, as in the case of transport systems, is likely though to enter decreasing returns once the physical and safety limits of the existing infrastructure are reached. While ICTs can push those limits further, one may think of 'smart' roads, electronically controlled rail and air-traffic control, there remain clear absolute physical limits beyond which usage of infrastructure cannot be expanded and safety limits linked to the human factor in complex systems, will remain the fundamental barrier. One should remember in this context that the currently, existing transport infrastructure whether canals, railroads or motor roads is of course the result of centuries of investment. Much of the economic growth over the last centuries has been the result of the continuous extension of the canals, railroad and road network infrastructure. They are also typical examples of path-dependent network infrastructures: the network advantages increased exponentially as more and more persons used the network until congestion and saturation started to set in, in the 1980s and 1990s.

It is important to realize that each of these transport systems contain a certain degree of flexibility, which is essential from the perspective of transport customisation and the extent to which ICTs can increase the efficiency of transport and distribution. The older the transportation system, the less flexible are its features. Thus, the railroad transport system is in many ways a truly 'industrial age' transport system. The word 'railroad' is illustrative: roads of fixed rails that determine the direction of movement and from which it is impossible to divert. The fast development of railroads in the nineteenth century was strongly linked to the industrialisation process and the necessity to get raw materials and other goods from far removed places. It was much cheaper than the digging of canals, which had characterized the first phase of industrialisation. Mountainous places could be reached which where impossible to reach by canal. Much has changed over the last century in the railroad transport system: the replacement of steam power, the containerisation of freight transport, the electrification and automation of signalling, the appearance of fast trains, the development of underground train transport, etc. Particularly the fact that stations where originally built into the centre of cities has emerged as one of the main advantages today for commuters using railroads as transportation system. It has also been the basis for the further development of underground 'lightrail' metro systems in most large cities across the world in the twentieth century. But the major disadvantages of rail transport have not disappeared. On the contrary, those disadvantages have become gradually more and more visible. First of all, railroads are by their nature dramatically inflexible. Apart from rail switches, which have been foreseen on the track at specific fixed places, there is indeed no possibility for trains to avoid unforeseen obstructions. The whole railroad system is particularly sensitive to the smallest obstruction, which can in no time have implications for the performance of the whole network. Railroads suffer from practically all imaginable disadvantages of an inflexible network. It is not like on the Internet where information packages can be sent through different 'routing' systems depending on congestion or even like aircraft transport, where possible alternative landing routes can be followed or planes can be diverted to other airports in case of unforeseen circumstances. As railroads are being used more intensively, the probability of delays hence increases disproportionately. A second factor relates to the simple physics behind rail transport. Pushing forward a massive amount of steel along rails requires a lot of initial energy, while coming to a stop requires a substantial amount of length. This means that important safety limitations influence the intensity of the use of a railroad track. Weight and speed determine the required distance between trains: a high speed train, such as the TGV, requires more than ten miles to come from its maximum speed to a stop; a light metro train will have a maximum speed of 60 km an hour and a stopping length of less than a hundred yards. The intensity of use of an underground metro track is hence much higher than that of a high-speed train track. The difference with a telecom network is huge. It is best illustrated by the success with which the telecom branch succeeded in developing year after year new compression techniques (ISDN, ADSL) so as to send larger and larger data volumes along existing 'upgraded' telephone lines and hence increase the use of the existing network in a dramatic fashion. From this perspective, railroads represent a typical old, network infrastructure, which is already today near to its congestion capacity despite the very limited use of its large, physical infrastructure.

A similar question can be raised with respect to road infrastructure. The flexibility in the use of physical infrastructure is obviously much larger here, so that in first instance the use of ICTs, such as information on traffic use, board computers and alternative routing advice will lead to a better and faster routing of transport over motorways. The increased use of ICTs is hence core to more efficient 'just-in time' stock management methods, whereby the road infrastructure is used more intensively. But here too, congestion limits will appear rather quickly. While overall, e.g. when distributed over the day and week-ends, road use still offers plenty of opportunities for increased usage, it will appear rather quickly that at certain moments of the day, the network will be overloaded and congestion will increasingly become translated in increased economic costs. In the case of road transport, it is the human individual which plays as independent 'free' driver a central role. The logical follow-up in automation such as in the case of 'clever' roads whereby drivers are no longer 'free' in their driving decisions, will hence crucially depend on the social acceptance and integration of the technology by individual drivers. While on the commercial transport side (freight transport, bus transport and other commercial transport of persons) such further automation of driving is likely to be accepted and integrated in a relatively smooth fashion, it is in the consumption sphere, including the daily commuting from home to work that acceptance is likely to be much more difficult. The fact that both transport models combine the same road infrastructure is likely to exacerbate the problem and slow down the diffusion of new road automation techniques.

These two examples illustrate the intrinsic limitations of the impact of ICTs on a better usage of existing road and transport infrastructure. And yet, the impact of ICTs is expected to increase, given the new, global transparency of, and access to markets, tradeable activities. The search for better distribution methods and systems is hence likely to continue to dominate the ICTs agenda for a long time to come. Ultimately, ICTs bring also the limits of the physical transportation of goods and persons to the forefront.

2.3.2 Information and Communication Technologies and Consumption

The consumption society, as it developed in the US and Europe after the Second World War was strongly influenced by the industrialisation and automation of household tasks, which itself led to a large increase in the demand for household equipment and machines (from washing machines, dish washers, fridges, freezers, magnetrons, etc.). The time saving which resulted from the use of such equipment opened up further the way to the growth of double income families and the 'outsourcing' of other household tasks, which could not be automated. As a result the individual choice possibilities of households with respect to consumption behaviour, living environment and in particular the distance to work, free time usage and the decision to carry out internally or outsource household activities, increased dramatically (See also Chap.14).

In terms of urban planning, these developments led to a large increase in the usage of physical space for consumption purposes. The emergence of shopping malls became a general trend with as essential condition easy access by car. Warehouses took advantage of the rapid growth in mass consumption thanks to their scale advantages, but also moved quickly to exploit some of the scope advantages through a continuous enlargement of the product range on offer, hence responding aptly to the growing individualisation trend of consumption behaviour. At the same time, the 'love of variety' of those consumers was cleverly used to realise through the notion of self-service a fundamental distribution chain reversal with consumers now spending themselves the time to select and carry the goods to the cashier. For most consumers those additional time costs were considered small compared to the cost advantages of such self-service systems, very quickly shopping became even a social activity for which citizens were prepared to use large parts of their free time. Similarly with respect to living conditions, physical space, or distance to nature became a premium with as a result a rapidly growing differentiation in house prices depending on the physical location of the object. In search of space people moved out of inner-cities with major implications for the social fabric of inner cities which became at night empty office working spaces. As in the case of shopping, the increased time needed for getting from home to work was made 'freely' available by the employee/consumer.

As a general trend, it could be argued that the development over the last century of consumption patterns and behaviour was both *space* and *time* extensive. The limits of such a development pattern have clearly not been reached as yet, but the increase in price of prime locations and of time, as reflected in the opportunity costs, indicate that space and time saving is increasingly becoming valued. Here too ICTs will offer as a complementary technology interesting opportunities. The very rapid diffusion of mobile phones and mobile equipment illustrates to some extent such underlying trends. As people put more and more time in commuting and the uncertainty with respect to the necessary time involved grows (congestion delays, etc.), mobile communication becomes a basic need. The trend towards the further '*mobilisation*' of ICTs equipment is undoubtedly also induced by the growing problems people are confronted with in terms of physical accessibility. The growing demand for mobile communication corresponds from this perspective to the same individual freedom of choice need, but this time more in terms of virtual contacts, as did the motor car in the previous century, the freedom to bridge physical distance. As a complementary technology, ICTs offers though no solution to the increasing pressures on space and time. To do so one will have to look more in detail at the substitution possibilities of the new digital technologies.

With respect to *space*, it is the underutilisation of space, both at home and at work that is so striking. As Frances Cairncross (1998) noted: "… Commuting wastes time and building capacity. One building – the home – stands empty all day; another – the office – stands empty all night", predicting that this phenomenon might become obsolete in the future decades. Furthermore and particularly when viewed from a longer time perspective, the question can be raised whether the typical factory organisation system which organised first blue collar labour so as to commute within easy distance from the home to the factory and later on organised white collar work on a nine to five basis, with commuting time part of the employee's own costs, is not likely to become increasingly eroded. New forms of household work have been growing rapidly reducing further the time spent at the office (Lindbeck and Snower 2000). In the emerging information society, the development of the household economy could well become a central societal trend, contributing in contrast to pre-industrial household production activities, directly to GDP and national income.

With respect to *time*, it is the change in the valuation of time by consumers, which is most characteristic of recent trends. With the increase in household income, the 'money' valuation of time increases also. One is becoming more aware of the opportunity costs of the time spent in traffic jams, while shopping. The time 'wasted' queuing at the cashier or in the parking lot, will become identified with inferior service. Mass-consumption itself in the sense of mass participation, mass tourism or mass congestion is undoubtedly driven by the greater transparency of information, but here too as a consequence of such greater transparency it can be expected that quality differentiation will emerge. With respect to the role of ICTs, and Internet in particular, it can be expected that such technologies will increasingly become less used for simple price transparency than for the evaluation of products and services.

More generally, the question can be raised whether the trend towards the externalisation of household tasks characteristic of the post-war period is not coming to an end thanks to a more efficient use of ICTs time use. As Assar Lindbeck and Solveig Wikström put it: "the new information and communication technology is likely to induce households to take over a number of production tasks earlier pursued by firms...while during the industrialisation period 'outsourcing' was a main development, 'insourcing' is instead encouraged by ICTs ..." (Lindbeck and Wikström 2001, p.23). One may think of financial services, health, and tourism.

2.4 Conclusions

The developments described above give a rather complex picture of the possible impacts of ICTs on physical space that cannot be summarized in a couple of sentences. We did not really discuss the impact on local and urban development, addressed in other chapters of this book, such as Chap. 7. However, many of the questions raised in those papers with respect to the future function of e.g. cities depend crucially on the inflexibilities of the current, physical transportation and distribution infrastructures to be able to deal with congestion as opposed to the reliability and new opportunities offered by ICTs.

After a century of continuous industrialisation, also of services, most of the basic needs of Western societies, consumers, and citizens appear fulfilled, their welfare has increased substantially, and the amount of 'free time' increased. The space and time extensive development path, which accompanied this industrialisation process, appears to run against natural limits. ICTs can expand these limits. But it can also, partially at least, destroy those limits. The first effect consists of what we have described here as the complementary effect of the use of ICTs on space, the second effect as the substitution effect.

The complementary effect of ICTs can be considered as a form of space and time augmenting technological change. Distance can, with the help of 'just in time' be made less relevant, the rate of return to the physical infrastructure increased. Mobile communication offers solutions to the time problem when access is becoming difficult because of congestion. As to the knowledge sector, which we did not discuss here, it can be expected that ICTs will augment the rate of return to knowledge investments. This holds for research and development, education and training, marketing, as well as information and communication more generally. In this sense the physical proximity to the access of codified knowledge and information no longer represents a limiting factor, but the distinction between knowledge in which physical proximity might be important, e.g. when based on informal and social contacts, and codified knowledge remains essential. It is only this last form of knowledge, which appears no longer restricted by geographical frontiers but in Marshallian terms appears worldwide 'in the air', can be bought or acquired and understood and maintained by communities. From this perspective, the relation between ICTs and space calls for a new concept of agglomeration in a world characterized by the 'death of distance'. And that that world is still heavily characterized by location and agglomeration effects is obvious from the continuous success of Wall Street or the City, which everybody can nevertheless bypass thanks to his mobile or PC anywhere, any place.

The impact of the substitution effect is more difficult to estimate. Here we argued that certainly from a long-term perspective, one should remain open to the possibility of changes in the organisational set-up of industrial production whereby household activities would start to play (again) a more important role. What the exact implications would be of such a development trend for urban planning is difficult to predict. In one case there might be a clear need for new urban housing planning with a focus on up-to-date ICTs connections, in other cases the opposite with much more attention for social contact independent of work. The ways in which ICTs leads to complementary or substitution effects in consumption behaviour or labour organisation will in the end crucially depend on the way these developments are embedded in the social and societal environment. Both labour and consumption play an essential role in the need for social contact of humans. One cannot expect that substitution effects would ever become totally dominant and replace the present mobile consumption society. Rather the question can be put whether the need for social contact will remain in the future a 'by product' of an increasingly time and space stressed work, family and consumption life or rather will become the 'core product'. So that the largest part of the week, important, more content-based work is carried out nearby the home, and that the formal working place is visited for complementary, more social activities. Just as when people shop on Sundays 'for fun' without buying something but will only buy something after carefully have acquired all relevant information, e.g. through the Internet.

References

Autor DH, Levy F, Murnane RJ (2000) 'Upstairs, downstairs': computer-skill complementarity and computer-labour substitution on two floors of a large bank. National Bureau of Economic Research (NBER) Working Paper 7890, National Bureau of Economic Research, Washington, DC

Bresnahan T, Trajtenberg M (1995) General-purpose technologies: engines of growth. Journal of Econometrics 65: 83–108

Cairncross F (1998) The death of distance: how the communication revolution will change our lives. Harvard Business School Press, Boston, MA

David P (1991) Computer and dynamo: the modern productivity paradox in a not-too-distant mirror. American Economic Review 80: 355–61

Dosi G (1984) Technical change and industrial transformation. Macmillan, London

Freeman C, Perez C (1988) Structural crises of adjustment: business cycles and investment behaviour. In: Dosi G, Freeman, C, Nelson R, Silverberg G, Soete L (eds) Technical change and economic theory. Pinter, London, pp 38–66

Freeman C, Soete L (1994) Work for all or mass unemployment? Computerised technical change into the 21st century. Pinter Publishers, London

Groot L, de Grip A (1991) Technical change and skill formation in the bank sector. Economics of Education Review 10: 57–71

Harris R (1998) The Internet as a GPT: factor market implications. In: Helpman E (ed) General purpose technologies and economic growth. MIT Press, Cambridge MA, pp 145–66

Helpman E (1998) General purpose technologies and economic growth. MIT Press, Cambridge, MA

Katz BG, Philips, A (1982) Government, economies of scale and comparative advantage: the case of the computer industry. In Nelson RR (ed) Government and Technical Process: A Cross-Industry Analysis. Pergamon Press, New York, pp 162-232

Lindbeck A, Wikström S (2001) How will ICTs change the border between households and organizations? Paper presented at the Infonomics/Merit Workshop on Digitisation of Commerce: e-Intermediation (DoC:e-I), November 23–24, 2001, Maastricht

Lindbeck A, Snower DJ (2000) Multitask learning and the reorganization of work: from Tayloristic to holistic organization. Journal of Labour Economics 18: 353–76

Triplett JE (1996) High tech industry productivity and hedonic price indices. In: Organisation for Economic Co-operation and Development (OECD), Industry productivity, international comparison and measurement issues. OECD, Paris, pp 119–142

Section A: Clusters, Innovation and Entrepreneurship

3 Clustering in Space Versus Dispersing Over Space

Karen R. Polenske

Department of Urban Studies and Planning, Massachusetts Institute of Technology

3.1 Introduction

In a previous study (Polenske 2001b), I have maintained that assets should form the base of a regional economic-development strategy, where assets include both tangible (e.g., physical infrastructure) and intangible (e.g., skills and knowledge) ones. I laid out the underlying institutional, economic, and physical factors needed to have successful development. In this chapter, I analyse regional economic development from a different, but related, perspective to examine the role played by economies of scale and innovation in making regions competitive and to help make regional economic development sustainable.

I hypothesize that two types of economies of scale may enhance regional economic growth. The first type is the well known 'agglomeration economies'. The second type is 'dispersion economies', a concept that I first introduced in an earlier paper (Polenske 2001a). Other analysts either have dealt with this concept only indirectly in their discussions of the grouping and dispersing of economic activities, or they have used it in a different sense than I use the term here. Storper (1997, pp. 299-300), for example, briefly discusses how agglomeration economies may be more regional than local or may operate at a "system-of-city level".

Also, in an earlier book, Storper and Walker (1989, pp. 70-71) discuss dispersing as one of four types of locational patterns of industries, calling it "deagglomeration". Analysts explain this process of growth, they say, using either neoclassical or product-life cycle theories. Of the five variants of their theories of growth, the third one (p. 83) comes closest to my dispersion economy perspective. They state that "...industry... has dispersed rapidly in the twentieth century thanks to the flexibility and speed of truck traffic". They cite various factors as causes of deagglomeration, such as deindustrialization processes (p. 97), core-periphery relations, (p. 180), and deskilling of labour (p. 181), but they do not think in terms of regional and global supply-chains.

Dispersion economies/diseconomies, as I define them, may occur if cost-savings/cost increases result when firms disperse their activities away from the home office, often along regional or global supply-chains. One typical cost-saving method is the potential reduction in inventories when suppliers and customers of a firm are distributed along a supply chain. The new information and communication technologies (ICTs) certainly play an important role in promoting the dispersion of firms over space, partly because they may allow firms to reduce costs, details of which I discuss later.

In contrast, cost savings/increases that occur when firms locate in one geographical location may create agglomeration economies/diseconomies. If firms belonging to the same sector locate in one area, they may take advantage, on one hand, of the same training facilities, reaping a savings for all firms of a given sector (locational economies) or for firms from all sectors in a given region (urbanization economies). On the other hand, by locating close to other firms producing similar goods, they may create so much traffic that the congestion increases the time to ship inputs and outputs (locational/urbanization diseconomies). Following Hoover (1937, pp. 90-91), in his now classic location study of the shoe and leather industries, I distinguish two types of agglomeration economies: locational and urbanization economies. I use locational economies for the agglomeration economies accruing when similar firms locate in one area and take advantage of the various facilities in the region (trade associations, training institutes, etc.) and urbanization economies for the agglomeration economies accruing to a firm from the many different suppliers and producers locating in a particular area, each of whom takes advantage of the presence of banks, universities, labour, etc. that service diverse industries.

Thus, the factors leading to agglomeration and dispersion economies differ. Such a distinction should help policy planners realize that they need not follow a clustering strategy in order to have increased regional growth. Rather, for some situations, analysts should consider dispersing activities to reap cost-savings and other benefits.

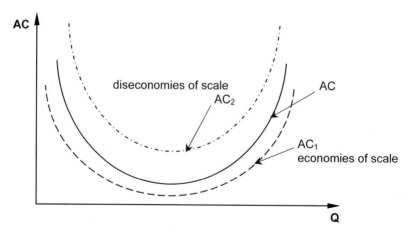

Fig.3.1. Agglomeration and dispersion economies and diseconomies of scale, AC = average cost, Q = quantity

An analyst can use the same theoretical structure, shifts in the average cost curve of the firm/industry, to measure both of these concepts. In other words, Fig. 3.1 represents both agglomeration and dispersion economies/diseconomies. A dispersion economy/diseconomy, for example, is external to the firm; thus, it moves the entire cost curve of the firm down (up) at all output levels, although the old and the new cost curves do not have to be parallel at different scales of output. An agglomeration economy/ diseconomy has the same effect on the cost curve. I stress, however, that the causes for the shifts from agglomeration economies usually differ from those for dispersion economies.

I explore factors creating the agglomeration and dispersion economies and the formation of world-class information and communication technologies and practices, regardless of size and type of industry, by examining (1) industrial clusters, industrial complexes, industrial districts, growth poles, and interfirm networks; (2) learning regions, (3) innovations; and (4) supply chains.

3.2 Industrial Clusters, Growth Poles, Industrial Complexes, Industrial Districts, and Interfirm Networks

Location theories are partially distinguished by the type of agglomeration economy emphasized, partially by whether they can account for both initial firm location and firm mobility, and partially by the focus on one or more of five major spatial concepts: (1) industrial clusters, (2) industrial complexes, (3) industrial districts, (4) growth centres/poles, and (5) interfirm networks. Many analysts seem to have gravitated to the use of the word 'cluster'. Martin and Sunley (2003, p. 2) effectively deconstruct the cluster concept to show the "many fundamental conceptual, theoretical and empirical questions", indicating that their concerns "relate to the definition of the cluster concept, its theorization, its empirics, the claims made for its benefits and advantages, and its use in policy-making". I would go even further than they have, because I believe that there is a strong similarity among the first four concepts I list above, including clusters, in the way in which they are used to define a spatial boundary. A discussion along similar lines can also be found in Chap. 7.

The "industrial-complex" and "industrial-district" concepts are very similar, in that both focus mainly on *localization economies/diseconomies*. Isard et al. (1959) and Isard and Vietorisz (1955), for example, use an input-output table to identify an "industrial complex" of interrelated Puerto Rican firms that have strong interindustrial linkages. To achieve high rates of economic growth, countries (regions) are advised to concentrate investments in firms located within the boundaries of this industrial complex in order to achieve agglomeration economies (Isard and Schooler 1959; Isard et al.1959). This type of industrial concentration is very similar to the "industrial districts", such as the Third Italy and Silicon Valley (Sabel 1989; Saxenian 1994), which became the centre of economic activity for certain types of industries, such as textiles, tiles, microcomputers, and electronics. One important difference between the two concepts is that most industrial-complex analysts use quantitative methods to group firms and conduct regional-development analyses, while industrial-district analysts most frequently use qualitative methods (e.g., case studies and firm surveys) to make and analyse the groupings.

Storper and Walker (1989), Porter (1985, 1990, 2000, 2001), and Markusen et al. (1999), for example, use the "industrial cluster" concept, which is based upon the "innovation cluster" concept of Schumpeter (1939, pp. 100-101). These two concepts are closely related to the "growth-pole (growth-centre)" concept (Perroux 1951) in that both are based upon the need for *urbanization economies*. Using an input-output table, growth-pole analysts select the key sector(s), not necessarily just one, and determine which ones have the highest backward linkages with suppliers and forward linkages with customers or consumers (Hirschman 1958), hence create the largest multiplier effects.

Analysts who discuss an industrial cluster generally include firms from a number of sectors, whereas when they discuss an industrial-complex, they refer to industries that form a single set of interrelated sectors (e.g., petrochemicals in the case of the Isard et al. (1959) study of Puerto Rico). For the remainder of this chapter, I will use the terms 'industrial cluster' and 'growth poles' interchangeably and the terms 'industrial districts' and 'industrial complexes' interchangeably. All four concepts help analysts define spatial economic boundaries around industrial activities. In terms of the focus of this chapter, I stress that all four concepts relate to agglomeration economies, so that I will later show that analysts conducting regional analyses tend to overlook the possibilities of regional growth occurring because of dispersion economies.

What about interfirm networks? The interfirm network concept is sometimes the same as and sometimes different from other industrial group notions. Interfirm networks, industrial clusters, and growth-poles all deal with the economic effects of spatial agglomeration of innovations with a given set of interorganizational (network) relationships (DeBresson and Amesse 1991, p. 364; Karlsson 1997). Markusen et al. (1999) maintain that interfirm networking occurs more within than across district boundaries. Their perspective of an interfirm network is therefore almost identical to an industrial cluster (district) or growth pole. Locke (1995), however, shows that more and more interfirm networking is occurring across industrial-district and national boundaries.

Interfirm networks, however, can be very different from an industrial cluster or growth pole. Locke (1995), for example, defines three ideal-types of interfirm networks: (1) hierarchical, (2) polarized, and (3) polycentric, which differ in regard to the structure of intergroup relations, patterns of association, and linkages of central policymakers. To participate in an interfirm network, industry managers do not necessarily need the same spatial location. Firms can network across geographic, social, and political boundaries (Messner 1997; Podolny and Page 1997). Thus, the information-economy revolution is allowing firms to develop national or global networks, which, at times, can assist and, at other times, hamper firm mobility and regional economic development (Castells and Hall 1994; Glaeser and Ellison 1997). Considerably more research is required concerning networks to determine (1) whether industrial clusters, industrial districts, or interfirm networks operate most efficiently in terms of agglomeration economies, especially in terms of reducing the average cost to the individual firm; (2) the relationship among distance, regional boundaries, and clusters/districts/networks for different types of interchange; and (3) the role of networking in helping clusters and districts to function effectively.

In Table 3.1, under Old Concepts, I show the relationship between these four grouping concepts and one or more of four types of agglomeration economies (diseconomies): (1) *scale*, (2) *localization*, (3) *urbanization*, and (4) *spatial-juxtaposition*, (the latter hereafter called *social*)[1]. Then, under New Concepts, I list some of the many types of chains that are discussed in the literature. Analysts should find the distinction among the four types of agglomeration economies and the four types of dispersion economies useful for developing new location theories, extending existing ones, testing the theories with empirical data, and providing appropriate industrial and regional-development advice to policy makers.

Because there is so much similarity among these industrial-concentration concepts, I discuss three major questions around which analysts can conduct systematic tests of the interaction between industrial concentration and innovation. First, do industrial concentration and innovation lead to new business growth, as posed by increasing-returns and some other location theorists?

Table 3.1. Agglomeration and dispersion economies/diseconomies

Agglomeration/Dispersion Concept	Type of Agglomeration/Dispersion Economies/Diseconomies and Networks
Old Concepts[a]	
Industrial Cluster	Internal, Urbanization, Scope
Industrial Complex	Internal, Localization, Social, Scope
Industrial District	Internal, Localization, Social, Scope
Industrial Growth Pole/Center	Internal, Urbanization, Scope
New Concepts	
Chain (Consumer-driven)	Dispersion, Scope, Horizontal Networks
Chain (Producer-driven)	Dispersion, Internal, Vertical Networks
Chain (Supply)	Dispersion, Internal, Vertical Networks
Interfirm Network	Dispersion, Scope

[a] Alfred Marshall (1890) is the first analyst to use the actual terms "internal economies" and "external economies". Alfred Weber (1929), the father of location economics, used these terms to help explain the concentration of small workshops in Germany.

DiPasquale and Wheaton (1996, pp. 170-172) conducted a test in eleven states, specifically to refute Krugman (1991). They used the 1987 share of national jobs for a given industry in each state and concentration ratios, i.e., the percentage of total jobs accounted for by a particular SIC (standard industrial classification) in-

---

[1] Spatial-juxtaposition economies/diseconomies, a distinction originated by Isard et al. (1959), are scale-economy (other than size) factors, such as quality control, training, and social-welfare economies that result when an industrial complex is located at only one site.

dustry. They conclude that for aggregate industries, concentration theory does not seem to hold, "but if done for four-digit SIC industries, it may hold" (p. 172). Even so, DiPasquale and Wheaton did not conduct a definitive test, partially because they were unable to control for industrial and subregional mixes. Also, their quantitative tests may not appropriately account for social and other agglomeration economies/diseconomies in the economy. Firms may cluster, for example, to take advantage of both physical and financial infrastructure support (Kaufman et al. 1994; Scott and Bergman 1995) and of external support organizations, such as trade and industrial associations, educational and training facilities, and research and development laboratories (Rosenfeld 1995; Sabel 1989; Saxenian 1994).

Concentration of firms may enhance the localization, social, and urbanization economies in the region. Over the last 70 years, for example, the Tooling and Manufacturing Association, to which many of Chicago's metalworking firms belong, helped to maintain the network of those firms as it went through various phases of a life cycle, enhancing its localization economies (McCormick 1996). Support systems, however, are sometimes inadequate. If industries are not making profits, for instance, the trade and industrial association formed by them will have a hard time to survive. Analysts testing statistically for concentration tendencies need to account for quantitative measures, such as profits, and other more qualitative measures, such as social networking.

Second, what other factors than transportation costs help firms determine whether or not to locate in a particular location? Labour costs usually represent a much larger cost to the firm than transport costs. In the United States in 1987, for example, transportation direct costs averaged less than three percent of total costs for all except one of 79 sectors, whereas labour direct costs were over 15 percent for most sectors (U.S. Department of Commerce 1994, pp. 64-71). Location theorists also can improve their theories by analysing not only transportation and labour costs, but also the relevance of various transportation characteristics. Supply-chain and other analysts (e.g., Pereria 1996; Polenske et al. 1996) show that for a significant number of firms, speed and reliability of shipments are of as much, or even more, concern than transport costs to both the shipping and receiving firm, with other attributes, such as accessibility, flexibility in delivery times, safety, and tracing of the shipments usually ranking high as well. These studies indicate that, although Glaeser and Ellison (1997) say that transportation cost is easy to model, it may not be the most critical location factor for most firms today.

Third, are dispersion economies benefiting regional development and, if so, how? Some evidence is surfacing that strong agglomeration tendencies seem to be counterbalanced by equally strong dispersion tendencies. Analysts, for example, find that industrial concentration in one region creates competitive disadvantages at given points of the business cycle and for large urban centres, especially if it is excessive. When technological change is rapid, the industrial complex of firms may be at a competitive disadvantage because firms resist, or do not have access to, information outside the complex (Glasmeier 1987; Glasmeier and Sugiura 1991). This resistance may also lead these firms to be less innovative than they otherwise would be (Harrison 1994, Chap. 4). These findings suggest that an agglomeration diseconomy may lead to firms moving to other locations in order to reap dispersion economies.

In addition, in countries as different as Brazil, Japan, Republic of Korea, and the United States, concentration of firms seems to create adverse economic impacts on urban size and income distribution among regions (Markusen et al. 1999). In some countries, the government may disperse industries from the core to the periphery, trading agglomeration economies for lower location costs and, if income distribution improves, helping to assure social and political stability. Industries may also disperse of their own accord. Another consideration is that excessive urbanization in New York and Pittsburgh was found to hinder the intergenerational transfer of entrepreneurial skills (Chinitz 1961).

Finally, firms usually concentrate in a region under distinct circumstances (Harrison et al. 1995; Harrison et al. 1996). If the economic activity does not already exist in a region, economic specialization in that activity is difficult to foster. An example is the lack of regional development in Appalachia (Hansen 1966). Analysts can devise ways to test for at least some of these agglomeration-dispersion tendencies.

In order to look at these concentration/dispersal tendencies in more detail, I first discuss analysts who have examined 'learning regions', which may be a leading example of an innovative concentration of firms taking advantage of agglomeration economies. I then contrast these agglomeration tendencies of the learning region with the dispersion tendency of regional and global supply chains, which are prime examples of some of the many ways firms are dispersing innovation across regions and the globe.

3.3 Learning Regions

I define regions to include communities, cities, provinces, and countries. Regardless of how analysts define a geographic region, in the learning region, the community/city/ province/country combines with academic institutions, firms, and government in the 'region' in collective-learning environments (Keeble and Wilkinson 1999). What is the purpose of a learning region? Do learning regions/communities initiate and sustain the development of ICTs? If so, how? How do they affect these technologies? What type(s) of assets (human, physical, and/or natural) help them to achieve sustainable development? To answer these questions, at least partially, I briefly review some of the extensive literature on learning regions/communities. Underlying my discussion are ideas obtained from Lundvall and Johnson's (1994) and Lundvall's (1996) classic articles on learning economies, supplemented with the extensive writing on learning regions by Asheim (1996, 1998, 1999, 2001a,b), including two of his latest joint articles (Asheim and Herstad 2002; Asheim and Isaksen 2002).

For the firms, the learning may be based on intrafirm, interfirm, and/or regional coalitions. Analysts emphasize the importance of knowledge and learning and the need to increase the rate of change of learning. In this respect, ICTs play an important role. As Lundvall (1996, p. 4) states, however, "The learning economy is affected by the increasing use of information technology, but it is not synonymous with what is often called 'the information society' ".

A learning region is one in which industry, community, government, and educational centres in a region all work together to help the region develop (Polenske 2004). It is characterized by a set of horizontal relationships among the actors, who exchange and compare knowledge and experiences, so that problems are solved by "...extracting the best out of a broad range of experiences and ideas" (Asheim 2001b, p. 9). Networks and organizations in the region share the knowledge interactively (Lundvall 1996, p. 2); thus, knowledge becomes one of the intangible collective assets of the region (Polenske 2001b).

Although the term 'learning region' is relatively new, it has important roots in the flexible production, flexible-specialization literature (Plummer and Taylor 2001), and even in writings of Alfred Marshall (Asheim 2000). Valuable discussions of the concept are included in many articles, including those by Asheim (2001a, b), Asheim and Dunford (1997), Boekema et al. (2000), Florida (1995), Lundvall (1996), Lundvall and Johnson (1994), and Morgan (1997), to name just a few. One view is that the idea of a learning region modified the interpretation of industrial districts by incorporating social relations, competitiveness, networks, learning, knowledge, and innovations. By locating in industrial districts, Piore and Sable (1984) indicated firms were able to achieve the multiplier effects and agglomeration economies of growth poles. Another perspective of the learning region is that it modified the way in which policy makers use 'flexible specialization' at a regional level. Thus, analysts, such as Sabel (1989), Hirst and Zeitlin (1992), and Best (1990), use the term 'flexible specialization' to show policy makers that small and medium-size firms, research and development institutes, and contractual relations are important elements of the way firms can share distribution, production inputs, information, and technologies.

Porter (1998, p. 78) represents another perspective. He defines clusters as "geographic concentrations of interconnected companies and institutions in a particular field. Clusters encompass an array of linked industries and other entities important to competition". According to Porter's definition, all learning regions are clusters. Even so, usually, not all clusters are learning regions. Ennals and Gustavsen (1999) define a different type of learning region, namely, development coalitions, indicating that these coalitions may range all the way from small and medium workplaces to regions and larger networks of firms to entire nations. According to Ennals and Gustavsen's definition, not all learning regions are clusters, which counters Porter's definition.

Asheim (1996, 2001a), Lundvall and Johnson (1994), and other European analysts indicate that regional policy makers need to establish learning regions in order to achieve community revitalization. Authors such as Lundvall (1996) emphasize the need to build social capital and to create educational initiatives. Lundvall (1996, p. ii) maintains that in the learning economy, "... the capacity to learn increasingly determines the relative position of individuals, firms, and national systems". For a learning region to be sustainable policymakers in the region must emphasize the distribution of capabilities to learn; otherwise the labour markets will become increasingly polarized. Concerning the learning, Lundvall and Johnson (1994) distinguish four types of knowledge: (1) *know-what* (knowledge of facts, which is easy to codify), (2) *know-why* (knowledge of principles that exist in nature, the human mind, and the society, some of which is relatively easy to codify), (3) *know-how* (knowledge of skills, capabilities, and other knowledge that in today's world creates incentives for firms to develop networks to exchange this know-how. Only some of this knowledge can be codified, (4) *know-who* (socially embedded knowledge, learned from customers, contractual arrangements, etc., that is difficult to transfer because it is tacit knowledge). The know-how and know-who forms of knowledge are playing increasingly important roles in society. Asheim (2001b, p. 10) maintains that, in a learning economy that is being globalized, there is a "transition from an internal knowledge base in specific industries (i.e., high-tech sectors) to a globally distributed knowledge base of firms, caused by the general increased knowledge intensity in post-Fordist learning economies"[2].

As the reader can see, these analysts are creating some confusion by calling the same notion by a different name, most with the word 'learning' attached. For example, Asheim uses the terms 'learning organizations', 'learning regions', 'learning systems', and 'development coalitions', but so far he has not clearly identified the differences, if any, among these concepts. He only says that a development coalition is one type of learning organization, which are organizations that are "fluid, transnational, continuously reshaping themselves to meet new challenges" (Asheim 2001b, p. 9).

What do these authors say about the effect of learning regions on the development of ICTs and vice versa? Lundvall (1996, p. ii) maintains that "the relationship between codified and tacit knowledge is symbiotic and that ... tacit knowledge and the learning of skills will be fundamental for the economic success of agents..." I leave the remainder of the answer to this question to the next section, because innovation is an important component of the ICT sector.

3.4 Innovation

The British government has called for an intensive investigation of the role that innovation is playing in regions in Britain and has provided a considerable amount of funding for studies of innovation and entrepreneurship in what is called CMI (an alliance between Cambridge University in England and the Massachusetts Institute of Technology in the United States). Fingleton et al. (2002, p. 1) state that high-technology production is increasing in economic importance for the biotechnology, telecommunications, electronics, and computer services sectors. As a result, the British government has declared knowledge to be the most important

---

[2] If this type of diffusion is occurring, then learning regions may be helped by dispersion economies, although my main argument in this section is that learning regions are prime examples of agglomeration economies.

'driver' of economic growth for economies that are trying to achieve an overall competitive advantage. This growth, they maintain, leads to geographically concentrated economic activity, that some economic analysts call 'high-technology cluster'.

Innovation is important to the survival of most firms, but the type of innovation that occurs differs from firm-to-firm and depends partially on the size of the firm (Keeble 1997)[3]. Some innovations seem to occur when firms locate in one region, while other types of innovation need firms to be dispersed.

One example of differences even when firms are clustered is the innovative, cooperative, collaborative aspects of firms in the Silicon Valley versus the hierarchical, centralized decision-making of the firms along Route 128 (Saxenian 1994). Firms in both regions started producing electronics: semiconductors (1960s) and chips (1970s) in the Silicon Valley and transistors and other solid-state devices (1960s) and microcomputers (late 1970s) along Route 128. According to Saxenian, however, Silicon Valley firms soon dominated the semiconductor field and also took a lead with small workstations and personal computers. Although firms in both regions were relatively clustered, Saxenian maintains that it was the type of decision-making, not the clustering, that helps one type to succeed better than the other.

Instead of looking at the success of a cluster of innovative industries in a particular region, Gertler (1993) looks at the restructuring of particular innovative sectors, such as advanced technology machinery producers. Gertler (1995) has an intriguing way of looking at the successful relationships between the producers and users of this machinery, showing that they are enhanced by three types of 'closeness': (1) physical (geographical) distance, (2) organizational (interaction, collaboration, shared workplace practices, and training) distance, and (3) cultural (common language, modes of communication, customs, conventions, and social norms) distance.

Gertler (1995, 1996) articulates his approach clearly. Each type of distance, he claims, has a strong influence on whether or not new technology will be adopted and, if it will, on the ease with which it is adopted. Through an extensive postal survey of 400 so-called "technology-implementation experiences" in 170 plants, combined with personal interviews in 20 plants, he finds that implementation difficulties are persistent and significant (1996, p. 20). The greatest difficulties were experienced by small plants, by firms using foreign (especially overseas) technology, and by firms using technology that had one or more of the three 'distance' attributes. Physical distance did affect implementation for all firms, but especially for small firms. This finding would imply that dispersion economies differ for large and small firms. Gertler also found that when the 'workplace culture' between the producer and the user of the technology is distinctly different (cultural distance), implementation is very difficult. Such differences may be related to physical distance, but more often are associated with social diseconomies. In addition, he determined that institutions and regulatory systems that assist firms in maintaining long-term relations with their employees are important factors that

---

[3] Schumpeter (1939) differentiates between innovations and entrepreneurship.

shorten the organizational distance and lead to effective implementation on a timely basis.

In summary, Gertler found that long and extended interactions between producers and users are very important for small enterprises and those that are domestically owned, single-plant establishments and that large distances (in any of the three meanings) reduced the effectiveness of the implementation. Even large enterprises feel the need for closeness, not only in terms of distance, but also organizationally and culturally. He would maintain, I assume, that distance does create extra costs for innovators.

Block (1990) presents a treatise that tends to destroy the traditional concepts of capital. Based upon Block's conceptions, Gertler discusses some of the qualitative changes that are occurring in process technologies, such as the use of microprocessors and electronic controls in industrial machinery[4]. The results of these changes include: lower machine prices and smaller size of plant (both of which lead to capital savings), lower capital/output ratios; and machines that are capable of producing a large number of products. At the same time, Gertler maintains that the plant size is being reduced (again creating cost savings) due to changes in the internal and interfirm organization of production, such as fewer inventories and fewer machines. He does not indicate however whether the decline in machinery costs is greater than the decline in plant costs.

If all of this is indeed occurring, physical accounts for the firm will show that fewer machines and floor space are needed than before such change occurred, and the value accounts of the firm will show a decline in the dollar value of investment. Yet, the productive capacity of a region where the firm is located will be greater than before. These and other dilemmas attached to accurate measurement have led some analysts, influenced by new growth theorists, to study only the machinery and equipment portion of annual investment, believing that technology and investment are closely linked, but their approach is still aggregate. Gertler favours examining the adoption of each new process technology individually, as he did in his survey discussed above, indicating that a socially constructed model of technology aids an understanding of the sectors and regions in which investment occurs and its relationship to the process of technological change.

Lam (1998a) has conducted an extensive study of an advanced information-technology Japanese and British firm who wish to collaborate to acquire skills and knowledge from each other. She finds that the socially embedded nature of knowledge can impede cross-national collaborative work and knowledge sharing. This is knowledge that "is not migratory, because it is embedded in complex social interactions and team relationships within organizations" (p. 10). In fact, the two firms have completely different methods of organizing work, with the Japanese having an 'organizational' method of structuring high-level work that relies on worker interaction and minimum hierarchy, thus relying on tacit knowledge that can mainly be obtained through experience. The British have a 'professional'

---

[4] Block supports his position by studies of the metalworking industries where productivity gains from these qualitative improvements range from 200 to 300 percent (Block 1990, pp. 142-143).

method in which workers rely on formulas, manuals, and blueprints. Considerable friction developed when the teams from each firm tried to work together, until finally, they divided most work between the two firms, rather than collaborating on it (Lam 1998a, b).

Her study is captivating because it lends yet one more example to the debate concerning whether tacit knowledge, as originally defined by Polanyi (1966) can be codified. Her example seems to say that it cannot be when the social differences are as great as those between Japan and Britain. She states that the "differences are deeply embedded in the contrasting national systems of skills formation, labour markets, and occupational structures", concluding that "there is no evidence in the present study that the two partner firms, despite their long years of close collaboration, have become more alike in their organisational forms or knowledge bases. On the contrary, the two firms appear to have become more divergent in their distinctive and complementary capabilities" (Lam 1998a, p. 36). Lam's findings are supported by her later study (Lam 1998b) and are partially based on the extensive study of these factors by Nonaka (1994) and Nonaka and Takeuchi (1995). Nonaka calls the Japanese type of factor "knowledge of experience", which is tacit knowledge learned within a particular context.

The Japanese style of management is one factor that analysts are examining. Gertler's research of German and Canadian firms tends to support Nonaka's findings in that German workers seem able to fix problems as they arise on the job, whereas for many problems, Canadian workers need to call in someone to fix the problem. Thus, whereas location theorists stress the need for geographic proximity among firms, Gertler, Nonaka, Lam and others stress organizational and cultural proximity as well. Fine et al. (1995, p. 5) add electronic proximity, which refers "to the form and intensity of electronic communication between economic agents". They indicate (1995, p, 11) that "...electronic proximity may act as a substitute or either physical or organization proximity, or both".

Lundvall (1996, p. 11) is less optimistic indicating that firms introducing new automation and information technology in Denmark initially elicit a significant slowing of productivity growth for at least four years compared with firms that do not use the new technology. This slowing is caused, he says, by many factors, but especially by firm workers needing to accept substantial organizational change in order to learn the new technologies. For those firms that simultaneously introduce the new technology and new forms of organization, the learning costs are significantly reduced.

Leamer and Storper (2001) are more upbeat in their discussion of the economic geography associated with the Internet.

Some scholars (e.g., DeBresson and Amesse 1991, p. 388) argue that a network of innovators is needed to ensure success. This network supposedly could be dispersed across space. Scholars maintain that a network can help reduce transaction costs, foster collective learning, link the innovation to the market, overcome failures in market creation for technological services, establish social norms and standards for the new market, and generate trust (Sabel 1992; Teubel et al. 1991). Continuous innovation, timeliness, and rapid product development, in turn, requires cooperation and trust among firms (Saxenian 1994). According to Schmitz

(1996), the basis of trust between firm owners, workers, and others changes over time and evolves from an "ascribed" trust among those in the same social group within a region to "earned" trust among outsiders in the global market.

Cooperation allows firms to share research and development costs, access to credit, training, etc. (Sabel 1992). This sharing reduces the production costs of each small firm, which otherwise would not have low-cost access to such services[5]. Firms in the Silicon Valley, for example, form a regional network where there is collective learning, dense social networks, open labour markets, with considerable horizontal communication among firm divisions and with outside suppliers, trade associations, and universities (Saxenian 1994). The Silicon Valley firms thus form a learning region. An important finding, if true, from the Silicon Valley case is that the firms were able to capture the economies of scale and scope simultaneously at the level of the district, not the individual firm.

Also, Porter (1998, pp. 85-86) maintains that "In fact, there is no such thing as a low-tech industry. There are only low-tech companies – that is, companies that fail to use world-class technology and practices to enhance productivity and innovation". If this is so, technological and biological firms are not the only ones that can be competitive, productive, and innovative in the new global arena. Rather, most firms with the right set of tangible and intangible assets can succeed.

So far, I have dealt with dispersion economies only briefly, yet I maintain that they are playing an increasingly important role in today's global economy, and I examine them through the concept of 'supply chains'.

3.5 Supply Chains

Earlier in Table 3.1, I listed supply chains and then two specific types of supply chains, producer-driven and consumer-driven. In addition to reducing costs, managers of consumer-driven supply chains have as one of the primary goals helping to create improvements in customer service. Either type of supply chain can be internal to a firm/region or extend beyond the boundaries of the firm/region to the nation or globally. In an earlier chapter (Polenske 2001a), I examined some of the factors affecting both the internal and external types of supply chains. Most analysts discuss producer supply chains, or discuss supply chains without differentiating them. I note that the supply-chain terms used by regional scientists and economists often differ from those used by management and transportation analysts. As an example, a customer-driven chain is often called a 'pull' system, while a producer-driven chain is called a 'push' system.

In this chapter, I concentrate on the global supply chain, although many dispersion economies/diseconomies affect regional or internal supply chains as well. Most global supply-chain analysts focus on the producer-driven supply chain, in

---

[5] A similar concept of sharing is behind the creation of the manufacturing centres in the United States that have been set up by the U.S. National Institute of Science and Technology (Sabel 1996).

which the producer is looking for ways to reduce costs, reduce the time it takes to get the product to market, and expand the market for the product(s).

In a different study (Polenske 2004), I differentiate three types of analysts who wrote about restructuring, namely: (1) Italian model, (2) Japanese model, and (3) Global Model. I call those who study the success of multinational corporations in the post-Fordist period the "global-model analysts", which include Amin and Robbins (1990), Gereffi and Korzeniewicz (1994), Harrison (1992, 1994), MacDuffie and Helper (1999), Martinelli and Schoenberger (1991), and Scott (1993). These global analysts disagree with those who emphasize the role of small firms in the restructuring of production, although they agree that restructuring is occurring and that flexibility is being incorporated into the production and distribution processes. Castells and Hall (1994) assert that networks among all sizes of firms are critical to allow flexible specialization to thrive.

The global firms are adopting supply-chain management techniques, enabling them to push risks and costs along the supply chain by just-in-time (JIT) production. Specifically, rather than to absorb the cost of warehousing or of having extra supplies on hand at the production site, the global analysts indicate that the suppliers and the customers are now having to cover these costs. Five chief characteristics are associated with these firms: (1) an increased internationalisation of capital, (2) more effective corporate integration, (3) increased control over markets and finance, (4) pushing of risks and costs along the supply chain onto small suppliers, and (5) the need for support from both the public and private sectors.

An important forerunner to the global perspective and supply chains is the work by Chandler (1977) on the rise of large firms. The managers of these firms created the hierarchically organized firm to achieve their dominant competitive position. They used producer-driven supply chains, where managers oversaw the entire supply chain from the raw-material supplier to the ultimate consumer. As a result, they were able to use these attributes and scientific-management procedures to reap 'economies of time'. Such an organizational structure seems to stand in sharp contrast to that proposed by the horizontal structure of the learning-region advocates.

Why is the large firm adopting more flexible production techniques and flourishing? Harrison (1994, pp. 9-10) argued as follows. First, they are downsizing both the number of activities and number of employees, thus reducing costs. Second, the directors of the large firms develop a core-periphery labour relationship. They segment the employees into a core group, who are kept at the headquarters, are paid high salaries, and collaborate in the production decisions, and a periphery group, who are dispersed to other locations or hired in locations distant from the plant, some of which may be overseas. I argue that this is one of several ways in which firms can reap dispersion economies. Third, they network both within their own corporation and with other corporations, through respective intrafirm and interfirm networks. Finally, managers are using computers increasingly both for manufacturing and management information systems to help coordinate and monitor their activities and employees and to increase the flexibility of production and marketing. Thus, firms are working not only to reduce costs, but also to disperse them along the supply chain.

As is the case of Harrison, many of these global analysts deal with regions in terms of the way the corporations develop a network of supplier firms across space and allocate core workers to the urban centres and peripheral workers to the suburbs or elsewhere. By incorporating the regional dimension, these analysts can determine the way the organizational boundary of the firm changes and the way costs are dispersed across regions. Ettlinger (1992) investigates the specific way in which large corporate organizations affect the regional geography. The Gereffi and Korzeniewicz (1994) research on global commodity-chains supports my contention that dispersion economies are helping to maintain a viable supply chain. They develop a global commodity-chain framework to study different segments of the chain, from the core region, where the innovating firms locate, to the peripheral regions, where the low-cost firms locate and employ low-skill workers. Rather than to look at networks of firms in a region, they study the network of large transnational firms and their customers across political boundaries.

Because large transnational producers control the supply chain, they disperse globally and control the way the costs are dispersed along the chain. Thus, they control many of the small firms. As I have stated in another paper (Polenske 2004), these large multinationals do interfirm networking within the large corporation, among other large firms, and between the large and the small firms, mostly through supply chains, with the spatial boundary being extended globally. The organizational boundary extends along the producer-supply chain, with the large producer controlling the market.

3.6 Conclusions

I began this chapter by hypothesizing that two types of economies are affecting regional economic growth, namely, agglomeration economies/diseconomies and dispersion economies/diseconomies. A number of analysts reviewed above show that this may be so. More empirical tests, however, still need to be made. No analyst has tested the hypothesis I put forth, partially perhaps because the concept of dispersion economies is only two-years old (introduced in 2003). I created the concept based on a belief that the economies from dispersing economic activity is an important factor affecting regional development, but regional analysts have not yet systematically examined the effects.

I think that the increasing number of global and regional supply-chain analyses may be a good place to start with the empirical tests. In fact, my own research staff and I have several case studies in the United States and the People's Republic of China (China) that may provide sources for such tests. We had a different objective for our work on supply chains for the Chicago metalworking sector (Polenske et al. 1996), but the plant surveys we conducted may provide some information we could use.

Likewise, I could glean some empirical data from our six-year environmental and energy study of the coke-making sector in the People's Republic of China in which we are conducting surveys of coke making township and village enterprises

(TVEs) and state-owned enterprises (SOEs). I can use these data to help determine whether or not dispersal of plants leads to cost savings—at least for the metal-working and coke making sectors.

I did not expect to find studies of dispersion economies, but I think it is important to measure empirically the cost-savings of the agglomeration/dispersion of firms. Fingleton et al. (2002) recently conducted some tests of cluster intensity. They are looking at a different question from mine, but they found that their econometric estimates "support the hypothesis that cluster intensity is a cause of employment growth, although there are important differences of scale at which this effect operates for the two sectors [computing services and research and development] considered" (Fingleton et al. 2002, p. 1).

Many analyses are needed to provide sufficient empirical evidence that will support or not support my hypothesis that both agglomeration and dispersion economies are important for regional economic development. The analyses should be both quantitative and qualitative. There is obviously considerable need for such studies. The results should be fascinating and will help policy makers as they make industrial policies.

Acknowledgements. I thank Natalia Sizov for technical assistance, and the two reviewers and Yu Li for insightful comments. For additional discussion of some of the restructuring literature, the reader is encouraged to refer to my paper on cooperation, collaboration, and competition (Polenske 2004).

References

Amin A, Robbins K (1990) The re-emergence of regional economies? The mythical geography of flexible accumulation. Environment and Planning: Society and Space 8: 7–34

Asheim BT (1996) Industrial districts as 'learning regions': a condition for prosperity? European Planning Studies 4: 379–400

Asheim BT (1998) Learning regions as development coalitions: partnership as governance in European workfare states? Paper Presented at the Second European Urban and Regional Studies Conference on "Culture, Place and Space in Contemporary Europe", September 17–20, University of Durhan, Durhan

Asheim BT (1999) Interactive learning and localised knowledge in globalising learning economies. Geography Journal 49: 345–352

Asheim BT (2000) Industrial districts: the contributions of Marshall and beyond. In: Clark GL, Feldman M, Gertler M (eds) The Oxford handbook of economic geography. Oxford University Press, Oxford, pp 413–431

Asheim BT (2001a) Learning regions as development coalitions: partnership as governance in European workfare states? Concepts and transformation. International Journal of Action Research and Organizational Renewal 6: 73–101

Asheim BT (2001b) Project organisation and globally distributed knowledge bases. Centre for Technology, Innovation and Culture Working Paper, University of Oslo, Oslo

Asheim BT, Dunford, M (1997) Regional futures. Regional Studies 31: 445–455

Asheim BT, Herstad S (2002) Regional clusters under international duress: between local institutions and global corporations. In: Asheim BT, Mariussen Å (eds) Innovations, regions and projects: studies in new forms of knowledge governance. NORDREGIO report R2003: 3, NORDREGIO, Stockholm, pp 203-239

Asheim BT, Isaksen A (2002) Regional innovation systems: the integration of local 'sticky' and global 'ubiquitous' knowledge. Journal of Technology Transfer 27: 77–86

Best M (1990) The new competition: institutions of industrial restructuring. Harvard University Press, Cambridge, MA

Block FL (1990) Postindustrial possibilities: a critique of economic discourse. University of California Press, Berkeley, CA

Boekema FK, Bakkers MS, Rutten R (2000) Knowledge, innovation and economic growth: the theory and practice of learning regions. Edward Elgar, Cheltenham

Castells M, Hall P (1994) Technopoles of the world: the making of 21st century industrial complexes. Routledge, London

Chandler AD Jr (1977) The visible hand. Harvard University Press, Cambridge, MA

Chinitz B (1961) Contrasts in agglomeration: New York and Pittsburgh. American Economic Review 51: 279–289

DeBresson C, Amesse F (1991) Networks of innovators: a review and introduction to the issue. Research Policy 20: 363–379

DiPasquale D, Wheaton WC (1996) Urban economics and real estate markets. Prentice Hall, Englewood Cliffs, NJ

Ennals R, Gustavsen B (1999) Work organisation and Europe as a development coalition. John Benjamin's, Amsterdam

Ettlinger N (1992) Modes of corporate organization and the geography of development. Papers in Regional Science 71: 107-26

Fine C, Gilboy G, Oye K, Parker G (1995) Technology supply chains: an introductory essay. Working Draft by the International Motor Vehicle Program at MIT Sloan School of Management, Cambridge, MA. Available at
http://imvp.mit.edu/papers/95/Fine/fine2.pdf

Fingleton B, Igliori DC, Moore B (2002) Employment growth of small high-technology firms and the role of horizontal clusters: evidence from computing services and R&D in Great Britain 1991–2000. Paper Presented at the "High-Technology, Small Firms One-Day Clusters" Conference, April 18, Manchester Business School, Small Business Service, Manchester

Florida R (1995) Toward the learning region. Futures 27: 527–536

Gereffi G, Korzeniewicz M (eds) (1994) Commodity chains and global capitalism. Praeger, Westport, CT

Gertler MS (1993) Implementing advanced manufacturing technologies in mature industrial regions: towards a social model of technology production. Regional Studies 27: 665–680

Gertler MS (1995) 'Being there': proximity, organization, and culture in the development and adoption of advanced manufacturing technologies. Economic Geography 71: 1–26

Gertler MS (1996). Worlds apart: the changing market geography of the German machinery industry. Small Business Economics 8: 87-106

Glaeser E, Ellison G (1997) Geographic concentration in U.S. manufacturing industries: a dartboard approach. Journal of Political Economy 105: 889–927

Glasmeier A (1987) Factors governing the development of high technology clusters: a tale of three cities. Regional Studies 22: 287–301

Glasmeier A, Sugiura N (1991) Japan's manufacturing system: small business, subcontracting, and regional complex formation. International Journal of Urban and Regional Research 15: 395–414

Hansen N (1966) Some neglected factors in American regional development policy: the case of Appalachia. Land Economics 62: 1–9

Harrison B (1992) Industrial districts: old wine in new bottles? Regional Studies 26: 469–483

Harrison B (1994) Lean and mean: the changing landscape of corporate power in the age of flexibility. Basic Books, New York

Harrison B, Glasmeier AK, Polenske KR (1995) National, regional, and local economic development policy: new thinking about old ideas. (Report prepared for the Economic Development Administration, U.S. Department of Commerce)

Harrison B, Kelley M, Gant J (1996) Innovative firm behavior and local milieu: exploring the intersection of agglomeration, firm effects, and technological change. Economic Geography 72: 233–258

Hirschman AO (1958) The strategy of economic development. Yale University Press, New Haven, CT

Hirst P, Zeitlin J (1992) Flexible specialization versus post-Fordism: theory, evidence, and policy implication. In: Storper M, Scott AJ (eds) Pathways to industrialization and regional development. Routledge, London, pp 70–115

Hoover EM (1937) Spatial price discrimination. Review Economic Studies 4: 182–191

Isard W, Schooler EW (1959) Industrial complex analysis, agglomeration economies, and regional development. Journal of Regional Science 1: 19–33

Isard W, Vietorisz T (1955) Industrial complex analysis and regional development, with particular reference to Puerto Rico. Papers and Proceedings of the Regional Science Association 1: 227–256

Isard W, Schooler EW, Vietorisz T (1959) Industrial complex analysis and regional development. John Wiley, New York

Karlsson C (1997) Product development, innovation networks, infrastructure and agglomeration economies. The Annals of Regional Science 31: 235–258

Kaufman A, Gittell R, Merenda M, Naumes W, Wood C (1994) Porter's model for geographic competitive advantage: The case of New Hampshire. Economic Development Quarterly 8: 43–66

Keeble D (1997) Small firms, innovation and regional development in Britain in the 1990s. Regional Studies 31: 281–293

Keeble D, Wilkinson F (1999) Collective learning in knowledge development in the evolution of regional clusters of high technology SMEs in Europe. Regional Studies 33: 295–303

Krugman P (1991) Geography and trade. MIT Press, Cambridge, MA

Lam A (1998a) The social embeddedness of knowledge: problems of knowledge sharing and organisation learning in international high-technology ventures. DRUID Working Paper No. 98–7, Danish Research Unit for Industrial Dynamics, Aalborg Copenhagen

Lam A (1998b) Tacit knowledge, organisational learning and innovation: a societal perspective. Danish Research Unit for Industrial Dynamics (DRUID) Working Paper No. 98–22, Danish Research Unit for Industrial Dynamics, Aalborg Copenhagen

Leamer E, Storper M (2001) The economic geography of the Internet age. National Bureau of Economic Research (NBER) Working Paper 8450, National Bureau of Economic Research, Washington, DC

Locke RM (1995) Remaking the Italian economy. Cornell University Press, Ithaca, NY

Lundvall BÅ (1996) The social dimension of the learning economy. Danish Research Unit for Industrial Dynamics (DRUID) Working Paper No. 96–1, Danish Research Unit for Industrial Dynamics, Aalborg Copenhagen

Lundvall BÅ, Johnson B (1994) The learning economy. Journal of Industry Studies 1: 23–42

MacDuffie JP, Helper S (1999) Creating lean suppliers: diffusing lean production throughout the supply chain. In: Liker, J, Adler P, and Friun M (eds) Remade in America: transplanting and transforming Japanese production systems. Oxford University Press, New York, pp 154-200

Markusen AR, Lee YS, DiGiovanna S (eds) (1999) Second-tier cities: rapid growth beyond the metropolis. University of Minnesota Press, Minneapolis, MN

Marshall A (1890) Principles of economics. Macmillan, London

Martin R, Sunley P (2003) Deconstructing clusters: chaotic concept or policy panacea? Journal of Economic Geography 3: 5–35

Martinell F, Schoenberger E (1991) Oligopoly is alive and well: notes for a broader discussion of flexible accumulation. In: Benko G, Dunford M (eds) Industrial change and regional development: the transformation of new industrial spaces. Belhaven Press/Printer, London New York, pp 117-133

McCormick LE (1996) The rise and fall of network production in twentieth century Chicago manufacturing. Ph.D. thesis, Massachusetts Institute of Technology, Cambridge, MA

Messner D (1997) The network society: economic development and international competitiveness as problems of social governance. GDI Book Series No. 10, Great Britain

Morgan K (1997) The learning region: institutions, innovation and regional renewal. Regional Studies 31: 491–503

Nonaka I (1994) A dynamic theory of organizational knowledge creation. Organization Science 5: 14–37

Nonaka I, Takeuchi H (1995) The knowledge creating company. Oxford University Press, New York

Pereira AE (1996) Implications for transportation planning of changing production and distribution processes. Ph.D. thesis, Massachusetts Institute of Technology, Cambridge, MA

Perroux F (1951) The economy of 20th century (in French). Presses Universitaires de France, Paris

Piore MJ, Sabel CF (1984) The second industrial divide: possibilities for prosperity. Basic Books, New York

Plummer P, Taylor M (2001) Theories of local economic growth (part 1): concepts, models, and measurement. Environment and Planning A 33: 219–236

Podolny JM, Page K (1997) Network forms of organization. Annual Review of Sociology 24: 57–76

Polanyi M (1966) The tacit dimension. Anchor Day Books, New York

Polenske KR (2001a) Competitive advantage of regional internal and external supply chains. In: Lahr M, Miller RE (eds) Essays in honor of Benjamin H. Stevens. Elsevier Publishers, Amsterdam, pp 259–284

Polenske KR (2001b) Taking advantage of a region's competitive assets: an asset-based regional economic-development strategy. In: Entrepreneurship, firm growth, and regional development in the new economic geography. Uddevalla Symposium 2000, June 15–17, Trollhättan, Sweden, pp 527–544

Polenske KR (2004) Competition, collaboration, cooperation: an uneasy triangle in networks of firms and regions. Regional Studies 38: 1029-1043

Polenske KR, McCormick LE, Perreira AE, Rockler NO (1996) Industrial restructuring, infrastructure investment, and transportation in the Midwest. Report to the Joyce Foundation, Chicago Manufacturing Center, and National Institute for Science and Technology, Chicago, IL

Porter ME (1985) Competitive advantage: creating and sustaining superior performance. Free Press, New York

Porter ME (1990) The competitive advantage of nations. Free Press, New York

Porter ME (1998) Clusters and the new economics of competitiveness. Harvard Business Review 76: 77–90

Porter ME (2000) Location, competition, and economic development: local clusters in a global economy. Economic Development Quarterly 12: 15–42

Porter ME (2001) Regions and the new economics of competition. In: Scott AJ (ed) Global city-regions. Oxford University Press, New York, pp 139–157

Rosenfeld S (1995) Industrial strength strategies: regional business clusters and public policy. The Aspen Institute Rural Economic Policy Program, Washington, D.C.

Sabel CF (1989) Flexible specialization and the re-emergence of regional economics. In: Hirst P, Zeitlin J (eds) Reversing industrial decline. Berg, Oxford, pp 17-70

Sabel CF (1992). Studied trust: building new forms of co-operation in a volatile economy. In: Pyke F, Sengenberger W (eds) Industrial districts and local economic regeneration. International Institute for Labour Studies, Geneva, pp 215–250

Sabel CF (1996) A Measure of federalism: assessing manufacturing technology centers. Research Policy 25: 281–307

Saxenian AL (1994) Regional advantage: culture and competition in Silicon Valley and Route 128. Harvard University Press, Cambridge, MA

Schmitz H (1996) From ascribed to earned trust in exporting clusters. Institute of Development Studies, University of Sussex, Brighton

Schumpeter, JA (1939) Business cycles. McGraw-Hill, New York

Scott AJ (1993) Technopolis: high-technology industry and regional development in Southern California. University of California Press, Berkeley, CA

Scott AJ, Bergman D (1995) The industrial resurgence of southern California? Advanced ground transportation equipment manufacturing and local economic development. Environmental Planning C (Government and Policy) 13: 97–124

Storper M (1997) The regional world: territorial development in a global economy. Guilford Press, New York

Storper M, Walker R (1989) The capitalist imperative: territory, technology, and industrial growth. Basil Blackwell, Oxford

Teubal M, Yinnon T, Zuscovitch E (1991) Networks and market creation. Regional Policy 20: 381–392

U.S. Department of Commerce (1994) The input-output structure of the U.S. economy, 1987. U.S. Department of Commerce, Bureau of Economic Analysis, Washington, D.C., pp 64–71

Weber A (1929) Theory of the location of industries (English Edition). University of Chicago Press, Chicago, IL

4 Regional Innovation Systems in Small and Medium-Sized Regions

Martin Andersson and Charlie Karlsson

Jönköping International Business School, Jönköping University

4.1 Introduction

Continuous product and process innovations are prerequisites for sustainable growth of both nations and regions. How such innovations are created and how successful innovation processes can be initiated are therefore extremely important questions. In recent years, it has been recognized that innovations are normally the result of ongoing and prolonged collaboration and interaction between firms and a variety of actors around them. These actors include customers, producers, subcontractors, consultants, public organizations, research institutes and universities, etc. Also, institutions interpreted as normative structures and 'rules of the game' are given an important role in promoting stable and efficient interaction and collaboration. Against this background, a systemic approach is argued to be most appropriate. An innovation system can in principle be described as the system in which the relevant factors (i.e. actors and institutions) in an innovation process interact.

A discussion on innovation as an interactive process in a regional innovation system is initiated in Chap. 3. The literature offers studies and conceptualisations of a number of different innovation systems. Four major types can be found in the literature: (i) *ational nno ation ystems* (NIS), (ii) *e ional nno ation ystems* (RIS), (iii) *ectoral nno ation ystems* (SIS) and (iv) *echnolo ical ystems* (TS)[1]. In addition to these, Fischer et al. (2001) conceptualised *etropolitan nno ation ystems* and Malecki and Oinas (2002) *patial nno ation ystems*. The NIS and RIS approach are similar in the sense that they do not focus on any particular industry or technology. Here, the whole set of industries in a nation or region with surrounding institutions are considered simultaneously (Breschi and Malerba 1997). These are the only types of innovation systems where, at least to some extent, the geographical boundaries are well defined. Both SIS and TS may or may not be spatially bounded. In the TS approach, the focus is on specific techno-industrial areas (Carlsson and Stankiewicz 1991). The main differ-

---

[1] Interested readers may consult inter alia Lundvall (1995) and Nelson and Rosenberg (1993) on NIS, Cooke et al. (1997, 1998) on RIS, Breschi and Malerba (1997) on SIS and Carlsson and Stankiewicz (1991) on TS.

ence between TS and SIS is that the latter focus on the competitive elements between firms while the former stress the networks among firms (see e.g. Breschi and Malerba 1997).

RIS have recently gained increased attention. The emphasis on regions has many grounds. Most important among them is that innovation systems are most easily observed at the regional level, since distance tends to decrease the frequency of interaction among individuals. Of significance is also the acknowledgement by researchers of the role of the regional economic milieu and geographical proximity for the innovativeness of firms. Informal routines and norms that are specific to each region are argued to play an essential role in the behaviour of firms and the form of collaboration between them. In addition, tacit and non-codified knowledge has been recognized as of importance in the innovation process while closeness and face-to-face contacts are prerequisites for the exchange of this kind of knowledge. Focusing mainly upon NIS, several important regional phenomena that facilitate innovation processes are ignored or not observed.

RIS have different characteristics in different regions depending on their industrial specialization. Innovation systems in high-technology regions are, for example, most likely different from the innovation systems in traditional regions specialized in, for example, wood and metal manufacturing. Moreover, due to regional specificities, such as routines and norms mentioned earlier, RIS can also possibly be very different between regions with similar industrial structures. One is also likely to observe substantial differences in the structure and functioning of RIS between large regions with many different economic activities and in small and medium-sized regions with a less diversified economic milieu.

Recognizing that innovations stem from co-operation between many different actors, it is reasonable to question the ability of smaller regions to generate innovations. Small and medium-sized regions that often are dominated by a limited number of industries and do not host actors such as universities and research institutes are naturally disadvantaged when it comes to innovations. What do RIS look like in regions that lack what is normally considered to be important actors in the innovation process? Can firms in such regions generate innovations in spite of the absence of certain regional strategic actors and lack of competence? What kind of innovations can they generate? These questions are of primary concern for smaller regions as well as national governments that actively try to harmonize regional disparities in innovation capacities. Acknowledging the role of RIS makes it natural to raise a question on whether they also need special regional innovation policies to function well. Of course, there are national innovation policies but these, probably in many cases, need to be complemented with regional innovation policies focusing on regional specificities. This question is particularly relevant to small and medium-sized regions lacking the diversified innovation infrastructure typical of larger regions.

The purpose of this chapter is to provide a theoretical overview and a critical examination of the concept of and theories on RIS, in particular in relation to small and medium-sized regions, to discuss how the function of RIS differs between regions with different industrial specialization and size and to draw conclusions about how regional innovation policies can help to develop and to improve RIS. SIS and TS are beyond the scope of the chapter.

The remainder of the chapter falls into five parts. Sect. 4.2 describes the basic principles of the old linear and the modern interactive innovation model and explains the differences between them. Sect. 4.3 gives a theoretical overview of the concept of RIS, in which both a region and an innovation is defined. Particular emphasis is placed on the relationship between RIS and clustering of economic activities. A presentation of different types of RIS is also given. Sect. 4.4 discusses RIS in regions with different industrial specializations, focusing on small and medium-sized regions. Sect. 4.5 discusses what role regional innovation policy can and should play for the creation and development of RIS. A series of conclusions of the chapter are given in Sect. 4.6.

4.2 The Linear Versus the Interactive (Non-linear) Model of Innovation

The modern interactive model of innovation, upon which the systemic approach to innovation is based, regards innovations as the outcome of an interactive process in which actors from a wide array of levels are involved. In contrast, the traditional linear model of innovation, developed in the Fordist era, is based on the idea that R&D is the key to innovations. In this model the innovation process is described as a chain that links different activities in a certain ordering (see e.g. Fischer 1999; Halvorsen and Lacave 1998), as visualized in Fig. 4.1. The chain starts with formal R&D activities followed by applied research and product development. The step after product development is commercialisation. According to the linear model of innovation, more R&D would generate more innovations. Hence, low R&D capacity could explain low innovative activity (Asheim and Isaksen 1996). The policy implication to be drawn from the linear model is rather straightforward; innovations rely on R&D promotion.

Fig. 4.1. The linear model of innovation

Criticism against the linear model of innovation emerged in the post-Fordist era when empirical studies showed that the innovation process did not work in such an order as described by the model (Fischer 1999). As far as the linear model of innovation can be considered as an 'orthodox' model[2], the work by Nelson and

---

[2] Nelson and Winter (1982) do not mention the linear model of innovation explicitly.

Winter (1982) constitutes an important part of the criticism[3]. The main arguments made by critics were that innovation processes do not take place from left to right and "...the starting point does not have to be academia, the impulses and ideas could just as well have come from the markets, or the production spheres", (Halvorsen and Lancave 1998, p.34). The model has also been criticized for its bias towards product innovations.

The criticism of the linear model spurred researchers to adopt the interactive model of innovation and "...today it is increasingly recognized that innovation extends beyond formal research and development (R&D) activities" (Mytelka and Farinelli 2000, p.8). According to the interactive model, there is no such thing as a general order of how innovations come about. Instead, the interactive model emphasizes feedback and interaction effects between market- and technology-related stages of the innovation process (Fischer 1999). Massey et al. (1992) have identified five differences between the linear and the interactive model of innovation:

1. There is not just one process of innovation from research to commercialisation; rather, ideas are generated and developed at all stages of innovation, including production.
2. Basic research is not the only initiator stage. This is not to imply that basic research pursued in laboratories is irrelevant to innovation.
3. Rather than just being used as the starting point of innovation, research results are used, in one form or another, at all stages of the innovation process.
4. The relationship between basic research and commercialisation is too complex to be understood as a straight-line relationship. There are feedback loops at all stages.
5. The linear model reduces the contribution of the people involved in innovation, to only the first stages, while the interactive model makes it clear that innovation can take place in all stages and by different professions involved.

4.3 Understanding 'Regional Innovation Systems'

The aim of this section is to define and discuss the concept of Regional Innovation Systems (RIS). Niosi (2000, p.8) states, "...any definition of RIS should start defining regions". This section starts by the region in the context of RIS and goes on to discuss innovations and innovation systems.

4.3.1 The Region – a Functional Entity

It is hard to find any explicit definition of the term region in the RIS literature. An attempt is made by Cooke et al. (1997, p.480), who states that a region should be

---

[3] However, their work amounts to much more than just criticism. They provide an alternative theoretical setting by, from an evolutionary perspective, stressing the role of search and selection processes for technological change and economic growth.

defined as "...a territory less than its sovereign state, possessing distinctive supra-local administrative, cultural, political, or economic power and cohesiveness, dif-ferentiating it from its state and other regions". We believe that a proper way to treat the concept of a region is to let it be synonymous with a functional region. This is because a functional region has characteristics germane to the mechanisms stressed to be important in the systemic approach. Specifically, a functional region is characterized by a high intensity of economic interaction (Johansson 1998) and consists of nodes, such as municipalities, connected by economic networks and networks of infrastructure (Johansson 1992). The borders of functional regions are determined by the frequency or intensity of economic interaction as shown in Fig. 4.2.

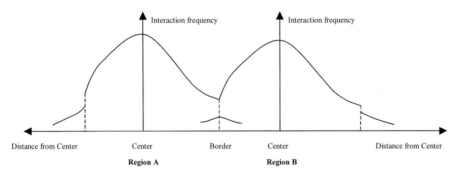

Fig. 4.2. Demarcation of functional regions. Source: based on Johansson 1992

Examples of economic interaction upon which the borders may be determined are intra-regional trade and labour commuting[4]. Commuting patterns is a common source for empirically identifying functional regions (Karlsson and Olsson 2000). The labour market is of special importance since the links between employers and employees create a rigid foundation of the economic network in a functional re-gion (Johansson 1992). These links are one type of ties that form a regional eco-nomic system (Johansson 1992). The latter can be described as a structure that is formed by interactive elements, which can be classified by means of geographical patterns and/or organizational couplings (Johansson 1993). Almeida and Kogut (1999) also recognize the importance of the labour market and maintain that flows of knowledge are embedded in regional labour networks. For these reasons, com-muting patterns can be regarded as the appropriate type of interaction to base the borders upon. Therefore, a region can be defined as a territory in which the inter-action between the market actors and flows of goods and services create a regional economic system whose borders are determined by the point at which the magni-tude of these interactions and flows change from one direction to another.

---

[4] Since it is likely that the borders of a functional region depend on the type of interaction studied, the borders are fluid to some extent.

4.3.2 The Concept of Innovation

The most fundamental feature of an innovation is that it is something new. It can be a new process, product or, following Schumpeter, a new combination. Straight-forward definitions of innovations include, "…putting new products and services on the market or new means of producing them" (Bannock 1992), "…the economic application of a new idea" (Black 1997), "…the implementation of changes in production (…) [or] the introduction of new types of commodities on the market" (Suranyi-Unger 1982). These definitions stress an important feature of an innovation, namely that it has to be used on the market to be classified as an innovation. Thus, it has to be involved in a commercial transaction. However, Freeman (1998, p.858) points out the twofold meaning of an innovation: "…the word is used both to indicate the date of the first introduction of a new product or process and to describe the whole process of taking an invention or set of inventions to the point of commercial introduction". Hence, it is important to distinguish between an innovation and an innovation process although it is emphasized that it is the innovation process that is important rather than the innovation as such (Lundvall 1995; Edquist 2000).

When market usage is imposed as a criterion for innovation, demand conditions will play an important role. Amendola and Bruno (1990) point out that what matters are not the environmental circumstances, in which an innovation is created, but rather the ability and willingness of consumers to adopt and use the innovation. The importance of demand and early adopters for innovations has been emphasized by authors such as Gregersen and Johnson (1996), Porter (1990), Rothwell (1992), Sölvell et al. (1991), and von Hippel (1998, 1988). These ideas can be related to the concept of the innovative milieu (Maillat 1993, 1995, 1998).

Three different kinds of innovations are generally identified in the literature. These are (i) radical innovations, (ii) major (or adaptive) innovations and (iii) incremental innovations (see e.g. Asheim and Isaksen 1996; Jonsson et al. 2000; Maillat 1993; Rothwell 1992). A radical innovation implies that a totally new product is developed, which can create a new area of business. The second class of innovations, major (adaptive) innovations, constitutes improvements of already existing products or new products and processes within an established business. Incremental innovations are small and often stepwise improvements of existing products and processes. Hence, a broad view on innovations is taken.

In addition to the types of innovation mentioned above, yet another type can be found in the literature. Bresnahan and Trajtenberg (1995) introduce the concept of General Purpose Technologies (GPT) and Freeman and Perez (1988) discuss the concept of Techno-Economic Paradigms (TEP). These two concepts are in principle equivalent and refer to key technologies, such as the steam engine and electricity. Fig. 4.3 visualizes the scope of the innovation concept. The different types of innovation are ordered in descending order according to their pervasive force. Naturally, GPT and TEP have the most far-reaching diffusion process, followed by radical innovations.

In connection with diffusion, it should be pointed out that established networks, such as links between customers and deliverers, both within and between firms are basic prerequisites for a smooth diffusion process, (Johansson 1993). For example, Karlsson (1988) showed that firms in the Information Technology sector use intra-firm links to diffuse new applications.

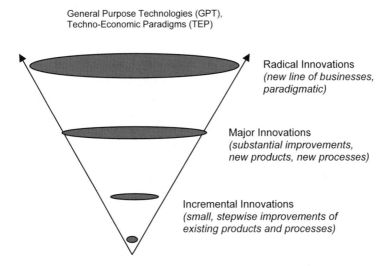

General Purpose Technologies (GPT),
Techno-Economic Paradigms (TEP)

Radical Innovations
(new line of businesses, paradigmatic)

Major Innovations
(substantial improvements, new products, new processes)

Incremental Innovations
(small, stepwise improvements of existing products and processes)

Fig. 4.3. The scope of the innovation concept. Source: Adapted from Jonsson et al. 2000

4.3.3 Innovation Systems

The concept of Innovation Systems (IS) is based upon the interactive model of innovation. The key feature of the concept is that the ability of an economy (regional or national) to generate innovations does not depend only on how individual actors (firms, universities, organizations, research institutes, governmental institutions, etc) perform, but rather on how they interact as parts of a system (Gregersen and Johnson 1996, Eriksson 2000). Meeus et al. (1999) point out that a firm should be considered an actor that interacts with an actor set, which facilitates and contributes to the innovation process. The actor set contains actors such as buyers, sellers, suppliers, local and national authorities and intermediate organizations, etc. Similarly, Koschatzky (1998a) stresses the importance of co-operation between firms for the generation of innovations points out that innovation networks are one of the most important types of business networks. Firms need external resources in the innovation and learning process and in order to access them, they need to be a part of a system that makes these external resources available (Oerlemans et al. 1998). The following points can be seen as 'foundations' of the concept of IS (de la Mothe and Paquet 1998, p.105):

- It emphasizes that firms must be viewed as part of a network of public and private sector organizations whose activities and interactions initiate, import, modify and diffuse new technologies.
- It emphasizes the linkages (both formal and informal) between organizations.
- It emphasizes the flows of intellectual resources that exist between organizations.
- It emphasizes learning as a key economic resource.

Lundvall (1995) stresses that an IS should primarily be thought of as a social system, since learning is the most central activity in the innovation process and involves interaction between people. As Meeus et al. (1999, p 6) put it, "...markets do not accumulate knowledge, they connect knowledgeable actors"[5].

Innovation Systems can be approached in a narrow or in a broad way (Gregersen and Johnson 1996). The narrow approach makes it possible to identify specific sectors that generate and distribute innovations when supported by specific institutions. In this context, an innovation system would have clear boundaries. With the broader approach, innovations can be generated by ordinary economic activities, such as procurement, production and marketing, in every part of an economy. The broader view is generally argued to be more appropriate to use when approaching IS (see e.g. Gregersen and Johnson 1996; Lundvall and Lindgaard-Christensen 1999). The narrow approach can be associated with the old linear model of innovation, (Asheim and Isaksen 1996). Definitions of IS when the broad view is taken include the following:

"...a system of innovation is constituted by the elements and relationships which interact in the production, diffusion and use of new, and economically useful, knowledge" (Lundvall 1995, p.2),

"...a system of actors (firms, organizations and government agencies) who interact in ways which influence the innovation performance" (Gregersen and Johnson 1996, p.484),

"...we will specify system as including all important determinants of innovation" (Edquist 2000, p.15),

"...a set of institutional actors that, together, plays the major role in influencing innovative performance" (Nelson and Rosenberg 1993, p.4).

Edquist (2000) emphasizes that the systemic approach to innovation is to a large extent holistic. The aim is to include all the important determinants of innovation. Gregersen and Johnson (1996) point out that the holistic approach should not be interpreted as if the innovation process depends on everything. The main point is that it provides a new perspective and understanding of the determinants in an innovation performance. Lundvall (1995) stresses that specific definitions must be adjusted to the processes studied, but emphasizes that the institutional set-up and the structure of production are universal components in all innovation systems.

---

[5] However, it is important to keep in mind that ordinary goods also contain and diffuse knowledge, such as technical know-how. For instance, Eli Heckscher stated that imports of goods could stimulate local production that substitutes imports (Johansson 1992).

The rather vague definitions of IS reflect the need for further research. Particularly, it is necessary to try to specify what factors are included in everything and what factors are more or less important. Thus, identifying necessary and sufficient requirements for innovation systems to function is a central research question, not least to be able to formulate regional innovation policies.

4.3.4 Regional Innovation Systems

Innovation systems are most often referred to as national systems (Asheim and Isaksen 1996; Freeman 1995). The definitions of innovation systems provided in the previous section are also originally given in connection to discussions of National Innovation Systems (NIS). As far as the processes maintained to be important are concerned, the basics of a RIS are in principle the same as for a NIS. For example, Meeus et al (1999, p.9) define a RIS as "...the innovating firms surrounded by a number of actors who are all in one way or another linked to the innovation process of a focal firm and to each actor". However, Wiig (1996) stresses that a RIS should be looked upon as analogous to definitions of NIS, but that they should not be considered only "micro-national systems". One can relate the NIS concept to regional institutions and actors but must at the same time recognize that regional systems may differ from the national standard. This in turn makes RIS different from each other[6].

Asheim and Isaksen (2002) designate RIS as regional clusters that are supported by surrounding organizations. They argue that a RIS has two key features. These are (1) firms in the regional core cluster and (2) an institutional infrastructure. The most obvious reason to focus on clusters is that they (as well as geographical proximity in general) tend to facilitate the key points made in the systemic approach, namely learning through interaction.

4.3.5 Clusters and Regional Innovation Systems

A cluster can be defined as a number of firms (within the same industry) that share the same location in space (Karlsson 2001). In each cluster, it is possible to observe a common labour market, a common market for input-deliveries to the firms and/or information- and technology-transfers between the firms. Many firms can, for example, together provide a large demand for specialized labour and create a pooled labour market, which secures the supply of labour for the firms as well as the supply of jobs for workers. When motivating the role of clusters, most of the literature emphasizes that clusters facilitate knowledge spillovers and knowledge transfers. The former is considered to be of special importance for the innovation process (see e.g. Breschi 1998; Koschatzky 1998b). In general, knowledge spillovers is referred to as a kind of informal diffusion of knowledge which takes place

---

[6] Radosevic (2002) maintains that RIS develops from interaction between determinants from different levels, e.g. national, sectoral and region-specific determinants.

most effectively when firms are located close to each other. As Feldman and Audretsch (1998, p.2) put it, "...knowledge may spill over, but the geographic extent of such knowledge spillovers is bounded". Knowledge transfers refer to more explicit and planned transmission of knowledge between economic agents. Transfers often involve a regular commercial transaction, which are obviously facilitated by proximity, but are not interchangeable with knowledge spillovers (Karlsson and Manduchi 2001).

In the context of innovation, it is usually maintained that much of the knowledge relevant for innovation processes is tacit. Tacit knowledge has been defined as semi- and unconscious knowledge that does not exist in explicit printed forms, (Leonard and Sensiper 1998). Skills and routines are examples of tacit knowledge (Lorenzen 1998). Its formation and use depend, to a large extent, on the social and institutional context in a region (Lam 1998). Several studies have also shown that informal oral sources of information are keys to successful innovations (Karlsson 2001). The main communication channels for tacit knowledge are employee mobility, informal personal relations and supervision (Lorenzen 1996). Hence, the transmission of tacit knowledge necessitates face-to-face contacts. Since firms and individuals in a cluster are by definition located in proximity to each other, it is evident that clusters facilitate both knowledge spillovers and knowledge transfers.

In addition, not only geographical proximity but also *relational* proximity has a role to play in improving the ease by which knowledge is transmitted (Capello 2001). The latter encompasses relations developed by integration of firms and socio-cultural homogeneity. Also, Wiig and Wood (1995) stress that the presence of mutual trust and collective tacit knowledge in a region tends to stimulate innovative activities. Mutual trust facilitates exchange of knowledge and diminishes uncertainties while collective tacit knowledge eases exchange of technological know-how, etc. Both these elements are likely to be developed in clusters if anywhere. For example, Storper (1995) emphasizes that every cluster develops its own specific rules, i.e. local institutions, which may include conventions and rules for developing, communicating, and interpreting knowledge. Storper refers to these relationships as untraded interdependencies between actors. This concept is equivalent to Maillat's (1995) concept of atmospheric externalities. It basically means that each cluster in a region has its own norms that "...stem from a shared technical culture, from interaction between, and mobility of, individuals on the labour market..." (Maillat 1995, p.161), which in turn "...facilitates the exchange of knowledge and makes it easier also to establish contacts and exchange information between persons and firms within an area" (Wiig and Wood 1995, p.3). Within this context, one may talk about a localized learning process in which the learning takes place locally with few external actors involved.

Furthermore, it should be noted that individuals must have relevant training to be able to absorb the knowledge they acquire (Karlsson and Manduchi 2000; Fischer 1999). To be able to make sense of high-level knowledge in engineering, an education in engineering is generally a prerequisite. Maurseth and Verspagen (1998, p.16) study knowledge spillovers in Europe and conclude, "...technology diffusion is in no sense automatic, but demands a certain level of economic development, in addition to innovative efforts and favourable institutional settings".

Moreover, Bottazzi and Peri (1999) find that knowledge spillovers between European regions are especially strong between technologically similar and geographically close regions. This suggests, not surprisingly, that the ability for a region/cluster (or rather the individuals residing in it) to adopt and use new knowledge partly depends on the education of the workforce in the region.

Having discussed the reasons for the emphasis on clusters for RIS, it is natural to ask if all clusters can be characterized as RIS. Even if clusters, as shown, play a key role, a regional cluster is not a sufficient condition for a RIS. For instance, Cooke et al (1997) stress the role of access to knowledge centres and the existence of a governance structure including private business associations, chambers of commerce etc. They also point out the role of a financial infrastructure.

Figure 4.4. describes what may be called a 'complete' RIS. The core is constituted by the firms in the regional cluster, surrounded by supporting as well as complementary firms. Institutions, as normative structures and 'rules of the game', are present which facilitate co-operation and knowledge spillovers and transfers. Likewise, an infrastructure of knowledge and technology as well as financial resources surrounds the firms.

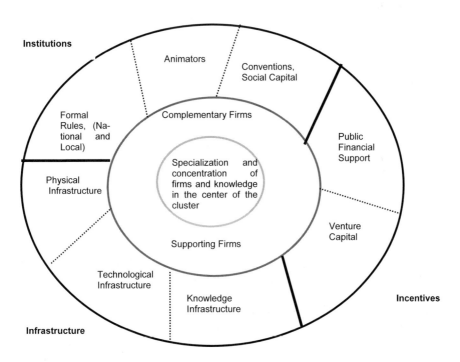

Fig.4.4. Components of a complete Regional Innovation System (RIS). Source: Adapted from Eriksson 2000

Figure 4.4 suggests a relationship between university, industry and government in a RIS. Etzkowitz and Leydesdorff (2000, p.111) refer to this relation as the

"Triple Helix". In their view, the "Triple Helix" generates "...a knowledge infrastructure in terms of overlapping institutional spheres, with each taking the role of the other with hybrid organizations emerging at the interfaces". Universities are maintained to play an essential role for the functioning of RIS. Of course, universities are not the only relevant knowledge provider. Application-oriented and non-university research institutes are also important in forming the knowledge infrastructure in a RIS. Koschatzky (2001, p.3) stresses that Higher Research Institutes (HEIs) generally fulfill two main functions in a region:

- To manage the common knowledge base of a region by producing and diffusing knowledge through education, by distributing scientific and technological information and by demonstrating and transferring technological or scientific solutions.
- To provide expertise knowledge by training, consulting, contract research and development, or by the transfer of services, taking into account the specific needs of single actors.

Since HEI's keep regional firms up to date regarding scientific solutions, etc, they facilitate necessary industrial transformations when new technologies are introduced. In that sense, they counteract lock-in situations. In addition, Koschatzky (2001) maintains that HEIs do not only act as knowledge providers, they are also incubators for new firms since they qualify and support potential entrepreneurs. HEIs thus help transform new scientific knowledge into commercialised products and create new businesses. Their presence also affects the location-choice of firms, at least high-technology firms, since they tend to regard them as a source for new knowledge and technologies (Varga 1998). Anselin et al. (1996) provide empirical support for that university research in a region has a significant positive impact on the innovative activities of the high-technology firms in that region.

4.3.6 Different Types of Regional Innovation Systems

The previous section focused on what may be called complete RIS. However, it is important to recognize that a RIS may be more or less complete. A region (or cluster) that has not all the characteristics listed in Fig. 4.2 may still be referred to as a RIS. Thus, there are different types of RIS. Asheim and Isaksen (1996, 2002) distinguish between three broad groups of RIS, (1) territorially embedded regional innovation networks, (2) regional networked innovation systems and (3) regionalized national innovation systems. These differ mainly in terms of their connection to knowledge-providers and actors outside the region as well as the form of co-operation in the innovation process. Table 4.1. lists the characteristics of each type of RIS in Asheim and Isaksen (2002).

For the first type of RIS, territorially embedded regional innovation networks, proximity (both geographical and relational), is the main stimulus for firms' innovative activities. Interaction with knowledge providers and their presence tends to be very modest.

Table 4.1. Some characteristics of the three main types of RIS

Main type of RIS	The location of knowledge organizations	Knowledge flow	Important stimulus of co-operation
Territorially embedded regional innovation networks	Locally, however, few relevant knowledge organizations	Interactive	Geographical, social and cultural proximity
Regional networked innovation systems	Locally, a strengthening of (the co-operation with) knowledge providers	Interactive	Planned systemic networking
Regionalized national innovation systems	Mainly outside the region	More linear	Individuals with the same education and common experiences

Source: Adapted from Asheim and Isaksen (2002)

Probably the best examples of this kind of systems are "…networking SMEs [small and medium-sized enterprises] in industrial districts, which build their competitive advantage on localized learning processes" (Asheim and Isaksen 1996, p.14). Firms in territorially embedded regional innovation networks rely upon locally developed knowledge and the untraded interdependencies discussed above tend to be strong. It seems therefore natural to suggest that learning-by-doing and learning-by-using are the key knowledge-generating mechanisms in these systems and that the innovations achieved are mainly incremental innovations. But these systems hold different types of knowledge. The authors maintain that while learning-by-doing and learning-by-using are primarily based on informal, practical and tacit knowledge, there is also a specific kind of knowledge that stems from "disembodied technical knowledge", which is mastered by firm-groupings through untraded interdependencies as well as formal exchange with other firms. This kind of knowledge is not mainly based on tacit knowledge. It is instead referred to as localized, codified knowledge. It may constitute the basis for interactive learning. Furthermore, "…according to modern innovation theory, interactive learning has the potential to produce radical innovations in addition to incremental ones," (Asheim and Isaksen 1996, p.15). However, the probability for these systems to produce radical innovations is low due to the lack of knowledge providers.

A danger with territorially embedded regional innovation networks concerns its ability to sustain the competitiveness of the firms in the system/region. For example, Asheim and Isaksen (1996) maintain that it is doubtful whether a territorially embedded regional innovation network is capable of avoiding lock-in situations by breaking path dependency and changing technological trajectory. Lack of co-operation with knowledge organizations may result in that firms are unable to catch up with new technologies and new knowledge. Close co-operation with research universities facilitates necessary industrial transformations when new technologies, etc, are introduced. Similarly, Asheim and Isaksen (2002) stress that the majority of firms do need access to universal knowledge (from e.g. national systems of innovation). This is especially true for SMEs. According to the authors, it is not possible to fully rely on localized learning, and tacit knowledge (as well as localized, codified knowledge) must in many cases be complemented with formal R&D-competence. This suggests that for this type of RIS, it is important that the regional actors develop external linkages and not only co-operate intra-regionally.

The second type of RIS, regional networked innovation systems, can be seen as an extension of the first type of RIS where the needs described above are satisfied. Asheim and Isaksen (2002) write that the basic features are the same as for the first type, but in this case the networking is better planned and more systemic. They maintain that this is achieved by means of a strengthened regional infrastructure, such as having more local organizations, e.g. R&D institutes and vocational training organizations, participating in the firms' innovative activities. Thus, in regional networked innovation systems the firms have access to local competence making the likelihood of lock-in situations lower (and the probability of radical innovations higher). Asheim and Isaksen (2002, p.83) argue that "…the networked system is more or less regarded as the ideal-typical RIS; a regional cluster of firms surrounded by a local supporting institutional infrastructure". Hence, this type of RIS is more or less synonymous with the type presented in Fig. 4.4.

Regionalized national innovation systems, the last category, are different from the other two in many aspects. Outside actors are involved in the firms' innovative activities and in the regional industry as a whole. The institutional infrastructure is also partly integrated with the national or even international innovation system. Therefore, it is close to a 'micro-national system'. Regional clusters in which the knowledge providers are first and foremost located outside the region are good examples, (Asheim and Isaksen 2002). Relevant examples also include R&D institutes and science parks with only some degree of linkages to the local industry. Asheim and Isaksen (2002) argue that co-operation between firms and knowledge organizations in regionalized national innovation systems are often related to specific projects with the aim of developing more radical innovations. They also point out that the innovation process is, to a greater extent, of the linear nature. The knowledge used is more formal and "…co-operation may be stimulated when people have the same kind of education (e.g. as engineers) and sharing the same formal knowledge, rather than belonging to the same local community" (Asheim and Isaksen 2002, p.84). Hence, the interaction between knowledge organizations and the firms appears to be primarily based on commissioned research work rather than on integration and continuous involvement.

The discussion above can be summarized in the following points:

- Interaction between agents is a necessary condition for a RIS to function.
- Such interaction can be achieved through clustering.
- Existence of knowledge-providers is not a prerequisite for a RIS.

- A necessary but not sufficient condition is that the actors within a RIS produce and diffuse knowledge among each other. It is not sufficient because it is the degree to which knowledge is produced and diffused that is relevant question [7].
- Different kinds of RIS can be identified based on the following:
  - How knowledge is produced.
  - The kind of knowledge produced.
  - How the interaction is organized.
  - The boundaries of the system, i.e. how 'regional' is the RIS?
- The nature of the knowledge available and produced partly determines the kind of innovations a RIS is able to produce. Hence, different RIS produce different kinds of innovations.

4.4 Regional Innovation Systems in Different Industries and Regions with Different Industrial Specializations

In this section, the focus is on Small and Medium-Sized Regions (SMRs) dominated by traditional manufacturing industries. There is an evident lack of general theories in the literature regarding how the function of RIS differs between regions with different industrial specializations. For many authors, the theory seems to be the arrival point and there is no real application of it. However, the different types of RIS based on Asheim and Isaksen (1996, 2002) discussed in Sect. 4.3.6 provide an overall idea. For example, it is sensible to assume that the innovation system in small and peripheral regions, that are likely to be without a research university, etc, are best described as territorially embedded regional networks, while the innovation systems in larger regions, with research universities and other knowledge providers/organizations, are likely to be synonymous with regional networked innovation systems. However, an examination of some empirical findings is necessary here due to the lack of general theories.

4.4.1 Theories and Empirical Findings

Breschi and Malerba (1997) point out that the technological knowledge in different sectors has different characteristics. They emphasize that the technological knowledge can be characterized according to the degree of:

1. Specificity: (the knowledge can be specific, i.e. connected to certain applications, or generic)
2. Tacitness: (the knowledge can be tacit and local or codified and easily transferable)

---

[7] Here it is possible to talk about a minimum degree of knowledge creation and diffusion, below which one cannot talk about a RIS.

3. Complexity: (e.g. the knowledge may stem from different disciplines to different extents)
4. Independence: (the knowledge can be identified easily or be embedded within a larger system)

They further provide examples of different sectors in which the knowledge is of a different character, constituting what they call different sectoral innovation system (SIS). They argue that the knowledge base of the innovative activities in the traditional (non-knowledge intensive) sector has a low degree of complexity and is easily codified and transferred. This implies that geographical proximity is not important for the actors and the authors argue that there is likely to be a high degree of geographical dispersion of the innovators. Mechanical industries and industrial districts make up another sector. Here, Breschi and Malerba (1997) maintain that the knowledge base for the innovative activities is characterized by a high degree of tacitness and specificity. There are many innovators and the boundaries of knowledge are local. Hence, geographical proximity is important for the firms in this sector. The authors identify two other sectors, the computer (hardware) industry, and the software (microelectronics, biotech) industry. Knowledge is highly complex in both sectors and they are generally considered to be knowledge-intensive. The hardware industry, which according to the authors has few innovators, is geographically concentrated and knowledge has global boundaries. The software industry, on the other hand, has many innovators, where a mixture of both tacit and codified knowledge makes geographical proximity very important. Knowledge boundaries are both local and global since they have both tacit and codified properties.

Similar ideas are put forward by Meeus et al (1999 p.10), who discuss how interaction with the actor set varies from one firm to another. For them, it is likely that "...supplier dominated and scale intensive focal firms interact less frequently with the actor set than focal firms in science based industries and specialized suppliers". They also state, "...radical innovations are associated with a higher frequency of interaction between the actor set and the focal firm than incremental innovations". In this sense, traditional industries, including many manufacturing industries, are less dependent upon the regional "milieu" for their innovative activities. This view is shared by Breschi and Malerba (1997).

Audretsch and Feldman (1996) make use of the Industry Life Cycle Theory[8], to analyse and explain spatial dimensions of innovative activity. Like Breschi and Malerba (1997), they argue that the nature of the knowledge is important for the spatial location of innovative activities. Their main hypothesis is that the tendency of innovative activity to cluster is strongest during the early stages of the industry life cycle. They state (p.259) that "...innovative activity should take place in those regions where the direct knowledge-generating inputs are greatest, and where knowledge spillovers are the most prevalent," an argument that concurs with the discussion above. The authors also argue that tacit knowledge is likely to play an especially important role in the innovation process in the early stage of the indus-

---

[8] Industry Life Cycle Theory is synonymous with the Product Life Cycle Theory.

try life cycle, since "...there are no widely accepted standards with respect to product specifications, so that obtaining information about what consumers want and how it can be produced demands proximity to knowledge sources". Since exchange of tacit knowledge demands geographical proximity and face-to-face contacts, one can draw the conclusion that the tendency for innovative activities to spatially cluster is strongest in the early stages of the cycle. Based on data for 210 U.S industries, which were classified into four stages of the industry life cycle, Audretsch and Feldman (1996) find evidence that the propensity of innovative activities to cluster is greatest in the early stages, while it is more dispersed in the mature and declining stages of the cycle.

Other empirical studies include Jonsson et al. (2000), who study the Swedish medicine-technology sector and find that the innovative activity is highly concentrated. They discover that five metropolitan and urban areas (Stockholm, Göteborg, Malmö, Uppsala and Halmstad) account for 80 percent of the creation of new products and processes. However, some degree of dispersion was observed with respect to improvements of existing products. Moreover, the manufacturing industry was found to be less concentrated than other industries within the sector. Similar core-periphery patterns are found for the manufacturing industry in Norway. For example, Wiig and Isaksen (1998) find a clear centre-periphery pattern when measuring different Norwegian regions' share of firms with innovation costs and share of firms producing new or significantly altered products. Peripheral regions had a substantial lower share of both. Moreover, Asheim and Isaksen (1996) show that the costs associated with innovation of firms in central areas are mainly made up by (or are related to) R&D, while the same costs of firms in peripheral areas are, on the other hand, mostly constituted by trial production and production start-ups. This suggests that firms in central areas are more concerned with radical innovations while firms in peripheral regions are skewed towards incremental innovations and tend to "...import and alter innovations from outside" (Asheim and Isaksen 1996, p. 23). Likewise, based on data from 100 manufacturing firms in a Norwegian peripheral region (Finnmark), Wiig (1996) finds that the typical innovative firm is larger than the average firm and that these sell the largest share of their total sales outside the region. That the innovative firm is larger than the average firm is in line with the reasoning in Audretsch and Feldman (1996).

From the discussion above, it is clear that high-technology industries using highly complex knowledge, such as computer hardware and software industries are in the greatest need of a rich regional milieu. These industries also interact most frequently with the regional milieu in the innovation process and the Triple Helix tends to be of special importance. As Breschi and Malerba (1997) point out, these industries are also dependent upon global knowledge, which implies that linkages to innovation systems in other domestic regions and abroad are likely to be important. It seems therefore sensible to suggest that RIS in these industries can be linked to what Asheim and Isaksen (1996) refer to as regionalized national innovation systems and regional networked innovation systems. For example, these industries tend to be located close to research universities and the high complexity of the knowledge involved is likely to result in limited linkages to the local industry in the region. This depends, however, on the level of education in the region. It is also apparent that this type of industries tends to cluster in larger regions. Against this background, high-technology industries seem to constitute the best basis for RIS.

In traditional sectors, on the other hand, a typical firm interacts less with different actors. Firms in these industries do not seem to need such a rich regional economic milieu. It has been shown empirically that the innovative activities of traditional industries are more geographically dispersed than in other industries. It has also been shown that the innovative activities of manufacturing firms in peripheral regions are less associated with formal knowledge compared to central regions, suggesting that peripheral firms are mainly concerned with incremental innovations and the import of novelties from other regions.

4.4.2 RIS in Small and Medium-Sized Regions Dominated by Manufacturing within Traditional Industries – an Elaboration

Empirical studies point out that large and central regions with a large knowledge base in relative terms are mostly involved with radical innovations. Moreover, knowledge-intensive (central) regions are also likely to be the first to adopt new techniques and new knowledge. Tödtling (1993) states that regions with large agglomerations of economic activity and knowledge providers tend to have the location requirements to constitute the earliest adopters of new techniques. Also, these regions tend to act as import nodes, from which novelties diffuse to other regions, Johansson and Westin (1987). In the subsequent discussion, SMRs dominated by manufacturing industries will be treated as receivers in such a diffusion process.

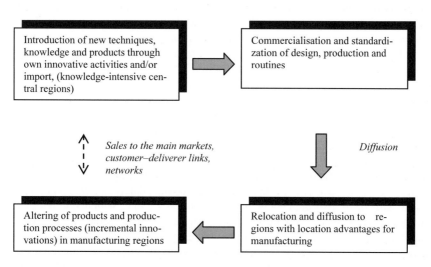

Fig.4.5. Diffusion and re-location of production of novelties

Based on the Spatial Product Cycle (SPC) theory, Fig. 4.5 provides a schematic picture of the diffusion and re-location of the production of novelties. A central idea in the SPC theory is that knowledge-intensive regions (import nodes) generate and import innovations, of which the production is then subsequently relocated to manufacturing regions with cost advantages when the products are standardized and certain routines are established, (Johansson and Westin 1987). Thus, in the mature phases of a product's life, SMRs (as defined above) usually have a location advantage. For the most part, such production is located in SMRs in order to produce more cheaply for other larger markets. Thus, the majority of the goods are shipped to large regions or exported abroad. Therefore, it may be assumed that the manufacturing firms in SMRs dominated by manufacturing are linked to larger regions via established networks, e.g. customer-deliverer links[9]. These links are likely to be of major importance for the innovative activities of firms in SMRs. Customer-deliverer links may, for example, work as channels through which demand for improvements of existing goods and new ideas diffuse from larger regions to firms in smaller regions. This may in turn stimulate improvements of products. As mentioned previously, a number of authors have stressed that a 'demanding demand' functions as an innovation-trigger (see e.g. Porter 1990). This type of demand structure, though rarely an endogenous phenomenon within SMRs, may thus be "imported" via networks. Hence, external linkages exist and should be of special importance for the innovation processes of firms in SMRs.

Based on this framework, how then can an innovation system in these regions be described? In principle, one is able to identify three types of manufacturing SMRs. First, there are SMRs with many manufacturing SMEs that form a cluster. An example of this type of SMRs is the Gnosjö region in Sweden (see e.g. Karlsson and Klaesson 2000). Second, there are SMRs with one (or a few) large manufacturing firm(s) surrounded by smaller local suppliers that together may form a cluster. Third, one finds manufacturing regions in which there is one large manufacturing firm with a few or non local subcontractors. Peripheral regions in the north of Sweden with a manufacturing division of a larger company are good examples. These three types are, in principle, identical to Markusen's (1996) industrial districts, namely Marshallian, Hub-and-Spoke and Satellite Platform industrial districts, respectively. It is questionable to talk about an innovation system in regions characterized by Satellite Platform industrial districts. Asheim and Isaksen (2002) argue that it is not appropriate to talk about RIS in regions that are dominated by branch activities of, for example, trans-national corporations and in regions having too few firms within the same sector to form a regional cluster. The reason is that there is generally no base to form regional innovation networks upon. Therefore, it is natural to focus upon the first two categories of SMRs.

The innovation system in this type of regions (Marshallian and Hub-and-Spoke) may best be described as territorially embedded. That is, knowledge providers play a minor (or no) role in the innovation process and knowledge is pri-

---

[9] One may also consider that larger firms sometimes out-locate the manufacturing division(s) to SMRs.

marily developed through learning-by-doing and learning-by-using. Exchange of knowledge is mostly informal and tacit, where untraded interdependencies are likely to play a key role. Both theories and empirical findings suggest that incremental innovations are the main type of innovations made. But in the light of the discussion above, some points need to be added to Asheim's and Isaksen's (2001) characterization. Firstly, information and demand, etc, transferred to the firms through external linkages are important stimulus for the innovative activities, in addition to social, cultural and geographical proximity. Secondly, firms do get access to universal knowledge and novelties through the process in which the production of novelties is out-located to these regions. As stressed earlier, one must keep in mind that new goods carry information about new techniques and technical solutions, etc. Relocation of the production novelties then implies that this new know-how is accessible to the firms in the manufacturing region and stimulates imitation, etc. Hence, these innovation systems are not as closed as it may be perceived. How they perform also depends on the innovative activities in larger regions and the import activity of import nodes since these activities have a strong influence on SMRs specialized in manufacturing.

Manufacturing SMRs that are characterized by Marshallian industrial districts are different from those characterized by Hub-and-Spoke industrial districts. The latter is obviously more dependent upon certain firms, i.e. the large manufacturing firm(s) in a region, than regions characterized as Marshallian industrial districts. The innovation process in the Hub-and-Spoke type of region is, for example, likely to be more dependent upon large firms'/the larger firm's ability to absorb new knowledge and recognize demands for improvements of products, etc.

Based on the above discussion, the conclusions drawn about RIS in manufacturing SMRs can be summarized in the following points:

- Clustering of manufacturing firms is the underlying mechanism that facilitates interaction and exchange of technical know-how.
- Endogenous knowledge-generating mechanisms are primarily learning-by-doing and learning-by-using.
- New knowledge and technical know-how are gradually introduced to the system by diffusion and relocation processes from larger regions to small and medium-sized regions specialized in manufacturing.
- Customer-deliverer links to other regions help to convey ideas about how to improve and alter existing products/production processes.
- The innovative activities mainly concern incremental innovations that stem from imitations and various improvements of existing products.

4.5 Regional Policy and Regional Innovation Systems

To reduce uncertainty by providing information, to regulate conflicts and cooperation and to provide incentives are basic functions of governmental institutions (Edquist 1997). These can be seen as universal missions for policy makers. They are, of course, also important for innovation systems, but what policies are more specific for RIS? In principle, regional innovation policies should take all elements in Fig. 4.3 into account. For example, access to venture capital and a good physical infrastructure are always important. However, some elements are more important than others. As the quotation above emphasizes, education should be one of the primary concerns for regional policy makers. To be able to absorb and develop new knowledge and new technical solutions a good education is of paramount importance. A regional innovation policy should therefore always aim to attract skilled labour and establish regional knowledge providers such as, universities and research institutes. This is especially important for SMRs specialized in manufacturing that have a workforce with a low knowledge-intensity. To develop the ideal type of RIS (regional networked innovation systems), tacit and local knowledge must be complemented with more formal knowledge, such as R&D-competence. A strengthening of the regional infrastructure should be a focal aim. But many regions are too small to be able to host a research institute or local research university. In such regions, it is important to develop linkages to new knowledge bases and knowledge providers in other regions, i.e. external linkages, (Echeverri-Carroll and Brennan 1999; Mytelka and Farinelli 2000). Having studied the innovation system in a Norwegian peripheral region (Finnmark), Wiig (1996, p.39) concludes that firms need:

a. Contact with relevant research milieux.
b. Technical institutions for innovation support.
c. Financial support for innovation.
d. Young educated people to start in industry.
e. New subjects at the technical colleges in the region.
f. To overcome network bottlenecks.

These findings support the fact that knowledge providers and skilled labour are the most important factors to consider. They also suggest that the needs of regional firms should be taken into account when formulating and implementing education policies. It is important that universities and policy makers recognize what kind of education and knowledge institutions that the firms in the region demand.

The existence of knowledge providers is, however, not enough for a successful regional innovation process. As stressed throughout the chapter, the systemic approach to innovation emphasizes the importance of interaction and collaboration between knowledge providers and the business sector. Regional policy makers should therefore try to establish networks between research universities and firms, and also try to integrate the regional public sector in the innovation process. That is, establish a well-functioning university-industry-government relation. This can, for example, include attempts to initiate different research projects that involve actors from all three sectors. Another important aspect is that businessmen, etc, need places to meet in order to exchange knowledge. It has, for example, been stressed that knowledge spillovers, especially in the context of tacit knowledge, are strongly facilitated by frequent face-to-face contacts. Establishing communities, arenas, and other arrangements that create a base and possibility for recurrent face-to-face contacts can therefore be effective tools to encourage such spillovers. By such arrangements it might also be possible to overcome network bottlenecks, such as found by Wiig (1996). Recall that one difference between territorially embedded regional innovation systems and regional networked innovation system (the ideal) is that the networking in the latter type of RIS is more planned and systemic.

Even if the theory emphasizes the importance of knowledge spillovers, it is important that policy makers pay attention to the balance between private and public dimensions of novelties and knowledge, i.e. the free-rider problem. Based on a postal survey from 121 manufacturing firms in two Norwegian regions (More and Romsdal), Wiig and Wood (1995) found that the "fear of imitation/risk associated with being first to innovate" was the most restrictive factor to product and process innovations. This implies that too effective policies to generate spillovers can have negative effects on firms' incentives to innovate. If newly created knowledge goes public after a short time, i.e. becomes freely accessible to everyone, which firm will be willing to bear the cost of developing it? Various rules for patent-regulations and property rights, etc, which prevent from too effective spillovers are most often determined at the national level, but an awareness of the issue at the regional level is nevertheless important.

In sum, a regional innovation policy directed towards the development and improvement of regional innovation systems should include measures that:

- Develop regional knowledge providers and/or link the firms to external knowledge sources,
- Attract skilled labour and promote the education of labour,
- Develop an institution responsible for scanning markets and technologies for regionally important clusters,
- Promote interaction and collaboration between firms, knowledge institutions and governmental institutions,
- Promote recurrent contact between businessmen, i.e. develop more formal and planned networking,
- Secure the supply of venture capital.

A final point to be made is that policies for regional innovation systems demand an extensive study of the regional economy. As mentioned earlier, each cluster in a region develops its own norms and informal routines. This implies that forms of collaboration and interaction are likely to be different between different clusters within and between regions. Careful considerations and studies must therefore be made before establishing a general regional innovation policy. Even if the aims should in many cases be the same, this may not be true for the instruments.

4.6 Conclusions

The purpose of this chapter was to present a state-of-the-art review and a critical assessment of current research about RIS with special focus on their role in small and medium-sized regions. We were particularly interested in finding out what policy conclusions could be drawn for regional innovation policies in small and medium-sized regions.

The results are partly disappointing. Current research on RIS suffers from a number of deficiencies. The theoretical base is not well developed and much of what has been written lacks the clarity that is necessary to really evaluate the research and formulate strong policy conclusions. It is inadequate to define a RIS as all those factors that influence the innovation process. Such definitions are not operational. For this reason, more and better research on RIS is necessary to be able to formulate guidelines for regional innovation policies, in particular, in small and medium-sized regions.

However, a number of conclusions can be drawn in the light of the review and assessment. Firstly, it seems clear that for regional innovation policies to be meaningful the regions in question must already have either one or several clusters of SMEs or one or several larger leading companies surrounded by clusters of suppliers and/or customers. Secondly, since most small and medium-sized regions do not have public research institutions, developing strong links to research universities in other regions are of paramount importance. Thirdly, for those small and medium-sized regions that have one or several institutions of higher education it is important to take special measures to adapt the educational profile to fit with the needs of the regional innovation networks. Fourthly, problems to recruit qualified personnel seem to hamper the regional innovation systems in many small and medium-sized regions. Special measures may often be needed to facilitate the recruitment of qualified personnel. Fifthly, since RIS to a large extent function via collective learning it is necessary to improve existing arenas and meeting places and also create new arenas and meeting places. Sixthly, because many innovations are best realized within new firms it is vital for the regional innovation systems to offer broad support to new entrepreneurial ventures. Seventhly, as conditions in each region have unique traits, it is necessary to base all regional innovation policies upon careful studies of the existing regional innovation systems, the way they function as well as their weaknesses. Eighthly, administrative and functional regions normally do not coincide. Since the functional region is the relevant region from an economic point of view, it is therefore of great importance to see to it that regional innovation policies are formulated and executed for functional regions.

References

Almeida P, Kogut B (1999) Localization of knowledge and the mobility of engineers in regional networks. Management Science 45: 905–917

Amendola M, Bruno S (1990) The Behavior of the innovative firm: relations to the environment. Research Policy 19: 419–449

Anselin L, Varga A, Acs Z (1996) Local geographic spillovers between university research
and high technology innovations. Journal of Urban Economics 42: 422–448

Asheim B, Isaksen A (1996) Location, agglomeration and innovation: towards regional innovation systems in Norway. STEP Report R-13, STEP Centre for Innovation Research, Oslo

Asheim B, Isaksen A (2002) Regional innovation systems: the integration of local sticky
and global ubiquitous knowledge. Journal of Technology Transfer 27: 77-86

Audretsch D, Feldman M (1996) Innovative clusters and the industry life cycle. Review of
the Industrial Organization 11: 253–273

Bannock G, Baxter RE, Davis E (1992) The Penguin dictionary of economics, 5th edn, Penguin Books, London

Black J (1997) A Dictionary of economics. Oxford University Press, Oxford

Bottazzi L, Peri G (1999) Innovation, demand and knowledge spillovers: theory and evidence from European regions. Centre for Economic Policy Research (CEPR) Discussion Paper Series No. 2279, Centre for Economic Policy Research, London

Breschi S (1998) Agglomeration economies, knowledge spillovers, technological diversity
and spatial clustering of innovations. LIUC (Libero Istituto Universitario Carlo Cattaneo) Papers in Economics, N.57, Carlo Cattaneo University, Castellanza

Breschi S, Malerba M (1997) Sectoral innovation systems: technological regimes, Schumpeterian dynamics and spatial boundaries. In: Edquist C (ed) Systems of innovation:
technologies, institutions and organizations. Pinter, London, pp 261-287

Bresnahan T, Trajtenberg M (1995) General purpose technologies – engines of growth?.
Journal of Econometrics 65: 83–108

Capello R (2001) Urban innovation and collective learning: theory and evidence from five
metropolitan cities in Europe. In: Fischer M, Fröhlich J (eds) Knowledge, complexity
and innovation systems. Springer, Berlin Heidelberg New York, pp 181-208

Carlson B, Stankiewicz R (1991) On the nature, function and composition of technological
systems. Journal of Evolutionary Economics 1: 93–118

Cooke P, Uranga MJ, Etxebarria G (1997) Regional innovation systems: institutional and
organizational dimensions. Research Policy 26: 475–491

Cooke P, Uranga MJ, Etxebarria G (1998) Regional systems of innovation: an evolutionary
perspective. Environment and Planning 30: 1563–1584

de la Mothe J, Paquet G (1998) National innovation systems, real economies and instituted
processes. Small Business Economics 11: 101–111

Echeverri-Carroll E, Brennan W (1999) Are innovation networks bounded by proximity?
In: Fischer M, Suarez-Villa L, Steiner M (eds) Innovation networks and localities.
Springer, Berlin Heidelberg New York, pp 28-49

Edquist C (1997) Institutions and organizations in systems of innovation: the state of the
art. Department of Technology and Social Change (TEMA T) Working Paper No. 182,
Department of Technology and Social Change, Linköping University, Linköping

Edquist C (2000) Systems of innovations – their emergence and characteristics. In: Edquist
C, McKelvey M (eds) Systems of innovations: growth, competitiveness and employment, vol 1, MPG Books, Cornwall, pp 3-37

Eriksson A (2000) Regional innovation systems – from theory to accomplishment (in
Swedish). Swedish Office of Science and Technology, Stockholm

Etkzkowitz H, Leydesdorff L (2000) The dynamics of innovation: from national systems and mode 2 to a triple helix of university-industry-government relations. Research Policy 29: 109–123

Feldman M, Audretsch D (1998) Innovation in cities: science-based diversity, specialization and localized competition. European Economic Review 43: 409–429

Fischer M. (1999) The innovation process and network activities of manufacturing firms. In: Fischer M, Suarez-Villa L, Steiner M (eds) Innovation, networks and localities. Springer, Berlin Heidelberg New York, pp 11-27

Fischer M, Revilla-Diez J, Snickars F (2001) Metropolitan innovation system: theory and evidence from three metropolitan regions in Europe. Springer, Berlin Heidelberg New York

Freeman C (1995) The national system of innovation in historical perspective. Cambridge Journal of Economics 19: 5–24

Freeman C (1998) Innovation. In: Newman P (1998) The New Palgrave dictionary of economics and law. Macmillian, London, pp 858-860

Freeman C, Perez C (1988) Structural crises of adjustment: business cycles and investment behavior. In: Dosi G, et al (eds) Technical Change and Economic Theory. Pinter Publishers, London, pp 38-66

Gregersen B, Johnson B (1996) Learning economies, innovation systems and European integration. Regional Studies 31: 479–490

Halvorsen K, Lacave M (1998) Innovation systems in urban areas. Norwegian Institute for Urban and Regional Research (NIBR) Working Paper 110, Norwegian Institute for Urban and Regional Research, Oslo

Johansson B (1992) Economic dynamics in Europe (in Swedish). Liber-Hermods, Malmö

Johansson B (1993) Economic networks and self-organization. In: Bergman E, Maier G, Tödtling F (eds) Regions reconsidered. Ipswich Book, Suffolk, pp 17-32

Johansson B (1998) Infrastructure, market potential and endogenous growth. Jönköping International Business School (JIBS), Jönköping

Johansson B, Westin L (1987) Technical change, location and trade. Papers of the Regional Science Association 62: 13–25

Jonsson O, Persson H, Silbersky U (2000) Innovativeness and the region – firms, processes and politics (in Swedish). Rapport 121, Swedish Institute for Regional Research, Östersund

Karlsson C (1988) Innovation adoption and the Product Life Cycle. Umeå Economic Studies, No. 185, University of Umeå, Umeå

Karlsson C (2001) The role of clusters for industrial and regional economic development (in Swedish). Mimeograph, Jönköping International Business School (JIBS), Jönköping

Karlsson C, Klaesson J (2000) Success in manufacturing employment in an industrial district: higher productivity or lower wages? Investigaciones Europeas de Dirección y Economía de la Empresa 6: 65–90

Karlsson C, Manduchi A (2001) Knowledge spillovers in a spatial context. In: Fischer M, Fröhlich J (eds) Knowledge, complexity and innovation systems. Springer, Berlin Heidelberg New York, pp 101-123

Karlsson C, Olsson M (2000) Methods for identifying functional regions – theory and applications. Jönköping International Business School (JIBS) Working Paper Series No 2000–3, Jönköping International Business School, Jönköping

Koschatzky K (1998a) Innovation networks of industry and business-related services – relations between innovation intensity of firms and regional inter-firm cooperation. European Planning Studies 7: 737–757

Koschatzky K (1998b) Firm innovation and region: the role of space in innovation processes. International Journal of Innovation Management 2: 383–408

Koschatzky K (2001) Regional development through entrepreneurship promotion? The role of higher education institutes for stimulating firm foundations. Paper presented at the 41st Congress of the European Regional Science Association (ERSA), 29 August- 1 September, Zagreb

Lam A (1998) Tacit knowledge, organizational learning and innovation: a societal perspective. Danish Research Unit for Industrial Dynamics (DRUID) Working Paper No. 98–22, Danish Research Unit for Industrial Dynamics, Copenhagen

Leonard D, Sensiper S (1998) The role of tacit knowledge in group innovation. California Management Review 40: 112–131

Lorenzen M (1996) Communicating trust in industrial districts. Paper presented at the Erasmus Intensive Seminar 'Local Production Systems and European Integration', July 4-12, Turin

Lorenzen M (1998) Localized learning – why are inter-firm learning patterns institutionalised within particular localities? Department of Industrial Economics and Strategy (IVS) Working Paper no. 98-10, Copenhagen Business School, Copenhagen

Lundvall B (1995) Introduction. In: Lundvall B (ed) National systems of innovation – towards a theory of innovation and interactive learning. Biddles, London, pp 1-19

Lundvall B, Lindgaard-Christensen J (1999) Extending and deepening the analysis of innovation systems – with empirical illustrations from the DISKO project. Danish Research Unit for Industrial Dynamics (DRUID) Working Papers No. 99–12, Danish Research Unit for Industrial Dynamics, Copenhagen

Maillat D (1993) The innovation process and the role of the milieu. In: Bergman E, Maier G, Tödtling F (eds) Regions reconsidered. Ipswich Book, Suffolk, pp 103-115

Maillat D (1995) Territorial dynamic, innovative milieus and regional policy. Entrepreneurship & Regional Development 7: 157–165

Maillat D (1998) Interactions between urban systems and localized productive systems: an approach to endogenous regional development in terms of innovative milieu. European Planning Studies 6: 117–129

Malecki E, Oinas P (2002) The evolution of technologies in time and space: from national and regional to spatial innovation systems. International Regional Science Review 25: 102–131

Markusen A (1996) Sticky places in slippery space: a typology of industrial districts. Economic Geography 72: 293–313

Massey D, Quintas P, Wield D (1992) High tech fantasies: science parks in society, science and space. Routledge, London

Maurseth P, Verspagen B (1998) Knowledge spillovers in Europe and its consequences for systems of innovation. Eindhoven Centre for Innovation Studies (ECIS) Working Paper No. 98.1, Eindhoven Centre for Innovation Studies, Eindhoven

Meeus M, Oerlemans L, van Dijck J (1999) Regional systems of innovation from within – an empirical specification of the relation between technological dynamics and interaction between multiple actors in a Dutch region. Eindhoven Centre for Innovation Studies (ECIS) Working Paper No. 99.1, Eindhoven Centre for Innovation Studies, Eindhoven

Mytelka L, Farinelli F (2000) Local clusters, innovation systems and sustained competitiveness. United Nations University/ Institute for New Technologies (UNU/INTECH) Discussion Paper 2000-5, United Nations University/ Institute for New Technologies, Maastricht

Nelson R, Rosenberg N (1993) Technical innovation and national systems. In: Nelson R. (ed) National innovation systems – a comparative analysis. Oxford University Press, New York, pp 3-21

Nelson R, Winter S (1982) An evolutionary theory of economic change. Harvard University Press, Cambridge, MA

Niosi J (2000) Regional systems of innovations – market pull and government push. Innovation Systems Research Network (ISRN) Working Paper 2000-4, University of Toronto, Toronto

Oerlemans L, Meeus M, Boekema F (1998) Does networks matter for innovation? – the usefulness of the economic network approach in analyzing innovation. Tijdschrift voor Economische en Sociale Geografie (Journal of Economic and Social Geography) 89: 289–309

Porter M (1990) The competitive advantage of nations. Macmillian, London

Rothwell R (1992) Successful industrial innovation: critical factors for the 1990s. R&D Management 22: 221–239

Radosevic S (2002) Regional innovation systems in Central and Eastern Europe: determinants, organizers and alignments. Journal of Technology Transfer 27: 87-96

Storper M (1995) The resurgence of regional economies, ten years later: the region as a nexus of untraded interdependencies. European Urban and Regional Studies 2: 191–215

Suranyi-Unger T (1982) Innovation. In: Greenwald D (ed) Encyclopaedia of economics. McGraw Hill, New York, pp 525-526

Sölvell Ö, Zander I, Porter M (1991) Advantage Sweden. Nordstedts, Stockholm

Tödtling F (1993) Spatial differentiation of innovation – locational and structural factors: results from an Austrian study. In: Bergman E, Maier G, Tödtling F (eds) Regions reconsidered. Ipswich Book, Suffolk, pp 215-233

Varga A (1998) University research and regional innovation – a spatial econometric analysis of academic technology transfers. Kluwer, Boston, MA

von Hippel E (1988) The sources of innovation. Oxford University Press, New York

von Hippel E (1998) Economics of product development by users: the impact of sticky local information. Management Science 44: 629–644

Wiig H (1996) An empirical study of the innovation system in Finnmark. STEP Working Paper R-09, STEP Centre for Innovation Research, Oslo

Wiig H, Isaksen A (1998) Innovation in ultra-peripheral regions: the case of Finnmark and Rural Areas in Norway. STEP Report R-02, STEP Centre for Innovation Research, Oslo

Wiig H, Wood M (1995) What comprises a regional innovation system? – an empirical study. STEP Working Paper R-01, STEP Centre for Innovation Research, Oslo

5 Relating Entrepreneurship to Economic Growth

Christian Friis[1], Charlie Karlsson[2] and Thomas Paulsson[3]

[1] LänsTeknikCentrum (LTC)
[2] Jönköping International Business School, Jönköping University
[3] AstraZeneca Sweden AB

5.1 Introduction

Not all economists grant the entrepreneur a central role to explain economic growth. However, some include the entrepreneur as one of the main characters. For example, Holcombe (1998, p. 60) claims, "the engine of economic growth is entrepreneurship". Others, not least neoclassic economists, place the entrepreneur in the wings.

The entrepreneur is an elusive character in economic theory due to the difficulty of providing an accurate description. It appears impossible to produce a single definition of entrepreneurship and most theoretical approaches yield operational difficulties. By the same token, most operational definitions are incomplete and cover only single parts of the concept[1].

Previous overviews on the topic of entrepreneurship include Goel (1997) who has made a comprehensive study of the entrepreneur in mainstream economic theory. Glancey and McQuaid (2000) offer a summary of how entrepreneurship is incorporated into economic and social theory. Yu (1997) presents some approaches to encompass entrepreneurship into the theoretical framework of economics. Two volumes of commonly cited articles are edited by Casson (1990) and Livesay (1995). Furthermore, Wennekers and Thurik (1999) attempt to identify the links between entrepreneurship and economic growth. The paper by Wennekers and Thurik is of particular relevance to this contribution as it provides an overview of studies of entrepreneurship in economic theory and a methodological reference. Henrekson (2002) dedicates a chapter to summarise effects of entrepreneurship on economic growth. Numerous empirical studies have examined the effects of en-

---

[1] In a similar way, economic growth is not an axiomatic concept. It could include an increase in per capita income, an outward shift of the production possibility frontier, greater purchasing power, an increase in average living standards, a sustained rate of innovation or capital accumulation as well as a higher share of employment.

trepreneurship, but few studies have been undertaken in order to summarise the empirical evidence and synthesize the theoretical framework and the empirical results.

The objective of this chapter is to provide a critical overview of recent empirical research on the relationship between entrepreneurship and economic growth. Therefore, regional growth may differ due to differences in the presence of entrepreneurship. The analysis in this chapter may be compared with the discussion in Chap. 10, where regional differences in creativity are related to growth differentials.

Section 5.2 discusses the role and definition of entrepreneurship. Section 5.3 gives an overview of theoretical schools and their explanations of economic growth with reference to entrepreneurship. The theories are outlined briefly and categorized. Following, in Sect.5.4 presents a summary of empirical studies of entrepreneurship and economic growth. This serves partly as a survey of recent research and partly as a method of identifying neglected aspects of research in entrepreneurship with respect to growth. The findings are analysed and discussed in Sect.5.5 and summarized in Sect.5.6 alongside with suggestions for further research.

5.2 The Role and Definition of Entrepreneurship

One aspect that might initially blur the concept of entrepreneurship is that it can be defined in a number of different ways. The hypothesis, that the role of entrepreneurship has changed, is presented in this section. Following, there is a selection of definitions of entrepreneurship along with a discussion of the importance of various aspects of the concept.

5.2.1 The Changing Role of Entrepreneurship

Looking into historical perspectives of entrepreneurship, Baumol (1993) makes two propositions. First, the rules of the game determining the payoff from entrepreneurial activity change and has been changing over time and from place to place. Secondly, entrepreneurial behaviour has been changing according to the rules of the game.

A number of studies indicate that there has been a structural shift in the OECD economies from large companies competing through mass production, product differentiation, and economies of scale, towards smaller companies relying on knowledge, initiative, and flexibility. This transition from a 'managed economy' towards an 'entrepreneurial economy' appears to have taken place between the mid 1970s and the early 1990s (Acs 1996, 1999; Acs and Audretsch 2001; Audretsch and Thurik 1997, 2001a, 2001b; Audretsch et al. 2002; Carree and Thurik 1998; Carree et al. 1999, 2002; Thurik 1996; Verheul et al. 2003). The economy, later to be labeled 'managed', was characterized by "[the] three-pronged investment in production, distribution and management that brought the modern industrial enterprise into being" (Chandler 1990, p. 8). The competitive advantage was in economies of scale or scope and a distributional network allowing the product to reach a large market. Thus, large firms were the engines powering the economy ahead. The entrepreneurial economy is described by a decentralized industry structure with knowledge and flexibility as key factors of production. Knowledge is, as a factor of production, characterized by uncertainty as well as being highly asymmetric between individuals and costly to transact (Audretsch and Thurik 2001a).

A number of variables are assumed to have caused this transition, among them increased global competition, changes in demand and demographics, intensified uncertainty and new technologies. Various aspects and explanations are discussed in Acs (1996), Acs and Audretsch (2001), Acs, Carlsson and Karlsson (1999), Acs, Morck and Yeung (1999), Audretsch and Thurik (2001a), Brock and Evans (1989), Carlsson (1992, 1996 and 1999), Carree and Thurik (1998), Carree et al. (2002), Eliasson (1994), Glancey and McQuaid (2000), Loveman and Sengenberger (1991) and Piore and Sable (1984).

5.2.2 Definitions of Entrepreneurship

This chapter makes a distinction between theoretical and operational definitions of entrepreneurship. In general, the theoretical definitions are wide, covering a number of entrepreneurial activities, whereas the operationalized definitions cover a singular aspect.

Glancey and McQuaid (2000) mention five definitions of entrepreneurship, while Wennekers and Thurik (1999) thirteen. For example, entrepreneurship could imply an economic function, as a bearer of uncertainty, a resource allocator, or an innovator. It could also refer to particular behaviour, intrinsic characteristics, the creation of new organizations, or the role of an owner-manager of a company. Baumol (1993), and subsequently Dejardin (2000), stress that entrepreneurial activities can also range from being productive to society at large to searching for surplus profits with negative consequences, all depending on the structure of incentives and possibilities.

In this chapter, there is a focus on the economic aspects of entrepreneurship, the entrepreneur in economic theory as well as on recent empirical evidence of the economic impact of entrepreneurship on economic growth. This does not imply that other aspects, such as e.g. sociological or psychological manifestations of entrepreneurship, are irrelevant. They are merely beyond the scope of this chapter. For more insights and references, consult e.g. Hébert and Link (1989).

The economic definition of entrepreneurship can be viewed from a theoretical and an operational context. Among the early theoretical definitions, Cantillon (1755) claims that "undertakers" are a class of economic agents, making decisions on market transactions in the face of uncertainty. Knight (1921) defines entrepreneurship as dealing with uncertainty, making a distinction between risk, which can be calculated, and uncertainty, which cannot. Schumpeter (1934) describes the entrepreneur as the bearer of the mechanism for change and economic development, and entrepreneurship as the undertaking of new ideas and new combinations, i.e. innovations. He makes the distinction between five different manifestations of entrepreneurship (Schumpeter 1934, p. 66), a new good, a new method of production, a new market, a new source of supply of intermediate goods, and a new organization. The role of the entrepreneur in a competitive market process is stressed by Kirzner (1973), who defines the entrepreneur as an individual that is able to identify and act on arbitrage opportunities available in a competitive market environment. More specifically, Kirzner (1973, p. 17) states, "The entrepreneur's activity is essentially competitive. [...] Or, to put it the other way around, entrepreneurship is inherent in the competitive market process". This definition is very wide and would imply that every agent on the market, every firm, making a profitable business is an entrepreneur.

Yu (1997) argues that Schumpeter's entrepreneur, the creative destructor, prevents the economy from reaching a stationary equilibrium, while Kirzner's entrepreneur is the one bringing the economy into equilibrium by spotting and profiting from disequilibria[2]. Holcombe (1998) claims that the actions of the Kirznerian and Schumpeterian entrepreneurs are no different. Both take advantage of unexploited profit opportunities and the actions undertaken by any of them will alter the future market environment. An attempt to synthesise the actions of the arbitrageur and the creative destructor is offered by Runge (2000, p. 38), who, among other things, defines entrepreneurship as the exploitation of differences in market prices and private values. Successful entrepreneurship then relates to the ability to convince the market that the value or price assigned to some private capital, goods, or service previously has been underestimated. A further implication of the Kirzner entrepreneur is that, without the presence of a Schumpeter creative destroyer, the role of the entrepreneur as an engine of economic growth would cease as the economy reaches equilibrium.

Vosloo (1994, p. 147) suggests that the entrepreneur might be an opportunity maximizer when defining an entrepreneur "as a person who has the ability to explore the environment, identify opportunities for improvement, mobilize resources and implement action to maximize those opportunities". In what appears as a synthesis of the previous suggested definitions, Wennekers and Thurik (1999, pp. 46-47) suggest that entrepreneurship is the established capacity of individuals or firms to:

- "Perceive and create new economic opportunities [...] and to
- Introduce their ideas in the market, in the face of uncertainty and other obstacles, by making decisions on location, form and the use of resources and institutions."

In a previous study (Wennekers et al. 1997, p. 5) a third aspect was included as well:

- "[...] -Compete with others for a share of that market."

---

[2] See also Kirzner (1973, pp. 72-73).

This definition might include many of the aspects of entrepreneurship but it is not operationally applicable. Most of the aspects are hard to identify and isolate, leading to various functional definitions describing individual aspects of the concept. Quantitative studies of entrepreneurship often focus on business start-ups or innovation in small enterprises. Both these measures have several limitations. According to Audretsch (1995), some of the shortcomings in using the measure of start-ups are methodological, i.e. only net entry of start-ups has been used, and entry has generally only been measured over a single time period. Net entry gives little information on volatility and could conceal a process of creative destruction. This problem has been addressed during the last few years, which could result in some interesting publications. The measure of start-ups excludes 'intrapreneurship', i.e. entrepreneurship within existing organizations.

Defining entrepreneurship as small-firm innovation might also be misleading. Large firms might exhibit entrepreneurial and innovative behaviour. There might also be non-innovative start-ups, which are entrepreneurial in the sense that they respond to disequilibria or profit opportunities. An additional obstacle regarding the process of innovation is to define meaningful measures of innovative inputs and outputs, e.g. a measure using R&D expenditures cannot account for innovation in small firms (Acs and Audretsch 1990, 2001). From this, an alternative classification emerges, distinguishing three breeds of entrepreneurs (Wennekers and Thurik 1999; Dejardin 2000).

The Schumpeterian entrepreneurs mainly operate in small, independent firms. Intrapreneurs are the innovators and creative leaders within existing organizations. Both are creative destructors and bearers of change. In contrast to this, there are the managerial business owners, who focus on coordination of production and distribution. Possibly, this might be more of a Kirznerian entrepreneur. There are numerous, at times even contradictory, definitions of entrepreneurship. Broadly, these definitions can be divided into two subcategories: those that are generally more encompassing theoretically and the more narrow operational ones. Thus, one conclusion is that it might be more fruitful to talk about entrepreneurial activities, at least from an operational point of view. The operational definitions, such as start-ups or innovative activities, each cover a limited range of entrepreneurial activities but might yield a more profound coverage in combination.

5.3 Theories of Entrepreneurship and Economic Growth

This section provides an outline of some of the basic approaches used to define the relationship between entrepreneurship and economic growth. For economy and comparison, this sketch of theories is for the most part parallel to the classification offered by Wennekers and Thurik (1999). However, some words of caution are warranted here. First, we do not fully and completely endorse the classification offered by Wennekers and Thurik (1999). However, it serves as a useful tool to identify connections between entrepreneurship and theories of economic growth. Second, the list and description of growth theories are by necessity neither complete nor extensive and detailed. The brief theoretical outlines are merely offered as an orientation of theories with a significant academic impact. These short descriptions subsequently lack the details and intricacies of the full models. Therefore, the interested reader probing deeper into this subject matter is advised to consult original references and/or advanced textbooks on economic growth.

5.3.1 Classifying the Theories

The study of entrepreneurship was central to a number of leading economic theorists in the early 20th century, then relatively neglected for some decades until it was rediscovered in the 1970s. Donald Sexton offers an account of the shifts in academic focus and advances in the study of entrepreneurship since 1980 (Sexton and Smilor 1997, Chap. 18).

In a recent study, Steele (2000) raises criticism against traditional theoretical approaches to economic growth. Dividing the contemporary account into two broad categories, mathematical macroeconomic models and institutional or historical accounts, Steele questions the underlying neoclassical assumptions of a social equilibrium and individual optimisation. Instead, economic growth is attributed to market disequilibria with entrepreneurship functioning as an equilibrating process. This view is an extension of Kirzner (1973, 1994). Besides Kirzner's adaptive entrepreneurship, Audretsch et al. (2001) mention Lebenstein's routine entrepreneurship, Baumol's imitative entrepreneurship, and Schumpeter's creative entrepreneurship. A more in-depth presentation and analysis of this classification can be found in Yu (1997).

Wennekers and Thurik (1999) offer an alternative systematisation of the field. They attribute economic growth through entrepreneurship to three main processes or entrepreneurial activities: enhanced competition, innovations, and employment growth through firm start-ups. It should be noted that these processes or activities might be overlapping and not mutually exclusive. From this perspective, the foci of explanation of the different schools of thought are mapped. While the assessment offered by Wennekers and Thurik can be questioned (or at least discussed) on some accounts, this systematisation is used throughout the chapter, as it appears to be a useful tool in identifying links between entrepreneurship and economic growth. A modification of this assessment is presented in Table 5.1.

In addition to the various schools of growth theory presented in the table, the model and theory of recombinant growth could be included. This model was initially proposed by Weitzman (1998) and further developed by Olsson and Frey (2002). The focus of the model concerns innovation. Management literature perspectives on entrepreneurship are, however, omitted in this study.

Table 5.1. Assessment of the role of entrepreneurship, drawn from several fields of research

The Nature of the Entrepreneur	Competition	Innovation	Firm Start-ups	Importance of Entrepreneurship for Economic Growth
The Creative Destructor (Schumpeter)	Explicit	Central	Implicit	Explicit
The Expert (Neoclassical Growth Theory)	Explicit	Implicit	Absent	Implicit
The Arbitrageur (Austrian School)	Explicit	Implicit	Absent	Explicit
The Profit Maximizer (Endogenous Growth Theory)	Implicit	Central	Absent	Implicit
The Law Abider (Economic History)	Explicit	Central	Implicit	Central
The Opportunity Maximizer (Industrial Economics)	Central	Central	Explicit	Central
The Fittest (Evolutionary Economics)	Central	Central	Central	Central

Source: A modification of Wennekers and Thurik 1999, p. 50

5.3.1.1 The Creative Destructor (Schumpeter)

The Austrian tradition with Schumpeter (1934)[3] and Baumol (1968) focuses on the entrepreneur as an innovator and inspirer, the implementer of creative destruction, creating instability, disequilibria, and economic development. Yu (1997) concludes that Schumpeter's objections to the orthodox system relate to the use of equilibrium models and static analysis as well as the assumptions of rational behaviour and profit maximization. Furthermore, Schumpeter (1934) argues that the risk of trying new combinations, i.e. being entrepreneurial, intrinsically falls on the capitalist and not on the entrepreneur.

5.3.1.2 The Expert (Neoclassical Growth Theory)

Wennekers et al. (1997) and Glancey and McQuaid (2000) mention that under traditional neoclassical assumptions, also labeled the Chicago tradition, there are limitations imposed on entrepreneurship by perfect competition, perfect informa-

---

[3] The importance of the entrepreneur is primarily stressed in Schumpeter's earlier work on competitive capitalism. In the later works on capitalism, large firms are seen as the vehicle of economic progress (Brouwer 2000).

tion, and rational behaviour. An alternative to the latter limitation could also be the absence of time lags between decision and outcome, as suggested by Lydall (1998). The primary analytical tool of neoclassical theory is a model in which equilibrium is attainable and with an invisible hand leading the market towards equilibrium. There have been a few attempts made to incorporate entrepreneurship into the neoclassical framework. Knight (1921) defines willingness to accept uncertainty as entrepreneurship. Some intuitive ability or non-universal knowledge gives the successful entrepreneur a superior ability to handle uncertainty. Introducing Knight's uncertainty into a Schumpeterian framework has spawned several models, e.g. Kihlstrom and Laffont (1979), Brouwer (2000) and Rigotti et al. (2001).

While there are several growth models that can be labeled (more or less) neoclassical, no single growth model have received as much attention and have had such an impact as the Solow (1956) growth model[4]. A fundamental conclusion of the Solow model is that accumulation of capital cannot account for neither historic growth of per capita income or substantial international differences in per capita output. The model is built around a standard CRS (constant returns to scale) production function, where output is a function of capital and 'effective labour'. Effective labour includes the knowledge or effectiveness of the labour force. Hence, output increases if either capital or effective labour increases. With given levels of capital and labour, growth can only occur through the expansion of knowledge, i.e. we have technological progress. Independent of its starting point, the economy eventually reaches its equilibrium of the balanced growth path where output, capital, and effective labour are growing at a constant rate. Here the growth rate is completely determined by advances in knowledge or technological progress.

The entrepreneur does not exist in the Solow model. The benevolent reader could possibly discern the existence of an implicit entrepreneur encompassed by the notion of *knowledge*. However, knowledge or effectiveness of labour is incompletely defined in the model and can, therefore, be attached to various and several factors (other than capital and labour) that possibly could influence output. Furthermore and as pointed out by Romer (1990), since the growth rate of knowledge is exogenously given, growth is modelled by assuming its existence.

5.3.1.3 The Arbitrageur (Austrian School)

The peculiar characteristic of the Austrian entrepreneur is the ability to perceive profit opportunities. Kirzner (1973) suggests that the connection between entrepreneurship and economic growth is founded on the entrepreneur spotting and profiting from a situation of disequilibrium by improving on market inefficiencies or deficiencies. In an extension of Kirzner's model, Holcombe (1998) argues that these opportunities must come from somewhere, namely the insights of other entrepreneurs. Entrepreneurship creates changes, and changes lead to more opportu-

---

[4] The model is sometimes referred to as the Solow-Swan growth model, due to Swan (1956). Hitherto, referring to the neoclassical tradition in relation to growth, we will refer to the Solow model.

nities for entrepreneurship. Thus, entrepreneurship generates more entrepreneurship. In a comment on Holcombe, Hülsman (1999) is critical to the notion of entrepreneurship as a perpetuum mobile of economic growth. Minniti (1999) reaches the same conclusion as Holcombe, but does also include a "network externality of entrepreneurship", i.e. a self-reinforcing culture of entrepreneurial spirit. Referring to Knight, Minniti also endows the entrepreneur with bearing some degree of uncertainty.

5.3.1.4 The Profit Maximizer (Endogenous Growth Theory)

The basic neoclassical theory of growth, such as e.g. the Solow model, explains growth as exogenously determined changes or levels of technological progress. As such the neoclassical model is limited because it tells us very little about the factors that shape and mould technological progress, and in the extension growth. This has spawned the development of a family of highly influential models, generally labeled endogenous growth or 'new growth' models. Some of the more pioneering and important contributions in this field include Romer (1986, 1990), Lucas (1988), Grossman and Helpman (1991), and Aghion and Howitt (1992). For an overview of these models and others, see Aghion and Howitt (1998) and Valdés (1999).

A unifying character of these models, which also distinguishes them fundamentally from the Solow model, is that knowledge is modelled as being endogenous[5]. Growth is generated by investments in knowledge and the models outline the determinants of investment decisions in knowledge. Furthermore, some of these models, such as e.g. Lucas (1988) differentiate between physical and human capital. This implies that the relative importance of capital could be substantially more important than acknowledged by the Solow model, especially if there exist positive externalities in accumulation of (foremost human) capital.

While technologies or knowledge may be of diverse types and have different sources, such as e.g. basic scientific research, private R&D and innovation, or learning by doing, the entrepreneur does not generally hold a central position (if any) in the endogenous growth models. There is e.g. no explicit entrepreneur in Romer (1986, 1990) and Lucas (1988). A notable exception, extending upon Segerstrom et al. (1990) and Aghion and Howitt (1992), is offered by Grossman and Helpman (1991) where all R&D and investment decisions are made by forward-looking profit maximizing entrepreneurs. Successive quality improvements are made of available goods and services, so called quality ladders. The model generates equilibrium with a deterministic aggregate level of innovation, which is constant in the steady state. While the model claims to capture several realistic aspects of the innovation process such as e.g. product life cycles, non-uniform de-

---

[5] Within the theoretical framework of endogenous growth, efforts have been made in order to formalise Schumpeter's model of creative destruction and innovation as a mean of capturing monopoly profits (e.g. Aghion and Howitt 1992). From this perspective, endogenous growth theory can be regarded as a synthesis and extension of the Austrian and Chicago schools.

velopment across sectors etc., the role and behaviour of the entrepreneur is relative simplistic and mimics the behaviour of the standard profit maximising firm.

5.3.1.5 The Law Abider (Economic History)

According to Gould (1972), there has been a synthesis of economics and economic history in order to extend the static equilibrium models of economic growth and development. In economic history, institutions are perceived as a major determinant of economic growth. According to North and Thomas (1973, p.2) growth is explained by the presence of efficient economic organisations and institutions that provide individuals with incentives for growth generating activities. From the point of view of competing/alternative schools of thought, factors such as e.g. innovation economies of scale, education, and capital accumulation are generally considered as being prerequisites/conditions for growth. North and Thomas, on the other hand, claim that change in these factors in fact constitute growth. In a subsequent study by North (1990, p. 83) there is an even more explicit link between economic growth and the entrepreneur; "The agent of change is the individual entrepreneur responding to the incentives embodied in the institutional framework." This is in contrast to Gould (1972) who de-emphasizes the importance of the individual when analysing the history of growths and inventions.

Baumol (1993) advocates the importance of institutions for productive entrepreneurship, i.e. economic growth. He offers an account of the conditions for entrepreneurship and its manifestations throughout history, from ancient Rome and Greece to the present time. Another approach to describing the history of entrepreneurship, also focusing on institutional settings, is offered by Cole (1949).

In a study aimed at identifying links between entrepreneurship and economic growth Wennekers et al. (1997) include a section on the role of entrepreneurship in European history. In accordance with North and Baumol, the institutional framework is here the major determinant of the manifestations of entrepreneurship.

5.3.1.6 The Opportunity Maximizer (Industrial Economics)

Michael Porter grants entrepreneurship a crucial role when considering economic growth from a national perspective (1990, pp. 125-126):

"Invention and entrepreneurship are at the heart of national advantage. [...] Our research shows that neither entrepreneurship nor invention is random; assigning a role to chance does not mean that industry success is wholly unpredictable."

Porter finds a great deal of explanatory power in a number of determinants, such as factor conditions, demand conditions, the firm's strategy, structure and rivalry, related and supporting industries as well as a government function. In order to gain a competitive advantage there must be an interaction between the determinants. An advantage in one single factor might not be sufficient. Wennekers et al. (1997) suggest using the model for analysing the relationship between entrepreneurship and economic growth to find out where entrepreneurship and innovation is most likely to occur.

5.3.1.7 The Fittest (Evolutionary Economics)

Abstracting from optimisation and market equilibrium Nelson and Winter (1982) were influential in developing the school of evolutionary economics, drawing inspiration from disciplines such as Darwinism. A core concept of the theory is the notion of bounded rationality; all individuals are different and are facing both uncertainty about the possible courses of action, as well as imperfect information about the consequences of their decisions. Each individual is endowed with a set of routines, which can only evolve gradually. In the market situation, different routines are tested and through a process of natural selection the most suitable for the given market environment survive and achieve. Grebel et al. (2001) make an attempt to encompass the entrepreneur into an evolutionary framework. In the model, each individual is endowed with entrepreneurial spirit, human capital, and venture capital.

Eliasson (1994) claims that competence is the crucial factor for firm survival, competence being the ability to profit locally on internationally available technology. There are a large number of ways to solve any particular problem, and more ways the more complex the problem. Some ways are better than others, but a priori, the different strategies cannot be ranked. This implies trial-and-error experimentation where the learning process, i.e. the accumulation of competence, is the determinant of success. A subsequent study by Eliasson and Braunerhjelm (1998) support this by claiming that economic growth stems from human-embodied tacit competencies.

5.3.1.8 The Innovator (Recombinant Growth)

The concept of recombinant growth is based on Schumpeter's notion on innovations as a result of new combinations. The model was introduced by Weitzman (1998) and extended to specifically explain entrepreneurship by Olsson and Frey (2002). The model by Olsson and Frey includes a combinatory process of existing ideas that take place in a multidimensional technology space where ideas are separated by technological distance. Any convexities in the technology frontier imply potential expansion possibilities of the technology set. In this model, the entrepreneur is given the role of combining new ideas, and thus expanding the technology set.

5.3.2 Summary

It should be emphasized that the classification used in this chapter is only one of several comprehensive options. The advantage of this classification is its coverage of influential theories and the wide variety of entrepreneurial functions described.

Entrepreneurial activities range from being a creative destructor and an innovator to dealing with uncertainty and spot profit opportunities. The innovating Schumpeter entrepreneur brings the economy out of equilibrium and is the catalyst for a reallocation of resources to better uses. Knight's successful entrepreneur has a special advantage when dealing with uncertainty, while Kirzner's entrepreneur is skilled at spotting and making profit from disequilibria in the economy. These different aspects might have opposite effects on the market but they are not mutually exclusive per se. Due to the diametrically diverse natures of the entrepreneurial activities, no attempt has been made to formulate a master theory incorporating all the various aspects.

The institutional framework is the form in which the manifestations of entrepreneurship are moulded. Imperfections in the institutions might lead to socially undesirable entrepreneurial activities.

5.4 Entrepreneurship and Economic Growth: Empirical Results

This section summarizes a number of recent empirical studies covering aspects of the changing importance of entrepreneurship and its links to economic growth. The section follows the division made by Wennekers and Thurik (1999), linking entrepreneurial activities to economic growth through competition, innovation, and firm start-ups.

5.4.1 Competition and Economic Growth

Acs (1996) suggests that one explanation for employment growth in the US is increased competition. Manifestations of increased competition include rising import competition, anti-trust, deregulation, new structures of vertical integration and reductions in economies of scale.

An econometric study by Geroski (1994, p. 88) leads to the conclusion that "[...] competition plays a significant role in stimulating productivity, with both new firms and new ideas provoking movements to, and outwards movements of, the production frontier which, the data suggest, would not have occurred in their absence". Furthermore, Geroski (p. 149) finds that innovative activities tend to de-concentrate markets and concludes that "it is almost certainly the case that small-firm and entrant activity drives the negative association between changes in concentration and innovative activity which appears in the data".

An econometric study of the US telephone industry by Gort and Sung (1999) yields the conclusion that increased competition has led to greater efficiency within the industry. Gort and Sung assume that competition can affect efficiency in four ways; greater incentive to stimulate demand, higher quality of capital inputs, lower monitoring costs, and greater efficiency of firm-specific organizational capital as well as rivalry stimulating innovation. Regarding the fourth effect, the authors mention that it is possible the incentive to innovate might be greater under monopolistic conditions due to better opportunities for capturing the returns from innovation. Furthermore, monopolistic enterprises might have more resources to invest in innovation.

Nickell (1996) finds, in a study of firms based in the UK, that there is only weak empirical evidence in favour of the hypothesis that competition improves corporate performance. On the other hand, when measuring competition, as either increased numbers of competitors or lower levels of surplus profits, it appears that there is a positive correlation between the level of competition and total factor productivity growth.

5.4.2 Innovation and Economic Growth

Novis Ordo Mundi (*The New World Order*), characterized by greater uncertainty, asymmetry, and reliance on knowledge as a factor of production, has increased the importance of small entrepreneurial firms[6]. Acs and Audretsch (2001) conclude that there are significant differences in the importance of small firms regarding innovative activity across sectors. Specifically, they mention computers and process control instruments as industries where new entrepreneurial firms are an important part of the innovation process. This adds to a list of Baldwin and Johnson (1999), who mention the importance of small firms regarding electronics, instruments, medical equipment, steel, and biotechnology. Acs (1996) presents an innovation measure, defined as the total number of innovations per 1000 employees in different industry sectors. Applying this measure on data on the US market 1982 indicates that small firms (less than 500 employees) produce more innovations in the fields of electronic computing equipment, process control instruments, electronic components, engineering and scientific instruments and plastics products. Suggested explanations for the relative importance of small firms might be diseconomies of scale in the production of innovations and knowledge spillovers.

Knowledge spillovers are considered explicitly by Acs et al. (1994) in a study of the pattern of innovations in the US in 1982. In an econometric analysis they conclude that the innovative output of small firms increase in the vicinity of universities. A similar study by Audretsch and Vivarelli (1996), covering 15 Italian regions over nine years, comes to the same conclusion.

In specific studies of the semiconductor industry through patent data between 1977-1989, Almeida and Kogut (1997) and Almeida (1999) argue that small firms tend to innovate in relatively unexplored fields of technology. In this way, they differ from large companies, which seem to concentrate their research, measured as patents, in more established fields. Rothwell and Zegveld (1982) made a study of 380 innovations made in US, UK, Germany, Japan, and France between 1953 and 1973. They found that small firms contributed 31 percent and large firms 54 percent of all innovations. In estimating how radical the innovations were they also concluded that the entire output of small firms in UK consisted of radical

---

[6] See the discussion on the changing role of entrepreneurship at the beginning of Sect. 5.2.

breakthroughs. The US small firms produced 27 percent of the "radical break-throughs" made in the country as well as 30 percent of the "major technological shifts" and 37 percent of the "improvement-type innovations".

Geroski (1994) finds a strong and negative relationship between market concentration and innovation. This conclusion receives support in a study of industry innovations in 1982 by Acs and Audretsch (1990). Furthermore, the latter support the notion of two technological regimes, an entrepreneurial one, and a routinized one. They note that the entrepreneurial regime, in which small firm innovation is of importance, is characterized by a relative reliance on skilled labour and that large firms control a significant share of the market. By contrast, the routinized regime is recognized as being capital-intensive, concentrated, unionised and producing differentiated products.

A study of growing small and medium sized enterprises (GSMEs) in Canada 1984-1988 by Baldwin (1995) indicates that the more successful firms are, on average, focusing on innovative strategies and activities to a greater extent than the less successful firms. In conclusion, innovation is found to be the most important determinant of small firm success.

5.4.3 Industrial Structure, Start-ups and Job Creation

Carree and Thurik (1998) identify a number of market conditions favouring either large or small firms. Effects stimulating size include economies of scale and scope as well as declining average costs with increasing experience. In favour of small firms, Carree and Thurik mention that customers have a preference for minimizing travelling distance when searching for supplies thereby justifying geographically dispersed small firms. Furthermore, the demand for variety creates small markets, which can only sustain small firms. Another proposed argument is that small firms might have lower adjustment costs and, finally, the effect of control by an energetic, motivating entrepreneur. A similar list of advantages of small-scale enterprises is made by Vosloo (1994). It includes advantages for small firms in developing economies, such as less capital per worker on average and 'grassroot' development overcoming the lack of formal training and education. Other, more general, advantages include greater flexibility, a higher propensity of innovations per employee, higher growth and job creation rates as well as being better suited to serving limited or specialized market niches. Finally, according to Vosloo, small firms enhance political stability by strengthening middle-class influence and distributing prosperity.

Audretsch et al. (2002) present an econometric study of 18 European countries indicating that there has been a reward in terms of economic growth for countries that have experienced a quicker decentralization of their industry structure, i.e. have gained a greater share of smaller firms. This supports a study undertaken by Carree and Thurik (1998) of 14 manufacturing industries in 13 European countries. There were indications that on average, the employment share of large firms had a negative effect on growth of output 1990-1994. In a descriptive study of small business activity in Germany, Wengenroth (1999, p. 131) concludes, "Small business was the catalyst of industrial growth in providing the background of skills and services which alone made possible the mass consumption of industrial product".

The relationship between entrepreneurship and unemployment is analysed by Audretsch et al. (2001) in an econometric model covering 23 OECD countries between 1974-1998. They find a complex relationship between the two variables. Defining entrepreneurship as firm start-ups there is both a positive effect of unemployment on entrepreneurship (the "shopkeeper" or "refugee effect") as well as a negative relation (the "Schumpeter effect").

The Global Entrepreneurship Monitor 2000 concludes that there is a strong relationship between entrepreneurial activities, defined as start-up activities, and economic growth (Reynolds et al. 2000). In the study, this definition of entrepreneurship is claimed to constitute the singularly most important factor for economic growth. In an econometric analysis of Sweden during 1976-1995, Fölster (2000) finds significant support for the hypothesis that an increase in self-employment has a positive effect on overall employment.

Another study of Sweden by Davidsson et al. (1994) finds that 70 percent of the new net jobs are generated in the small business sector in the period 1985-1989. A further emphasis is that most of the new firms are not growth oriented, but are founded on a hobby or subsistence motive. Thus, small firms are important to the economy because of their large number but a vast majority of the upstarts will remain micro firms. Blanchflower (2000) does not support the hypothesis that increases in the level of self-employment increase the real growth rate. Furthermore, making a comparison of the level of self-employment in 23 OECD countries for the years 1966, 1976, 1986 and 1996, Blanchflower finds that the level of non-agricultural self-employment has decreased in most of the countries.

The relative importance of small firms is not undisputed as Davis et al. (1996) and Bednarzik (2000) remark in their studies. Although important, entrepreneurship through start-ups is claimed to make a smaller contribution to job growth than expansion within existing firms in the US. Davis et al. draw their conclusion from a study of data from the US Census Bureau during 1972-1988, whereas Bednarzik has studied the mid 1990s. Although smaller firms have a higher gross job creation rate, large firms supply more in terms of net job creation. In a comment on Davis et al. (1996), Carree and Klomp (1996) contest its conclusion, arguing that small firms created more net jobs during the 1972-1988 period relative to their employment share. Davidsson et al. (1998) empirically test the regression fallacy[7]. The test by Davidsson et al. covers Sweden 1989-1996 and concludes that the bias does not imply a qualitative change on the overall result. Baldwin and Picot (1995) have studied the Canadian manufacturing sector 1970-1990 and in order to avoid a regression-to-the-mean bias three different methods of estimation are used. A consistent finding is that small firms have a higher gross volatility in job growth and destruction but also a higher net employment growth than large firms.

---

[7] The regression fallacy, or the regression-to-the-mean bias, is the practice of measuring firm size changes from a base-year. This magnifies the importance of the small firms according to the authors.

While an international comparison of the relative importance of small firms with respect to net job creation is interesting, the results are likely to differ between countries due to institutional reasons. For example, Davis and Henrekson (1999) show that the Swedish institutional environment prior to the economic crisis at the beginning of the 1990s significantly disfavoured Swedish intensive-intensive, small, and/or managed-owned family businesses as well as entry of new firms compared to similar types of firms in the United States and other European countries.

In a test of the growth of micro and small firms, Heshmati (2001) calculates five different asset growth model parameter estimates on a large sample of firms in the county of Gävleborg in Sweden during the period of 1993-1998. The conclusion of the study is that the relationship between growth, size, and age of firms is highly specific to the method of estimation as well as the functional form and definition of size and growth. This conclusion lends supports to a study of the job flow dynamics in the US economy by Acs et al.(1999). In a regression using longitudinal data the authors find great differences in the results depending on whether mean or initial firm size was used. It is suggested that this might account for the conflicting findings regarding the relationship between net growth and size.

Kwoka and White (2001) find that there are significant variations in the share of small businesses across industrial sectors. Referring to Sutton (1998), the authors suggest that sunk costs might explain the differences but suggest further studies in the topic. The variations might also correlate with varying degrees of small firm innovation, which is described in the section discussing innovation and economic growth. Furthermore, there are also claimed to be considerable differences in the share of small firms across nations (e.g. Acs 1996).

A study of job creation by Andersson and Delmar (2000), covering firms with more than 20 employees in Sweden 1987-1996, produces the conclusion that the high-growth firms are underrepresented in the smaller size class and over-represented in the medium (50-249 employees) size class. High-growth firms are defined as the top ten percent of job creators in absolute numbers[8]. Furthermore, the high-growth firms are primarily found in young and growing industries, such as the knowledge-intensive service, education, and health care industries. It is, however, yet again hard to make a general case for these findings in an international comparison. This may, due to institutional reasons, be a special feature of the Swedish case, which is indicated by e.g. Storey (1994), who finds high growth firms in all types of industries in the cases of the UK and the US.

Using data from the US manufacturing sector 1972-1993 Haltiwanger and Krizan (1999) find that young firms exhibit high average net employment growth rate but also high volatility compared to mature establishments. Furthermore, among newly started firms there is no evidence of any systematic pattern by employer size of net employment growth. The conclusion is that in the context of employ-

---

[8] It should be noted that this measurement creates a powerful bias against small firms. On the other hand, a straightforward percentage growth measurement would provide a bias in favour of smaller firms. A definition of high growth firms independent of firm size would have been ideal.

ment growth, the age of firms appears to be more important than size, with the caveat that attributing a principal role to a single factor might be misleading.

5.4.4 Summary

A number of studies indicate that there has been a structural shift in the industrial sector towards a higher dependence on flexibility and knowledge-intense production. In general, this is considered to have made entrepreneurial activities a more important feature of the economy. However, this is not uncontroversial.

Empirical studies show that increased competition has been found to increase employment as well as enhance growth in total factor productivity. Small firms produce a large share of the total number of innovations, given sectoral differences, and are found to innovate in relatively unexplored fields. Examples include computers, electronics, and biotechnology. Innovation is also claimed to be a fundamental feature of successful small firms.

There is more controversy regarding the impact of small firms on net employment creation and as a generator of economic growth. The small firm sector is characterized by a high rate of gross job creation but also high volatility and destruction of firms. One explanation for the different outcomes in the empirical studies might be found in the different estimation techniques used. A cautious conclusion is that both small and large firms might be of importance for economic growth.

5.5 Entrepreneurship and Economic Growth: Discussion

The first part of Sect.5.5 discusses some of the implications of the selected categorization in Sect. 5.3. The division of entrepreneurship into economically gainful entrepreneurial activities creates three interdependent variables. The second part of this section analyses the focus of the theories, finding a bias towards stressing innovative activities as the engine of economic growth. In the third part, the empirical evidence is categorized and it is concluded that the empirical studies are biased towards start-ups.

5.5.1 Implications of the Categorization

Although the categorization of the effects of entrepreneurship on economic growth is functional and intuitively appealing from a theoretical standpoint, it does imply practical difficulties. Most of the processes identified as generators of economic growth are combinations of entrepreneurial activities. Fig. 5.1 is an attempt to illustrate this problem.

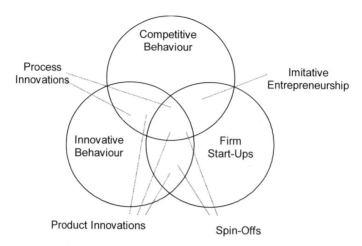

Fig. 5.1. The complexities associated with the categorization of entrepreneurial activities, including some examples of cross-category entrepreneurial processes

The complex nature of the entrepreneurial processes might result in a simplification, in which the processes are attributed to a single entrepreneurial activity. This might understate the total impact of the activities as well as ignore the aspects that are notoriously hard to define, such as competitive activities. It is less than straightforward to identify an operational measure of competitive behaviour and competitiveness as well as find comparable markets with different degrees of competition. Geroski (1994, p. 88) makes the following suggestion for a measure: "As entry and the innovation process are undoubtedly intertwined, the effect of competition might best be measured as the joint effect of the two, in which case it is clearly substantial."

However, the position of Geroski may seem overly optimistic with respect to net growth effects following innovation and entry, if acknowledging the impact of "business stealing" effects in the spirit of Aghion and Howitt (1992) – where innovation (and entry) destroys monopoly rents and eventually leads to sub-optimal levels of innovations.

5.5.2 Positioning the Theories Concerning Entrepreneurial Activities and Economic Growth

Even without a generally acceptable definition of entrepreneurship, it might be possible to discern a number of manifestations of entrepreneurial activity. Competition, innovation, and job creation through firm start-ups are assumed to affect economic growth. An unbalanced amount of attention has been devoted to theoretical vis-à-vis empirical treatments of these activities.

Table 5.1 demonstrates the foci of the different theories that have been used in the attempt to formalize entrepreneurial activity into models. This is summarized and illustrated in Fig. 5.2, adding the theory of recombinant growth.

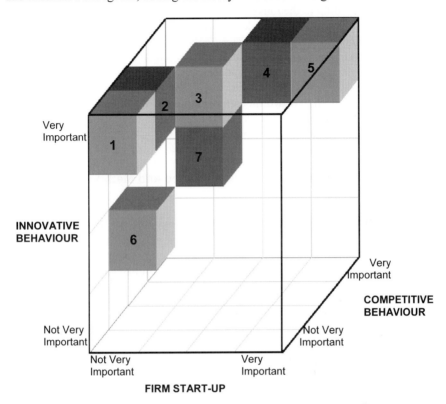

Fig. 5.2. The relative explanatory power of a number of different theories regarding innovation, competition and firm start-up. Legend: *1* – recombinant growth, *2* – endogenous growth theory, *3* – Schumpeter / Baumol and economic history, *4* – industrial economics, *5* – evolutionary economics, *6* – neoclassical (Solow), and *7* – Austrians

It should be emphasized that the authors have some objections to the ranking of the different theories as suggested by Wennekers and Thurik (1999, p. 50). For instance, competition and innovation is in our view considerably more central to the Austrian school than compared to the neoclassical Solow model. Therefore, we have chosen to make a sharper distinction between the two different traditions in the Fig.5.2, in comparison with the one offered by Wennekers and Thurik[9].

---

[9] Any classification of schools of thoughts as the one offered by Wennekers and Thurik (1999), represented by Table 5.1 and Fig. 5.2, is, of course, subject to some arbitrariness. It should, therefore, be understood as an indication of emphasis and direction.

As demonstrated, the main theoretical focus is on innovation. Innovation carries more weight in theory formulations than firm start-ups or competition, which in most cases is assumed to be monopolistic competition in the context of entrepreneurship. According to the ranking by Wennekers and Thurik (1999), six of the eight schools of thought have provided innovation as a "pivotal" element (Schumpeter/Baumol, endogenous growth theory, economic history, management literature, industrial economics and evolutionary economics), two include competition in this category (industrial economics and evolutionary economics) and one comprises firm start-up (evolutionary economics). Three of the theories do not consider firm start-up at all and two include it implicitly. Considering the amount of attention dedicated to firm start-up in empirical studies this discrepancy between theory and practice might be unfortunate.

5.5.3 The Relevance of the Empirical Studies and Methodological Problems

Regarding an operational measure of entrepreneurship, it is generally more straightforward to find statistics describing the number of firms entering and leaving the market than finding reliable data on innovation or competition. Fig. 5.3 illustrates the distribution of the empirical studies scrutinized for this chapter as well as the theoretical focus[10]. The outcome should not be generalized but might offer an indication of the allocation of research efforts.

A methodological problem with most of the empirical studies undertaken in the field is the aggregate level of the data. It conceals regional differences, which are supposedly sometimes larger than the differences between countries. Concerning firm start-ups it also leads to difficulties in discriminating between the potential 'gazelles', such as a biotech spin-off, and the no-growth firms, for instance a hairdresser or a pizza baker. One noticeable exception to this is provided by Fölster (2002), who compares two data sets – one aggregate international country comparison and one national disaggregate regionalized national comparison – in which the relationship between tax rates and levels of self-employment is analysed. While both data sets generate similar results, i.e. that lower tax rates seem to favour levels of self-employment, only the latter set seem to be statistical reliable and robust to statistical testing; hence, this highlights some of the problems with aggregation.

---

[10] The theoretical emphasis-line is subjectively derived from Table 5.1 and Fig.5.4. That is, it is our conjecture that innovative behaviour carries the heaviest weight in the theoretical growth literature. Competition is moreover treated as relatively important whereas the explicit emphasis and importance placed on new firm creation is virtually ignored. The theoretical emphasis can be compared with the focus adopted by the empirical studies considered for and referred to in this chapter. Here, the overall emphasis lies on new firm creation and considerably less on innovation and competition. This mismatch implies that hypotheses and predictions of theoretical models are not (sufficiently) tested.

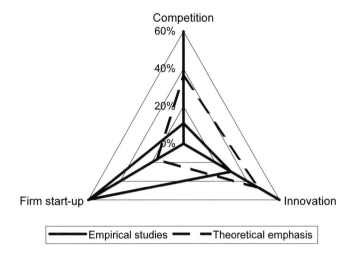

Fig. 5.3. The relative frequency of empirical studies and theoretical contributions covering different entrepreneurial activities

The firm and the creation of firms have long played an ambiguous role in economic theory but have nevertheless been used as an important measure in empirical studies. Coase (1937) suggests that the function of the firm is to minimize transaction costs. In a functioning market, more firms will ensure more employment opportunities and fiercer competition. Innovative activity is, furthermore, an ambiguous unit of measurement, especially concerning small firms. Neither R&D expenses nor patents might do small firms full justice. Reasons for this might include the existence of knowledge spillovers from universities and large corporations as well as diminishing returns to R&D, as suggested by Acs (1996). To counter this, Acs suggests using an innovation measure defined as the number of innovations produced per 1000 employees. Unfortunately, the author omits to include a definition of what constitutes an innovation[11].

In a similar way, the degrees of competition as well as its effects are difficult to measure. Nickell (1996) suggests using an increased number of firms in an industry and the level of surplus profits generated as measures of competition. Regarding an increased number of firms in an industry the picture might not be complete without some additional information about the distribution of firm size. Low or decreasing levels of surplus profits may be indeed a sign of increasing competition, but they might be also be the characteristics of a dying industry, the final phase in the cycle of creative destruction. A different approach is offered by Baumol (2002). Here innovation is the method to avoid price competition and to main-

---

[11] Most likely, the definition used is the one described in Acs et al. (1994), where the measure represents the number of innovations recorded in 1982 by the US Small Business Administration. The sources used are technology, engineering, and trade journals in each manufacturing industry. Even so, this measure does not appear clear.

tain monopoly rents. Innovation is the tool to deter entry, in which case rents would be eroded and the rate of innovation would thereby decline.

The conclusion appears to be that there is a lack of theoretical treatments explicitly dealing with the relationships between entrepreneurship and economic growth through entrepreneurial activities such as e.g. innovation, competitive behaviour, and firm start-ups. Furthermore, there appears to be a need for research on firm start-ups and job creation on a regional basis. The innovative activity of small firms could also be further studied and additional operational terms could be developed. Finally, there is a void regarding empirical tests of the links between competition and economic growth, especially in the context of entrepreneurship. To use Kirzner's words (1973, p. 8): "And I will argue further that the role of entrepreneurship in relation to competition has been virtually ignored." Kirzner aired this opinion in 1973; the statement still carries validity today. A final emphasis should be put on the importance of studying regions rather than nations. Aggregate studies reveal little of the enigmatic nature of Silicon Valley, Third Italy or the Gnosjö area in Sweden.

This chapter was initiated by a quotation by Holcombe and thus it appears appropriate to conclude the overview by completing the circle (Holcombe 1998, p. 58): "The engine for economic growth is not better inputs, but rather an environment in which entrepreneurial opportunities can be capitalized upon."

5.6 Conclusions

This chapter has provided an overview of the research on the relationship between entrepreneurship and growth. The emphasis on entrepreneurial activities in the context of growth-oriented theories has been outlined and brief overviews and main findings of relevant and recent empirical studies have been presented.

There exist an abundant number of definitions of entrepreneurship describing a wide array of economic activities and functions. In this chapter, a distinction has been made between theoretical definitions, which tend to cover a number of different aspects without being operationally applicable, and empirical definitions covering individual elements of entrepreneurial activities. Entrepreneurial activities range from creative destruction and innovation to dealing with uncertainty and spotting profit opportunities. Three links are emphasized through which those activities affect economic growth, firm start-ups, and innovative and competitive behaviour. These entrepreneurial activities form the methodological foundation of this chapter. In spite of the weaknesses of the classification, we have not found a better systematisation to identify the links between entrepreneurship and economic growth.

Theories of growth generally have an emphasis on innovation as the main explanatory engine for growth. Empirical contributions, on the other hand, most often have a focus on the relationship between new-firm creation and net employment growth. If entrepreneurship can be defined as the activities outlined above, there seem to be an obvious discrepancy between the theoretical and empirical literature with respect to the relationship between entrepreneurship and growth.

When it comes to the empirical studies, there is some controversy regarding the impact of small firms and start-up activities on net employment growth (e.g. Audretsch et al. 2001; Bednarzik 2000; Davidsson et al. 1994; Davis et al. 1996; Fölster 2000). Competition appears to correlate positively with both employment levels and growth in total factor productivity (e.g. Acs 1996; Geroski 1994; Nickell 1996). Small firms are found to produce a large share of the total number of innovations but there are significant sectoral differences (e.g. Acs and Audretsch 2001; Baldwin and Johnson 1999). They are also found to innovate in less explored fields of technology (e.g. Almeida and Kogut 1997; Almeida 1999). This generally involves greater uncertainty but higher potential for growth.

As illustrated in Fig. 5.2 the theoretical literature linking entrepreneurial activities to economic growth is skewed towards innovation. This calls for a discussion about the relationship between entrepreneurship and competition, as well as between competition and economic growth. Under favourable circumstances, firm start-ups appear to affect economic development through both job creation and increased competition. However, given that innovations are inducing growth and that innovation is the means to avoid price competition, increased competition may, via a 'business stealing' effect, erode economic rents and lower innovation rates (Aghion and Howitt 1992; Baumol 2002). Net effects on growth following increased competition might, therefore, be ambiguous. This is an interesting and highly relevant area of research, but currently a relatively unexplored one.

A great variety of instruments and methods has been used in the empirical studies undertaken so far. It would probably be beneficial to make an evaluation of the different approaches and compare their relative performance. Such an evaluation might assist in constructing operational tools for future studies. Corporate entrepreneurship and intrapreneurship are other promising themes for further research efforts, both with a theoretical as well as with an empirical foundation. Fig. 5.3 suggests, furthermore, that there is a need for additional empirical tests to support the theories linking entrepreneurship and innovative activity. The correspondence between entrepreneurial activities and competition is another topic for future explorations.

One specific topic of interest would be to identify whether there is a correlation between the numbers of firms created as a function of the existing number of firms in a regional framework. Regional studies and cluster studies could also be undertaken to study the dynamics of the creation and destruction of firms, simultaneously studying net changes and gross volatilities. The regional or cluster perspective seems essential since there are substantial differences between regions in their ability to stimulate entrepreneurial activities under seemingly (but not identical) similar institutional settings (Fölster 2002). A better understanding of how different regional economic milieus influence entrepreneurial behaviour seems to be necessary in order to better understand the links between entrepreneurship and economic growth.

The main focus of this contribution has been the empirical and theoretical relationship between entrepreneurship, or entrepreneurial activities, and economic growth. Some attention has been given to the importance of the institutional framework in supporting and enhancing entrepreneurship and growth. It is questionable whether a majority of the empirical results presented in this chapter carries any generality unless the institutional framework in which the study was undertaken is taken into account. The contributions of e.g. Baumol (1993, 2002), Bergström (2000), Davis and Henrekson (1999), Fölster (2002), and Henrekson (2002) suggest that levels of entrepreneurial activities and rates of growth should be understood in relation to the incentives provided by the institutional setting in each nation or region.

If the implications of the research efforts on entrepreneurship were to be translated into policy formulation, it would be injudicious to make entrepreneurship policy equivalent to policy for small firms and firm start-ups. This would imply that several aspects of entrepreneurial behaviour would be lost, aspects that are likely to affect economic growth positively. Furthermore, and given the contributions discussed in the paragraph above, it seems clear that one of the main objectives for policy in relationship to entrepreneurship, and in the extension to growth, is to organize the institutional rules of the game in such a way as to provide and support the incentives for innovation and facilitate entry and growth of new and small firms. It follows from Baumol (1993) that adoption of new technology and levels of innovations could e.g. be facilitated by supporting 1) immigration of individuals with key knowledge, 2) education and training of national in foreign countries where new critical technology and knowledge is being used, and iii) loan guarantees for a rapid adoption of critical foreign technology. From e.g. Davis and Henrekson (1999), Henrekson (2002), and Fölster (2002), it follows that entry and growth of new and small firms could significantly be improved via policy measures. Predominantly taking a Swedish perspective, they among other things suggest that: 1) the wage formation and labour market in general should be deregulated. This would support growth of firms by making it easier to hire (and fire) staff. 2) The tax system should be reformed not to disfavour small and new firms. Income taxes need, furthermore, to be cut in order to make it possible to accumulate wealth, which is fundamental for the birth of new firms. 3) Entry of firms should be free in the entire economy, i.e. regulated public sector monopolies should be abolished. While potentially wide-ranging, this is only an example of potential policy measures suggested to support entrepreneurship and growth in general. Anyone with an interest in growth will generally not disagree.

References

Acs ZJ (1996) Small firms and economic growth. In: Acs ZJ, Carlsson B, Thurik R (eds) Small business in the modern economy. Blackwell Publishers, Oxford, pp 1–62

Acs ZJ (1999) The new American evolution. In: Acs ZJ (ed) Are small firms important? Their role and impact. Kluwer Academic Publishers, Dordrecht, pp 1–20

Acs ZJ, Audretsch DB (1990) Innovation and small firms. MIT Press, Cambridge, MA

Acs ZJ, Audretsch DB (2001) The emergence of the entrepreneurial society. Swedish Foundation for Small Business Research, Stockholm

Acs ZJ, Audretsch DB, Feldman MP (1994) R&D spillovers and innovative activity. Managerial and Decision Economics 14: 131–138

Acs ZJ, Armington C, Robb A (1999) Measures of job flow dynamics in the U.S. economy. Discussion Paper 9907, Centre for Research into Industry, Enterprise, Finance and the Firm (CRIEFF), Fife

Acs ZJ, Carlsson B, Karlsson C (1999) The linkages among entrepreneurship, SMEs and the macroeconomy. In: Acs ZJ, Carlsson B, Karlsson C (eds) Entrepreneurship, small and medium sized enterprises and the macroeconomy. Cambridge University Press, Cambridge, pp 3–42

Acs ZJ, Morck R, Yeung B (1999) Evolution, community, and the global economy. In Acs ZJ (ed) Are small firms important? Kluwer Academic Publishers, Dordrecht, pp 147–157

Aghion P, Howitt P (1992) A model of growth through creative destruction. Econometrica 60: 323–351

Aghion P, Howitt P (1998) Endogenous growth theory. MIT Press, Cambridge, MA

Almeida P (1999) Semiconductor start-ups and the exploration of new technological territory. In: Acs Z J (ed) Are small firms important? Their role and impact. Kluwer Academic Publishers, Dordrecht, pp 39–50

Almeida P, Kogut B (1997) The exploration of technological diversity and the geographic localization of innovation. Small Business Economics 9: 21–31

Andersson P, Delmar F (2000) The characteristics of high-growth firms and their job contribution. In: Delmar F (ed) Innovation, growth and entrepreneurship. ESBRI 2000/5, Entrepreneurship and Small Business Research Institute (ESBRI), Stockholm, pp 204–213

Audretsch DB (1995) Innovation and industry evolution. MIT Press, Cambridge, MA

Audretsch DB, Thurik AR (1997) Sources of growth: the entrepreneurial versus the managed economy. Discussion Paper TI 97–109/3, Tinbergen Institute, Tinbergen

Audretsch DB, Thurik AR (2001a) What is new about the new economy: sources of growth in the managed and entrepreneurial economies?. Industrial and Corporate Change 10: 267–315

Audretsch DB, Thurik AR (2001b) Capitalism and democracy in the 21st century: from the managed to the entrepreneurial economy. In: Mueller DC, Cantner U (eds) Capitalism and democracy in the 21st century. Springer, Heidelberg Berlin New York, pp 23–40

Audretsch DB, Vivarelli M (1996) Firms size and R&D spillovers: evidence from Italy. Small Business Economics 8: 249–258

Audretsch DB, Carree MA, Thurik AR (2001) Does entrepreneurship reduce unemployment?. Discussion Paper 2001–074/3, Tinbergen Institute, Tinbergen

Audretsch DB, Carree MA, van Stel AJ, Thurik AR (2002) Impeded industrial restructuring: the growth penalty. Kyklos 55: 81–97

Baldwin JR (1995) Innovation: the key to success in small firms. Research Paper Series No. 76, Analytical Studies Branch Statistics Canada, Ottawa

Baldwin JR, Johnson J (1999) Entry, innovation and firm growth. In: Acs ZJ (ed) Are small firms important? Their role and impact. Kluwer Academic Publishers, Dordrecht, pp 51–77

Baldwin JR, Picot G (1995) Employment generation by small producers in the Canadian manufacturing sector. Small Business Economics 7: 317–31

Baumol WJ (1968) Entrepreneurship in economic theory. American Economic Review 52: 64–71

Baumol WJ (1993) Entrepreneurship, management and the structure of payoffs. MIT Press, Cambridge, MA

Baumol WJ (2002) The free-market innovation machine: analysing the growth miracle of capitalism. Princeton University Press, Princeton

Bednarzik RW (2000) The role of entrepreneurship in U.S. and European job growth. Monthly Labor Review 123: 3–16

Bergström F (2000) Capital subsidies and the performance of firms. Small Business Economics 14: 183–193

Blanchflower DG (2000) Self-employment in OECD countries. Labor Economics 7: 471–505

Brock WA, Evans DS (1989) Small business economics. Small Business Economics 1: 7–20

Brouwer M (2000) Entrepreneurship and uncertainty: innovation and competition among the many. Small Business Economics 15: 149–160

Cantillon R (1755) The circulation and exchange of good and merchandise. In: Casson M (ed) (1990) Entrepreneurship. Edward Elgar, Hants, pp 5–10

Carlsson B (1992) The rise of small business; causes and consequences. In: Adams WJ (ed) Singular Europe: economy and polity of the European Community after 1992. University of Michigan Press, Ann Arbor, pp 145–169

Carlsson B (1996) Small business, flexible, technology and industrial dynamics. In: Acs ZJ, Carlsson B, Thurik R (eds) Small business in the modern economy. Blackwell Publishers, Oxford, pp 63–125

Carlsson B (1999) Small business, entrepreneurship, and industrial dynamics. In: Acs ZJ (ed) Are small firms important? Their role and impact. Kluwer Academic Publishers, Dordrecht, pp 99–110

Carree M, Klomp L (1996) Small business and job creation: a comment. Small Business Economics 8: 317–322

Carree M, Thurik AR (1998) Small firms and economic growth in Europe. Atlantic Economic Journal 26: 137–146

Carree M, van Stel A, Thurik R, Wennekers S (1999) Business ownership and economic growth: an empirical investigation. Research Report 9809/E, EIM Business and Policy Research, Zoetermeer

Carree M, van Stel A, Thurik R, Wennekers S (2002) Business ownership and economic growth in 23 OECD countries in the period 1976–1996. Small Business Economics 19: 271–290

Casson M (ed) (1990) Entrepreneurship. Edward Elgar, Hants

Chandler A (1990) Scale and scope: the dynamics of industrial capitalism. Harvard University Press, Cambridge, MA

Coase RH (1937) The nature of the firm. Economics New Series 4: 386–405

Cole AH (1949) Entrepreneurship and entrepreneurial history. In: Livesay HC (ed) (1995) Entrepreneurship and the growth of firms, vol I, Edward Elgar, Hants, pp 100–122

Davidsson P, Lindmark L, Olofsson C (1994) New firm formation and regional development in Sweden, Regional Studies 28: 395–410

Davidsson P, Lindmark L, Olofsson C (1998) The extent of overestimation of small firm job creation – an empirical examination of the regression bias. Small Business Economics 11: 87–100

Davis S, Henrekson M (1999) Explaining national differences in the size and industry distribution of employment. Small Business Economics 12: 59–83

Davis S, Haltiwanger J, Schuh S (1996) Small business and job creation: dissecting the myth and reassessing the facts. Small Business Economics 8: 297–315

Dejardin M (2000) Entrepreneurship and economic growth: an obvious conjunction? DP 2000–08, Indiana University, Bloomington

Eliasson G (1994) The theory of the firm and the theory of economic growth. In: Magnusson L (ed) Evolutionary and neo-Schumpeterian approaches to economics. Kluwer, Boston, pp 173–201

Eliasson G, Braunerhjelm P (1998) Intangible, human-embodied capital and firm performance. In: Eliasson G, Green C, McCann CR Jr (eds) Microfoundations of economic growth: A Schumpeterian perspective. The University of Michigan Press, Ann Arbor, pp 389-405

Fölster S (2000) Do entrepreneurs create jobs?. Small Business Economics 14: 137–148

Fölster S (2002) Do lower taxes stimulate self-employment?. Small Business Economics 19: 135–145

Geroski P (1994) Market structure, corporate performance, and innovative activity. Oxford University Press, Oxford

Glancey KS, McQuaid RW (2000) Entrepreneurial economics. Macmillan, London

Goel U (1997) Economists, entrepreneurs and the pursuit of economics. European University Studies. Peter Lang, Frankfurt aM

Gort M, Sung N (1999) Competition and productivity growth: the case of the U.S. telephone industry. Economic Inquiry 37: 678–691

Gould JD (1972) Economic growth in history. Methuen, London

Grebel T, Pyka A, Hanusch H (2001) An evolutionary approach to the theory of entrepreneurship. Discussion Paper Series 206, Augsburg University Institute for Economics, Augsburg

Grossman GM, Helpman E (1991) Quality ladders in the theory of growth. Review of Economic Studies 58: 43–61

Haltiwanger J, Krizan CJ (1999) Small business and job creation in the United States: the role of new and young businesses. In: Acs ZJ (ed) Are small firms important? Their role and impact. Kluwer, Dordrecht, pp 79–97

Hébert RF, Link AN (1989) In search of the meaning of entrepreneurship. Small Business Economics 1: 39–49

Henrekson M (2002) Entrepreneurship - a weak link in the mature welfare state. Working paper No 518, Stockholm School of Economics, Stockholm

Heshmati A (2001) On the growth of micro and small firms: evidence from Sweden, Small Business Economics 17: 213–228

Holcombe RG (1998) Entrepreneurship and economic growth. The Quarterly Journal of Austrian Economics 1: 45–62

Hülsman JG (1999) Entrepreneurship and economic growth: comment on Holcombe. The Quarterly Journal of Austrian Economics 2: 63–65

Kihlstrom RE, Laffont JJ (1979) A general equilibrium entrepreneurial theory of firm formation based on risk aversion. In: Casson M (ed) Entrepreneurship. Edward Elgar, Hants, pp 19–48

Kirzner IM (1973) Competition & entrepreneurship. The University of Chicago Press, Chicago

Kirzner IM (1994) The Entrepreneur in economic theory. In: Dahmén E, Hannah L, Kirzner IM (eds) The dynamics of entrepreneurship. Crafoord Lectures 5, Lund University Press, Lund, pp 45–59

Knight FH (1921) Risk, uncertainty and profit. In: Casson M (ed) (1990) Entrepreneurship. Edward Elgar, Hants, pp 11–18

Kwoka JE, White LJ (2001) The new industrial organization and small business. Small Business Economics 16: 21–30

Livesay HC (ed) (1995) Entrepreneurship and the growth of firms. Edward Elgar, Hants

Loveman G, Sengenberger W (1991) The re-emergence of small-scale production: an international comparison. Small Business Economics 3: 1–37

Lucas RE Jr (1988) On the mechanics of economic development. Journal of Monetary Economics 22: 3–42

Lydall H (1998) A critique of orthodox economics: an alternative model. Macmillan, London

Minniti M (1999) Entrepreneurial activity and economic growth. Global Business and Economic Review 1: 31–42

Nelson RR, Winter SG (1982) An evolutionary theory of economic change. Harvard University Press, Cambridge, MA

Nickell SJ (1996) Competition and corporate performance. Journal of Political Economy 104: 724–746

North DC (1990) Institutions, institutional change and economic performance. Harvard University Press, Cambridge, MA

North DC, Thomas R P (1973) The rise of the Western world: a new economic history. Harvard University Press, Cambridge, MA

Olsson O, Frey B (2002) Entrepreneurship as recombinant growth. Small Business Economics 19: 69–80

Piore MJ, Sabel CF (1984) The second industrial divide; possibilities for prosperity. Basic Books, New York

Porter ME (1990) The competitive advantage of nations. Macmillan, London

Reynolds PD, Hay M, Bygrave WD, Camp SM, Autio E (2000) Global entrepreneurship monitor. 2000 executive report, Babson College, Wellesley, MA

Romer P (1986) Increasing returns and long run growth. Journal of Political Economy 94: 1002–1037

Romer P (1990) Endogenous technological change. Journal of Political Economy 98: 71–102

Rigotti L, Ryan M, Vaithianathan R (2001) Entrepreneurial innovation. Working Paper E01–296, University of California, Berkeley

Rothwell R, Zegveld W (1982) Innovation and the small and medium sized firm. Pinter Publishers, London

Runge I (2000) Capital and uncertainty. Edward Elgar, Cheltenham

Schumpeter JA (1934) The theory of economic development. In: Casson M (ed) (1990) Entrepreneurship. Edward Elgar, Hants, pp 105–134

Segerstrom PS, Anant TCA, Dinopoulos E (1990) A Schumpeterian model of the product life cycle. American Economic Review 80: 1077–1091

Sexton DL, Smilor RW (eds) (1997) Entrepreneurship 2000. The Erwing Marion Kauffman Foundation, Upstart Publishing Company, Chicago

Steele CN (2000) Entrepreneurship, institutions, and economic growth. UMI Dissertation Services, Ann Arbor

Solow RM (1956) A contribution to the theory of economic growth. Quarterly Journal of Economics 70: 65–94

Storey DJ (1994) Understanding the small business sector. Routledge, London

Sutton J (1998) Technology and market structure. MIT Press, Cambridge, MA

Swan TW (1956) Economic growth and capital accumulation. Economic Record 32: 334–361

Thurik AR (1996) Small firms, entrepreneurship and economic growth. In: Acs ZJ, Carlsson B, Thurik AR (eds) Small business in the modern economy. Basil Blackwell, Oxford, pp 126–152

Valdés B (1999) Economic growth: theory, empirics and policy. Edward Elgar, Cheltenham

Verheul I, Wennekers S, Audretsch D, Thurik R (2003). An eclectic theory of entrepreneurship: policies, institutions, and culture. In: Audretsch DB (ed) The globalization of the world economy. Edward Elgar, Cheltenham, pp 536-606

Vosloo WB (ed) (1994) Entrepreneurship and economic growth. HSRC Publishers, Pretoria

Weitzman ML (1998) Recombinant growth. Quarterly Journal of Economics 113: 331–360

Wengenroth U (1999) Small-scale business in Germany: the flexible element of economic growth. In: Odaka K, Sawai M (eds) Small firms, large concerns. Oxford University Press, New York, pp 117–139

Wennekers S, Thurik R (1999) Linking entrepreneurship and economic growth. Small Business Economics 13: 27–55

Wennekers S, Thurik R, Buis F (1997) Entrepreneurship, economic growth and what links them together. EIM Strategic Study, EIM Business and Policy Research, Zoetermeer

Yu TFL (1997) Entrepreneurship and economic development in Hong Kong. Routledge, London

6 Industrial Cluster Analysis and Technology Policy Decisions in Functional Regions

Roger R. Stough

School of Public Policy, George Mason University

6.1 Introduction

In the 1970s and 1980s, a widely adopted strategy for addressing rapid deindustrialization in the U.S. was the initiation of technology-driven economic development policies and programs at the state and local level. Interest in this approach grew from an assumption that it would produce high wage jobs, which of course, were being lost as manufacturing competitiveness waned in the face of strong foreign competition that was delivering less expensive and often superior goods and services to the domestic U.S. market. These strategies, when implemented at the state level took a variety of forms, including departments or programs within state government, quasi stand alone non-profit corporations, and commissions or authorities. By 2004, technology-oriented development programs had been created in every state in the U.S. (Riggle and Stough 2003).

The experience of these programs has been mixed, but in most cases, state legislatures have become impatient waiting for measured and validated job and wealth creation data. While the logic that technological change can drive development is generally unchallenged and success stories exist (e.g. Silicon Valley; Bangalore and Hyderabad in India), state programs have generally had limited demonstrated positive results from efforts to target their technology investments in support of economic development goals (Riggle and Stough 2003). Further, there is validated evidence of how these state programs have contributed to job and wealth creation at the sub-state regional level, if at all. This is important especially for this chapter in that state level economies are often, if not always, somewhat structurally diffuse. Only when state economies are disaggregated to the sub-state regional level do they acquire the attributes of structural definition that defines a cohesive integrated economic system. Thus, it is of considerable importance that state development policy in general and state development policy based on technology policy be guided by and implemented in terms of sub-state regional conditions, economic structure and traditions. Without such tailoring, results will be less than expected from any policy designed only at the state level. This chapter is important because it illustrates a methodology for achieving state policy tailoring for implementation at the sub-state level. Its purpose is to provide an industrial cluster-based methodology for identifying and measuring propulsive sub-state regional industrial clusters and for using the results to inform sub-state regional technology policy and program development. Analyses to this end were conducted for the nine economic regions in the State of Virginia (Stough et al. 2000). Two of these cases are presented in this chapter to illustrate the methodology and how it can be used to inform technology and economic development policy and program development at the sub-state regional level.

6.2 Methodology

A considerable amount of traditional economic development effort has focused on job creation via relatively indiscriminant business attraction and retention policies and efforts. Thus, opportunities for expanding growth in higher wage and more propulsive sectors, the so-called new economy (Atkinson et al. 1999), may not be optimised. It is argued however, that industry cluster analyses that focus on identification and definition of emergent or propulsive clusters of industries can be used to develop investment incentive policies for such groupings and in particular, guide technology investment decisions in support of their development. Successful implementation can result in job growth in higher wage/salary sectors and can help fuel increasing returns to employees, companies and the regional community overall. With such an approach, the initial focus is on identifying propulsive industries and their supporting institutions.

Regional industry clusters are geographically concentrated groups of industries that are highly interdependent in that they buy and sell from each other, their products tend to be functionally interrelated and there are supporting institutions, e.g., associations related to cluster functions (see Feser and Sweeney 2002; Stimson et al. 2002; Doeringer and Terkla 1995). Industrial sectors in the core of a cluster, for the most part, produce for the market outside the local region and thus are mostly export base industries. There are different types of industrial clusters including but not limited to ones focused on the dominant industry in a region, new emergent or propulsive clusters and service-based clusters, etc.

Diverse methodological approaches have been employed to conduct industrial cluster analyses. These include simple approaches employing expert judgment, raw employment and earnings data and more sophisticated approaches that employ concentration indexes (e.g., location quotients, and wage or earnings indexes) and interdependency measures such as coefficients in input-output models (see Begman and Feser 1999; Bergman et al. 1996; Bosworth and Broun 1996; Glasmeier and Harrison 1997; Gordon and McCann 2000; Held 1996; Jacobs and De Man 1996; Porter 1990; Rosenfeld 1995, 1996, 1997; San Diego Regional Technology Alliance 2000; Saxenian 1994; Sternberg 1991; Stimson et al. 2002). The methodology employed and advocated in this analysis, because it is replicable and systematic, uses a combination of the above approaches.

The first stage of the analysis identifies emergent or propulsive sectors of the regional economy with the aid of a propulsiveness index (PI). The PI value is defined as a weighted combination of a sector's employment size (50 percent), relative wage (30 percent) and employment change (20 percent) over a time (all weightings are applied to standardized values on these variables). This weighting or allocation was made for the current study by the author based on his knowledge of the state's economy and the goal to identify propulsive clusters. It was made in collaboration with state technology and economic development officials in Virginia, the site where the methodology was to be employed. For applications in other regions or for identification of non-propulsive clusters, a different weighting scheme would likely be more appropriate. Ideally, time periods for such studies would span a recent growth period. The PI values should be computed for all industrial sectors at the two-digit industrial code level (or a finer level of disaggregation, if possible). Given that wage and employment change are included in the index, propulsive industries tend to have the highest PI values. Thus, sectors with the highest PI values are defined as a region's propulsive industries.

The second stage of the analysis uses input-output modelling to measure interdependence among propulsive industries and other sectors. Such a model provides measures of interdependency among all sectors in a regional economy. Of particular interest are interdependencies among propulsive industries themselves and with their supporting industries. When the largest propulsive industries (sectors) are highly interrelated, only a few (one or two) clusters are expected. Where the level of interrelation among propulsive industries is less concentrated (more fragmented), it will tend to be more clusters. When these have been identified, the industrial structure of a cluster(s) is defined. Thus, with the aid of input-output analysis and the PI values initial clusters are systematically defined and can be separated by others using this same analytical routine. However, because the data is known to have some measurement error and is dated, clusters identified in this way are only approximations. Consequently, a third methodological or analysis element is required.

The purpose for the third stage of the analysis is in part to help validate the identified cluster(s) and to surface and establish strategy elements for strengthening and extending the development of the cluster, including identifying ways that technology can contribute. This involves systematically collecting the opinions and judgments of local experts (e.g., CEOs), heads of associations (e.g., chambers of commerce), public officials and university researchers that have specific knowledge about the industries in the cluster(s) and the regional economy and those outside the region that make resource allocation decision with respect to companies in the cluster, e.g. loan officers in commercial banks and executives in the headquarters of the company to which the branch office belongs in the region. This final stage of the analysis involves the use of focus groups, interviews and roundtable discussions to achieve a data-supported cluster definition that is adjusted and then supported by the views of regional experts. Several iterations of this process may be required to reach a consensus.

6.3 Case Studies

Two case studies from a larger study of the nine economic regions of the State of Virginia in the U.S. are reported and discussed to illustrate the application of the methodology. The study period for the analysis is 1992-1999, a period of steady economic growth nationally and in Virginia. Employment rates of change have been annualised over this period. The purpose of the case studies is to illustrate the methodology and how the research results can be used to generate proposals for technology policy and development action at the functional region level.

The nine Virginia economic regions: Northern Virginia, Hampton Roads, Greater Richmond, Lynchburg (Virginia' Region 2000), Danville (South Piedmont), Southwest Virginia, Roanoke (New Century), Charlottesville (Piedmont), and Harrisonburg-Winchester (Shenandoah). The regions are functional economic regions in that they are defined around major population centres that dominate the region and provide a degree of cross-region homogeneity in the labour force. The two regions selected for this chapter are the Shenandoah and Northern Virginia regions. The Shenandoah Region is long and narrow and has several population centres organized along the corridor that defines it. Historically, the Shenandoah Region was dominated by agriculture and related pursuits, more recently expressed in the emergence of a food processing industry. Other elements of the regional economy include light manufacturing and fabrication and a growing concentration of retirement communities.

The Northern Virginia region is a relatively large urbanized area (more than 1.5 million in population) that is part of the U.S. National Capital metropolitan region and has experienced significant and rapid growth over the past several decades due to its location adjacent the national centre of the U.S. federal government. Further, it has the largest concentration of the Washington region's technology sector (Stough 1998). Analyses of the two cases follow.

6.3.1 The Shenandoah Regional Industrial Cluster Analysis

The Shenandoah Region stretches more than one hundred miles along Route I-81 that runs parallel to the Shenandoah River and the Blue Ridge Mountains. Given that the region is quite extended in a north-south direction and somewhat impermeable in an east-west direction suggests that it has more than one labour pool. This may explain why the region has four industrial clusters rather than a more limited number.

Four clusters in the Shenandoah Valley were identified. These are: Cluster 1- Food Products; Cluster 2 – Printing and Publishing; Cluster 3 – Health Services; and Cluster 4 – Chemicals, Textiles and Rubber Manufactured Products. Due to space limitations for this chapter, only the first cluster will be analysed in detail in Sect. 6.3.1.2. The results of the analysis of the other three clusters are presented in summarized form in Table 6A.1.

6.3.1.1   Cluster 1:   The Food Products Cluster

The food products cluster employs 11,605 with an increasing location quotient[1] of 4.1 (See Table 6.1.).

Table 6.1. Selected statistics on industrial sectors in the Shenandoah food products cluster, 1999

SIC Code	Description	Sum of AVG EMP	LQ	AGE (%)	AVGW98 (USD)	REL_W98 (%)	WAGE-TO-STATE (%)
20	Food and Kindred Products	11605	4.05	5.5	25,047	105	93
17	Special Trade Contractors	6981	1.09	5.9	24,105	101	88
28	Chemicals and Allied Products	3345	2.25	8.5	60,207	252	125
42	Trucking and Warehousing	3502	0.95	5.6	27,807	117	109
49	Electric, Gas and Sanitary Services	1356	0.88	4.9	32,597	137	76
50	Wholesale Trade-Durable Goods	3724	0.52	1.7	26,774	112	65
73	Business Services	6765	0.44	10.2	15,108	63	40

SIC Code Standard Industrial Classification code, *Sum of AVGEMP* employment in the industry, *LQ* location quotient, *AGE* (%) employment annualised percentage change, *AVGW98(USD)* average annual earnings(in dollars), *REL_W98(%)* average earnings relative to regional average, *WAGE-TO-STATE* average earnings relative to state average

The average annual wage for this cluster is USD 25,047 that is 105 percent of the regional average and 93 percent of the state wide industry average. Employment increased at an annual rate of 5.5 percent. In short, it is a fairly propulsive cluster. Its sectoral composition is heavily dominated by meat and poultry products (64 percent of cluster employment). At the same time, it exhibits rich diversity with a number of smaller industry components including beverages, sugar confectionary products, bakery products and dairy products. The full list of sectors, along with employment share appears in Fig. 6.1.

Support industries for this cluster employ 25,673 and have an average location quotient of one. Employment had been increasing in all of the eight support industries with business services the greatest at 10.2 percent per year and wholesale trade in durable goods the least at 1.7 percent (Table 6.1.). The average annual earnings are all above the regional average except business services that is at 63 percent of the regional average.

---

[1] A location quotient (LQ) is the ratio between the share of an industry in the regional gross product and the share of that industry in the national gross product. If the LQ is greater than one, than the analysed industry is an export sector in the region.

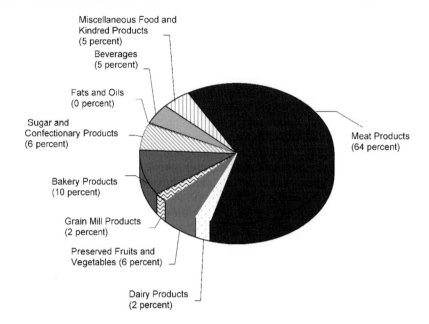

Fig. 6.1. Composition of Shenandoah Valley cluster 1 (employment, 1999).The total cluster industry employment is 11,605 for the year 1999

However, only chemicals and allied products and trucking and warehousing are above the state wide industry average earnings. The largest supporting industries are special trade contractors (27 percent of support industry employment), business services (26 percent), wholesale trade in durable goods (15 percent), trucking and warehousing (14 percent) and chemicals (13 percent) as illustrated in Fig. 6.2.

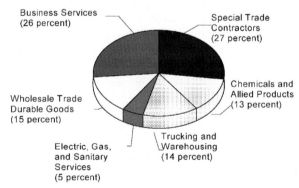

Fig. 6.2. Composition of support industry employment in Shenandoah Valley cluster 1, 1999. The total cluster support industry employment is 25,673 for the year 1999

The food products cluster is propulsive as are its supporting industries. It is a relatively dynamic set of industries with relatively high wages. However, the average earnings in the chemicals and allied products sector at USD 60,207 is nearly twice as high as for any other supporting industry and for the dominant cluster itself.

Despite employment growth, three of the supporting industries' location quotients have been decreasing, indicating that while they are growing they are doing so at a slower rate than the national average. One of these industries, business services, has a wage level that is far below the regional average and even further below the state wide industry average. Despite these qualifying observations, the food products cluster exhibits propulsiveness.

6.3.1.2 Focus Groups and Interpretative Analysis

Once the formal analysis was completed and examined for content and patterns, focus group meetings were organized with industry representatives and leaders from the region. The focus group meetings began with participants completing a survey of competitive strengths and weaknesses of the regional economy. An example of survey results appears below in the discussion of the Northern Virginia Case Study. The second part of the meeting involved eliciting and evaluating ideas about future directions of investment in cluster and related industries. A modified nominal group technique (Delp et al. 1977) was used to surface and obtain this information.

We do not present all of the results from the focus group meetings because there is insufficient space. However, one part of that discussion is shared to show how this process produced information essential for the initiation of technology policy at sub state level.

One of the CEOs of a meat processing company told the group that his corporation had just outsourced all of its logistics (acquisition of inputs and delivery of outputs to the market) to a large global logistics firm. This resulted in statements from three other CEOs that their companies were in the midst of making the same decision. This further solidified observations from the logistics integration literature (Stough 2001) and from what was learned in analyses of other Virginia economic regions that logistical outsourcing was a major and rapidly evolving new element of business process in the states as in many other parts of the country and the world. Yet all of the outsourcing of this function was to large national and international logistics services providers. None goes to local Virginia providers. Upon investigation, it was learned that no such company was headquartered in Virginia. Thus, it was recognized that a significant part of the operations of Virginia businesses were being outsourced, i.e. exported, to companies in at least other parts of the U.S. and with it jobs and wealth.

A related recommendation resulting from the focus group meeting was that the State of Virginia needed to either create and/or attract a large national level logistics firms to the state. In short, import substitution was viewed as an option to help keep the logistics part of business process in Virginia. On a national and global level, logistics and outsourcing of logistics is a technology-intensive and propulsive new emergent industry and, if seeded in Virginia, could help to retain large numbers of jobs (and wealth) that were being lost through large-scale outsourcing of these functions. Furthermore, it could, over time, become an industry that would create new, high-quality jobs and wealth.

6.3.1.3 Conclusions for the Shenandoah Valley Case Study

The general pattern of the Shenandoah Region economy is that it is somewhat more fragmented that other regional economies in Virginia. This is supported by the identification of four clusters. This relatively high level of definition may be attributable to the size and shape of the region that appears to support more than one labour pool and that in turn helps define the clusters. In short, historical patterns influenced by geography may be a major reason for the relatively large number of industry clusters.

Despite this cluster fragmentation, all of the clusters exhibit the same pattern, namely, the presence of relatively homogeneous propulsive industries and somewhat less dynamic supporting industries. These clusters have wage levels above the regional average (which is somewhat low compared to the state average) but below state wide industry averages. This places the region in a competitive position and explains why growth is occurring throughout dominant and supporting industries.

At the same time, the dynamics include a trend to outsource logistics on the part of the core cluster industries. This pattern has been observed to be occurring in other parts of the state and as well as nationally and globally. Given that the major logistics companies were located outside the state, it was important to try to create or attract one or more of the major companies to build a logistics support industry and to thereby retain the economic activities (job, earnings and wealth creation) that were already being exported from the state.

6.3.2 The Northern Virginia Regional Industrial Cluster Analysis

In addition to being one of the nation's fastest growing regions over the past three decades, Northern Virginia has a population of nearly 2 million and has among the highest family earnings and levels of educational attainment in the U.S. In 2001, the average household income was USD 112,380 and per capita income was USD 43,620. Further, nearly 5 percent of the region's households registered incomes greater that USD 150,000. Finally, about 25 percent of the labour force is in technology intensive work positions. These facts are not surprising, as national capital regions throughout the world and their component regions (such as Northern Virginia in the case of the U.S. National Capital Region) have long been known to disproportionately attract highly-educated workers who also command high earnings. However, these earnings and education attributes have more recently been accentuated in the U.S. National Capital region, and particularly in Northern Virginia, by the growth of a technology services business sector (Stough 1998) that forms along with federal contracting, the core of the region's economic base. The region also has a significant transportation infrastructure including the nexus of several express quality highways and a modern heavy rail transit system that connects it to the rest of the region. It is also the home of George Mason University with nearly 30,000 students and with more than 11,000 in graduate-level degree programs. The Northern Virginia Community College system offers training to nearly 40,000 students each year, of which an increasingly significant educational focus is technical education.

6.3.2.1 Cluster 1: The Technology Services Cluster

One large industrial cluster dominates the Northern Virginia economy. This cluster is sometimes called the Info-Com (information and communications) cluster. Here it is called the technology services cluster. The two largest and most dominant industries in this cluster are high-end and technology intensive business services and engineering and management services that together employ 149,740 and 87,040, respectively. A third but smaller sector is communications with 23,829 employees (Fig. 6.3.). The total employment of this cluster is 260,609 or about 40 percent of total regional employment. While production for commercial markets has increased in the region over the past decade or two, the dominant market is still the federal government sector (Fuller 2002). As technology became a more important factor in the overall economy, its presence and impact in the federal sector simultaneously increased as well.

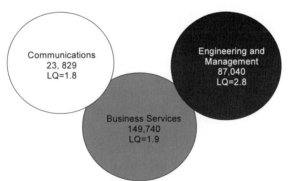

Fig. 6.3. Northern Virginia cluster 1– components, employment, and location quotients. *LQ* location quotient. The total cluster industry employment is 260,609

The technology services form a robust cluster with an average location quotient of 2.1 across the sectors that define it and it is propulsive. Business services grew at a rate of 8.5 percent per year over the study period (See Table 6.2.). The growth rate for engineering and management services was 5.3 percent. However, employment in the communications sector changed little (0.1 percent increase). At the same time the average wages in these sectors were far above the regional average at 136 percent (business services), 138 percent (engineering and management services) and an impressive 174 percent in communications. All three have average annual wages well above the state wide average. In short, this is one of the most powerful and propulsive clusters identified in any of the nine Virginia economic regions.

Table 6.2. Selected statistics on industrial sectors in the Northern Virginia technology services cluster, 1999

SIC Code	Description	Sum of AVG EMP	LQ	AGE (%)	AVGW98 (USD)	REL_W98 (%)	WAGE-TO-STATE (%)
73	Business Services	149740	1.85	8.5	53,765	136	141
87	Engineering and Management Services	87040	2.82	5.3	54,874	138	113
48	Communication	23829	1.75	0.1	68,825	174	134
27	Printing and Publishing	12813	0.89	0.6	44,128	111	131
36	Electronic and Other Electric Equipment	8282	0.54	13.4	48,173	122	128
42	Trucking and Warehousing	8619	0.44	6.3	28,682	72	112
50	Wholesale Trade-Durable Goods	29393	0.78	4.8	54,250	137	132
61	Non-Depository Institutions	12038	2.13	6.4	64,776	163	118
62	Security and Commodity Brokers	2564	0.41	10.3	102,016	257	121
67	Holding and Other Investment Offices	1335	0.43	−11.8	100,200	253	109
17	Special Trade Contractors	38125	1.12	7.1	31,900	80	117
65	Real Estate	16536	1.17	−0.5	37,776	95	131

SIC Code Standard Industrial Classification code, *Sum of AVGEMP* employment in the industry, *LQ* location quotient, *AGE* (%) employment annualised percentage change, *AVGW98(USD)* average annual earnings(in dollars), *REL_W98(%)* average earnings relative to regional average, *WAGE-TO-STATE* average earnings relative to state average

Business Services: The largest sector in business services is computer and data processing services (82,531 employees) (See Fig. 6.4.) that grew at a rate of nearly 10 percent per year and had a location quotient of 5.5, down from 7.7 in 1992. This is the technical intensive core of the business services. The largest sub-parts of the computer and data processing services sector are computer programming services (24,250 employees), other computer services (18,001 employees), computer integrated systems design (12,841 employees), prepackaged software (8,879 employees), data processing and preparation (8,278) and information retrieval services (7.148). All of these were growing between four to 40 percent annually. The fastest growing is information retrieval services. All of these sectors have large location quotients with the lowest at 2.5 and the highest at 9.4 (information retrieval services).

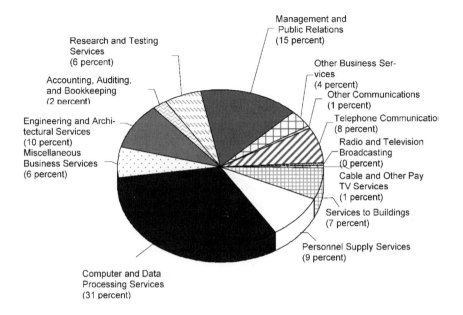

Fig. 6.4. Composition of Northern Virginia cluster 1 (employment, 1999). The total cluster industry employment is 260,609 for the year 1999

The second largest sub-part of the business services segment of the cluster is personnel supply services. Employment agencies (3,349 employees with a location quotient of 1.1) and help supply services (20,927 employees and a location quotient of 0.66) are the two major components of the personnel supply services sector. Both of these have been growing rapidly (11.9 percent and 13.8 percent respectively) but employment agencies have been more dynamic with an annual increase in the location quotient of 15.8 percent per year. This dynamism reflects an effort to attract an increasing number of technical workers.

Engineering and Management Services: This part of the technology services cluster is comprised of management (and public relations), engineering (and architecture), and research and testing services (See Fig. 6.4.). The management and public relations sector employs 15 percent of all employment in the cluster. Its employment has grown from 22,890 in 1992 to 40,637 in 1998 (an average annual growth of ten percent). With a location quotient of 3.8 this is a much more important sector in the region than nationally. Its largest constituent sub-parts are management consulting services (26,211 employees), other business consulting services (6,002), management services (5,296) and facilities support services (2,365). All of these sectors have large location quotients and increasing employment. With rapid growth in technical sectors like computer programming services and engineering services, as well as growth in the technically intense Internet and E-commerce sectors, management assistance has been in high demand.

The other large component of the engineering and management services part of the cluster is engineering and architectural services (ten percent of total cluster employment) with 25,462 employees (up slightly over 25,256 in 1992) and a location quotient of 2.8 that is down from 4.1 in 1992. This sector has been declining since the early 1990s.

The next largest sub-part of the technology services cluster is research and testing services. Commercial physical research is the largest component industry (employs 8,110). However, employment in this sector has been declining at a rate of 0.5 percent per year and its location quotient of 4.6 is down from the 1992 figure of 6.7 percent. Besides this component, the research sector includes other two dynamic parts; one is non-commercial research organizations with 4,398 employees and the other is commercial non-physical research with 1,970 employees. These sectors have location quotients of 5.4 and 1.6, respectively and have employment growth higher than 12 percent per year (14.6 and 12.5 percent average annual growth). It is apparent that these sectors exhibit dynamic behaviour. The fact that growth is occurring in the non-physical research area suggests that research is growing in areas that support the new commercial side of the region's economy, namely Internet and E-commerce. This is further confirmed by the presence of a large business-consulting sector (not elsewhere classified) that employs 6,002 and is growing at a rate of ten percent per year. It also has a large and growing location quotient (5.6). Such a large sector that is 'not elsewhere classified' suggests that it is composed of new industries (Internet and E-commerce related) that are difficult to classify in the Standard Industrial Classification (SIC) system at that time and even now in the new North American Industry Classification (NAIC) system.

Communications: The communications sector is the smallest of the three dominant industries in the technology services cluster (Fig. 6.5.). It employs 23,829 and is composed primarily of a large telephone communication sector that employs 17,211 (not including radio-related communication). It has been growing at about one percent per year and has a location quotient of 2.3 that has been decreasing. That employment in this area has been rising rather slowly is somewhat surprising given that the region claims communications as one of its core economic base activities. At the same time, much organizational rationalization and consolidation has been occurring as several large or super-large corporations have been created out of mergers and acquisitions. Such mergers are often accompanied with workforce reductions in pursuit of scale economies.

Support Industries: There are nine supporting industries for the business, engineering and management services and communications cluster as shown in Fig. 6.6. (See Table 6.2. also). The supporting industries have 129,705 employees and an average location quotient of about one.

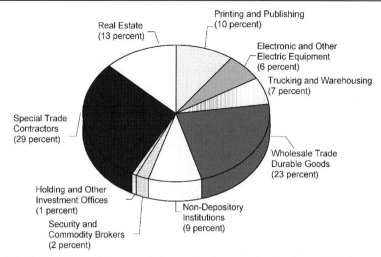

Fig. 6.5. Composition of Support Industry Employment in Northern Virginia Cluster 1, 1999. The total cluster support industry employment is 129,705 for the year 1999

The nine supporting industry sectors include electronics, non-depository financial institutions, security and commodity brokers, printing and publishing, trucking and warehousing, special trade contracting, real estate, wholesale trade and durables and holding and other investment offices. Most of these sectors have been growing at a rapid rate (average rate of employment growth is four percent per year) and have wage levels well above the regional and state industry averages.

Conclusions on Northern Virginia Technology Services Cluster Analysis: It is important to note that the supporting industries are, with only two exceptions, increasing their employment base. Further, they had very high wages relative to the regional average and even more so compared to the state wide industry average. Both the dominant industries and the supporting industries exhibited considerable propulsiveness.

6.3.2.2 Cluster 2: Membership Organization Cluster

A large number of regional, national and international organizations are located in the Washington D.C. area. Over the past two decades, these organizations, like many other activities, have been migrating to the sub-urban parts of the region. Initially, this locational diffusion was mostly to the inner suburbs (Arlington and Alexandria). More recently, however, some of the outer suburbs of the region have witnessed growth in this industry activity. As a consequence, it is no surprise that the membership organization cluster has emerged from the analysis.

This cluster has 18,327 employees with most of the employment concentrated in three sub-areas: business associations (37 percent of cluster employment), professional organizations (23 percent of cluster employment) and civic and social associations (19 percent of cluster employment) (Fig.6.6.). The location quotient for this sector is 0.8 and employment has been increasing at a rate of 6.3 percent per year. Along with some propulsiveness, this industry has a high level of average earnings at USD 42,970 that is 108 percent of the regional average and 136 percent of the state average for membership associations. Thus, Cluster 2 exhibits propulsiveness although not nearly as strong as for Cluster 1. The strong growth in this sector is tied in part to the region's proximity to the National Capital Region and in part to the strength of its growing commercial sector.

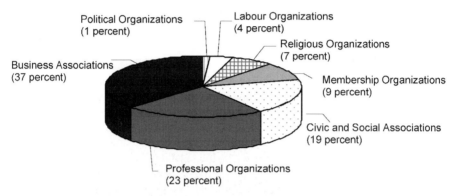

Fig. 6.6. Composition of Northern Virginia cluster 2 (employment, 1999). The total cluster industry employment is 18, 327 for the year 1999

6.3.2.3 The Federal Cluster?

Another important sector in the Northern Virginia region is the federal government. Despite the fact that the direct employment of the federal government sector has been decreasing over the last decade in the Greater Washington Region, it still maintains a dominant role. The latest estimations show that its direct and indirect contribution to the regional economy through employment and contracting is as high as 50 percent (Fuller 2005). This level of influence has been maintained and perhaps increased over recent years by a rapid increase in federal contracting in the region (Stough 2005). If during the mid 1980s the Northern Virginia firms had seven percent of all federal contracting, the percentage has risen to more than eleven percent currently.

6.3.2.4 Focus Groups and Interpretive Analysis: Creating New Opportunities

Eleven focus groups representing different parts of the Northern Virginia regional economy (e.g., information and communication technologies (ICTs), systems integration, aerospace, associations, and biotechnology) were held in the Northern Virginia study described above. Most of the participants were CEOs or senior executives of companies, part of the twelve industry sectors and other professionals with intimate knowledge of the regional economy, e.g. bankers, economic development director and local economist(s). At the beginning of the meetings, participants were asked to assess competitiveness factors of the regional economy with respect to their industry segment.

On the basis of the cluster analyses several visual displays showing the structure of the Northern Virginia economy were created. The ICTs components of the economy (with various other elements) from both the core technology cluster (Cluster 1) and its main supporting industries are presented in Fig. 6.7.

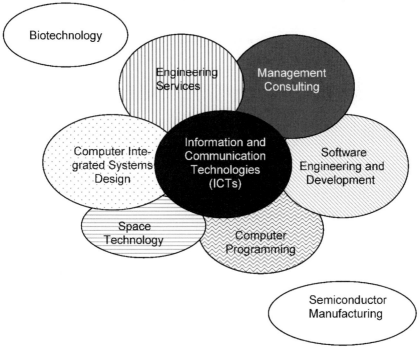

Fig. 6.7. The core industries of the Northern Virginia economy

A number of other quasi-clusters of activity was identified by disaggregating the sectoral components of the two main clusters and their supporting industries and these were then arrayed as "satellite" activities that were loosely connected to the ICTs core (Fig. 6.8).

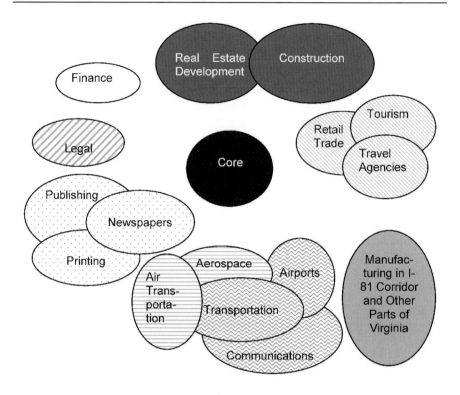

Fig. 6.8. Core and other important sectors of the Northern Virginia economy

These visual illustrations of the economy were then used to describe the basic structure of the regional economy to the different focus group participants and as elements for driving an exercise designed to identify opportunities for future development and deepening of the region's economy by the participants. This exercise is the basic method developed to support policy implementation and design at the sub-state regional level.

The Northern Virginia economy as noted above grew very rapidly from a modest bedroom community in the U.S. National Capital region to the centre for the large technology services industry in the region over the past 25 years. Because of this rapid development, the economy is not well integrated because there has not been time for the deep inter industry links that exist in mature economies to develop. Consequently, a major problem for the region is to broaden and deepen the existing industry in a way that creates a more integrated economy and thus one that is better able to manage cyclical and other shocks.

A major goal of the focus group meetings for this region was to identify directions and initiatives for broadening and deepening the technology services core of the region's economy and thus to achieve a more integrated economy. The methodology developed selects several sub-sectors randomly from the various industrial sectors included in the region's two major clusters in the region and their associated supporting industries. For example, in Fig. 6.9., one of these groups of sub-sectors includes ICTs, systems integration and health/medicine. This grouping was presented to several of the focus group participants and in response to a question about how these three sub-sectors might be used to spawn a new industry or activity they responded with the suggestion of telemedicine applications (See Fig. 6.9).

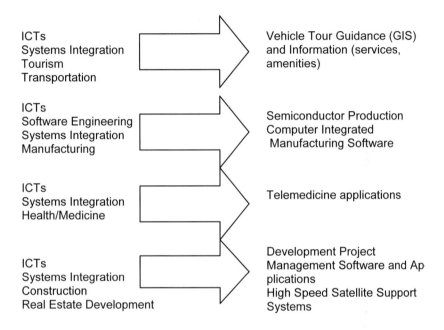

ICTs
Systems Integration
Tourism
Transportation

Vehicle Tour Guidance (GIS) and Information (services, amenities)

ICTs
Software Engineering
Systems Integration
Manufacturing

Semiconductor Production
Computer Integrated
 Manufacturing Software

ICTs
Systems Integration
Health/Medicine

Telemedicine applications

ICTs
Systems Integration
Construction
Real Estate Development

Development Project Management Software and Ap plications
High Speed Satellite Support Systems

Fig. 6.9. Intersectoral linkage development

Through many such exercises and related discussions it was possible to take core sectors of the Northern Virginia clusters and create working hypotheses (opportunities) for future development. For example, the integration of the results across all groups to opportunities related to the ICTs sector resulted into a ICT cluster including: wireless communication, regional electronic computer enhanced networks, Internet II, network products and services, telemedicine support systems, telework support systems and bio-informatics applications. Similar exercises were conducted with computer integrated systems design and legal services.

The above examples illustrate ways created to broaden existing sectors that define the core of the major industrial cluster in the region. However, questions remain about how to deepen some of the less well represented subsectors, such as finance. The larger region to which Northern Virginia belongs has historically been a government services economy and thus did not develop a strong commercial banking sector. Notwithstanding, because the National Capital Region has a nearly five million population and there has been considerable growth in the technology services sector, there is concern regarding the development of the banking sector as a supporting industry. The result of focus group exercises targeting the banking sector yielded some interesting and useful concepts about the opportunities to further develop this sector and its links to other parts of the economy.

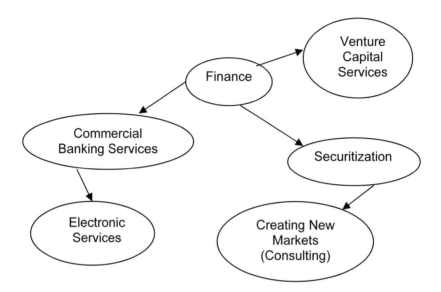

Fig. 6.10. Financial sector specialization development in the Northern Virginia region

As shown in Fig. 6.10 some of these opportunities for specialization include electronic services for commercial banking, venture capital services, and further development of the securitization industry that is well seeded in the region with the activities of Fannie Mae and Freddie Mack financial organizations. Given the presence of these securitization industries, it is possible for the region to become a knowledge centre for creating new markets, at large.

6.3.2.5 Conclusions for the Northern Virginia Case Study

The purpose of this case analysis was to show how the identification of propulsive clusters and their associated supporting industries could be used to find opportunities to broaden and deepen a technology services intensive cluster. A qualitative focus group approach was demonstrated as a way to accomplish this objective of the research. Various examples were provided to illustrate specific opportunities. This case study, conducted in 1999, is of additional interest because many of the identified opportunities have been developed, but also because some of them have not. Each of them is in itself a case study of how local leadership and initiatives either developed the opportunities or failed to develop them. Nonetheless, the employed method is a systematic way to identify potential opportunities for broadening and deepening the economic structure and therefore the basis for creating strategic economic development objectives.

6.4 Conclusions and Implications of the Findings

This chapter begins with a general assessment of the performance of state level efforts in the U.S. to design and implement technology policy in support of economic development. It is argued, in light of earlier research, that many of these efforts failed to bring anticipated benefits (Riggle and Stough 2003). Further, part of this outcome is attributed to the fact that most state economies are not single integrated economies, but rather a collage of individual sub-state region specific economies that are much more internally coherent than at higher levels of aggregations, e.g., at the state level. Thus, it is argued that there is a need for tailored implementation at the local regional level for optimal impact. Two case studies are conducted to illustrate an industry cluster based methodology that is augmented with a qualitative element that amplifies the quantitative results with industry leaders' opinions.

The first case study on the Shenandoah Valley region illustrates how this region, with its fairly mature economy based on food processing and light manufacturing, responds to globalisation and related competitive forces. The core industries in the region are significantly outsourcing both their inputs and outputs to national and global logistics firms. This is recognized to be a much larger problem in that it was occurring in most other parts of the state of Virginia as well as beyond and globally. Part of the region's and the state's economic capacity is outsourced to providers located outside the Shenandoah Valley and Virginia market areas. This case points to the need for concerted state leadership to help create or attract a major logistics firm in Virginia. Further, it showed both the need for and the opportunity to achieve import substitution and thus stem the flow of state capital and productive power to other places.

The second case study on the Northern Virginia region illustrates in more detail the region specific benefits of the multi-stage methodology developed in this chapter. In this analysis, numerous working hypothesis opportunities that could be used to broaden and deepen an emergent technology intensive economy are identified. Thus, it provides an example of identification and selection of strategy elements for the strengthening of a developing regional economy. Moreover, it is an illustration of how technology policy and initiatives can be guided and implemented at the sub-state regional level for development.

These examples illustrate the great need at the state level for technology policy to be disaggregated for implementation at the local regional level. There is need for a broad and deep study of this issue.

References

Atkinson RD, Court R, Ward J (1999) The State new economy index. Progressive Policy Institute Policy Report (July), Washington, DC

Bergman EM, Feser EJ (1999) Industry clusters: a methodology and framework for regional development policy in the US. In Roelandt T, den Hertog P (eds) Boosting innovation: a cluster approach. Organisation for Economic Cooperation and Development, Paris, pp 243-268

Bosworth B, Broun D (1996) Connect the dots: using cluster-based strategies to create urban employment. Firm Connections 4(2): 1-6

Stimson RJ, Stough RR, Roberts B (2002) Regional economic development: analysis and planning strategy. Springer, Berlin Heidelberg New York

Delp P, Thesen A, Motiwalla J, Seshadri N (1977) Systems tools for project planning. Pasitam, Bloomington, IN

Doeringer PB, Terkla DG (1995) Business strategy and cross industry clusters. Economic Development Quarterly 9: 225-237.

Bergman E, Feser E, Sweeny S (1996) Targeting North Carolina manufacturing: understanding the state's economy through industrial cluster analysis. University North Carolina Institute for Economic Development, Chapel Hill, NC

Glasmeier AK, Harrison B (1997) Response: why business alone won't redevelop the inner city: a friendly critique of Michael Porter's approach to urban revitalization. Economic Development Quarterly 11(1): 28-38

Gordon IR, McCann P (2000) Industrial clusters: complexes, agglomeration and/or social networks? Urban Studies 37 (3): 513- 532

Feser EJ, Sweeney (2002) Theory, methods, and a cross-metropolitan comparison of business clustering. In McCann P (ed) Industrial location economics, Edward Elgar, Cheltenham, UK, Northampton, MA, pp 222-259

Fuller SS (2002) The economic outlook for the Washington Area economy. In Stough RR (ed) Forecasting the Greater Washington economy: 2002 "Tracking the recovery". The Mason Enterprise Center, George Mason University, Fairfax, VA, pp 1-49

Fuller SS (2005) The economy in 2005 and beyond. Paper presented at the 13th Annual George Mason University "Forecasting the Greater Washington Area Economy", 6 January 2005, Fairfax, VA

Held JR (1996) Clusters as an economic development tool: Beyond the pitfalls. Economic Development Quarterly 10:249-261

Jacobs D, De Man AP (1996) Clusters, industrial policy and firm strategy: a menu approach. Technology Analysis and Strategic Management 8(4): 425-437

Porter ME (1990) The competitive advantage of nations. Basic Books, New York

Rosenfeld SA (1995) Industrial strength strategies: regional business clusters and public policy. Aspen Institute, Washington, DC

Rosenfeld SA (1996) Overachievers, business clusters that work: prospects for regional development. Regional Technology Strategies, Chapel Hill, NC

Rosenfeld SA (1997) Bringing business clusters into the mainstream of economic development. European Planning Studies 5(1): 3-23

San Diego Regional Technology Alliance (2000) Industry Clusters. Available at http://www.sdrta.org/sdrta/clusterdata/industriescluster.html

Saxenian AL (1994) Regional advantage: culture and competition in the Silicon Valley and Route 128. Harvard University Press, Boston, MA

Stough RR (1998) Endogenous Growth in a Regional Context. The Annals of Regional Science, Endogenous Growth Special Edition 32 (1): 1-5

Stough RR, Kulkarni R, Riggle J (2000) Technology in Virginia's regions. The Virginia Center for Innovative Technology, Herndon, VA

Stough RR (2001) New technologies in logistics management. In Bremer AM, Button KJ, Hensher DA (eds) Logistics and supply chain management. Pergamon, London, pp 513-520

Stough RR (2005) Vulnerability of the greater Washington regional economy in the 21st century. Paper presented at the 13th Annual George Mason University "Forecasting the Greater Washington Area Economy", 6 January 2005, Fairfax, VA

Riggle JD, Stough RR (2003) Evaluating state cooperative technology programs: With a Virginia case study, and comparative data from Illinois. Technological Forecasting and Social Change 70 (7): 639-651

Sternberg E (1991) The sectoral cluster in economic development policy: lessons from Rochester and Buffalo, New York. Economic Development Quarterly 5(4): 342-356

Annex

Table 6A.1 Selected statistics on industrial sectors in the Shenandoah clusters 2,3, and 4 for the year 1999

Cluster	Sector	Employment	Location Quotient	Share of the industry
2	PRINTING AND PUBLISHING	4734	1.80	100
	Books			49
	Commercial Printing			34
	Newspapers			13
	Business Forms			3
	Supporting Industries			100
	Special Trade Contractors	6981	1.10	25
	Business Services	6765	0.40	24
	Durable Goods	3502	1.00	13
	Trucking and Warehousing	3502	1.00	13
	Chemical and Allied Products	3345	2.30	12
	Utilities	1356	0.90	5
	Other	2170		8
3	HEALTH SERVICES	15702	0.70	100
	Hospitals			54
	Nursing and Care Facilities			16
	Medical Doctors and Clinics			15
	Other			15
	Supporting Industries			100
	Business Services	6765	0.40	39
	Chemical and Allied Products	3345	2.25	19
	Engineering and Management	1903	0.30	11
	Communication	1793	0.70	10
	Real Estate	1640	0.60	9
	Utilities	1346	0.90	8
	Legal Services	757	0.40	4
4	CHEMICALS, TEXTILES AND RUBBER	12897	2.40	100
	Miscellaneous Plastics			50
	Others (14 sectors)			50
	Supporting Industries			100
	Special Trades	6981	1.10	23
	Business Services	6765	0.40	23
	Durable Goods	3724	0.50	12
	Trucking and Warehousing	3502	1.00	12
	Industrial Machinery	3264	0.90	11
	Engineering and Management	1903	0.30	6
	Real Estate	1640	0.60	5
	Utilities	1356	0.90	5
	Legal Services	757	0.40	3

Section B: Location and Dynamics of Information and Communication Technology (ICT) Industries

7 Spatial Clusters of ICT Industries

Börje Johansson

Jönköping International Business School, Jönköping University

7.1 Introduction

7.1.1 Models of Cluster Economies

One basic observation is that economic activities are clustered in space. This may be seen as a prerequisite for the existence of agglomerations. In McCann (2001) industrial clustering is described as place-specific increasing returns to scale, due to positive externalities that co-located activities generate. As such, it is closely related to the phenomenon known as agglomeration economies with roots in Marshall (1920) and promoted by Krugman (1991). A closely related but distinctly different approach is due to Hoover (1948). In both cases, agglomeration effects accrue inside an urban region sometimes referred to as an industrial district.

In Marshall's theoretical scheme, there are three sources of agglomeration economies, namely (i) non-traded local inputs, (ii) local skilled-labour supply, and (iii) information spillovers. In the subsequent analysis, the first category is relabelled to read distance-sensitive inputs. Because of high geographic transaction costs, these inputs are more expensive when delivered from sources outside the region. Hence, proximity becomes an advantage when supplier and customer firms are co-located. The second category is related to a firm's labour acquisition costs. In a region where a large share of the labour force already has specialized skills, the costs of the firm to expand its labour force may be lower than otherwise. For example, search and retraining costs can be assumed to be lower when the labour pool is large.

According to the above arguments, proximity to specialized input suppliers and specialized labour supply will imply that inputs can be acquired at lower total prices for given quality levels. Because of this, the described phenomena are called pecuniary externalities. On the other hand, information spillovers have a non-pecuniary character. In some sense, the agglomeration information is locally available as a public good, and brings benefits that are not charged any price, except (possibly) in the form of land prices.

The spillover phenomenon refers to inter-firm externalities that can generate incremental as well as more radical innovations with regard to firm routines and product attributes. In this context there are two competing hypotheses. The first, which is attributed to Marshall, emphasizes localization economies, and the second, attributed to Jacobs (1969, 1984), stresses urbanization economies. With localization economies spillover is fostered by similarity among firms in a cluster, whereas urbanization economies imply that spillover is a diversity phenomenon. With pecuniary externalities it is equally relevant to distinguish between localization and urbanization economies (McCann 2001).

A recent article by Gordon and McCann (2000) provides a comprehensive assessment of various theoretical frameworks in which economic clusters have been discussed and researched. They find a tendency to use terms such as agglomeration, clusters, industrial districts, economic milieu, and industrial complex more or less interchangeably, and with little concern of how to operationalize the ideas. They suggest that the literature contains three basic notions of clustering: (i) the classic model of pure agglomeration, (ii) the industrial-complex model, and (iii) the network or club model focusing on social ties and trust. In this study, the two first notions are considered. In the pure agglomeration model, externalities arise via the local market and local spillovers. The industrial-complex model stresses the role of trading links that help to reduce transaction costs and ascertain input quality. The two notions merge in the sense that local markets and local transaction links can exist side by side in a functional region.

In concordance with the suggestions in Chap. 8, proximity to input suppliers and to customers are here introduced as important aspects of agglomeration economies. Proximity in these two respects can be substituted by supplier-customer links which are formed in order to reduce transaction costs and hence to eliminate the influence of distance on the interaction between seller and buyer. Such links can develop into networks that have similar properties as clusters although the networks extend across regional boundaries. Proximity does not exclude that local networks are formed. However, proximity implies that it is easier to establish links for transactions and cooperation, and hence, it is also easier to rearrange such links more frequently. In the subsequent analysis, it is important to recall this distinction between networks and clusters. This is emphasized by using the term spatial clusters.

Cluster formation can be described as a location process. At each point in time, we may look for a static picture of co-located (localized) industries and co-located firms. One may interpret such location patterns as an equilibrium outcome. However, it may also be conceived as a momentary picture of a dynamic location process, where an attractor drives the dynamics, and this attractor may have equilibrium properties. Although the statistical sources in this chapter can be used to examine change processes, the empirical analysis is a static cross-section exercise that represents a first step of a more comprehensive study.

7.1.2 The ICT Sector and Spatial Structure

In this chapter, ICT is used as an acronym for information and communication technology. During the 1990s, ICT was considered as a specific growth factor in the "digital economy" and the "new economy", bringing about a radical transformation of the economic system (e.g. Gordon 2000). The ICT sector is a great candidate for examining cluster phenomena, partly because it may be decomposed into a whole set of interlinked sub sectors, ranging across manufacturing, wholesale and service activities. In this study, there 27 industries: eight manufacturing, eight wholesale, and eleven service industries (See Table 7A.1). The location patterns are examined for the year 1999.

The basic observation unit is an industrial establishment, where a firm (company) may have several establishments. Each industry consists of establishments that produce similar, but possibly differentiated, products. The focus is on industries, and analytically each industry is characterized by a representative firm of that industry.

In the empirical analyses, the Swedish economic space is decomposed into 81 functional (urban) regions, labeled LA-regions[1]. These regions are functional in the sense that they correspond to local labour-market regions. Each such region consists of a set of integrated municipalities, and the average distance between such pairs of municipalities is 25-30 minutes by car. Starting in any particular municipality in a normal region, the distance to the border of the region is 45-60 minutes or less. This means that for almost all regions, the maximum distance between a municipality pair is 45-60 minutes, although a few regions have much longer time distances. Short time distances between municipalities of a region imply not only that the labour markets are integrated; time distances are also short as regards face-to-face interaction between firms in the same region. For a firm in a given industry, face-to-face contacts may be necessary when the firm buys certain inputs, which can be labeled distance-sensitive inputs. Such contacts may likewise be frequent when the same firm delivers its output to customers. In this case we observe distance-sensitive outputs.

Further, location patterns of regions are compared. In the theoretical models outlined, the geography is decomposed in an extremely simplified way. A distinction is made between supply and demand (i) inside an LA-region and (ii) outside the region. Proximity to suppliers and customer of a firm (or industry) applies when the firm (industry) and its suppliers and customers are located in the same region. Throughout there are two sectors: the ICT sector and the rest of all other industries not included in the ICT sector. With this background, we ask two simple questions: (i) is the location of an ICT industry in a region affected by the size of the ICT sector in the region, and (ii) is the same location affected by the size of the economy in the region. In other words, is the clustering of industries caused by localization or urbanization economies?

The study tries to shed light on these questions in two different ways. First, a model structure is outlined to formally describe input deliveries and customer sales, and to formulate a random-choice model of location behaviour. The model sheds light on the possibility to distinguish between localization and urbanization economies. The associated model discussion shows that in general both phenomena are likely to be active side by side and hence difficult to disentangle empiri-

---

[1] LA is the Swedish abbreviation for local labour market.

cally. Second, a set of regression analyses is used to empirically illustrate this formal conclusion. One set of regressions focuses on the location measured by the number of jobs in a region and another set focuses on the number of establishments in each region. Third, the formal models are also used to demonstrate that the existence of internal scale economies will cause scale effects in the location pattern, such that location is unlikely in regions with too small intra-regional demand. Fourth, the location selectivity of each industry is examined empirically.

It could be observed that the present study does not investigate some the alternative issues in cluster analysis. For example, it is possible to ask which specific groups of ICT industries tend to agglomerate together in space. In this case, one might employ statistical cluster analysis. It is also possible to contemplate if there are industries outside the ICT sector that may be correlated in space with certain ICT industries. In addition, one may ask if the size of a cluster is correlated with the growth of the pertinent industries. Instead, the analysis is solely focused on the question: do individual ICT industries locate in regions with a large ICT sector or in regions with a large economy?

7.1.3 Outline

Section 7.2 starts with a brief discussion of models of externalities that can be associated with the concept of sectoral cluster. The section outlines two models that can help us to understand input-based and output-based localization and urbanization economies. These models also contain a simple representation of intra-industry spillover and scale effects. The model formulations form a simple background to the empirical analysis in Sects. 7.3 and 7.4.

Section 7.3 examines clustering of ICT industry employment. It starts by characterizing the location pattern of the ICT sector and individual ICT industries. In a second step, a simple regression is employed to show that the size of the entire ICT sector is dependent on the size of the region. In a third step the same technique is applied to all the individual ICT industries as a means to determine which of these industries tend to be located in proportion to the size of the entire economy of a region. A similar exercise is also employed to illustrate the relation between individual ICT industries and the size of the entire ICT sector (localization externalities). This leads to an examination of how many regions that host each specific industry. This form of location selectivity is interpreted as a scale effect. Finally, it is shown that one cannot exclude the presence of localization economies.

Section 7.4 examines the clustering of ICT establishments. First, it examines to what extent individual industries consist of many establishments that are limited in size. This is important, because the random-choice model that is suggested relies on an assumption that firms in the same industry have approximately the same size. Next, two regressions are carried out showing how the number of establishments in an individual industry depends (i) on the total number of ICT establishments and (ii) the total size of ICT employment. These exercises are used in a final discussion of scale effects and their effects on location patterns.

The fifth and concluding section (7.5) discusses the relative importance of the two location impact factors: localization and urbanization economies. This section also outlines options to utilize the existing data set to further improve and enrich the empirical analysis. The conclusions end with a suggested scheme for a systematic assessment of cluster formation.

7.2 Models of Sectoral Clusters

7.2.1 External Economies and Clusters

In Sect.7.1 it has been stressed that the analysis of agglomeration economies and cluster economies can be seen as a heritage from Marshall (1920). In recent decades, this form of regional specialization has been advocated as a key force of economic growth in contrast to Heckscher-Ohlin comparative advantages. In this perspective, it is interesting to note that Ohlin (1933) outlines a scheme for analysing agglomeration economies, with the following four categories:

1. Internal economies of scale, associated with the technique or production function of the individual firm;
2. Localization economies, which affect the individual firm as an influence from the industry to which the firm belongs;
3. Urbanization economies, which arise from the size of the regional economy and hence are external to the industry and its firms;
4. Inter-industry linkages of input-output type, where proximity to suppliers of intermediate inputs reduces the price of such inputs.

In the classification above the focus is on how the individual firm is affected by each agglomeration factor. In the Hoover (1948) setting, internal returns to scale are firm specific, localization economies are industry specific and urbanization economies are specific for each urban region. The distinctions made in this chapter relate to Hoover but have a special twist:

1. The ICT sector consists of a set of industries. Localization economies are defined as a positive externality such that an individual industry benefits by having a large ICT sector in the same region. When many or all industries in the sector have an advantage of being located together with a large ICT sector they are classified as a cluster;
2. An industry in the ICT sector can also get an advantage by being located in a large region. This is considered as a result of urbanization economies.

With reference to Ohlin's classification, this study examines localization economies that affect the individual firm in an industry (or the industry as a whole) as an external influence from the ICT sector to which the industry is assumed to belong. A regression technique is suggested as a method to assess whether the industry in question actually belongs to the sectoral cluster. The alternative assumption is that industries are clustered together because of urbanization economies. In this case, a similar regression technique is used to examine the existence of urbanization economies. As will be shown the employed technique can only provide limited answers to the questions posed, therefore, the concluding section of the presentation will suggest a set of complementary statistical methods to generate more conclusive results.

How does the Ohlin structure relate to the analysis in this chapter? First, inter-industry linkages describe technology conditions about intermediary deliveries with relevance for a firm's inputs as well as its output. An inter-industry link of this kind has implications for spatial clustering to the extent that the pertinent delivery is distance sensitive (or is likely to have proximity-dependent spillovers). Second, the existence of internal scale-economies is uncontroversial in the sense that it can be combined with both localization and urbanization economies. At the same time, internal scale economies in combination with distance sensitivity implies that the size of demand inside the urban region becomes essential, and this is a form of urbanization economies in its own right.

In view of the above discussion, the subsequent analysis will consider two main cluster factors. The first is accessibility to input suppliers; the second is accessibility to customers. A third factor, labelled interaction and spillover phenomena, is presented in Fig. 7.1. This factor is present in the analysis as a stimulus between firms in the same industry. The theoretical analysis concentrates on pecuniary cluster effects, which operate via the market and market prices.

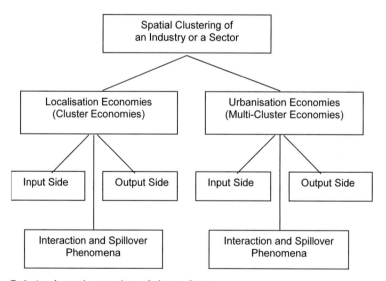

Fig. 7. 1. A schematic overview of cluster factors

A second alternative would be to analyse knowledge (technology) spillovers from customers to firms in an industry as well as from input suppliers to firms in an industry. These aspects are not treated in this chapter.

We should observe that one could identify an input side (accessibility to suppliers) and an output side (accessibility to customers) both for localization and urbanization economies. Moreover, interaction and spillover phenomena can occur both in a sectoral context (localization economies) and in a multi-sector context (urbanization economies). This is described in Fig. 7.1, which provides a schematic view of how a sectoral cluster may be analysed and understood.

The focus in the present contribution is on the ICT sector. In this perspective, localization economies are thought of as input, output, and interaction effects within the ICT sector.

Urbanization economies will in turn be thought of as input supply, customer demand, and interaction of ICT industries with other sectors and the regional economy as a whole. In Fig. 7.1, localization economies represent cluster economies, whereas urbanization economies – stressing diversity –may be interpreted as 'multi-cluster economies'. In the same figure, localization and urbanization economies on the input and output side refer exclusively to pecuniary externalities. It is worthwhile to observe that spillover of information and knowledge can take place in relation to both input and output contacts, and they would then represent vertical spillovers. Spillover externalities between firms in the same industry on the other hand represent horizontal spillovers.

The present study focuses on pecuniary externalities and the additional consequences of internal scale economies. In this context, one may observe that there is a more narrow form of localization economies than the one explored in this study. Localization could be confined to horizontal externalities between firms in the same industry. In the empirical assessment, this phenomenon may be reflected by location selectivity, such that an industry is present only in a subset of regions and such that some of these regions might have high location quotients.

In the subsequent model formulation, industries of the economy are organized in two sets. The first set consists of industries that belong to the ICT sector (A-sector), and the second set consists of all other industries (B-sector). For each ICT industry, a representative firm is modelled, while a deviation for an individual firm is represented by a random deviation-term. In this way, the location pattern of every industry can be derived from a random-choice model. Firms in each industry are assumed to have some form of scale economies, possibly a combination of internal and external economies of scale. In the statistical exercise, scale phenomena within an industry are examined especially for those industries, which are located only in a clear minority of all regions.

7.2.2 Proximity to Input Suppliers

Proximity is a key issue in this study. An individual firm (individual industry) can have short distance to suppliers, customers, and other kinds of interacting agents. In this context two variables are basic. The first is A_R, which signifies the size of the ICT sector in region R. The second is B_R, which signifies the size of the rest of the economy in the same region. The size of a sector refers to its supply capacity and may at the same time reflect the diversity of supply.

In the subsequent analysis, proximity to input supply from the A-sector and from the rest of the economy (B-sector) is recognized as large values of A_R and B_R, respectively. The same variables will also be used later to identify proximity to demand arising from the ICT sector and the entire economy. Proximity to supply and demand is important to the extent that inputs and outputs are distance sensitive. The main focus is input-based pecuniary localization economies.

In this subsection, two aspects of input-supply proximity are examined. Both aspects are reflected in a cost function, where the price of inputs varies with the proximity to supply and where the possibility to rely on local supply of inputs depends on the size of the A-sector and the B-sector. In the latter case, the usefulness of the inputs depends on their degree of variety, which is assumed to increase with the size of input supply. One remark is necessary. In principle, a firm has three alternatives with regard to inputs from the A-sector: (i) it may buy from local suppliers, (ii) it may buy from suppliers outside the regions, and (iii) it may produce the input itself, i.e., it may integrate part of the input process. This third option is not modelled in the subsequent analysis, because the intention is to isolate the trade-off between the first two options.

As described above, proximity to the supply of A-inputs can provide an advantage to a specific industry, k, in the A-sector given that the input delivery is distance sensitive. In this case, we observe input-based localization economies of industry k. The distance-sensitive deliveries may also have their source outside the ICT sector (B-inputs). In that case, we face input-based urbanization economies.

The intention here is to outline a very simplified cost structure of a representative firm. The cost of a firm k in industry i has three components, C^*_{iAR}, C^*_{iBR} and W^*_{iR}. The first component refers to inputs from the A-sector and the second to inputs from the B-sector. The third component reflects internal and external scale economies – to the extent that these are present.

The cost component C^*_{iAR}, reflects pecuniary (or market based) localization economies. These economies reflect an externality such that the A-sector reduces the costs of industry i as A gets larger. The importance of this first cost component depends on the size of the input coefficient b_{iAR}, which informs us about the input to industry i from the A-sector per unit output in a firm in industry i. First, we shall assume that every firm in industry i buys the same composition of A-inputs. However, we also have to consider the share, $0 \le \alpha_{iR} \le 1$, that is bought from suppliers in R, and the share, $(1-\alpha_{iR})$, that is bought from suppliers outside the region. A fundamental assumption is that $\alpha_{iR} = \alpha_i (A_R)$ is an increasing function of A_R.

Why does it matter from where inputs are delivered? It matters for inputs that are distance sensitive. Consider first the price of inputs that can be obtained when buying A-inputs from sources outside the region. Let this price be $\hat{p}_{AR}$ and consider the price of the same inputs when these are bought from suppliers inside the region, signified by p_{AR}. If the delivery is distance sensitive, we should expect that $\hat{p}_{AR} > p_{AR}$. When this holds, region R provides an advantage when α_{iR} is large.

Equation (7.1) describes the cost of A-inputs and the variables in the equation are presented in Table 7.1.

$$C_{iAR}^k = \alpha_{iR} p_{AR} b_{iA} + (1 - \alpha_{iR}) \hat{p}_{AR} b_{iA} \tag{7.1}$$

Table 7.1. The cost of A-inputs

b_{iA}	Input coefficient for delivery of A-inputs per unit output of a firm in industry i
α_{iR}	Share of A-inputs from suppliers inside region R, where $d\alpha_i/dA_R > 0$ as $\alpha_R < 1$
$1 - \alpha_{iR}$	Share of A-inputs from suppliers outside region R
$\hat{p}_{AR}$	The lowest price of A-inputs that can be obtained when buying from suppliers outside region R
p_{AR}	The price of A-inputs when these are bought from suppliers inside region R

In relation to Table 7.1, one may remark that the decomposition of costs makes sense only when the inputs are sufficiently distance sensitive. A relative measure of this sensitivity is expressed by the following formula:

$$q_{AR} = (\hat{p}_{AR} - p_{AR}) / \hat{p}_{AR} \tag{7.2}$$

Observe that if the A-sector is small, the level of p_{AR} may be high due to unexploited scale economies of local A-sector firms. In such cases, q_{AR} will be negative and the region has no advantages to offer. This observation also relates to path dependence. If some exogenous factor would make the A-sector larger, q_{AR} might turn positive and this could stimulate further growth of the A-sector.

Our next concern is the cost of B-inputs. In this case, it seems more natural than in the previous case to exclude the option of a firm to produce such inputs itself. Hence, there remains a choice between intra-regional and extra-regional suppliers. This choice is reflected by the cost component C_{iBR}^k, which has a similar structure as the function in Eq. (7.1). First, the price variables p_{BR} and $\hat{p}_{BR}$ are introduced to represent the price of B-inputs when delivered from suppliers inside and outside the region, respectively. Moreover, b_{iB} describes the input coefficient with respect to B-inputs. Finally, we need the variable β_{iR}, which reflects the share of B-inputs that are delivered by suppliers inside region R. This variable is assumed to depend on the urbanization economies in region R. Hence, it is assumed to be an increasing function of B_R, such that $\beta_{iR} = \beta_i(B_R)$, with $d\beta_i/dB_R > 0$ as $\beta_{iR} < 1$. With these ingredients the following cost component can be introduced, with all variables collected in Table 7.2:

$$C_{iBR}^k = \beta_{iR} p_{BR} b_{iB} + (1 - \beta_{iR}) \hat{p}_{BR} b_{iB} \tag{7.3}$$

Table 7.2. The cost of B-inputs

b_{iB}	Input coefficient for delivery of B-inputs per unit output of a firm in industry i
β_{iR}	Share of B-inputs from suppliers inside region R, where $d\beta_i/dB_R > 0$ as $\beta_{iR} < 1$
$1-\beta_{iR}$	Share of B-inputs from suppliers outside region R
$\hat{p}_{BR}$	The lowest price of A-inputs that can be obtained when buying from suppliers outside region R
p_{BR}	The price of B-inputs when these are bought from suppliers inside region R

In Eq. (7.3) the crucial condition for input-based urbanization economies is that the intra-regional input price, p_{BR} is lower than the extra-regional price, $\hat{p}_{BR}$. When this is true, there is an urbanization advantage associated with being located in a region with a large supply of B-inputs. Under such conditions one can observe that $q_{BR} > 0$, where

$$q_{BR} = (\hat{p}_{BR} - p_{BR})/\hat{p}_{BR} \qquad (7.4)$$

When $q_{BR} > 0$ the advantage of a location in region R depends on the input coefficient b_{iB} and on the size of β_{iR}, which is assumed to increase as B_R increases. In the two cost components presented in Eqs. (7.1) and (7.3) the input coefficients b_{iA} and b_{iB} are taken as given. There is a vast literature (e.g. Baptista 1998) about how a cluster milieu can positively affect technical improvements in a spill-over process. As long as such influences concern process innovations or process changes, they imply that our two input coefficients should have a tendency to be lower in regions where similar firms cluster together. Part of this phenomenon can be introduced with the help of a third cost component, specified as follows:

$$W_{iR}^k = W_i(x_{iR}^k, x_{iR}) \qquad (7.5)$$

Where x_{iR}^k denotes the output of firm k in region R and industry i, and where x_{iR} denotes the output from all firms in industry i and region R. The cost component in Eq. (7.5) may be used to include the technique influence from internal and external scale-economies. For example, we could have that $dW_{iR}^k/dx_{iR}^k < 0$ up to some level $\bar{x}_{iR}^k$, which would reflect internal scale-economies. Moreover, $dW_{iR}^k/dx_{iR} < 0$ would reflect non-pecuniary external scale-economies, such as technology spillover between firms in industry i. One may observe that x_{iR} reflects total demand that is available for firms in region R, whereas x_{iR}^k is the part of this demand that is captured by firm k.

With the help of the three cost components in Eqs. (7.1), (7.3) and (7.5) the following systematic cost function can be introduced:

$$V_{iR}^k = C_{iAR}^k + C_{iBR}^k + W_{iR}^k \tag{7.6}$$

The cost expression in Eq. (7.6) is called systematic cost, since in the next section a random element is added in a discrete-choice formulation. The localization economies that are included in the formula imply that regions with a large A_R will attract firms in industry i to locate and expand in region R – to the extent that there is sufficient demand for the output from industry i. Now, if such localization economies are present for many industries in the A-sector, many of these industries may grow such that $\Delta x_{iR} > 0$, and this implies that the entire A-sector grows and thus making A_R larger. As a consequence, we can observe cumulative growth. It also implies that at any particular moment in time x_{iR} is likely to be large in a region R where A_R is large. In the empirical parts of the chapter, the latter phenomenon is studied, not the dynamic process itself. Obviously, the above outline of cumulative properties of localization economies can be repeated for urbanization economies.

Consider now that spillover interdependencies imply that b_{iA} and b_{iB} reduce over time in a region R. Such a change will force us to index the input coefficients to read b_{iRA} and b_{iRB}, because now the implemented techniques are not same in all regions. We can still conclude that such a cost advantage would be represented in Eq. (7.6). This argument will not be pursued any further.

7.2.3 A Random-Choice Model of Cost-Minimizing Firms

The conclusions about localization and urbanization economies in the preceding sub section can be interpreted as follows. Suppose that each firm in industry i has a random choice preference function on which the individual firm bases its location decision. As a first step we assume that all firms k in industry i have equal size, which means that the number of firms in an industry also provides information about the number of persons employed. The preference function is assumed to have the form $U_{iR}^k = -V_{iR}^k + \varepsilon_{iR}^k$, where the last term is an extreme-value distributed random term. Such a function implies that firms are cost minimizers. With these assumptions firm k in industry i will select a location in R with the probability P_{iR}, specified as follows (e.g. Ben-Akiva and Lerman 1985):

$$P_{iR}^k = \exp\{-V_{iR}^k\} / \sum_R \exp\{-V_{iR}^k\} \tag{7.7}$$

The decision criterion behind Eq. (7.7) gives priority to locations that offer low production costs options. The random term can reflect relevant individual characteristics of each firm that are not observable. The formulation makes it possible to draw the following conclusion:

Remark 1: Let Eq. (7.7) represent the outcome of cost assessments of individual firms. One should then expect to find firms (and industries) located also in places with less favourable conditions, but with a lower frequency than in those places which have cost advantages. Observing the number of firms in industry i or the size of the industry in a region will, with this formulation, reveal localization economies better than what is revealed by comparing unit cost levels or productivity levels of regions.

One may understand the conclusion in the following way. For any particular location, there may be a firm with an unobservable firm-specific (or region-specific) asset that makes ε_{iR}^k large and explains that $U_{iR}^k = -V_{iR}^k + \varepsilon_{iR}^k$ becomes large. However, such cases will be rare, and will occur with a low probability. But they can be observed.

Consider now how Eq. (7.7) can be used. With a given population of firms in industry i, one can multiply the number of firms by the probability in Eq. (7.7) to express the expected number of firms in each region. If the average firm size (number of employees) is approximately the same in each region, one may also calculate the expected number of persons employed in each industry and region. Our major concern is how the size of an industry in region R, A_{iR} depends on the size of the A-sector, A_R, and the size of the rest of the economy, B_R, in region R. In the empirical part of the chapter all these three variables will be measured in terms of employment figures.

Let us assume that a share coefficient expresses the expected share, given the size of A_R, such that $\alpha_{iR} = \alpha_i(A_R)$ and $d\alpha_i / dA_R > 0$ as long as $\alpha_{iR} < 1$. With this assumption, we can use Eq. (7.7) to derive

$$dP_{iR} / dA_R = P_{iR}(1 - P_{iR})\alpha_{Rr}b_{Ai}(\hat{p}_{AR} - p_{AR})d\alpha_i / dA_R > 0 \qquad (7.8)$$

Where the inequality holds as long as $\hat{p}_{AR} > p_{AR}$. Equation (7.8) implies (i) that P_{iR} is monotonically increasing in A_R, and (ii) that this increase is large for small P_{iR} and then becomes smaller as P_{iR} becomes closer to unity. Hence, the value of P_{iR} follows an S-shaped curve as described by Fig. 7.3.

In summary, pecuniary input-side localization economies imply that industry i will increase in size as A_R gets larger. The same conclusion can be replicated for input-side urbanization economies, such that industry i will increase in size as B_R gets larger. This type of conclusions could form the basis for the regression analyses that are carried out in Sects. 7.3 and 7.4. However, the outline in this subsection remains unrealistic, because it neglects the effect of accessibility to customers and hence the proximity to demand.

7.2.4 Proximity to Customers

In this subsection the cost expression in Eq. (7.6) is taken as given. In this way the demand side can be emphasized in an analysis of how the proximity to customers can influence the sales volume of firms in each ICT industry. As sales and output expand, individual firms can exploit internal scale economies and they can benefit from external economies of scale. The focus on the demand side thus puts output-based localization economies in the forefront. Before the pertinent model formulations are specified in any detail one may immediately observe that according to the assumptions underpinning Eq. (7.1), an individual ICT industry is a customer to firms the A-sector. The importance of their presence in region R could then be explained by an assumption that their output is distance sensitive. Hence, their sales to industry i requires proximity.

To be more specific, suppose that industry i has a distance-sensitive output. In that case, the industry benefits from having a large intra-regional demand for its output. In the model outlined here, the regional demand is related to the size of the A-sector and the B-sector in the region. The first demand component consists of A-sector firms in a region that demand inputs from a particular A-sector industry in the same region. The second component reflects indirectly how the rest of the regional economy generates a demand for the output from industry i. The third demand component represents extra-regional demand. For outputs (products) that are not distance sensitive, extra-regional customers will have the major influence on demand, and this dominance will be greater, the smaller the region is.

In order to distinguish between the A-sector's supply capacity in region R, A_R, and the demand that is generated from the same sector and region, the latter is represented by the variable $\tilde{A}_R$. Analogously, the demand from the B-sector in region R is denoted by $\tilde{B}_R$. However, implicitly it is assumed that $\tilde{A}_R$ is proportional to A_R, and that $\tilde{B}_R$ is proportional to B_R.

The model outlined in this sub section is intended to reflect output-based localization economies. The output price of a firm in industry i and region R is denoted by p_{iR}. This price is a mill price and delivery costs are assumed to be smaller inside than outside the region. According to the preceding discussion, each industry has two customer groups in the regional market, A-sector and B-sector customers. Total demand in the A-sector is denoted by $\tilde{A}_R$ and the demand for industry i's output is given by $f_{iA}\tilde{A}_R$, where f_{iA} is a demand coefficient for industry i. Total demand in the rest of the economy is denoted by $\tilde{B}_R$ and this generates the demand $f_{iB}\tilde{B}_R$ for industry i's output, where f_{iB} is a demand coefficient of industry i. With a given price level p_{iR}, industry i will capture the share m_{iAR} of the demand $f_{iA}\tilde{A}_R$ and the share m_{iBR} of the demand $f_{iB}\tilde{B}_R$. Total demand for the output from industry i in region R, D_{iR}, can then be specified as follows:

$$D_{iR} = m_{iAR} f_{iA} \tilde{A}_R + m_{iBR} f_{iB} \tilde{B}_R + M_{iR} \qquad (7.9)$$

Where the parameters and variables in Eq. (7.9) are defined in Table 7.3.

Table 7.3. Components of the demand expression for industry i in Eq. (7.9)

f_{iA}	Share of the demand $\tilde{A}_R$ that is directed to industry i's output
f_{iB}	Share of the demand B_R that is directed to industry i's output
m_{iAR}	Share of the market $f_{iA}\tilde{A}_R$ acquired by industry i suppliers in region R

Table 7.3. (cont.)

m_{iBR}	Share of the market f_{iB} B_R acquired by industry i suppliers in region R
M_{iR}	Extra-regional demand for the output from industry i in region R

The coefficients f_{iA} and f_{iB} are assumed to be given parameters. However, the market share variables m_{iAR} and m_{iBR} are assumed to depend on the price level that firms in industry i of region R can offer. In principle, a similar analysis can be carried out for the extra-regional demand variable M_{iR}. However, that is beyond the scope of this chapter.

Consider now the cost component $W_{iR}^k(x_{iR}^k, x_{iR})$ in Eq. (7.6). This component reflects the presence of scale economies. With the help of the demand expression in Eq. (7.9), the cost component can be reformulated as follows: $W_{iR}^k(x_{iR}^k, x_{iR}) = W_{iR}^k(D_{iR})$. Scale economies are then active if $dW_{iR}^k / dD_{iR} < 0$. As a consequence, the cost per unit output in Eq. (7.6) can be reformulated as follows:

$$V_{iR}^k = v_{iR}^k + W_{iR}^k(D_{iR}) \tag{7.10}$$

Where $v_{iR}^k = C_{iAR}^k + C_{iBR}^k$. With the structure introduced it is now possible to express the profit per unit out for a firm k in region R and industry i:

$$\pi_{iR}^k = p_{iR} - v_{iR}^k - W_{iR}^k(D_{iR}) \tag{7.11}$$

This profit expression should be interpreted as the systematic part of random-choice profit function. In this context the following remark can be made with regard to small regions with a limited demand:

Remark 2: Suppose that D_{iR} is small. That may imply that W_{iR}^k is large and hence π_{iR}^k will be strongly negative. This suggests that the probability of location in region R will be very small. Thus, for a distance-sensitive product i with a demand-sensitive W_{iR}^k-function (e.g. internal scale economies) one may conjecture that product i is located with a low frequency in small regions.

What are the relevant assumptions with regard to the profit formula in (7.11)? From the above subsections 7.2.2 and 7.2.3, we have that

$$\partial v_{iR}^k / \partial A_R < 0 \text{ when input-side localizations economies apply} \tag{7.12a}$$

$$\partial v_{iR}^k / \partial B_R < 0 \text{ when input-side urbanization economies apply} \tag{7.12b}$$

$$\partial W_{iR}^k / \partial \tilde{A}_R < 0 \text{ when output-side localization economies apply} \tag{7.12c}$$

$\partial W_{iR}^{k} / \partial \widetilde{B}_{R} < 0$ when output-side urbanization economies apply $\qquad$ (7.12d)

Conditions in Eqs. (7.12a) and (7.12b) can be assumed to hold when inputs from the A-sector and the B-sector, respectively, are distance sensitive. In that case the additional assumptions are (i) that $d\alpha_i / dA_R > 0$ as $\alpha_R < 1$, and (ii) that $d\beta_i / dB_R > 0$ as $\beta_{iR} < 1$, as described in Tables 7.1 and 7.2. The two conditions in Eqs. (7.12c) and (7.11d) follow from the fact that in Eq. (7.9) D_{iR} $= m_{iAR} f_{iA} \hat{A}_R + m_{iBR} f_{iB} B_R + M_{iR}$. First, it is obvious that demand gets larger as A_R and B_R gets larger. Second, this observation brings us to the issue of the market share variables, m_{iAR} and m_{iBR}. Consider that the output price p_{iR} reduces as $V_{iR}^{k} = v_{iR}^{k} + W_{iR}^{k}(D_{iR})$ falls. As long as this adjustment mechanism is active, an ongoing increase in A_R and B_R will make the market-share variables grow. Positive scale economies will then in a cumulative way improve the profit outcome, as expressed in Eq. (7.11).

Remark 3: Suppose that A_R and $\widetilde{A}_R$ tend to be large when B_R and $\widetilde{B}_R$ are large, i.e., when a region is large. Then it will be difficult to empirically distinguish the effects in Eqs. (7.12a) - (7.12d).

7.2.5 Proximity to Suppliers and Customers in a Random-Choice Setting

The model exercise in Sects. 7.2.2 and 7.2.3 shows how the location of firms in individual ICT industries can be derived from cost minimization behaviour. Now we can combine this analysis with the observations in Sect. 7.2.4 and determine the compound effect of proximity to (i) input suppliers and (ii) output customers. This composite analysis is described in Fig. 7.2.

Figure 7.2 summarizes the preceding analysis in section 7.2.2 – 7.2.4. The figure describes two avenues for spatial clustering. Along the first line, the size of the A-sector generates costs advantages, as illustrated by the upper left box in the diagram. However, the size of the A-sector can also provide demand advantages. When these two phenomena are in force, the profit level of the individual firm will be positively affected. Both these endogenous effects can be classified as cluster economies.

Along the second avenue, the size of the B-sector is assumed to bring about both cost and demand advantages, again with positive consequences for the profit level and the size of profits. What shall we think about firms in a sector that cluster together due to urbanization economies? This is agglomeration economies but not cluster economies. However, one of the basic questions that this chapter attempts to examine empirically is whether one can distinguish localization from urbanization economies. The basic hypothesis is that localization economies and the associated cluster relations have a special importance when explaining the spatial concentration of ICT industries.

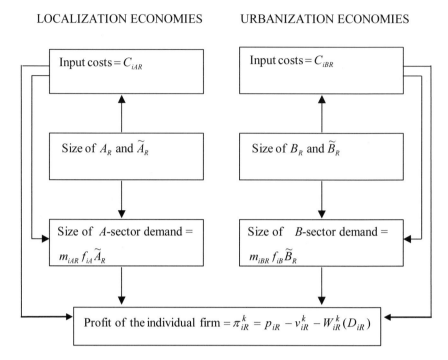

Fig.7.2. Mechanisms of localization and urbanization economies

Our next task is to formulate a profit function that reflects a random choice situation of firms in the various A-industries. The starting point is the profit expression in Eq. (7.11). This is considered as the systematic part of a random choice function, $\Pi_{iR}^k = \pi_{iR}^k + \varepsilon_{iR}^k$, where the last term is assumed to be extreme-value distributed. In this way Eq. (7.13) obtains:

$$\Pi_{iR}^k = p_{iR} - v_i^k - W_{iR}(D_{iR}) + \varepsilon_{iR}^k = \pi_{iR}^k + \varepsilon_{iR}^k \qquad (7.13)$$

Assume first that internal scale economies imply that firms in the same industry have the same size. Then the number of location opportunities of each region will be proportional to the size of D_{iR}. Adding the previous assumption about the error term implies that one can express the probability of finding firm k in industry i located in region R as follows:

$$P_{iR}^k = D_{iR} \exp\{\pi_{iR}^k\} / \sum_R D_{iR} \exp\{\pi_{iR}^k\} \qquad (7.14)$$

Equation (7.14) has the same theoretical background as Eq. (7.7). It applies if we make the assumption that for each industry there N_i firms of approximately equal size to be located across the existing regions. The probability expression in Eq. (7.14) is affected by localization economies in two ways. The first operates via A_R and reduces costs of A-inputs. The second operates via A_R and increases demand for the industry i's output. In order to find out how the value of P_{iR}^k behave as A_R varies, one can examine the derivative in Eq.(7.15).

$$\partial P_{iR}^k / \partial A_R = -P_{ir}^k (1 - P_{ir}^k)[\partial v_{iR}^k / \partial A_R + \partial W_{iR}^k / \partial A_R] > 0 \qquad (7.15)$$

The expression in Eq. (7.15) has similar properties as the one in Eq. (7.8). It is positive, because $\partial v_{iR}^k / \partial A_R = -\alpha_{iR} b_{iA}(\hat{p}_{AR} - p_{AR})\partial \alpha_i / \partial A_R < 0$ and $\partial W_{iR}^k / \partial A_R = [\partial W_{iR}^k / \partial D_{iR}][\partial D_{iR} / \partial A_R] < 0$. Given these observations, we can conclude that P_{iR}^k is an S-shaped function of A_R, as long as our assumptions about cluster economies hold true. This is described in Fig. 7.3.

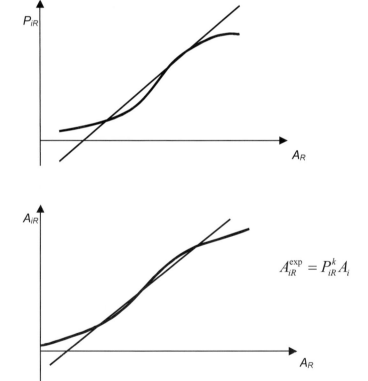

Fig.7.3. A linear representation of an S-shaped curve

According to Eqs.(7.8) and (7.15) P_{iR}^k is logistic (S-shaped) function of the size of A-sector in region R. This observation could be used to formulate a logistic regression as a means to examine empirically the relation between the location pattern of each ICT industry and the size of the entire ICT sector. However, this would require more observations than is available and therefore another approach will be undertaken. Moreover, it should be observed that the result in Eq. (7.15) can be replicated for the case when urbanization economies applies, again implying an S-shaped form. In order to transform the location probability to location patterns, the following assumption is used:

There are N_i firms in industry i in Sweden as a whole, and the firms   (7.16)

have the same size, measured in terms of numbers of persons
employed.

Let us now examine Eq. (7.14) further. Suppose that the effects on profits of localization and urbanization economies are fairly weak. Then the formula tells us that the expected location is close to proportional to the size of demand share, $D_{iR} / \sum_R D_{iR}$, of each region R. If in addition the demand is primarily generated from inside the region, location will roughly proportional to the size of each region. On the other hand, one can also draw the following conclusion:

Remark 4: Suppose that π_{iR} is strongly negative for small values of A_R and/or B_R and remains invariant and non-negative as A_R and/or B_R increase beyond a certain level. Then one should expect a very small location probability for regions below a certain level. Moreover, for regions above a certain size the location probability would become almost proportional to the size of the region.

To examine the conjecture in Remark 4 two investigations will be made. One task is to examine to what extent location is infrequent in small regions. The second task is to examine if location of each industry, A_{iR} is proportional to either A_R or B_R. In Sect. 7.2.3 A_{iR} is measured as the number of persons employed in industry i, and region R. In Sect. 7.2.4 A_{iR} is represented by the number of establishments in industry i, and region R. If the assumption in Eq. (7.16) is valid, the results in the two sections should be compatible.

Consider the approach of Sect. 7.2.3, and let A_{iR} be measured by the number of persons employed in sector i in region R, and let A_i denote the number of persons employed in the industry in the whole of Sweden. Then the assumptions in Eq. (7.16) imply that the expected value of A_{iR}, $A_{iR}^{\exp}$, satisfies $A_{iR}^{\exp} = P_{iR}^k A_i$, where A_i / N_i is the average size of a firm in industry i. Based on this the following regression equation is suggested:

$$A_{iR} = \alpha_0 + \alpha_1 A_R \qquad (7.17)$$

If the true relation is S-shaped and remains almost flat for small values of A_R, then we might expect that $\alpha_0 < 0$ as described in Fig. 7.3. In the following sections, this observation will be used as an assessment criterion. As a regression result, a negative value of the intercept, α_0, indicates that a scale effect is present.

7.3 Urbanization Economies and ICT Clustering

This section starts by asking to what extent the entire ICT sector is influenced by urbanization economies. The next question is about the number of ICT industries in each region. Does this diversity indicator depend on the size of the region? In a following step, a linear regression is used to examine how the size of each industry in a region depends on (i) the size of the region and (ii) the size of the ICT sector in the region. If there are strong signs of urbanization economies, localization economies may still be present but will obviously play a less significant role. In response to this, an attempt is made to find additional signs of localization economies, with a focus on location selectivity.

The empirical analyses examine individual industries and the four groups (i) manufacturing, (ii) wholesale, (iii) network services, and (iv) other services. The reader should observe that the statistical analysis uses the size of the entire economy as explanatory variable instead of the size of the B-sector. Since the ICT sector is such a small part in each region's economy, this deviation from the theoretical formulation has no significant consequences for the interpretation of the results. Throughout Sect. 7.3 as well as Sect. 7.4, the empirical observations are collected from establishment statistics produced by SCB (Statistics Sweden).

7.3.1 Urbanization Economies and the Location of the ICT Sector

Suppose that we find that many ICT industries seem to be attracted by the size of the ICT sector as a whole. Then this may be a result of urbanization economies to the extent that the ICT sector itself is affected in its location by urbanization economies. With this in mind this sub section starts by matching the size of the ICT sector in each region, A_R , against the size of the entire economy in the same region, L_R . In this analysis, the variable A_R signifies the number of persons employed in the ICT sector in region R, and L_R signifies the number of persons employed in the entire economy in region R. There are 81 regions, so-called LA-regions. This small number of observation units has motivated the use of a linear regression of the following kind:

$$A_R = \beta_0 + \beta_1 L_R + \varepsilon_R \qquad (7.18)$$

Where the error term ε_R is assumed to be normally distributed with zero mean. The regression result is presented in Table 7.4 and shows that there is a strong correlation (R^2-value) between the size of the ICT sector and the size of the economy in each region.

Table 7.4. The size of the A-sector as a function of the size of the regional economy, 1999

	β_0 (Intercept)	β_1 (Urbanization)	R^2 -adjusted
Region	−1472.15 (−5.22)	0.14 (42.12)	0.96

t-values in parentheses. 81 observations for each equation.

What are the conclusions from Table 7.4? The first observation is that there is a very strong correlation between the size of the ICT sector and the size of the economy. The second observation is that negative intercept. In Sect. 7.2 it was established in Eqs. (7.8) and (7.15) that our theoretical model predicts an S-shaped relation between A_{iR} and A_R. With similar arguments one may derive that (in the case of urbanization economies) there should be an S-shaped relation between A_R and L_R. In view of this, the negative intercept implies that the initial phase of the S-curve is very flat, which can be interpreted as an indication of very small location probabilities for small regions.

The result in Table 7.4 means that the location probability is small in small regions. This result should also imply that the location probability of any individual ICT industry is also small. As a consequence, the number of different industries should be size dependent in a similar way. This conclusion is illustrated in Table 7.5, where industry diversity is illustrated for three metropolitan, 20 medium-sized and 58 small regions. Medium-sized regions have more than 100 000 inhabitants and less than 500 000. Small regions have less than 100 000 and half of them have less than 30 000 inhabitants. Table 7.5 shows a similar urbanization effect as indicated by the regression in table 7.4.

Table 7.5. Information and communication technology (ICT) industries' diversity in three size classes of regions, in percentage, 1999

Number of indus-tries (diversity)	Metropolitan regions, percent	Medium-sized regions, percent	Small regions, percent
2 – 14	0	0	76
15 – 24	0	65	24
More than 25	100	35	0
Sum	100	100	100

7.3.2 Location of ICT Industries and Urbanization Economies

Section 7.3.1 indicates that urbanization economies have a clear influence on the size of a region's ICT sector. We may now examine the same relation for each individual ICT industry. Can the employment industry i, A_{iR}, be described as linear function of the total employment in the region, L_R? To investigate this, the following equation has been estimated for each of the 27 ICT industries:

$$A_{iR} = \beta_i + \gamma_i L_R + \varepsilon_{iR} \qquad (7.19)$$

Also for Eq. (7.19) one can formulate the hypothesis that each intercept, β_i, is negative as an indication of very low location probabilities for small regions. The hypothesis is rejected for industry i if the parameter β_i is not significantly different from zero and negative. At the same time, the results in Table 7.5 have to be recognized. They imply that many industries will be absent in a large set of regions. This in turn implies that Eq. (7.19) may be biased for several industries due to lack of both normality and homoskedasticity. Hence, t-values and R^2-values should be interpreted with this in mind.

In the assessment of the regression results, one group of industries is classified as not influenced by urbanization economies. Such industries satisfy a non-significant γ-value in combination with a low R^2. The assessment is based on the regression results in Table 7.6.

Table 7.6. Regressions according to Eq. (7.19), reflecting urbanization economies, 1999

Industry	β (t-value)	$\gamma\ 10^{-3}$ (t-value)	R^2-adjusted	Number of regions hosting the industry
Manufacturing				
30010	60.7 (2.15)	0.04 (0.19)	0.00	22
30020	−0.4 (−0.02)	1.40 (6.72)	0.48	50
31300	131.1 (3.66)	0.10 (0.34)	0.00	35
32100	−33.0 (−1.21)	3.80 (13.90)	0.88	56
32200	−150.4 (−0.50)	19.00 (8.54)	0.72	30
32300	−8.4 (−0.20)	2.80 (8.17)	0.65	38
33200	27.8 (0.44)	5.10 (8.55)	0.59	52
33300	24.9 (1.01)	0.46 (2.06)	0.09	45
Wholesale				
51431	−16.4 (−2.93)	1.00 (19.90)	0.90	47
51432	−31.3 (−4.77)	1.40 (25.07)	0.94	42
51433	−40.4 (−3.56)	1.10 (14.76)	0.91	23
51434	−21.2 (−1.43)	3.40 (22.50)	0.90	58
51640	−341.0 (−5.43)	19.00 (27.58)	0.92	68
51651	−59.9 (−5.28)	2.30 (24.04)	0.94	39
51653	−129.3 (−4.80)	6.50 (23.29)	0.90	61
51659	−55.6 (−5.06)	8.70 (69.53)	0.99	73
Network services				
64201	−99.0 (−3.98)	12.00 (40.65)	0.95	81
64202	−9.1 (−2.26)	6.00 (16.70)	0.87	45
64203	−6.2 (−3.22)	3.00 (26.45)	0.98	18
Other services				
71330	−10.2 (−2.57)	0.40 (12.94)	0.88	24
72100	−9.3 (−0.31)	1.80 (6.00)	0.41	54
72201	−486.6 (−5.13)	36.00 (32.96)	0.93	81
72202	−91.9 (−5.38)	7.40 (40.64)	0.96	64
72300	−67.0 (−3.30)	5.00 (24.95)	0.92	56
72400	−23.2 (−2.15)	1.20 (17.17)	0.94	21
72500	−3.4 (−0.61)	1.10 (20.57)	0.90	50
72600	−10.5 (−3.65)	0.60 (24.20)	0.94	42

t-values in parentheses. The number of observations for each sector is 81 (LA-regions).

Industries that are possibly influenced by urbanization economies should have (i) a positive and significant parameter γ, (ii) a high R^2-value, and (iii) the industry should be present in most of the regions.

Our first observation is that the intercept is negative for all industries outside the manufacturing sector. With two exceptions, the intercept is also significantly different from zero. For all manufacturing industries, the intercept has either a low t-value or a positive sign or both. For many of the estimated equations, normality is not fully satisfied and there are signs of heteroskedasticity. Such deficiencies are especially serious for the industries 30010, 31300, 33300, and 64202.

Applying the introduced criteria, the following industries do not reveal urbanization economies:

30010 = Manufacture of office machinery
31300 = Manufacture of insulated wire and cable
33300 = Manufacture of instruments for control of industrial processes
72100 = Hardware consultancy

In the list above of excluded industries, one may observe that these industries, with one exception, are only present in a minority of regions. Hence, they reveal location selectivity. The same conclusions can be made for a second set of industries. These are

32200 = Manufacturing of TV and radio transmitters, and telephony apparatus
32300 = Manufacturing of TV and radio receivers, and sound apparatus
51432 = Wholesale of TV and radio receivers
51651 = Wholesale of measurement and precision instruments
64203 = Cable TV
71330 = Renting of office equipment including computers
72500 = Maintenance and repair of office equipment including computers

The above set of industries may indeed be influenced by urbanization economies. For the wholesale and service industries the demand intensity may be so low that the demand will be large enough only in the largest urban regions. With regard to the two manufacturing industries, they both display clear internal scale economies by having a large average size of their establishments.

For the remaining 16 industries, the observations do not allow us to reject the hypothesis of urbanization economies.

7.3.3 Information and Communication Technology (ICT) Industries and Localization Economies

Having investigated the presence of urbanization economies, the next step is to examine how the location of each industry in the ICT sector is influenced by the location of the entire ICT sector in each region. Through this examination, one may discuss to what extent our empirical observations indicate the existence of a compound ICT cluster.

In the assessment of localization economies, we are able to draw special con-clusions about cluster phenomena. For each industry, we examine to what extent A_{iR} is correlated with A_R in regression equations. Both these variables are measured in terms of persons employed in each region. If a large share of the in-dustries in the A-sector displays this kind of correlation, one may conjecture that they mutually support or influence each other. This phenomenon could then be in-terpreted as the existence of an ICT cluster.

In Sect.7.3.2 the existence of urbanization economies is assessed through re-gression technique. The reason for examining both localization and urbanization economies is that these two phenomena easily can be confused with each other. The first task is to investigate how well A_{iR} can be described as a linear function of A_R. This is accomplished by estimating the Eq. (7.20) for each of the 27 ICT industries.

$$A_{iR} = \alpha_i + \sigma_i A_R + \varepsilon_{iR} \qquad (7.20)$$

Where ε_{iR} is a random error term, for which the same problems appear as in Eq. (7.19). Comparing Eqs. (7.20) with (7.19) it is obvious that A_R is much smaller than L_R. Hence, we can conjecture that α_i is larger than β_i for all industries. The regression results are presented in Table 7A.2 and show that this conjecture holds universally. In fact α_i is negative only for ten industries. In the wholesale industries, the α -parameter is significant and negative in five out of eight cases. As already observed, this reflects that the values of the A_R -variable vary over a much smaller range than the values of L_R -variable. As a consequence, the σ_i - value in Eq. (7.20) is much larger than the γ_i -value in Eq. (7.19).

In general, the results in Table 7A.2 are quite similar to those in Table 7.6, which is natural in view of the strong correlation between A_R and L_R that is shown in Table 7.4. However, one may investigate the seven industries for which strong location selectivity was observed (32200, 32300, .51432, 51651, 64203, 71330 and 72500). In all these cases the localization equation Eq. (7.3) generates clearly higher t-values and higher R^2 –values. Remembering previous reservations about these statistics, one may still interpret this as a weak sign of the presence of localization economies.

7.3.4 Cluster Economies and Location Selectivity

Location selectivity may be considered as a clear sign of a cluster phenomenon. However, the selectivity may also be related to the size of a regional economy, and then it only reflects a scale effect, such that an industry has a very low prob-ability of being located in a region that is not large.

The models in the background literature that are used as a reference in this chapter are not very explicit about any specific level of aggregation for the analy-sis of cluster economies. Certain models and theoretical frameworks may be interpreted in a more narrow sense than the current chapter has done. One such option is that certain ICT industries exist only in a few places, because the cluster phenomenon takes place with reference to each specific ICT industry itself. In a strict sense, this idea can be spelled out as the following statement: A_{iR} is large in a region whenever it exists in the region.

To shed some light on this intra-industry phenomenon one may select those industries that are not present at all in a majority of regions. Hence, we shall investigate industries that are not present in 62 percent or more of all regions. This means that our investigation concerns industries that are hosted by 30 regions or less. This amounts to the following six industries:

30010: Office machinery, 22 regions
32200: TV and radio transmitters, telephony/telegraphy apparatus, 30 regions
51433: Wholesale of phonograms and video cassettes, 23 regions
64203: Cable TV services, 18 regions
71330: Renting of office machinery and equipment, incl. computers, 24 regions
72400: Data base activities, 21 regions.

The location selectivity of these industries may reflect intra-industry clustering. It may also reflect strong internal scale economies combined with distance-sensitive output, which implies that the industries primarily can be found in the largest regions. In view of this, the following hypothesis is examined: These industries are concentrated in a very small number of regions, with only negligible activities in the remaining regions.

To carry out the described analysis, consider the following variables:

L_i = Number of persons employed in ICT industry i in the country as a whole.
L^1_i = Number of persons employed in ICT industry i in the region with the largest employment.
L^4_i = Number of persons employed in ICT industry i in the four regions that have the largest employment.

Hence, to obtain L^4_i, all regions are ranked in descending order according to the size of sector i, and then one adds the employment in the first four regions.

Table 7.7 presents a set of measures describing the concentration of each industry. It is evident from the table that all industries studied are characterized by a strong spatial concentration. However, these measures do not allow us to distinguish between internal and external scale economies. Both these return-to-scale phenomena are compatible with the observed pattern. At the same time the result in the table contradicts the linear regression form applied in Eqs. (7.19) and (7.20).

The second column in table 7.7 shows the employment share in the region with the largest industry concentration. The third shows the same share for the four regions that have the largest concentration. The forth column provides information about how important the three metropolitan regions Stockholm, Göteborg and Malmö are as places of location.

Our first observation is that the wholesale and service industries in Table 7.7 display stronger concentration than do the two manufacturing industries. We can also see that the metropolitan regions are stronger attractors for the non-manufacturing industries.

Table 7.7. Concentration measures of possible intra-industry localization economies, 1999

Industry	L_i^1 / L_i	L_i^4 / L_i	Metropolitan share,	Size of L_i
	percent	percent	percent	
30010	31.3	74.2	35.8	1394
Office machinery				
32200	44.4	77.3	50.3	31653
TV and radio transmitters, line				
telephony/telegraph apparatus				
51433	70.8	86.7	84.6	1046
Wholesale of phonograms and				
videocassettes				
64203	55.8	85.3	76.7	346
Cable TV services				
71330	63.7	87.3	82.7	369
Renting of office machinery and				
equipment, including computers				
72400	55.2	87.0	81.3	1375
Data base activities				

Moreover, the column L_i^1 / L_i refers to the Stockholm region with the exception of 30010 (office machinery), which is not influenced by urbanization economies.

How can the result in Table 7.7 be interpreted? Basically, it says that four industries with a strong location selectivity are clustered in the largest urban regions, and especially in Stockholm (the largest region). The implicit message is that also in this case we are not able to distinguish between clustering due to localization and urbanization economies. However, this observation is indeed a lesson. The observations in the table also indicate that a complete study should include the same type of investigation for all industries, including those for which location selectivity is not obvious.

7.4 Clustering of Establishments

In this section, localization economies of ICT industries are examined from another perspective. First, do the location measures applied in the previous section indicate the location of many establishments or do they reflect the location of few and large establishments? Second, the formulations of location probabilities are based on the assumption that each industry consists of many firms that have approximately the same size. Does this assumption have any empirical support?

7.4.1 Manufacturing ICT Industries

How many establishments can we find in the manufacturing ICT industries? This is the first question to be examined. The second task is to transform the localization regressions in Sect. 7.3 in such a way that the number of establishments in an industry is the dependent variable instead of the number of persons employed. To examine these two related issues the following notations are introduced for this analysis:

A_{iR} = The number of establishments in industry i, and region R.

S_{iR} = The number of persons employed in industry i, and region R.

A_R = The number establishments in the ICT sector, and region R.

S_R = The number of persons employed in the ICT sector, and region R.

In six of the manufacturing industries the number establishments is fairly large. Moreover, the average size of an establishment can be considered as quite large in one case only (32200). This industry also has a large number of establishments.

The clustering of establishments is examined with the help of the following two regression equations:

$$A_{iR} = a_i + b_i (S_R - S_{iR}) + \varepsilon_{iR} \qquad (7.21)$$

$$A_{iR} = d_i + e_i (A_R - A_{iR}) + \varepsilon_{iR} \qquad (7.22)$$

Equation (7.21) relates the number of establishments in industry i to the employment in the ICT sector, excluding industry i itself. Equation (7.22) relates the same variable to the number of establishments in the ICT sector. These two regression equations should be compared with Eq.(7.20). Such a comparison shows that both Eqs. (7.21) and (7.22) generate better t-values and higher R^2-values than the previous estimation of Eq. (7.20) as presented in Table 7A.2. Thus, with the new equations we obtain similar results as in Sect. 7.3. This means that a concentration of employment in a region usually also implies a cluster of several establishments. Just as in Sect. 7.3, normality and homoskedasticity are not satisfied fully for Eqs. (7.21) and (7.22).

7.4.2 Wholesale, Network Services, and Other Services

The analysis in Sect. 7.4.1 can be repeated for the three categories of ICT services, which are (i) wholesale, (ii) network services, and (iii) other services. For these industries, the number of establishments is indeed large for all industries except 64202, 64203, and 71330. Moreover, the average establishment size tends to be very small, often with less than ten employees per establishments, never above 20.

This implies that the probability formulations in Sect. 7.2 are compatible with the existing industrial structure.

Equations (7.21) and (7.22) are applied to the 19 service sectors. Both sets of regressions yield similar results, and the estimated parameters in Eq. (7.21) are presented in Table 7.8. These results should be compared with the results in Table 7A.2. A major result is that the number of persons employed in the ICT sector predicts both the employment in individual industries and the number of establishments in the same industry.

Table 7.8. Estimation results for Eq. (7.21)

Industry	a_i (t-value)	$b_i\ 10^{-3}$ (t-value)	R^2
Wholesale			
51431	−0.37 (−1.6)	0.95 (36.1)	0.94
51432	−0.77 (−3.6)	1.12 (43.9)	0.96
51433	−1.14 (−5.5)	0.80 (36.6)	0.93
51434	−0.89 (−3.6)	2.75 (92.7)	0.99
51640	−11.96 (−6.6)	12.08 (55.6)	0.97
51651	−3.28 (−7.1)	2.62 (47.4)	0.97
51653	−7.63 (−6.3)	5.71 (39.7)	0.95
5659	−1.98 (−1.2)	11.33 (55.2)	0.97
Network services			
64201	8.01 (8.3)	3.50 (30.2)	0.92
64202	0.41 (5.4)	0.13 (14.7)	0.73
64203	0.09 (1.3)	0.09 (10.0)	0.55
Other services			
71330	−0.44 (−3.6)	0.39 (26.9)	0.90
72100	−1.90 (5.0)	2.27 (50.3)	0.97
72201	−60.67 (−5.6)	47.31 (35.8)	0.94
72202	−4.28 (−5.8)	5.53 (63.2)	0.98
72300	−2.32 (−4.3)	2.46 (37.7)	0.95
72400	−0.73 (−6.2)	0.55 (39.3)	0.95
72500	0.99 (3.7)	0.99 (31.0)	0.92
72600	−1.13 (−5.9)	0.97 (42.4)	0.96

t-values in parentheses. These values as well as the R^2-values should be interpreted with some caution.

The two network industries 64202 and 64203 have both a rather limited number of establishments, and this may also be reflected in the lower R^2-value for these two industries. The overall conclusion from Table 7.8 is that the signs of industry concentration or clustering detected in Section 7.3 are primarily clustering of establishments and not location of large single-establishments.

7.5 Conclusions

The introduction of this chapter makes a reference to Gordon and McCann (2000). They find three basic notions of clustering. These are the model of pure agglomeration, the model emphasizing delivery links between firms, and the social network model. The model emphasizing delivery links (industrial-complex model) has inspired researchers to use information from input-output tables as a means to identify industries, which constitute possible cluster groups. The idea is that cluster effects occur between industries that form a network with strong inter-industry links. This chapter suggests an alternative approach, according to which one should search for industries that mutually exhibit a strong tendency of being co-located. This is suggested as an initial step to identify a group of industries, which are cluster candidates. Having found this group, further analysis of the cluster interdependence between these industries can be examined. Such further analyses could include input-output information as wells as in formation about size distribution and number of firms.

The approach described above is applied to the ICT sector. Industries in this sector are assumed to influence each other in a positive way. For this to be true, firms in these industries must show a high tendency of localization. This is tested by estimating how each individual ICT industry's probability of being located in a region depends on the size of the entire ICT sector in the same region. Using this method, it was possible to identify a large set of ICT industries with signs of mutual attraction.

The outcome of the regressions is that the location of individual ICT industries is far from random in Sweden for the year 1999. At the same time, the chapter shows that the location of the ICT sector as a whole is strongly influenced by urbanization economies. Hence, the question arises: can one distinguish the effects of localization economies from the effects of urbanization economies. The answer in the chapter is that such a distinction is possible only to a limited extent. Thus, the analysis does not reject the hypothesis that cluster-like localization economies are present. At the same time, neither does the analysis reject the hypothesis that the localization effects are reflections of urbanization effects. A preliminary conjecture from the analysis is that input externalities (localization economies) are combined with output, customer-related, externalities (urbanization economies). Analyses that elaborate similar issues are also carried out in Chaps. 8, 9, and 10.

A clear drawback in the analyses that have been carried out is that linear regression is not really appropriate. A remedy would be to instead use logit and probit models. These could also help to determine scale or threshold phenomena. Such models would also be more suitable to examine the S-shaped location probability-pattern that is suggested in the theory part of the chapter.

The empirical analysis of the chapter can be extended in several ways. A first option is of course to carry out a dynamic analysis that can show how the location of ICT industries over time is influenced by the size of the ICT sector. Such an analysis can show to what extent the size of the ICT sector functions as a location attractor. A second option is to study the identified cluster in more detail so that external economies of scale are separated from internal scale economies. In this case, one may count the number of firms in each industry and examine their size distribution Moreover, the composition of the ICT sector in each region can be characterized in more detail. Suppose that the composition is not important. Then one may conjecture that a large ICT sector generates a favourable labour market for ICT industries in general. If, on the other hand, the composition has importance, then this provides an incentive to look for finer groups of cluster.

Acknowledgements. The present study is part of the research accomplished in the MUTEIS (Macroeconomic and Urban Trends in Europe's Information Society) project that has received funding from the European Union

References

Baptista R (1998) Clusters, innovation, and growth: a survey of the literature. In: Swann GMP, Prevezer M, Sout D (eds) The dynamics of industrial clustering. Oxford University Press, Oxford, pp 12-51

Ben-Akiva M, Lerman SR (1985) Discrete choice analysis. MIT Press, Cambridge, MA

Gordon RJ (2000) Does the 'new economy' measure up to the great innovations of the past? Journal of Economic Perspectives 14: 49–74

Gordon IR, McCann P (2000) Industrial clusters: complexes, agglomeration and/or social networks? Urban Studies 37: 513–532

Hoover EM (1948) The location of economic activity. McGraw-Hill, New York

Jacobs J (1969) The economy of cities. Random House, New York

Jacobs J (1984) Cities and the wealth of nations. Random House, New York

Krugman P (1991) Geography and trade. MIT Press, Cambridge, MA

Marshall A (1920) Principles of economics. Macmillan, London

McCann P (2001) Urban and regional economics. Oxford University Press, Oxford

Ohlin B (1933) Interregional and International Trade. Harvard University Press, Cambridge, MA

Statistics Sweden (1999) Regional statistics. Available at
    http://www.scb.se/templates/Listning1_____19854.asp#statistik

Annex

Table 7A.1. Classification of ICT industries according to industry code *SNI92*

Industries	Number of host regions
Manufacturing	
30010 Office machinery	22
30020 Computers and other information processing equipment	50
31300 Insulated wire and cable	35
32100 Electronic valves and tubes and other electronic components	56
32200 Television and radio transmitters, line telephony/telegraph apparatus	30
32300 Television and radio receivers, sound or video recording apparatus	38
33200 Equipment for measurement, control and testing	52
33300 Equipment for control of industrial processes	45
Wholesale	
51431 Household machinery and apparatus	47
51432 Radio and TV receivers	42
51433 Phonograms and video cassettes	23
51434 Electrical equipment	58
51640 Office machinery and equipment, including computers	68
51651 Measurement and precision instruments	39
51653 Electronic components and telecommunication products	61
51659 Other machinery for industry and transport	73
Network services	
64201 Telecommunication, network operation	81
64202 Telecommunication, radiation	45
64203 Cable TV	18
Other services	
71330 Renting of office machinery and equipment, including computers	24
72100 Hardware consultancy	54
72201 Software Consultancy	81
72202 Software production and supply	64
72300 Data processing	56
72400 Data base activities	21
72500 Maintenance and repair of office, accounting and computing equipment	50
72600 Other computer-related services	42

SNI92 Swedish industry classification code 1992 (Standard för svensk näringsgrensindelning 1992). Source: Statistics Sweden (SCB), 1999.

Table 7A.2. Regressions according to Eq. (7.20), reflecting localization economies, 1999

Industry	α (t-value)	σ 10^{-3} (t-value)	R^2-adjusted	Number of regions hosting the industry
Manufacturing				
30010	62.6 (2.35)	0.1 (0.07)	0.00	22
30020	23.6 (1.07)	8.4 (5.62)	0.40	50
31300	131.3 (3.87)	0.9 (0.45)	0.01	35
32100	13.2 (0.65)	27.0 (18.61)	0.87	56
32200	98.8 (0.45)	137.0 (11.96)	0.84	30
32300	34.4 (1.02)	20.1 (10.10)	0.74	38
33200	120.0 (1.83)	32.0 (7.08)	0.50	52
33300	30.7 (1.32)	3.3 (2.18)	0.10	45
Wholesale				
51431	1.1 (0.20)	6.7 (18.87)	0.89	47
51432	−7.6 (−2.00)	9.9 (41.70)	0.98	42
51433	−17.6 (−2.87)	7.4 (26.25)	0.97	23
51434	28.1 (1.93)	22.9 (21.67)	0.89	58
51640	−112.3 (−3.85)	134.0 (58.41)	0.98	68
51651	−20.9 (−3.27)	15.6 (40.86)	0.98	39
51653	−48.0 (−3.61)	46.3 (46.63)	0.97	61
51659	52.2 (2.59)	58.3 (35.05)	0.95	73
Network services				
64201	−29.2 (1.69)	84.4 (57.21)	0.98	81
64202	−0.6 (−0.19)	4.2 (22.50)	0.92	45
64203	0.5 (0.32)	2.0 (33.07)	0.99	18
Other services				
71330	−3.6 (−1.37)	2.3 (18.81)	0.94	24
72100	24.6 (0.78)	10.1 (4.58)	0.29	54
72201	−118.4 (−3.42)	258.0 (86.63)	0.99	81
72202	7.9 (0.40)	49.9 (32.92)	0.95	64
72300	2.6 (0.21)	35.1 (40.03)	0.97	56
72400	−2.0 (−0.23)	7.8 (20.56)	0.96	21
72500	13.2 (2.87)	7.4 (23.70)	0.92	50
72600	−0.4 (−0.13)	4.0 (19.84)	0.91	42

t-values in parentheses. The number of observations for each sector is 81 that is the number of LA-regions.

8 Local and Regional ICT Service Sector Markets in Sweden

Johan Klaesson and Lars Pettersson

Jönköping International Business School, Jönköping University

8.1 Introduction

The Information and Computer Technology (ICT) sector was a fast growing sector during the 1990s in Sweden. The growth was stimulated by a high demand on the world market. Swedish manufacturing industry for telephones, radios, television products and other electronics increased from 11.1 percent of total export in 1990 to 24.7 percent in 2000. The real export value for these branches increased by more than 400 percent during the 1990s. The only sector that matches this performance in relative terms during the 1990s in Sweden is the medical sector.

The study of the spread and diffusion of the sector is interesting since this is an example of implementation of new technology and far reaching changes of the way the economy is working. In particular, services that are connected to the sector can be assumed to have influence of fundamental conditions in the regional economic milieu that are of concerns for economic growth. On the firm level, both internal and external conditions have to be considered in regards to economies of scale. In the process of expansion of the production volume, special attention should be paid to the question of internal scale efficiency. Externally, firms ought to reconsider the possibilities to exploit advantages from localization economies, arising from the size of the local industry, and from urbanization economies, due to the size of the local economy. Such external conditions for production can be assumed to be dependent on the supply of services on the regional and local level.

As already discussed in Chap.7, for different service industries, the closeness to ICT service providers is considered to be of great importance, especially those branches of these industries where purchases are accompanied by physical interaction between buyer and seller. Although the digitalisation of the economy has created new market places, there are still market activities that are not suitable for electronic commerce. This is the case for both consumer- and producer- oriented services.

The purpose of this analysis is to explore the existence and the magnitude of the external economies of scale to individual firms in a selection of ICT service sectors. If this type of scale effects proves essential to the firms in these sectors, it will affect firms' location decision; hence, it will have an impact on the local and regional economy. Given that the size of the local market determines the variety of services supply, then this also constitutes important features of the local production and consumption milieu.

The presence of scale economies and price competition (both real and potential) are important factors to acknowledge in explaining the provision of services. Connected to these are the possibilities to benefit from large volumes and closeness to the market. In particular, for several service markets (such as face-to-face activities) accessibility determined by time-distance between customer and the service supplier is more important than geographical distance. Improvements in infrastructure and accessibility serve thereby as a driving mechanism to regional development. In Sweden, several improvements have been made in the transportation networks during the 1990s, which have had a positive influence on the accessibility for a large number of municipalities. As a consequence, it can be assumed this policy to strengthen the importance of urbanization economies.

In this chapter, we focus on services within the ICT sector. Following a former study of the authors (Klaesson and Pettersson 2001) we place the centre of attention in the study on services that are very much 'trapped' in their locations and highly dependent on the local market. The analysis is concerned with location of activities that are dependent on physical interaction between buyer and seller and how such activities are distributed with respect to access to markets of different size.

In the empirical analysis, we explore the relation between the presence of a particular branch of the service sector and the size of the local market. Market size is expressed in two ways: either (1) the size of the population in a municipality in Sweden, or (2) accessibility to population with respect to transportation by car. In our analysis, we are particularly interested in 'marginal industries' and the municipal 'size range' where many sectors are affected. By this we mean industries that can be assumed to be especially sensitive to changes in market size.

In the statistical analysis, we study the probability that a certain type of service branch in the ICT sector is established in the local market with respect to market size. The analysis is based on a probability distribution and employs a binomial logit-model. We also investigate the dynamic changes over time by comparing the situation in 1993 with the one in 1999. 1993 is chosen as a reference year based on the consideration that the Swedish economy had a deep recession this year. In the latter half of the 1990s the Swedish economy has been 'booming'. This means that the study can be assumed to capture the expansionary side of the structural change that has been taking place during the chosen time-period. The two years are starting points and end points in the most recent business cycle respectively. Another motive behind the selection years is that we have access to data from these two points in time. We do not have a complete data panel for the whole time period between 1993 and 1999.

In the empirical part of the chapter, we also distinguish between the local municipal market, the market size of the functional region and external markets outside the functional region. The probability of existence of the respective service sectors is analysed with respect to access to these three types of market size. From this analysis, we are able to study how the different sectors are more or less dependent on access to the local market in the municipality compared to the regional market and the external markets.

The chapter is structured into four sections. In the Sect. 8.2 a theoretical background is presented that considers monopolistic competition and increasing returns to scale. Section 8.3 contains the empirical analysis of the specific branches that are focused. In the final section (8.4) we summarize our findings.

8.2 Market Size and Market Accessibility

The ICT service establishments are most dependent on their choice of location. The size of the trading area and local geographical market determine basic conditions that put limitations on potential turnover and sales volume, profits etc. Gravity models, explaining how customers are attracted to establishments that are closer than competitors, have been used for analysing trading areas.

In the frameworks that utilize gravity models, distance (or travelling time) is naturally an important explanatory variable together with population size (or market size in terms of purchasing power). In this chapter, we will found the theoretical discussion on the contemplation that market size can be assumed to have significant influence on the attributes in the economic milieu of a region. The size of the market is assumed to have a positive effect on the diversity of services offered in a local market.

The consideration of agglomeration economics is most important. The perception builds on the recognition of cost reductions or revenue increases that can be realized when activities are located in one place. When fixed costs can be split on a large number of units, it is possible to lower the price (and still cover the total costs) and in larger markets, it is possible to have higher turnovers than in smaller markets.

External economies and the driving mechanisms that explain agglomeration in space of activities are focused very much in the field of so-called new economic geography. This phenomenon is frequently explained by the appearance of increasing returns, market size and transportation costs (accessibility). A survey of literature in this field is presented in Fujita et al. (1999).

The central-place theory provides a useful fundament for studies of regional and urban land use. Spatial interactions of agents in the economy are depicted in models of central-place systems. In such systems, cities are portrayed as nodes in a geographical network, where the links are the transportation network. The result of such model of the economy can be viewed as a hierarchical ranked structure of cities and urban regions. Large cities are likely to be linked closely to cities of a smaller size and hence one can say that the larger cities serve as engines to regional growth (in a hierarchical way). This structure of geographical ordering of cities is sometimes referred to as the rank-size rule. Related to this analysis is the concept of marginal goods, which denotes the marginal effects on the supply side for a city, or a region, in terms of difference in variety in goods and services between cities of different rank-ordering (Dicken and Lloyd 1990)[1]. Moving from a lower rank to higher rank in the ordering of central-places is presumably accompanied with an increase of the number of services provided.

The algebraically model we present in this section is intended to form a theoretical fundament for our analysis. We use a model, which utilize monopolistic competition and increasing returns, in the tradition that springs from Lancaster (1975) and Dixit and Stiglitz (1977). A wanted and important element of the model is the acknowledgement of benefits from diversity, which also generates agglomeration and hence growth of market size. The model also highlights the importance of complementarities between different ICT services.

The analysis in this section, and in the entire study, at large may also be seen as a progress from an earlier work made by the authors (Klaesson and Pettersson 2001). In this previous work, the centre of attention was put on the concept of 'the regional economic milieu', which focuses on both the production and consumption sides of the local economies when the regional development is investigated. The model is also in line with the seminal model presented by Rivera-Batiz (1988). The model presented in Sect. 8.2 can also be associated to another work made by one of the authors (Klaesson 2000) where an analogous model is used in purpose to investigate the concentration in production with respect to transportation costs. In the model we use in this chapter, we focus on the demand side of the market, when we explore the importance of increasing returns and monopolistic competition. The algebraically approach of monopolistic competition is based on a Chamberlinian-type of model.

In this case, we consider a typical household that maximize utility U from a bundle of goods A and ICT services S. The utility function is homogenous of degree one and is expressed as in Eq. (8.1) below:

$$U = A^\alpha S^\beta \qquad (8.1)$$

α and β are non-negative constants and $\alpha + \beta = 1$. We assume that the corresponding sub-utility, with the centre of attention on ICT services is specified by Eq. (8.2) that has constant elasticity of substitution (CES-form):

$$S = \left(\sum_1^n s_i^{1-\frac{1}{\sigma}} \right)^{\frac{\sigma}{\sigma-1}}, \sigma > 1 \qquad (8.2)$$

where σ is elasticity of substitution between i different ICT services s. The ICT services may be seen as different intermediates for buyers in the market. If we

---

[1] Empirical studies, for example the frequently cited study by Noyelle and Stanback (1983) for the US economy, support the existence of the rank-size rule.

shall allow some s_i to be zero, σ needs to be larger than one. This means that buyers do not necessary need to purchase every service that is offered. σ is large when the services are close substitutes to each other. In other words, in situations when σ is large preferences for variety is not very significant and when σ is close to one variety in ICT service provision is important and can been seen as complementary to each other.[2] One should notice that we use the assumption of constant marginal utility as consumption of a particular service increases. All services are symmetric, and hence, have identical cost- and production functions. This assumption simplifies the algebraic expressions and by using these postulations, we can redefine the sub-utility function for services as Eq. (8.3) below:

$$S = n^{\frac{\sigma}{\sigma - 1}} s \qquad (8.3)$$

From the simplified expression in Eq. (8.3) it is most obvious that S becomes small when σ is large. On the other hand, as σ approach to one, the power will be of substantial size. This consideration shows that if complementarities are strong between ICT services, the corresponding utility among buyers will be positively affected by high accessibility to a large variety of such services. In order to explore the properties of Eq. (8.3) further we may assume that there are a total number of inputs for ICT service providers M in their sub-utility function. Let $M = ns$ be the total number of input services for the ICT sector. We can then rewrite Eq. (8.3) as:

$$\frac{S}{M} = n^{\frac{1}{\sigma - 1}} \qquad (8.4)$$

where S/M denotes the utility per service in average. It is interesting that Eq. (8.4) is increasing in n, which means that there exist increasing returns for utility, with respect to number and diversity of services. From this it follows that a regional market that host a large number of services can be assumed to be more attractive for ICT service firms than a regional market with fewer services.

The cost function for the typical firm in the ICT service industry is the same as for the total sector. We assume a most common version of the cost function written as:

---

[2] This means that we take substitutability into consideration. A desirable feature of the model is that it takes into account both substitutability and acknowledge if different service are complements to each other. However, one ICT service does not need to be a substitute of complement for another. It is possible to think of both services that have close substitutes/complements, and services that do not have any substitutes/ complements.

$$TC = n(as + F)$$ (8.5)

where TC is total costs, a is variable costs (equal to marginal costs) and F is fixed costs. As indicated from the cost function we assume constant returns to scale in production of services. Moreover, we assume that TC is proportional to the market size and thereby determined by the underlying market conditions in the region. This condition can be written as Eq. (8.6) below:

$$bLw = TC$$ (8.6)

or

(8.7)

$$\frac{TC}{L} = bw$$

where L is the population size in the region, b is the share the 'regional budget' spent on ICT service sector (all ICT services in aggregate) and w is the average wage (for the whole population). Equation (8.5) can be rewritten as:

$$\frac{TC}{n} = as + F$$ (8.8)

or

(8.9)

$$s = \frac{1}{a}\left(\frac{TC}{n} - F\right)$$

Equation (8.8) can then be substituted into Eq. (8.3) and we get:

(8.10)

$$S = \frac{n^{\frac{\sigma}{\sigma-1}}}{a}\left(\frac{TC}{n} - F\right)$$

or

(8.11)

$$S = \frac{n^{\frac{\sigma}{\sigma-1}}}{a}\left(\frac{bLw}{n} - F\right)$$

Equation (8.10) can be rewritten as:

$$S = \frac{bLwn^{\frac{1}{\sigma-1}}}{a} - \frac{Fn^{\frac{\sigma}{\sigma-1}}}{a} \qquad (8.12)$$

Differencing Eq. (8.9) with respect to n and setting $\delta S/\delta n=0$ we find out that optimum number of ICT services in a local market. Optimal number of services established in a market is:

$$n = \frac{bLw}{\sigma F} \qquad (8.13)$$

From Eq. (8.13) we find that the optimum number of ICT services in market is determined from the population size (L), the level of the average wage (w), the budget share spent on ICT services in the region (b), the size of the fixed costs in the ICT service industry (F) and the elasticity of substitution between ICT services (σ). The relation between the different determinants for the number of ICT services can be summarized as in Table 8.1 below.

Table 8.1. Relationship between number of services and selected variables

Variable	Change in Variable	Effect on Utility in Region r
Population size (L)	L↑	n↑
Average wage (w)	w↑	n↑
Share of budget spent on ICT services (b)	b↑	n↑
Fixed costs in the ICT service industry (F)	F↑	n↓
Elasticity of substitution between services (σ)	σ↑	n↓

A change in any variable causes an effect on the market conditions for services as indicated in Table 8.1. From the results of this model we conclude that market size and the local circumstances in the regional economies can be assumed to have significant influence on important conditions that determine the potential for ICT services to be established in a specific location.

It is most reasonable to assume that market size can be measured as population size (given that there are no substantial income differences between regions) and/or in combination with spatial accessibility. The regional differences in income per capita in Sweden are relatively small in an international comparison. However, regional differences exist. From our data set we find that industrial mix and regional size can explain such differences. Given these facts we use *access to aggregated wage sum* in order to account for these regional differences in the analysis.

8.3 Assessing the Influence of the Accessibility to the Market

The purpose with this empirical analysis is to investigate the probability for presence of establishments in the ICT sector in municipalities with respect to market size and accessibility. Market size is defined as access to purchasing power, measured as wage-sum. This means that both population size and income per capita is taken into account. The analysis covers ten selected branches of the ICT sector, which are described in Table 8A.1.

The selection of services has been made with respect to identifying branches and activities that are assumed to be sensitive to market size. A common characteristic of the services is that they can be assumed to represent 'marginal services', analogues to the concept stated from the rank-size distributions (Dicken and Lloyd 1990).

The method we use is to estimate a binary logit-model, using the probability distribution:

$$P_i(x) = \frac{1}{1 + e^{-(\alpha + \beta x_i)}} \tag{8.14}$$

where P_i is the probability that a service sector is present in municipality i. x_i is the size of municipality i in terms of population or in terms of access to purchasing power. α and β are estimated parameters. $P_i=1$ (0 otherwise) if the particular service sector is present (if there exists at least one establishment).

If we set

$$\frac{dP_i^2(x_i)}{dx^2} = 0 \tag{8.15}$$

and solve for x_i, we obtain

$$x_i = -\frac{\alpha}{\beta} \tag{8.16}$$

Equation (8.16) gives the x_i-value where the slope of the probability curve attains its maximum value. That is, at that x_i-value the effect of purchasing power (size of market) on the probability of presence of service sector i is at its highest. If we solve for x_i directly from Eq. (8.14) we obtain

$$x_i = -\left(\frac{\alpha}{\beta}\right)\left(1 + \frac{1}{\alpha}\ln\left(\frac{1-P_i}{P_i}\right)\right) \qquad (8.17)$$

From Eq. (8.17), we can calculate the market size (purchasing power) that is required for every level of probability for the presence of service sector i. When market size is measured in terms of accessibility, we use the following definition:

$$X_i = \sum_j x_j e^{-\lambda t_{ij}} = x_i e^{-\lambda t_{ii}} + \sum_{j \in R} x_j e^{-\lambda t_{ij}} + \sum_{j \notin R} x_j e^{-\lambda t_{ij}} \qquad (8.18)$$

where X_i is the accessibility to purchasing power measured as wage-sum in municipality i, x_j is purchasing power (or market size) in municipality j, λ is a distance decay parameter and t_{ij} is the time-distance between municipalities i and j if one travels by car. Internal accessibility is given by the same formula and t_{ii} measures the average time-distance between zones in municipality i. In the estimations performed with accessibility measures x_i is substituted by X_i in Eqs. (8.14) to (8.17).

We focus the analysis to the difference between the situation in 1993 and 1999. Our choice of years is motivated by the changes in the Swedish economy. A substantial recession occurred in the Swedish economy during the first years of the 1990s. The situation culminated in the autumn of 1992 when fixed exchange rate regime had to be abolished (November 19, 1992). From 1993 and onwards the economy then starts to recover and in the last years of the 1990s a boom occurred. This means that we have chosen to compare the situation when the economy was in the very lowest level of the business cycle (1993) and a peak year (1999).

Table 8.2. Employment dynamics of the ten ICT service sectors

Sector[a]	Employ-ment 1993	Employment 1999	Change in Employment	Change in Employment (percent)
Softw Con.	19,241	50,781	31,540	163.9
Softw Sup.	3,676	12,064	8,388	228.2
Data Process.	4,679	8,240	3,561	76.1
Wholesale Tel.	5,084	7,543	2,459	48.4
Hardw Con.	1,201	3,645	2,444	203.5
Retail Comp.	2,156	2,576	420	19.5
Maintenance	1,601	2,341	740	46.2
Retail Tel.	178	1,700	1,522	855.1
Data Base Ac.	788	1,375	587	74.5
Other	446	876	430	96.4
All ICT Services	39,050	91,141	52,091	133.4

[a] The full names of the sectors are presented in Table 8A.1. Data source: Statistics Sweden 2001

As shown in Table 8.2 all the chosen branches increased in number of employees. The ten branches increased by 133 percent and increased in absolute number of employees from around 40, 000 to 90,000 during the time period. In absolute numbers, *Software Consultancy* increased most of the ten branches, and by far dominates the growth in employment between 1993 and 1999.

Retail Sale of Telecommunication Equipment experienced the strongest relative increase in employment, around 850 percent during the particular time period. The branches that had the strongest relative increase in employment were *Retail Sale of Telecommunication Equipment, Software Supply, Hardware Consultancy and Software Consultancy.* All these branches grow by more than 100 percent.

After presenting the changes in employment, we then turn to the distribution of the ICT sector. We limit the analysis by study the number of municipalities where the different branches are present. The total number of municipalities in Sweden is 289 and the most widely spread branch is *Software Consultancy* (Table 8.3). On one hand, branches that have many employees tend to have a wide spread distribution, for example *Software Consultancy* and *Software Supply*. On the other hand, branches such, as *Data Processing* do not have the same high rank in Table 8.3 as in Table 8.2. Moreover, *Retail of Computers, Office Machinery and Computer Programs* is highly ranked in terms of number of municipalities were it is present, despite its relatively lower number of employees. On average, 14 persons per municipality are employed in the branch *Retail of Computers, Office Machinery and Computer Programs*, which could be compared with 180 of *Software Consultancy*.

Table 8.3. Number of municipalities where the ten ICT service sectors are present

Sector[a]	Number of Municipalities 1993	Number of Municipalities 1999	Change	Percentage Change (percent)
Softw Con.	222	281	59	26.6
Softw Sup.	130	177	47	36.2
Data Process.	84	173	89	106.0
Wholesale Tel.	125	156	31	24.8
Hardw Con.	57	145	88	154.4
Retail Comp.	93	131	38	40.9
Maintenance	39	113	74	189.7
Retail Tel.	89	108	19	21.3
Data Base Ac.	15	47	32	213.3
Other	24	82	58	241.7
All ICT Services	222	281	59	26.6

[a] The full names of the sectors are presented in Table 8A.1. Data source: Statistics Sweden 2001

As shown in Table 8.2 and Table 8.3 there are substantial differences between the different sectors. Using the binary logit-model we estimate the probability of presence for each sector related to access to market. Accessibility is defined as in

Eq. (8.18), and we focus on the access to (i) the market within the municipality, (ii) the regional market in the specific functional region (the labour market region), and (iii) to external markets outside the labour region. We also compare the situation 1993 with the one in 1999. This means that we are comparing a situation when the economy was in recession (1993) with a booming situation (1999). The analysis captures the expanding phase of the business cycle from the 1990s in Sweden for the ICT service sectors.

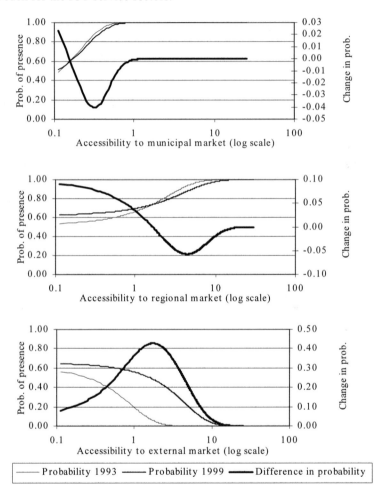

Fig. 8.1. Probability of presence in municipalities in 1993 and 1999 for *Wholesale of Telecommunication Equipment and Electronic Components*, billions of euros in yearly income

The results from the empirical analysis can be presented in both graphs and tables. We present the graph for one sector. Fig. 8.1 shows the probability of presence in municipalities for the sector *Wholesale of Telecommunication Equipment and Electronic Components.* When we first analyse the presence of the sector related to the accessibility to the local market within the municipality we find that there is no major difference between 1993 and 1999. The presence of the sector is positively related to accessibility, and the probability of presence is equal to one when the local market size (as we measure it) is approaching 1 billion euros[3] (10 billion SEK) in yearly income (the sum of per capita income). Turning to access to the regional market (the functional region) we find that the probability function is less step and approaches one when the regional market is around 10 billion euros (100 billion SEK) in yearly income.

All ICT service sectors are included in the empirical analysis presented in Table 8.4. Table 8.4 shows the results from the statistical estimations using the binary logit-model where we use the probability distribution from Eq. (8.14).

Table 8.4. Results of the logit estimations predicting ICT service sectors probability of municipal presence in 1993 and 1999

Independent variable	Constant[a]	Accessibility to market within municipality[a]	Accessibility to market within region[a]	Accessibility to market outside region[a]	McFadden R^2	Prediction (percent)[b]
Wholesale Tel.1993	1.35 (0.24)	−1.10 (0.22)	−0.06 (0.02)	0.21 (0.12)	0.27	75.7 (56.6)
Wholesale Tel.1999	1.16 (0.22)	−0.87 (0.18)	−0.04 (0.01)	0.04 (0.07)	0.23	74.0 (51.0)
Retail Comp. 1993	1.80 (0.28)	−2.20 (0.35)	0.00 (0.01)	0.10 (0.12)	0.32	79.5 (54.9)
Retail Comp. 1999	1.35 (0.24)	−1.69 (0.29)	0.01(0.01)	0.01 (0.07)	0.26	73.6 (51.7)
Retail Tel. 1993	2.17 (0.29)	−0.44 (0.09)	0.02 (0.01)	0.25 (0.17)	0.16	88.2 (86.5)
Retail Tel. 1999	1.97 (0.28)	−1.89 (0.29)	0.03 (0.01)	0.26 (0.11)	0.37	82.3 (66.0)
Hardw. Con. 1993	2.75 (0.31)	−0.52 (0.10)	−0.03 (0.01)	−0.13 (0.11)	0.26	85.4 (80.2)
Hardw. Con.1999	1.79 (0.25)	−1.06 (0.20)	−0.04 (0.01)	−0.04 (0.07)	0.30	76.4 (56.3)
Softw. Con. 1993	−0.05 (0.25)	−2.10 (0.52)	−0.08 (0.05)	0.18 (0.12)	0.21	77.4 (77.1)
Softw. Con. 1999	−1.29 (0.33)	−1.20 (0.59)	−0.14 (0.11)	0.00 (0.13)	0.14	92.0 (92.0)
Softw. Sup. 1993	2.18 (0.29)	−1.07 (0.19)	−0.02 (0.01)	0.09 (0.13)	0.31	84.0 (70.8)
Softw. Sup.1999	1.49 (0.25)	−1.45 (0.28)	−0.04 (0.02)	−0.04 (0.07)	0.29	75.7 (53.5)
Data Process.1993	1.76 (0.26)	−0.72 (0.14)	−0.05 (0.01)	0.13 (0.12)	0.26	79.9 (67.7)
Data Process.1999	1.81 (0.26)	−1.12 (0.21)	−0.04 (0.01)	0.07 (0.09)	0.32	79.5 (59.0)
Data Base Ac.1993	3.61 (0.54)	−0.17 (0.07)	−0.03 (0.01)	0.20 (0.30)	0.24	94.8 (94.8)
Data Base Ac.1999	3.07 (0.35)	−0.37 (0.08)	−0.02 (0.01)	0.04 (0.11)	0.28	90.6 (86.8)
Maintenance1993	2.49 (0.31)	−1.69 (0.27)	0.00 (0.01)	0.05 (0.13)	0.37	83.3 (69.1)
Maintenance1999	2.16 (0.27)	−0.96 (0.16)	0.00 (0.01)	−0.03 (0.07)	0.29	83.0 (68.1)
Other 1993	3.85 (0.47)	−0.44 (0.10)	−0.03 (0.01)	−0.06 (0.17)	0.30	91.7 (91.7)
Other 1999	2.51 (0.29)	−0.49 (0.09)	−0.02 (0.01)	−0.03 (0.08)	0.28	84.4 (77.4)

[a] Estimated coefficients, standard errors in brackets
[b] The correct prediction in percentage compared to the naive model in brackets

As can be seen in Table 8.4 there are variation between these sectors. *Retail of Computers, Office Machinery and Computer Programs* has a high probability of

---

[3] The original figures were expressed in Swedish Kronor (SEK), but they were transformed into euros using the exchange rate 1 EUR = 9 SEK

presence with respect to access to municipal market already at a small size of the local market. This can be compared with other sectors. A sensitivity analysis reveals that the probability of presence in a market with respect to the purchasing power in the municipality approaches one on a somewhat higher level for the sector *Retail Sale of Telecommunication Equipment*. The same situation is also found in the sector *Data Base Activities*, and *Other Computer Related Activities*.

From Table 8.4 we also find that the probability approaches one for the sectors who have significant estimates for the variable *Accessibility to Regional Market* when the size of the market is around 10 billion euros (100 billion SEK) in yearly income. This is the situation for the sectors *Wholesale of Telecommunication Equipment and Electronic Components* (Fig. 8.1), *Hardware Consultancy, Software Supply*, *Data Processing*, and *Other Computer Related Activities*.

From the statistical estimation we find that access to purchasing power in both the local market in the municipalities, and the regional markets (more than half of the cases) are statistical significant at five percent level. However, when we study access to external purchasing power the relationship is not significant at the same high level.

The variable *Accessibility to Market within Municipality* is significant at five percent level in all cases. Concerning the variable *Accessibility to Market within Region* that is the functional region (the labour market), the picture is a bit mixed. This variable is significant at five percent level for the sectors *Wholesale of Telecommunication Equipment and Electronic Components, Hardware Consultancy, Software Supply, Data Processing,* and *Other Computer Related Activities*. Access to the regional market is not significant for the remaining five out of the ten sectors. One observation is that when the variable *Accessibility to Market within Region* is significant at five percent level, this is the case for both of the years 1993 and 1999. The sensitivity to access to the regional market has not changed substantially for these sectors over time.

As we expected, *Accessibility to Market Outside Region* does not yield significant estimations of the same magnitude. We suppose it is because we have focused our analysis on service sectors, which we assume are sensitive to the demand in the local market. When we study the statistic results for all three variables in Table 8.4, our interpretation is that the strength of the respective markets depends on the local and regional demand in relation to demand from other regions.

Five sectors show significant signs for the variable *Accessibility to Market within Municipality* but not for the other variables. Three of these sectors (*Retail of Computers, Office Machinery and Computer Programs, Software Consultancy*, and *Maintenance and Repair of Office, Accounting and Computing Machinery*) show comparably high values of the estimated coefficients for the variable *Accessibility to Market within Municipality*. Overall, we find higher estimates for the variable *Accessibility to Market within Municipality* compared to the other variables. This is also interpreted as an indication of a higher dependency of the local markets compared to other markets.

The McFadden pseudo R^2 is applied to indicate a measure of fit for the estimated models. This measure yields values around 0.3 for most of the models. The percentage of correct predictions is also reported in Table 8.4.

Concerning the variable *Accessibility to Market Outside Region* we find only one significant estimate at five percent level, which is for the sector *Retail Sale of Telecommunication Equipment, Software Supply, Hardware Consultancy and Software Consultancy*. This estimate also has the opposite sign compared to the significant parameters for the variables *Accessibility to Market within Municipality* and *Accessibility to Market within Region*. Our conclusion in this particular case is that the positive sign reveals a competition effect. Therefore, this sector is sensitive to competition located in other regions.

The results presented in Table 8.4 reveal the spatial dimension of the service markets we have analysed. It is evident that the economies of scale related to purchasing power external to the firms are most important in their close surrounding. For the branches *Hardware Consultancy* and *Data Processing*, the market areas expand more than for other services, including the region level. One explanation to this can be that these services are somewhat more specialized and do not reach the same volume in production per employee. The fixed cost may therefore be of a larger size ('burden') compared to services that have a larger share of 'traditional retailing'.

It is also self-evident that *Wholesale of Telecommunication Equipment and Electronic Components* is dependent on a larger geographical area, as long as market region level deals with wholesale. This branch is not directly dependent on where consumers are located, only indirectly. Although one can assume that the importance of economies of scale (how fixed cost can be distributed with respect to number employed) is of significance for the wholesaling firms and thereby there is a geographical constraint, the wholesaling firms serve other firms in the retailing business that is more dependent on where consumers and the purchasing power are located.

It should be reminded that the results in Table 8.4 acknowledge the dynamics in the economy during a catch-up part of the business cycle (in the 1990s). Therefore, the expansionary phenomenon in the economy during a boom is captured in the results. We cannot make any statements about the development during times of recession.

8.4 Conclusions

The focus of this chapter is on ten service branches in the ICT sector in Sweden. This sector has been growing very fast in Sweden during the 1990s. The service branches we have chosen to study are assumed to be dependent on the demand from the local market. Moreover, we recognize them as important characteristics of the supply side in the local economic milieu. From a theoretical perspective, it is reasonable to assume that the presence of the service industries can be explained by the size of the local and regional markets, conclusion that may be compared with findings in Chap. 7.

In the empirical analysis, we study the relationship between accessibility to municipal market, regional market, and external markets and the probability of presence of the respective service industries in municipalities. The market potential at a location is defined as accessibility to purchasing power (aggregated income). In this study, we use a binary logit-model. According to the results from the statistical estimations, all selected service industries are dependent on access to the local market. The regional market (functional region) is also important. The estimations yield significant parameters at five percent level, in half of the cases at regional level and in all cases at local level. Access to external regions appears to be of less importance, and does not result in significant estimates except for one case.

From this study, one can dwell on a policy aspect: The access to the local market in the municipal is of high importance. This means that regional and local development can be assumed to be self reinforced in a cumulative way. An increase in the market potential attracts new firms and thereby the variety of the supply side will grow. A more diversified supply of services will then attract new households and firms, etc. In a dynamic perspective, growth can be promoted by investments in infrastructure, which reduce time distances.

If one would like to promote entrance of this particular type of service industries it is important to acknowledge locations with good access to the local (municipal) market. Furthermore, some of the branches require access to a larger market size than other branches. For a number of branches (in this case more than half of the industries) access to a regional market of substantial size is also important. For the branches that showed significant signs of dependency on the regional market, the size of the market had to be around 10 million euros (100 Million SEK) per year in aggregated income (for the probability of presence to approach one).

The study only concerns the recovery part of the business cycle. This constitutes a limitation of the analysis. We cannot make statements regarding the situation might be in a recession phase. However, by the way the study is carried out we are able to understand some of the spatial dynamics in times of recovery. Since the focus is on ICT service sectors we have been able to catch the development of a strong growing sector that sprawled in the economy when the new information technology were adopted widely in the economy.

References

Dicken P, Lloyd PE (1990) Location in space – theoretical perspectives in economic geography. Harper Collins Publishers, New York

Dixit AK, Stiglitz JE (1977) Monopolistic competition and optimum product diversity. The American Economic Review 67: 297–308

Fujita M, Krugman P, Venables A (1999) The spatial economy – cities, regions, and international trade. The MIT Press, Cambridge, MA

Klaesson J (2001) A study of localisation economies and the transport sector. Jönköping International Business School (JIBS) Dissertation Series No. 006, Jönköping University, Jönköping

Klaesson J, Pettersson L (2001) Regional Development – The importance of production and consumption milieu. In Uddevalla Symposium 2000: Entrepreneurship, firm growth and regional development in the new economic geography. Research reports 01:1, University of Trollhättan/Uddevalla, Trollhättan, pp 413- 432

Lancaster K (1975) Socially optimal product differentiation. The American Economic Review 65: 567–585

Noyelle T, Stanback T (1983) The economic transformation of American cities. Rowan and Allanheld, Totowa, NJ

Rivera-Batiz FL (1988) Increasing returns, monopolistic competition, and agglomeration economies in consumption and production. Regional Science and Urban Economics 18: 125–153

Statistics Sweden (2001) Employment in municipalities and counties 1999 – labour statistics on administrative sources. Statistical Letter No. 0101, Statistics Sweden, Stockholm

Annex

Table 8A.1. Description of the ICT service sectors

SIC Code	Description	Abbreviation
51653	Wholesale of telecommunication equipment and electronic components	Wholesale Tel.
52493	Retail sale of computers, office machinery and computer programs	Retail Comp.
52494	Retail sale of telecommunication equipment	Retail Tel.
72100	Hardware consultancy	Hardw Con.
72201	Software consultancy	Softw Con.
72202	Software supply	Softw Sup.
72300	Data processing	Data Process.
72400	Data base activities	Data Base Ac.
72500	Maintenance and repair of office, accounting and computing machinery	Maintenance
72600	Other computer related activities	Other

9 Growth Dynamics in a Municipal Market-Accessibility Hierarchy

Martin Andersson and Johan Klaesson

Jönköping International Business School, Jönköping University

9.1 Introduction

The relationship between market-size and the location of economic activities is well established in the literature, both theoretically and empirically. In principle, this has been the major theme of the models of the new economic geography (NEG), starting with the seminal work of Krugman (1991a, b). Such models are based on increasing returns, which are necessary in order to explain geographical concentration (Johansson and Karlsson 2001). In the presence of increasing returns, market-size can be regarded as a measure of the 'competitiveness' of a region as regards its ability to attract firms and industries. Clearly, any firm with internal scale economies seeks closeness to large markets. However, the role of market-size is not constrained to be the supply of potential customers in a proximate geographical area, though this ought to be the major factor for service industries such as retail and wholesale, (c.f. Klaesson and Pettersson 2001). It should be noted, though, that the ideas behind the NEG-approach have a long history. Weber (1929), for example, maintained that regional location factors, i.e. those involved in the minimization of transport costs when choosing location, can create concentrations if similar firms find their individual optimal location to be in proximity to each other. Clearly, market-size is an excellent example of such a regional factor relevant for most types of firms. Furthermore, in his famous book on *Location theory and the Shoe and Leather Industries,* Hoover (1937) elaborated and popularised Ohlin's (1933) concepts of localization and urbanization economies. Hoover's definitions are used to this present day.

Several empirical studies point in the direction that the richness in the regional economic milieu and market-size (e.g. in population terms) tend to go hand in hand (see *inter alia* Kjellgren 2002). Thus, agglomeration economies, such as access to various business services, labour supply and transportation networks, etc., tend to be strong in regions with a large market potential. Consequently, not only firms with internal scale economies benefits from being located in proximity to a large market (see e.g. Feser 2001). Any firm can in principle reap the advantages from agglomeration economies. Moreover, a majority of empirical studies point in the direction that there is also a strong relationship between size and growth, (see e.g. Beeson et al. 2001; Glaeser 1998; Quigley 1998). In Sweden, for example, the tendency in the late 1990s has been that large municipalities get larger and small get smaller. In 1999, the percentage increase in employment was largest in large municipalities, while small municipalities on average experienced a decline in employment, (Statistics Sweden 2001). Furthermore, the four largest municipalities accounted for about 50 percent of the total increase in employment. Thus, in line with results presented in Chaps. 7-8, size seems to be important for both the location and growth of economic activities. However, Fujita and Thisse (2002) note that much work needs to be done on the theoretical side.

In this chapter, municipal growth across Swedish municipalities is related to municipal, intra regional and extra regional market-size, where market-size is defined as the accessibility to wage-sum. An accessibility-based hierarchy is constructed, such that the municipalities are divided into different categories based on their market-size. This allows for a structured way to investigate the relationship between market-size and growth. We explore the growth in (i) population, (ii) employment, and (iii) commuting patterns. These variables are perceived as being dependent on a municipality's location in the hierarchy. The purpose of the chapter is twofold: first, to reveal systematic regularities in growth performance across Swedish municipalities and second, to relate the overall pattern of change to the performance of the information and communication technology (ICT) service sectors. In this manner, we are able to ascertain whether a similar process governs these sectors.

The justifications for studying the ICT service sectors separately are many. In a Swedish context, the regional spread of the ICT service sectors is of great interest. The Swedish government, for example, has a stated aim that all households in Sweden should have access to broadband (Government Offices of Sweden 2000). One of the reasons for this aim originates from the apprehension that ICT-industries are distance insensitive. Hence, the prevalent view was (and at least in part is) that an ICT firm can in principle locate anywhere as long as they are connected to the Internet. Therefore, many believed that the ICT sectors could solve unemployment and development problems in peripheral parts of Sweden if the government provided the appropriate ICT infrastructure. Hence, the question whether the ICT service sectors follow the same pattern as other sectors or not as regards growth is of great concern from a Swedish perspective.

The study is based on data describing the growth in Swedish municipalities between 1993 and 1999. This time period is chosen in order to capture how the Swedish aggregate growth was allocated across municipalities.

The remainder of the chapter is organized in the following fashion; Sect. 9.2 presents the definition of the ICT service sectors used in the chapter as well as some descriptive statistics of the development of the sectors in Sweden 1993-1999. In Sect. 9.3.1, a model of consumer service location is presented, which relate diversity to market-size. Sect. 9.3.2 describes the method of analysis and the construction of the market-size hierarchy of municipalities. The relationship between market-size and employment growth is explored. Cross-sectional regression analysis is applied to the overall growth performance across Swedish municipalities and the ICT-service sectors. The ICT service sectors are analysed both individually and as a group. The conclusions and policy implications drawn from the findings are presented in the last section, 9.4.

9.2 Definition of the ICT Service Sectors and General Observations

The definition of the Information and Communication Technology (ICT) service sectors used in this chapter follows that of OECD (1998, p.7): "for service industries", it is maintained, "the products of a candidate industry must be intended to enable the function of information processing and communication by electronic means". Acknowledging this requirement, it is possible to identify ten ICT service sectors in Sweden using the SNI-92 classification system at the five-digit level. However, one sector, *Other Computer Related Activities*, was excluded from the analysis. The reason is that it cannot properly be understood what activities the sector is constituted by, which make the sector inherently difficult to analyse. Thus, nine ICT service sectors are considered in this chapter.

Table 9.1. Descriptive statistics of selected ICT service sectors 1993 and 1999

Sector[a]	Employment			Average estimated size			Gini-coefficient[b]		
	1993	1999	Δ%	1993	1999	Δ%	1993	1999	Δ%
Wholesale tel.	5 084	7 543	48.4	7.47	9.30	24.6	0.17	0.22	28.9
Retail comp.	2 156	2 576	9.5	5.96	4.49	·24.7	0.27	0.24	·13.4
Retail tel.	178	700	855.1	3.07	6.12	99.3	0.41	0.22	·46.1
Hardw. Con.	1 201	3 645	203.5	0.35	8.76	·15.4	0.39	0.33	·14.9
Softw. Con.	9 241	50 781	63.9	6.31	7.55	1 9.6	0.10	0.07	·29.2
Softw. Sup.	3 676	2 064	228.2	3.67	1.63	·14.9	0.27	0.19	·30.4
Data Process	4 679	8 240	76.1	5.91	9.30	21.3	0.25	0.27	5.9
Data Base Ac.	788	375	74.5	31.52	7.63	·44.1	0.38	0.34	·11.0
Maintenance	601	2 341	46.2	5.28	7.12	34.7	0.22	0.27	23.3
ICT-9	38 604	90 625	34.8	7.49	8.46	1 3.0	0.22	0.22	· 2.8

Δ% annual growth rate (percentage). [a] A list with the formal definitions and abbreviations of the nine ICT service sectors considered in this chapter is provided in Table 9.A1. [b]The calculations of the Gini-coefficients follow the method in Krugman (1991)[1]. A value of 0.5 indicates complete concentration and 0 complete dispersion. The calculations are made using municipalities as geographical entities. Data source: Statistics Sweden 2001.

---

[1] The calculation of the Gini coefficient can be expressed by $\int_{0}^{1}(f(x) - x)dx$, where x is the cumulative share of the employment in an industry and $f(x)$ gives the cumulative share of the employment in a sector belonging to the industry. The x inside the brackets indicates the straight line from the southwest to the northeast corner whose slope is 1.

In Table 9.1, the number of persons employed, average establishment size and the Gini coefficient in 1993 and 1999 of the nine ICT service sectors are presented. The ICT service sectors have experienced a rapid growth in Sweden between 1993 and 1999. Although there are quite substantial differences between the growth rates of the individual sectors, the overall pattern reveal a drastic increase in employment. Total employment in the ICT-9 increased from 38 604 to 90 625, which corresponds to a percentage increase of 134.8 percent. At the same time, the overall employment growth in the total private sector in Sweden was 16.7 percent. Hence, the ICT service sectors have performed very well relative to the Swedish average in the 1990s. Of the nine sectors, *Retail sale of telecommunications, Software consultancy, Hardware consultancy* and *Software supply* experienced the fastest growth in employment. The aggregate growth of these four sectors amounted to 180.7 percent. It is worthwhile to note that the employment growth in *Retail sale of telecommunications* was extraordinary during the time period. The total employment grew from 178 to 1,700, representing a percentage growth of 855.1. The growth in this industry reflects the increased use of various telecommunication equipment and related services, in particular mobile phones. The growth of the other three fast growing sectors is connected to the increased usage of computers, which produces a great demand for both hardware and software.

On reasonable grounds, it can be assumed that a fast growth at the national level is coupled with regional diffusion. However, services can at least partly be considered as non-tradable, which means that they to a certain extent are constrained to the local markets offered by the municipalities in which they are located. The size of the fixed costs associated with an establishment should determine the market-size required for a feasible location due to internal scale economies. Thus, the larger the fixed costs, the less dispersed an industry ought to be. Average establishment size in the table above is a rough proxy of the size of the fixed costs. The figures do not reveal any clear-cut relationship between the degree of dispersion, as measured by Gini-coefficients, and average establishment size. Hence, there is no systematic pattern showing that those sectors with a large average establishment size have a corresponding relatively high Gini-coefficient, as expected from the above reasoning. However, the four ICT service sectors experiencing a decrease in the average establishment size between 1993 and 1999 also experienced a decrease in the Gini-coefficient, indicating increased dispersion. This implies that the new plants established between 1993 and 1999 were on average smaller than those existing in 1993 were and that the establishments of the new plants were spread across space. Only in two out of nine cases did the two measures develop in opposite directions, i.e. an increase in the average establishment size and a decrease in the Gini-coefficient. Such a picture point towards a rapid growth of employment in initial establishments coupled with new start-ups in several regions. This pattern also holds for the nine ICT service sectors as a whole (ICT-9).

The Gini-coefficients in the former table reveal that three sectors, *Wholesale of telecommunication equipment, Data processing* and *Maintenance & repair* became more concentrated between 1993 and 1999. However, Gini-coefficients must be consulted with care, since they do not take the number of locations of a sector into account. A simple calculation of the number of municipalities in which the selected ICT sectors were present in 1993 and 1999 shows that in this respect, all sectors became more dispersed. Again, as depicted in Table 9.2, *Retail sale of telecommunications, Software consultancy, Hardware consultancy* and *Software supply* stand out, this time showing a strong dispersion measured by the absolute change in the number of locations.

Table 9.2. Geographical spread and the degree of urbanization of the ICT service sectors in 1993 and 1999[a]

Sector[b]	Number of municipali- ties 1993	Number of municipali- ties 1999	Δ	Δ %	Urb.93 (%)	Urb.99 (%)	Δ
Wholesale tel.	125	156	31	24.8	47.64	43.84	−3.8
Retail comp.	130	177	47	36.2	24.58	35.09	10.5
Retail tel.	39	113	74	189.7	29.21	41.94	12.7
Hardw. Con.	57	145	88	154.4	72.36	64.77	−7.6
Softw. Con.	222	281	59	26.6	52.95	55.01	2.0
Softw. Sup.	84	173	89	106.0	44.61	53.03	8.4
Data Process	93	131	38	40.9	38.30	32.44	−5.9
Data Base Ac.	15	47	32	213.3	39.85	55.56	15.7
Maintenance	89	108	19	21.3	39.66	36.14	−3.5
ICT-9	255	281	26	10.2	47.80	50.92	3.1

Δ change of the indicator between 1993-1999, Δ% growth rate (percentage) between 1993-1999, *Urb.93 (%)* share of the five largest Swedish municipalities employment in the total employment of the sector in 1993, *Urb.99 (%)* share of the five largest Swedish municipalities employment in the total employment of the sector in 1999.[a] The maximum number of municipalities is 288.[b] A list with the formal definitions and abbreviations of the nine ICT service sectors considered in this chapter is provided in Table 9.A1. Data source: Statistics Sweden 2001

Urb.93 and *Urb.99* measure the five largest municipalities' (in terms of population) share of the total employment in the sectors in the respective years[2]. This is a simple way to measure the degree of urbanization of the sectors. Looking at the figures, it is evident that the ICT service sectors are highly urbanized. In 1993 the ICT service sectors related to retail sale showed the lowest level of urbanization. Yet, about a fourth of the total employment was found in the five largest municipalities. The share also increased with approximately 43 percent to 1999. In 1999, *Data processing* showed the lowest degree of urbanization. Still, as much as 32.44 percent of the total employment was to be found in the five largest municipalities. Only four out of the nine sectors decreased the level of urbanization. Relative to those sectors that experienced an increase in urbanization, the decrease in urbanization must be considered as low. Moreover, the overall pattern of the ICT-9 reveals a trend towards increased urbanization.

---

[2] The five largest municipalities (in terms of population) in 1993 and 1999 were Stockholm, Göteborg, Malmö, Uppsala and Linköping.

The description at hand reveals that the ICT service sectors experienced a rapid growth in employment compared with the national average between 1993 and 1999. Interestingly, it has been observed that two very different systematic processes have concurrently taken place during the 1990's, (i) a diffusion process and (ii) an urbanization process. Between 1993 and 1999, large amounts of new establishments have been made across Swedish municipalities, indicated by both the Gini-coefficients and the number of municipalities in which an industry were present. At the same time a majority of the ICT service sectors became more urbanized. Hence, a vast majority of the selected ICT sectors grew fastest in large municipalities between 1993 and 1999. This observation goes against the conventional view that it is declining sectors in metropolitan regions that diffuse throughout the regional hierarchy, such as predicted by the Spatial Product Cycle (SPC) theory, (see e.g. Karlsson 1999).

9.3 Market-Size and Regional Growth Dynamics

In this section, the relationship between market-size and growth in employment between 1993 and 1999 in the ICT service sectors across a market-size hierarchy of 288 Swedish municipalities is investigated. The section starts by presenting a model building upon the assumption that utility increase with diversity, which illustrates the role of market-size for the location of consumer service sectors.

9.3.1 A Model of Consumer Service Location, Diversity and Market-Size

The following model builds upon monopolistic competition and increasing returns. The model is static in the sense that it only considers one point in time. However, it clearly evaluates the relationship between market-size and the location of consumer service sectors[3] and, hence, the location of the employment opportunities in those sectors. We consider a typical household that resides in municipality m. Each such household is assumed to maximize it's utility U_m from a bundle of goods A_m and consumer services S_m that are available for consumers in municipality m. The utility function is homogenous of degree one and is expressed as in Eq. (9.1) below,

$$U_m = A_m^\alpha S_m^\beta \qquad (9.1)$$

---

[3] The service sectors considered in this chapter are not only consumer services, but also producer services. A discussion of how the model can be reformulated to be valid also for producer services is given in the subsequent text.

where α and β are non-negative constants and $\alpha + \beta = 1$. The sub-utility function for consumer services that corresponds to Eq. (9.1) is of the constant elasticity of substitution (CES) form, as specified in Eq. (9.2),

$$S_m = \left(\sum_{i=1}^{n} s_{im}^{1-\frac{1}{\sigma}} \right)^{\frac{\sigma}{\sigma-1}}, \sigma > 1 \tag{9.2}$$

where σ is elasticity of substitution between n different consumer services s. The consumer services may be viewed as different intermediaries for consumers in their consumption process. In order to allow some s_{im} to be zero, σ needs to be larger than one. This means that consumer's do not necessarily need to consume every service that is offered. σ is large when the services are close substitutes to each other. In other words, in situations where σ is large, preference for variety is not very significant and when σ is close to one variety in consumer service provision is important and can been seen as complementary to each other.

All services are symmetric, and hence, have identical cost- and production functions. This assumption makes it possible to simplify Eq. (9.2). The sub-utility function for services can be redefined to read:

$$\tag{9.3}$$

$$S_m = n_m^{\frac{\sigma}{\sigma-1}} s_{im}$$

From the simplified expression in Eq. (9.3) it is obvious that S_m becomes small when σ is large (holding n_m and s_{im} constant). On the other hand, as σ approaches one, the power will be of substantial size. This consideration shows that if complementarities are strong between services, the consumer's utility will be positively affected by high accessibility to a large variety of services.

In order to explore the properties of Eq. (9.3) further, we let $M_m = n_m s_{im}$ be the total amount of services used. We can then rewrite Eq. (9.3) as:

$$\frac{S_m}{M_m} = n_m^{\frac{1}{\sigma-1}} \tag{9.4}$$

In Eq. (9.4), S_m/M_m denotes the average utility per service. It is interesting that equation (4) is an increasing function of n, which means that there exist increasing returns with respect to number and, hence, diversity of services. From this follows that a regional market hosting a large number of services might be assumed to be more attractive for consumers than a regional market with fewer services.

The cost function for the typical firm in the consumer service industry is the same for all firms. We assume a very common version of the cost function written as:

$$TC_m = n_m \left(as_m + F_m \right) \tag{9.5}$$

In Eq. (9.5) TC_m is total costs for the production of all consumer services in municipality m, a is variable cost (equal to marginal cost) and F_m is fixed cost. As indicated from the cost function we assume constant returns to scale in production of services.

Now, we assume that consumers are not forced to purchase services produced in the own municipality only. Consumers are free to buy services from neighboring municipalities as well. However, we assume that the propensity to purchase services from other municipalities diminishes with distance from the own municipality. Thus, the probability that a consumer purchases a given service decreases with the time distance to the service provider. From the viewpoint of the producer of consumer-services the market can be viewed as a market-potential surface. The best location for a producer to allocate the production facility is then where the market potential is at its highest. But, since the fixed costs have to be recovered a certain share of the market has to be secured. This prevents the possibility that all producers locate at the same spot. Since all firms have the same demand on market size, it is the market-potential at each location that determines the number of firms that can be accommodated. This requires that at each location (municipality) all n producers of consumer services, aggregate total costs must be equal to the market-potential in that location. This condition can be written as Eq. (9.6) below:

$$\beta Acc_{tot}^m = TC_m \tag{9.6}$$

In Eq. (9.6) β is the share of the consumer's budget spent on consumer services, for simplicity assumed to be equal across households, and Acc_{tot}^m denotes the total accessibility to the market (or market potential) in municipality m. Acc_{tot}^m is defined as:

$$Acc_{tot}^m = \sum_{l=1}^{N} L_l w_l \exp\{-\lambda t_{ml}\} \tag{9.7}$$

In Eq. (9.7), N is the total set of municipalities. l denotes any municipality in the set N and, hence, can also be municipality m. L_l is the population in municipality l and w_l is the average wage in municipality l. λ is a distance-decay (or distance-friction) parameter that determines the inhibiting effect of distance on consumers' propensity to purchase consumer services at a distance. Eq. (9.5) can be rewritten as:

$$S_m = \frac{1}{a}\left(\frac{TC_m}{n_m} - F_m\right)$$

(9.8)

Eq. (9.6) is then substituted into Eq. (9.8) and the result is further substituted into Eq. (9.3) and we obtain:

$$S_m = \frac{n^{\frac{\sigma}{\sigma-1}}}{a}\left(\frac{\beta Acc_{tot}^m}{n_m} - F_m\right)$$

(9.9)

Eq. (9.9) can be rewritten as:

$$S_m = \frac{\beta Acc_{tot}^m n_m^{\frac{1}{\sigma-1}}}{a} - \frac{F_m n_m^{\frac{\sigma}{\sigma-1}}}{a}$$

(9.10)

At this point it is possible to optimise the consumer utility of consumer services w.r.t the number, i.e. variety, of consumer services n, given the requirements on the market-size that follows from the definition of the cost function of a typical firm. This leads to:

$$\frac{\partial S_m}{\partial n_m} = \frac{n^{\frac{1}{\sigma-1}}}{(\sigma-1)a}\left(\beta Acc_{tot}^m n_m^{-1} - \sigma F_m\right) = 0$$

(9.11)

Since is $\sigma > 1$, n and a are non-negative, it must be $\left(\beta Acc_{tot}^m n_m^{-1} - \sigma F_m\right)$ that makes $\partial S_m / \partial n_m$ to be zero. Thus, we have:

$$n_m = \frac{\beta Acc_{tot}^m}{\sigma F_m}$$

(9.12)

From Eq. (9.12), we find that the optimum number of consumer services in a market is determined by the market accessibility (Acc_{tot}^m) the budget share spent on services by consumers (β), the size of the fixed costs in the consumer service industry (F) and the elasticity of substitution between consumer services (σ). If we assume that β, σ, and F_m are equal across regions Eq. (9.12) can be rewritten as:

$$n_m = K_m Acc_{tot}^m, \ \forall m \tag{9.13}$$

where $K_m = \beta/\sigma F_m$ and m denotes municipality m. Eq. (9.13) says that the number of consumer services available in municipality m is proportional to the total wage-sum available at that municipality.

With Eq. (9.13) as a base, it is possible to explore the role of relative market-size, as measured by accessibility to wage-sum, across municipalities for the number of consumer services present in the municipalities. Such an exploration necessitates the assumption that K is identical across the municipalities. This would imply that consumer service firms', in their search for a location, is invariant to K and only take the total market-size Acc_{tot}^m into account. Consider two municipalities m and k and assume that the total market-size of each municipality incorporates the market of the other municipality. Hence, we can establish:

$$Acc_{tot}^m = L_m w_m \exp\{-\lambda\,t_{mm}\} + L_k w_k \exp\{-\lambda\,t_{mk}\} \tag{9.14a}$$

$$Acc_{tot}^k = L_k w_k \exp\{-\lambda\,t_{kk}\} + L_m w_m \exp\{-\lambda\,t_{km}\} \tag{9.14b}$$

Where Eqs. (9.14a) and (9.14b) represent the total market-accessibility of municipality m and k respectively. From the assumption that K is equal across municipalities, it follows that,

$$\tilde{n}_m = \frac{Acc_{tot}^m}{\sum_{m,k} Acc_{tot}}, \ 0< \tilde{n}_m <1 \tag{9.15}$$

where $\tilde{n}_m = n_m / (n_m+n_k)$. Eq. (9.15) simply means that the relative market-size determines the relative number of consumer services. Assume that wages are equal across regions $w_m=w_k$ and the time distance between the two municipalities are identical $t_{mk}=t_{km}$, such that any change in t has the same impact on each direction $\Delta t_{mk}=\Delta t_{km}$. Then it holds that $\partial \tilde{n}_m /\partial t_{mk} > 0$ and consequently $\partial \tilde{n}_k /\partial t_{mk} < 0$, as long as the intra municipal market-size is larger in municipality m than in municipality

k, thus that $L_m \exp\{-\lambda t_{mm}\} > L_k \exp\{-\lambda t_{kk}\}$. This implies that the lower the time distance between the municipalities, the more the smaller municipality will benefit relative to the larger municipality. The reason is straightforward, while the large municipality gets increased access to something small; the small municipality gets increased access to something large. This result suggests that there are positive backwash-effects from being located in close proximity to a large neighbour[4]. However, it is important to recognize that the two municipalities essentially compete for the same customers. By stressing agglomeration economies, for example, it could be argued that the large (small) municipality would benefit (detriment) from a reduction in the inter-municipal time distance. Thus, customers in the smaller municipality can cross the municipal borders to explore the diverse set of services available in the larger municipality. In this respect, the small municipality can be characterized as being under the influence of an agglomeration-shadow, (cf. Krugman 1993). Our framework, however, does not allow for a theoretical consideration of these effects.

A similar model as the one presented above can be constructed with producer-services in mind. Eq. (9.1) is then substituted by a Cobb-Douglas production function with a CES-sub-production function for producer services. Also, in such a model it is necessary to assume that the market for producer services is proportional to the aggregate wage-sum. This would lead to the same result as above, as regards the number of producer services available in a municipality.

9.3.2 Employment Growth and Market-Size – an Empirical Assessment

To empirically assess the relationship between market-size and employment growth each municipality's accessibility to wage-sum is calculated. Wage-sum is an appropriate base to form market-size upon since it basically measures access to purchasing power. Clearly, it is purchasing power rather than the sheer number of customer that ought to be relevant for providers of advanced services. Moreover, wage-sum does not only reflect purchasing power. It can also be seen as an indication of the size and value of the production in a municipality. Hence, the demand for various producer services is likely to be high where the wage-sum is high. Following Johansson et al. (2002), the total market-accessibility of each municipality is divided into three components, as shown in Eq. (9.16).

$$Acc_{tot}^m = Acc_{im}^m + Acc_{ir}^m + Acc_{er}^m, \quad \forall m \qquad (9.16)$$

---

[4] Note that it is required that $L_m = L_k$ and $t_{mm} = t_{kk}$ for $\tilde{n}_m$ and $\tilde{n}_k$ to be equal, see Eqs. 9A.1.-9A.4.

In the above equation, Acc_{im}^m refers to intra municipal, Acc_{ir}^m to regional and Acc_{er}^m to extra regional market-accessibility. Intra regional accessibility refers to the market-accessibility to other municipalities within the functional economic region (FER) in which the municipality in question belongs to. Note that this method makes it possible to find out to what extent there is a competition- or backwash-effect between the municipalities as regards the location of ICT service establishments, as discussed earlier. Normally, such effects are studied by means of simultaneous equation systems (see e.g. Schmitt and Henry 2000; Henry et al. 1999; Henry and Barkley 1997). The interest of these studies, however, lies on the interaction between employment and population.

Let m denote a municipality within a FER denoted by R and l another municipality; the formal definition of the three components in Eq. (9.16) can be expressed as follows,

a. Intra Mun. market accessib. $\Rightarrow Acc_{im}^m = w_m \exp\{- \lambda_{im} t_{mm}\},$

b. Intra Reg. market accessib. $\Rightarrow Acc_{ir}^m = \sum_{l \in R} w_l \exp\{- \lambda_{ir} t_{ml}\},$ $\left. \right\} \forall m, m \neq l$

c. Extra Reg. market accessib. $\Rightarrow Acc_{er}^m = \sum_{l \notin R} w_l \exp\{- \lambda_{er} t_{ml}\},$

In the formulas above, w is the wage-sum of a given municipality. t is the travel time by car between two municipalities and accordingly, λ is a time distance sensitivity parameter[5]. Three different values of λ are used, i.e. one for each component. The value of the respective λ is estimated based on commuting flows within and between Swedish municipalities by means of a doubly constrained gravity model, (see Johansson et al. 2003). λ_{im} (intra municipal) is set to 0.02, λ_{ir} (intra regional) to 0.1 and λ_{er} (extra regional) to 0.05. These are the values found by Johansson et al. (2003), which used Swedish commuting data for 1998. While these estimates are not directly related to the sensitivity to travel time as regards accessing a service provider, it can be assumed that the time-budget needed to access a service provider are to be found within the time frame valid for commuting.

To structure the analysis and make it possible to reveal if the influence of market-size is different across municipalities with different characteristics, each municipality is ordered in an accessibility-based hierarchy. The hierarchy is constructed by dividing the municipalities into eight different categories based on the size of each of the three kinds of accessibilities as shown in Fig 9.1.

The municipalities are categorized based on the size of each type of accessibility. With respect to each type of accessibility, we make a distinction between

---

[5] The time distance within a municipality is the average travel time by car between zones within the municipality.

small and large. In this manner we end up with eight (2*2*2 =8) municipal categories.

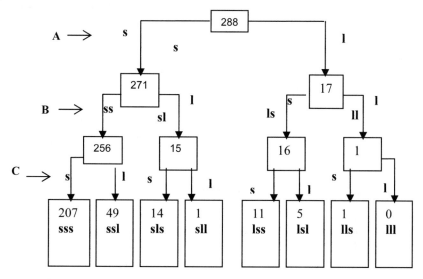

Fig.9.1. The formation of a market accessibility hierarchy (the number in each box represents the number of municipalities in each category), *A* division between small (s) and large (l) based on intramunicipal accessibility, *B* division between small (s) and large (l) based on intraregional accessibility, *C* division between small (s) and large (l) based on extraregional accessibility

As shown in Fig.9.1, we start by dividing the municipalities into small and large based on the intramunicipal accessibility indicated by *A* in the figure. Next, for both of these categories we make a further division between small and large based on the intraregional accessibility, indicated by *B* in the figure. The result is four categories. Then, we make a final division based on the extraregional accessibility for all four categories (*C* in Fig.9.1) and end up with the eight municipal categories.

The division into small and large was made in a stepwise manner. First, each municipality's share of all the municipalities' total accessibility was calculated. Second, the municipalities were ranked in descending order based on their share of the total accessibility. Third, the cumulative sum of the shares was calculated. The cut-value for the cumulative sum was set to 0.5. Thus, the municipalities constituting 50 percent of all municipalities' total accessibility were considered as having a large market-accessibility and the other 50 percent as having a small market-accessibility. This method was applied to the three types of accessibility. As can be seen in Fig. 9.1, according to this classification only 17 municipalities have a large intra municipal market-accessibility, which reflects the Swedish phenomenon of concentration of economic activity to a small set of municipalities. Moreover, no municipality qualified as having a large value of all the three types of accessibilities simultaneously. Hence, only seven categories will be considered in the study. With the categorization explained above as a base, the subsequent analysis will explore the patterns of growth across the eight different categories. Table 9.3 provides an overall description of the different municipal categories.

Table 9.3. A description of the eight municipal categories

Market accessibility	sss	ssl	sls	sll	lss	lsl	lls	lll
Intra Municipal	s	s	s	s	l	l	l	l
Intra Regional	s	s	l	l	s	s	l	l
Extra Regional	s	l	s	l	s	l	s	l

s small, *l* large

9.3.2.1 The Growth Dynamics in the Municipal Hierarchy in the 1990s

The tree diagram presented in Fig.9.2 provides a general picture of the private employment 1993 across the municipal categories. The tree diagram follows the hierarchy outlined in Fig. 9.1: the dots represent the municipal categories. For each municipal category the diagram shows the mean private employment in 1993. The four horizontal lines represent the level of division. At the bottom line, no division is made and, hence, the dot on the line shows the mean employment of all municipalities. At the second horizontal line from below, *A*, municipalities are divided into small and large based on the intramunicipal accessibility. Two dots can be found on this line, one for municipalities with a large intra-municipal accessibility and one for municipalities with a small, which represent the mean employment in each category. One the third horizontal line from below, *B*, a further division is made based on the intra regional accessibility and there are now consequently four dots. Finally, the fourth horizontal line shows the final division taking the extra regional accessibility into account. Here, there are seven dots on the line representing the eight municipal categories. The names of the categories are presented in Table 9.3.

From the structure of the tree diagram, it is evident that there are substantial differences across the categories[6]. Not surprisingly, there is a striking difference between the categories based on a small intra municipal market accessibility (the s-group) and those based on a large market accessibility (the l-group). The municipal categories based on a small intra municipal market-accessibility seems to be a rather homogeneous group since there are no major differences between them when they are further divided based on the intra and extra regional market-accessibility. The same is not true for the categories based on a large intra munici-pal market-accessibility. However, the mean figures are here based on less number of observations per category, which obviously has an effect on the divergent pat-

---

[6] Tables with the actual figures behind the tree diagrams presented in this section can be found in Table 9A.2.

tern. Overall, the intra municipal market-size seems to be the primary determinant of the size of the employment.

Municipal category

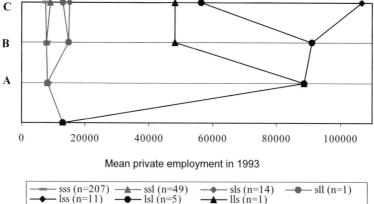

Mean private employment in 1993

——— sss (n=207)	—▲— ssl (n=49)	—◆— sls (n=14)	—●— sll (n=1)
—◆— lss (n=11)	—●— lsl (n=5)	—▲— lls (n=1)	

Fig. 9.2. Tree diagram of the mean private employment in 1993 across the seven municipal categories (*n* number of municipalities in each category), *A* division between small (*s*) and large (*l*) based on intramunicipal accessibility, *B* division between small (*s*) and large (*l*) based on intraregional accessibility, *C* division between small (*s*) and large (*l*) based on extraregional accessibility

Turning to the absolute growth in total private employment, the basic pattern is the same. When dividing the municipalities into small and large intra municipal market-accessibility it is apparent that the growth primarily took place in the municipal categories based on a large market-accessibility, the *l*-group. Again, the **s**-group seems to be quite homogeneous, but this time to a less extent. For this type of municipalities, proximity to large municipalities in the same functional region seems to stimulate the overall employment growth, which can be seen as an indication of a positive backwash effect.

For the *l*-group, on the other hand, the *lss*-category has experienced the largest growth while the *lsl*-category experienced the lowest. In fact, there is a substantial difference between the two municipal categories during the time period[7]. This hints at a possible competition effect caused by proximity to large municipalities in other regions, (cf. Cheshire and Gordon 1998).

Having observed the general pattern of private total employment in the categories presented in Fig.9.3, the next step is to relate it to the ICT service sectors. In Fig. 9.4, the mean total employment in the nine ICT service sectors across the seven municipal categories is presented.

---

[7] In exact figures, the mean absolute growth in the *lls*-category amounted to 12, 038 while the same figure was 2037 for the *lsl*-category.

Municipal category

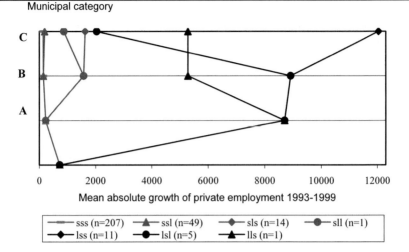

Fig. 9. 3. Tree diagram of the mean absolute growth of private employment 1993-1999 across the seven municipal categories, *A* division between small (*s*) and large (*l*) based on intramunicipal accessibility, *B*   division between small (*s*) and large (*l*) based on intraregional accessibility, *C* division between small (*s*) and large (*l*) based on extraregional accessibility

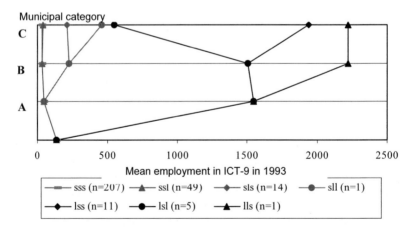

Fig. 9.4. Tree diagram of the mean employment in the ICT-9 in 1993 across the seven municipal categories, *A*   division between small (*s*) and large (*l*) based on intramunicipal accessibility, *B* division between small (*s*) and large (*l*) based on intraregional accessibility, *C* division between small (*s*) and large (*l*) based on extraregional accessibility

The pattern in Fig.9.4. is basically a mirror image of that in Fig. 9.2., on the to-tal private employment. Thus, in 1993 the ICT service industry was distributed in the same fashion as the overall economic activity. However, both the **s**-group and the *l*-group show a larger degree of heterogeneity when the municipalities are fur-

ther divided according to intra and extra regional market accessibility. The similarities between the ICT service sectors and the total private employment are also
present when looking at the employment growth. Figure 9.5. shows the tree diagram for the mean absolute employment growth 1993-1999 in the nine ICT service sectors. It is evident that the growth pattern for the ICT service sectors is exactly the same as for the total employment.

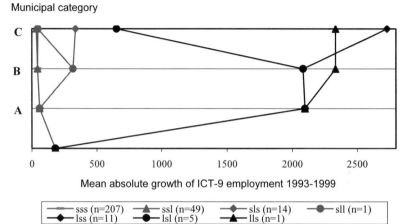

Fig.9.5. Tree diagram of the mean absolute growth of employment in the ICT-9 1993-1999
across the seven municipal categories, A division between small (s) and large (l) based on
intramunicipal accessibility, B division between small (s) and large (l) based on intraregional accessibility, C division between small (s) and large (l) based on extraregional accessibility

In Figs. 9.4. and 9.5., we treated the nine ICT service sectors at the aggregate
level. In order to explore the differences between the nine ICT service industries,
we make use of a simple correlation analysis. For each industry, we calculate the
correlation coefficient between the mean absolute growth across the municipal
categories, the mean absolute aggregate growth of the nine ICT service sectors
(ICT-9), and the mean absolute growth of the total private sector. Such an analysis
tells us to what extent the individual ICT service sectors follow both the overall
pattern of ICT-9 and the total private sector across the eight municipal categories.
The results in Table 9.4 indicate that the growth in the majority of the ICT service
sectors follow overall pattern of growth in both ICT-9 and the total private sector.
Thus, if the total employment in the private sector and the ICT-9 grew at a certain
speed, so did most of the individual ICT service sectors.

Six out of the nine industries have a correlation coefficient equal to or larger
than 0.9 for both the ICT-9 and the total private sector. This points in the direction
that a majority of the ICT service industries are complementary.

Table 9.4 The correlation between the absolute growth 1993-1999 in each ICT service sector, the overall ICT services and the total private employment across the municipal categories

ICT Service Sector	ICT-9	Total Private Sector
Wholesale tel.	0.93	0.92
Retail comp.	0.71	0.66
Retail tel.	0.90	0.95
Hardw. Con.	0.99	0.99
Softw. Con.	0.97	0.99
Softw. Sup.	0.99	1.00
Data Process	0.80	0.85
Data Base Ac.	0.97	0.96
Maintenance	0.41	0.47

However, if one considers total private employment growth as a rough measure of the overall demand in the economy, the strong correlations provided in the table should be expected. The industries showing the highest correlation to the ICT-9 and the total private sector, *Hardware consultancy, Software consultancy, Software supply* and *Data base activities*, are all closely coupled to computer usage. *Retail sale of computers, office machinery and computer programs, Maintenance & repair* and *Data processing* show a relatively low correlation with the overall absolute employment growth in both the ICT-9 and the total private sector.

What conclusions can be drawn from the descriptive analysis presented above? First and foremost, it can be concluded that market-accessibility seems to be important for both the size of employment and the growth in employment in the ICT-service sectors as well as the overall employment. Moreover, it is clear that the distinction between different types of market-accessibilities reveals interesting differences across municipalities. Primarily, it seems as if proximity to larger markets stimulates growth for small municipalities but have a negative effect for larger municipalities. Also, it has been shown that most of the ICT service sectors are homogeneous as regards their growth experience across the eight municipal categories. Their growth seems to reflect the overall demand in the economy. Also, it has been indicated that they can be seen as complementary to each other. However, the result must be consulted with care due to the aggregation of the figures.

9.3.2.2 Exploring Systematic Regularities in Municipal Growth Patterns – How Well Do the ICT Service Sectors Fit?

In this section, we extend the empirical analysis in order to explore the extent to which the growth pattern of the ICT service sectors corresponds to the overall regularities in Swedish municipalities. Cross-sectional regression analysis is applied. The absolute employment growth between 1993 and 1999 in each ICT service sector is regressed on the three types of market-sizes set out in Eq. (9.16). Both dummies and interaction variables are included in the regression model to control for the eight municipal categories established in Fig. 9.1, (see Table 9A.3). The regression model is presented in Eq. (9.17).

$$\Delta Y = \alpha + \beta_1 Acc_{im} + \beta_2 Acc_{ir} + \beta_3 Acc_{er} + \gamma_1 D_{im} + \gamma_2 D_{ir} + \gamma_3 D_{er} \qquad (9.17)$$
$$+ \theta_1 I_{im} + \theta_2 I_{ir} + \theta_3 I_{er} + \varepsilon$$

Where the error-term ε is assumed to be normally distributed such that $\varepsilon \sim N(0, \sigma^2)$. The variables denoted by I represent the interaction variables and are defined as below.

$$I_{im} \equiv Acc_{im} \times D_{im}, \ I_{ir} \equiv Acc_{ir} \times D_{ir}, \ I_{er} \equiv Acc_{er} \times D_{er} \qquad (9.18)$$

Based on the model above, 14 regressions are made. The independent variables are the same for all the regressions. Table 9.5 describes the dependent and independent variables used in the analysis. As seen in the table, the three accessibility measures are based on 1993. Thus, it is assumed that the effects of the structure of the market-accessibilities take place with a time lag.

Table 9.5 Variables in the regression analysis, their notation and meaning[a]

Variable	Description
ΔY	Absolute change in total population, employment, in- and out-commuting, ICT-9 and employment in each of the nine ICT service sectors 1993 -1999
Acc_{im}	Accessibility to market within the municipality 1993
Acc_{ir}	Accessibility to market within the region 1993
Acc_{er}	Accessibility to market outside the region 1993
D_{im}	1 if the municipality had a large intra municipal market size 1993, 0 otherwise
D_{ir}	1 if the municipality had a large intra regional market size 1993, 0 otherwise
D_{er}	1 if the municipality had a large extra regional market size 1993, 0 otherwise
I_{im}	Interaction variable for intra municipal market size
I_{ir}	Interaction variable for intra regional market size
I_{er}	Interaction variable for extra regional market size

[a] The division of the municipalities into small and large market-size is the same as the one explained in Sect. 9.3.2.

As stated above, the growth in the ICT service sectors will be compared with the overall pattern of change. Therefore, in addition to the growth in the nine ICT service sectors, the model above is regressed on the absolute change in *total population, total private employment*[8], and *total in- and out-commuting* in each of the 288 municipalities in the study. The change in these variables is perceived as being dependent on the character of a municipality as regards the size of the three market-sizes. By regressing on these variables, we should be able to reveal sys-

---

[8] The public sector was deleted in the analysis since the same processes do not govern it as the private sector in general.

tematic regularities across the municipal categories. Hence, the method makes it possible to ascertain whether similar processes govern the chosen ICT service sectors or not.

The use of the change in population and employment needs little justification. These are the primary indicators of overall growth performance. Thus, these are the variables to reveal systematic regularities in the general growth patterns across the municipalities in the study. Furthermore, the motivation for the use of in- and out-commuting is straightforward. Firstly, the commuting patterns across the municipalities in the study disclose how the impact of neighbouring municipalities differs across the municipal categories as regards employment opportunities, i.e. the existence of competition/backwash effects. For example, municipalities with a large in-commuting benefit in the sense that their potential labour supply is large. Secondly, these patterns will also hint at the potential patterns of mobility of consumers searching for services. For example, the time distance relevant for a consumer when it comes to travel to a service provider is most likely germane to the time distance pertinent for commuting. This implies that it can be expected that service providers located in municipalities with large in-commuting from surrounding municipalities regard the individuals in the surrounding municipalities as potential customers. In-commuting implies by definition that a municipality experiences an inflow of potential customers each day.

Starting with the overall growth pattern across the 288 municipalities, the results of the regressions on the absolute change in total population, total employment and in- and out-commuting are presented in Table 9.6.

Table 9.6 Regression result of the 288 municipalities based on Eq. (9.17) for the absolute change in population, private employment and in- and out-commuting between 1993 and 1999[9]

	ΔPopulation		ΔEmployment		ΔIn-commuting		ΔOut-commuting	
α	−0.64*	(−5.62)	−265.48*	(− 4.02)	−197.28*	(−3.03)	−52.07	(−0.97)
Acc_{im}	0.19	(1.13)	270.94*	(3.09)	238.33*	(3.02)	178.08*	(2.10)
Acc_{ir}	0.05*	(3.69)	27.97*	(4.06)	22.72*	(2.71)	13.23**	(1.69)
Acc_{er}	0.03	(0.23)	130.94**	(1.74)	143.69**	(1.94)	105.66**	(1.81)
D_{im}	−1.60	(−1.33)	−5197.78*	(−9.49)	−4189.73*	(−7.07)	−2368.38*	(−4.95)
D_{ir}	3.08**	(1.87)	346.77	(0.34)	82.39	(0.08)	110.26	(0.14)
D_{er}	−1.88*	(−2.85)	−87.17	(−0.32)	176.27	(0.67)	−214.87	(−0.54)
I_{im}	0.52*	(3.02)	779.59*	(8.72)	583.97*	(7.12)	391.02*	(4.45)
I_{ir}	−0.05	(−1.49)	−16.06	(−0.81)	−9.75	(−0.46)	3.35	(0.22)
I_{er}	0.50*	(2.23)	−101.99	(−1.02)	−197.39*	(−2.09)	−33.83	(−0.24)
R^2 adj.	0.86		0.97		0.96		0.95	
N	288		288		288		288	

t-values are in parentheses.* denotes significance at the 0.05 level.** denotes significance at the 0.1 level.

---

[9] All regressions are made using the Robust Errors technique outlined in White (1980) and pedagogically explained in Greene (2000).

The goodness of fit indicators (R^2 adjusted) of the regressions is gratifying. At the lowest, the model explains 86 percent of the variation in the dependent variable, leaving not much room for alternative model specifications.

According to the estimation, the three market accessibilities have a positive effect on the growth in total private employment and in out - and in -commuting. The significance of the interaction variable for the intra municipal market-accessibility ($I_{im,}$), shows that the initial intra municipal market accessibility has a stronger impact on the growth for the municipalities with a large such market accessibility, i.e. the l-group[10]. Hence, being initially large seems to foster growth in these variables. For the in-commuting, it is evident that municipalities located in proximity to municipalities in other functional economic regions have experienced a lower growth, indicating a competition-effect.

This is given by the significantly negative estimate for I_{er}. The intra-municipal market-accessibility has no impact on the population growth. It neither adds nor subtracts anything from the growth performance. This is only true, however, for the municipalities with a small intra municipal market-size, the s-group. Thus, also here the initial size is important, since the estimate for I_{im} is significantly positive. The same result applies to the extra regional market-accessibility.

Turning to the estimates for the ICT service sectors presented in Table 9.7, we can see that the intra municipal market-accessibility is the major determinant for the employment growth in these sectors. Looking at the ICT-9 as an aggregate, the intra-municipal market-accessibility spurs growth across all types of municipalities.

Table 9.7 Regression result of the 288 municipalities based on Eq. (9.17) for the absolute employment change in the ICT-9 and the individual ICT service sectors between 1993 and 1999[a]

	ΔICT-9	ΔWhole-sale	ΔRetail Comp.	ΔRetail Tel.	ΔHardw. Con.	ΔSoftw. Con.	ΔSoftw. Sup.	ΔData process.	ΔData base	ΔMain-tenance
α	−3.34	−3.14	−1.74	−0.27	−0.02	11.27	−10.46	3.58	−1.16	−1.40
	−0.25	−1.37	−0.86	−0.53	−0.01	1.28	−1.67	0.92	−0.78	−0.91
Acc_{im}	74.28*	0.80	−1.10	4.07*	5.23*	36.77*	17.23*	10.11**	1.64	−0.47
	4.36	0.27	−0.84	6.37	2.41	2.44	2.07	1.90	1.63	−0.50
Acc_{ir}	1.57	0.33	0.01	−0.06	−0.20	−0.42	1.59	0.20	0.24	−0.13
	0.97	1.74	0.17	−1.44	−0.93	−0.60	1.07	0.54	1.53	−1.45
Acc_{er}	−9.43	3.02**	1.83	−0.80	−0.52	−10.18	2.37	−8.69**	0.08	3.45
	−0.59	1.68	0.86	−1.52	−0.43	−0.95	0.33	−1.92	1.53	1.51
D_{im}	−894.4*	−71.72*	−5.89	−20.5*	1.49	−681*	−107**	38.66	−56.4*	8.42
	7.17	−4.05	−0.33	−2.85	0.04	−7.44	−1.96	0.94	−3.11	1.30
D_{ir}	−468.0**	76.87	6.11	−3.65	−5.11	−491*	−78.82	−14.3	23.59	19.07
	−1.75	0.85	0.69	−0.82	−0.38	−2.26	−1.42	−0.18	1.31	0.91

---

[10] Observe that the significantly negative dummy for the municipalities with a large intra municipal market-accessibility should *not* be interpreted as that those municipalities on average have a lower grower. The dummy is negative due to the steeper relationship for these municipalities, which presses down the intercept.

Table 9.7 (cont.)

	ΔICT-9	Δ Whole-sale	Δ Retail Comp.	Δ Retail Tel.	Δ Hardw. Con.	Δ Softw. Con.	Δ Softw. Sup.	Δ Data process.	Δ Data base	Δ Main-tenance
D_{er}	−89.44*	6.94	3.24	0.50	−12.2**	−67.0*	−20.8**	−7.07	0.69	6.29
	−3.27	1.36	0.70	0.23	−1.90	−3.01	−1.67	−0.47	0.23	1.46
I_{im}	152.13*	9.89*	3.40*	1.97*	2.38	115.4*	17.07**	−2.97	3.8*	1.20
	8.27	2.97	2.26	2.17	0.50	6.96	1.91	−0.54	3.00	1.27
I_{ir}	8.53**	−0.62	0.04	0.04	0.27	9.83*	−0.26	−0.12	−0.7**	0.01
	1.83	−0.53	0.28	0.48	1.16	2.61	−0.14	−0.10	−1.83	0.05
I_{er}	17.01	−4.36*	−1.64	0.61	3.14	15.29	−1.03	8.87**	0.25	−4.13**
	0.97	−2.02	−0.78	1.03	1.49	1.27	−0.13	1.69	0.18	−1.73
R^2 adj.	0.98	0.67	0.31	0.90	0.34	0.97	0.87	0.40	0.64	0.14
N	288	288	288	288	288	288	288	288	288	288

[a] All regressions are made using the *Robust Errors* technique outlined in White (1980) and pedagogically explained in Greene (2000). T-values are written in italics.* denotes significance at the 0.05 level.** denotes significance at the 0.1 level.

As was found for the overall pattern, the effect is stronger for the municipalities with a large intra municipal market-accessibility. Similarly, only for municipalities with a large intra regional market accessibility the estimate is significant. We may interpret this as indicating that closeness to large municipalities in the same functional economic region stimulated the diffusion of these sectors during the time period. Hence, signs of path-dependence are present for the ICT service sectors also. For six out of the nine ICT service sector it is found that the effect of the intra municipal market accessibility is larger for municipalities with a large such market-accessibility, which is in line with the overall pattern. It is evident that the growth in employment in these sectors is primarily dependent on the initial market conditions internal to the municipalities.

9.4 Conclusions and Policy Implications

Our endeavour in this study has been to reveal systematic patterns of growth in the ICT service sectors across Swedish municipalities and relate these to the overall growth in the Swedish economy. Explaining the employment growth with different types of market-accessibilities, it was found that the growth in the ICT service sectors coincides with the overall private employment growth. In this way the present chapter extends the conclusions in Chap. 7. During the 1990s, a vast majority of the ICT service sectors displayed a rapid diffusion process. This was shown using multiple measures. However, regional diffusion was coupled with increased employment in the metropolitan and urban areas.

As a vehicle for the detailed analysis, the Swedish municipalities where ordered in an accessibility-based hierarchy with eight categories. The intra municipal market-accessibility is the most important determinant for the employment expansion.

The analysis showed that both general employment increases and ICT employment growth differed substantially across the municipal categories. This is evident from the frequent occurrence of significant estimates for both the intercept and the slope dummies. Since the overall pattern suggests that municipalities with larger initial market accessibilities grow faster, the study supports the presence of a self-strengthening cumulative process. This result implies that the size distribution of municipalities is becoming more uneven over time.

In this analysis market size is formulated as an accessibility measure where time-distance, and hence infrastructure, plays a central role. From a policy point of view, this means that market size can be altered through infrastructure investments. Thus, infrastructure improvements can increase the market accessibility for a particular municipality. However, infrastructure investments are costly and in order for these investments to have a sufficient impact on accessibility, the original time distance should not exceed one hour. This statement is dependent on the magnitude of the distance decay parameter. This means that for many municipalities in Sweden where the economic density is low infrastructure improvements are not enough to turn around a negative development. Nevertheless, for some municipalities such investments can be useful. If the municipality is not too small and neighbouring municipalities are not too far away, shorter time-distances can have a decisive impact.

References

Beeson P, DeJong D, Troesken W (2001) Population growth in U.S. counties 1840–1990. Regional Science and Urban Economics 31: 669–699

Cheshire P, Gordon I (1998) Territorial competition: some lessons for policy. Annals of Regional Science 32: 321–346

Feser E (2001) Agglomeration, enterprise size and productivity. In: Johansson B, Karlsson C, Stough RR (2001) Theories of endogenous regional growth – lessons from regional policies. Springer, Berlin Heidelberg New York, pp 231–251

Fujita M, Thisse JF (2002) Economics of agglomeration: cities, industrial location and regional growth. Cambridge University Press, Cambridge

Glaeser E (1998) Are cities dying? Journal of Economic Perspectives 12: 1139–1160

Government Offices of Sweden (2000) An information society for all (in Swedish). Law No 86, 1999/2000, Government Offices of Sweden, Stockholm. Available at http://www.regeringen.se/content/1/c4/21/80/bf3285d6.pdf

Greene WH (2000) Econometric analysis, 4 edn. Prentice Hall, Englewood Cliffs, NJ

Henry M, Barkley D (1997) The Hinterland's stake in metropolitan growth: evidence from selected southern regions. Journal of Regional Science 37: 479–501

Henry M, Schmitt B, Kristensen K, Barkley, D, Bao S (1999) Extending the Carlino-Mills models to examine urban size and growth impacts on proximate rural areas. Growth and Change 30: 526–548

Hoover EM (1937) Location theory and the shoe and leather industries. Harvard University Press, Cambridge, MA

Johansson B, Klaesson J, Olsson M (2002) Time distance and labour market integration. Papers in Regional Science 81: 305–327

Johansson B, Klaesson J, Olsson M (2003) Commuters' non-linear response to time distances. Journal of Geographical Systems 5:315-329

Johansson B, Karlsson C (2001) Geographic transaction costs and specialization opportunities of small and medium-sized regions: economies of scale and market extension. In: Johansson B, Karlsson C, Stough RR (2001) Theories of endogenous regional growth – lessons from regional policies. Springer, Berlin Heidelberg New York, pp 150–180

Karlsson C (1999) Spatial industrial dynamics in Sweden – urban growth industries. Growth and Change 30: 184–212

Kjellgren J (2002) Essays on agglomeration and sectoral diversification in Sweden. Licentiate Thesis, Jönköping International Business School, Jönköping

Klaesson J, Pettersson L (2001) Regional dynamics of service markets in Sweden – a probability approach exploring the presence of consumer services. Mimeograph, Jönköping International Business School, Jönköping

Krugman P (1991a) Increasing returns and economic geography. Journal of Political Economy 99: 483–499

Krugman P (1991b) Geography and trade. The MIT Press, Cambridge, MA

Krugman P (1993) On the relationship between trade theory and location theory. Review of International Economics 2: 110–122

Organisation for Economic Co-operation and Development (OECD) (1998) Measuring the ICT sector. OECD Report, Paris

Ohlin B (1933) Interregional and international trade. Harvard University Press, Cambridge, MA

Quigley JM (1998) Urban diversity and economic growth. Journal of Economic Perspectives 12: 127–138

Schmitt B, Henry M (2000) Size and growth of urban centres in French labour market areas: consequences for rural population and employment. Regional Science and Urban Economics 30: 1–21

Statistics Sweden (2001) Employment in municipalities and counties 1999 – labour statistics on administrative sources. Statistical Letter No. 0101, Statistics Sweden, Stockholm

Weber A (1929) Theory of the Location of Industries. University of Chicago Press, Chicago

White H (1980) A Heteroscedasticity-Consistent Covariance Matrix Estimator and a Direct Test for Heteroscedasticity. Econometrica 48: 817–838

Annex

Table 9A.1 Description of the ICT service sectors

SIC-code	Description	Abbreviation
51653	Wholesale of telecommunication equipment and electronic components	Wholesale tel.
52493	Retail sale of computers, office machinery and computer programs	Retail comp.
52494	Retail sale of telecommunication equipment	Retail tel.
72100	Hardware consultancy	Hardw Con.
72201	Software consultancy	Softw Con.
72202	Software supply	Softw Sup.
72300	Data processing	Data process
72400	Data base activities	Data Base Ac.
72500	Maintenance and repair of office, accounting and computing machinery	Maintenance

Annex 9A.1. Derivation resulting from Eq. (9.15)

Eq. (9.15) can be written as:

$$\tilde{n}_m = \frac{L_m e^{-\lambda m} + L_k e^{-\lambda t}}{L_m e^{-\lambda m} + L_k e^{-\lambda t} + L_k e^{-\lambda k} + L_m e^{-\lambda t}} \tag{9A.1}$$

In the Eq. (9A.1), m and k denote the intra municipal time distance of the two municipalities respectively. t denote the time distance between the two municipalities. Derivation of the expression above w.r.t t leads to:

$$\frac{\partial \tilde{n}_m}{\partial t} = \frac{\lambda e^{-\lambda t} \left(-L_k^2 e^{-\lambda k} + L_m^2 e^{-\lambda m} \right)}{\left(L_m e^{-\lambda m} + L_k e^{-\lambda t} + L_k e^{-\lambda k} + L_k e^{-\lambda t} \right)^2} \tag{9A.2}$$

From the expression above it is evident that for $\partial \tilde{n}_m / \partial t$ to be equal zero, L_k must be equal to L_m and m must be equal to k. Thus,

$$- L_k^2 e^{-\lambda k} + L_m^2 e^{-\lambda m} = 0 \qquad (9A.3)$$

$$\frac{L_m^2}{L_k^2} = \frac{e^{-\lambda k}}{e^{-\lambda m}} = e^{\lambda(-k+m)} \qquad (9A.4)$$

Table 9A.2. Presentation of the figures/statistics for Figs. 9.2-9.5.

Municipal category	Private Employment 1993	ΔEmployment 1993-1999	Employment ICT-9 1993	Δ Employment ICT-9 1993-1999
No division				
All munici-palities	13 054.1	732.1923	134.0417	179.3785
1st division				
s	8 284.885	228.6394	45.4059	59.13653
l	88 519.94	8 700.176	1 547	2 096.176
2nd division				
ss	7 900.941	148.9882	34.71094	44.08203
sl	14 786.33	1 577.4	227.9333	316.0667
ls	91 039.13	8 913.375	1 505	2 081.375
ll	48 213	5 289	2 219	2 333
3rd division				
sss	7 637.33	138.37	33.92	46.46
ssl	9 032.29	194.56	38.06	34.04
sls	14 919.5	1 627.07	211.21	335.43
sll	12 922	882	462	45
lss	106 802.4	12 038.82	1 938	2 730.64
lsl	56 360	2 037.4	552.4	653
lls	48 213	5 289	2 219	2 333

Data source: Statistics Sweden 2001

Table 9A.3. Explanation of the dummy variables in Eq. 9.17

D_{im}	D_{ir}	D_{er}	Municipal category
0	0	0	sss
0	0	1	ssl
0	1	0	sls
0	1	1	sll
1	0	0	lss
1	0	1	lsl
1	1	0	lls
1	1	1	lll

Section C: Telecommunication and Policy

10 Cities in the Internet Age

Edward J. Malecki

Department of Geography, The Ohio State University

10.1 Introduction

Recent literature in the social sciences suggests that a 'new geography' has emerged – one that marks a break from past geographies. Cities are central to the 'new geography', particularly global or world cities and their surrounding urban regions. This chapter attempts to synthesize the new realities of cities and the new urban geographies that have appeared during the past decade or two. Recent research at both the interurban scale of city systems and at the intra-urban scale of the individual metropolis makes claims that new trends, patterns, and processes are operating. Both scales of analysis are foci of this chapter, centred around aspects of technology and its effects on cities. In this way the presentation relates to problem formulations that are introduced in Chap. 2 of this book.

Far from diminishing the attraction of large cities, the combination of new technology and the need for face-to-face contact continue to favour large cities. Storper and Venables (2002) attribute this to 'buzz', or the advantage of face-to-face contact, which they assert is the mechanism at the heart of urban agglomeration. However, other forces pull to some degree toward new 'edge cities' or new clusters of economic activities outside the urban core but within the metropolitan region.

The chapter begins with a survey of the 'new geography' and the technological, social, and political forces that have created it. Next, the chapter turns to the urban hierarchy and the largest urban regions, or world cities, in particular. In both the new geography and the evolving world city hierarchy, there appear to be winners and losers, a pattern reinforced by the 'new economy' and its effects on cities. The chapter then focuses on the shape of the postmodern metropolis, with attention paid to 'edge cities' and the polynuclear urban form found increasingly throughout the world. The chapter ends with an assessment of challenges for urban planning in the context of 'splintered urbanism', the trend toward social, economic, and spatial bifurcation of urban spaces.

10.2 A New Geography?

We live in "an urbanized world of sprawling metropolises" Castells (2001, p. 224). Urban economies are "the information-switching centers of the global economy" (Graham and Marvin, 1996). These metropolises are also the locus of contradictions, where all do not benefit equally from the new economy. "The Internet allows segregated, affluent enclaves to remain in contact with each other, and with the world, while severing ties with their uncontrolled, surrounding environment" (Castells 2001, p. 240).

In his description of "the new geography", Kotkin (2000) points out that geography has not diminished in importance, but its significance has changed in nature. If people, companies, or industries can locate anywhere, or choose from a multiplicity of places, the question of where they locate becomes increasingly contingent on the specific attributes of any given location. What have changed are the rules that govern geography, and the rules that make of successful and unsuccessful places. Perhaps the key rule is based on the realization that "where information-processing companies, related services, and skilled professionals choose to locate will increasingly shape the geographic importance of future cities and communities" (Kotkin 2000, pp. 6-7).

Companies, under constant pressure to create new products and services, and the skilled professionals, on whom they depend for creativity, gravitate toward large, amenity-rich urban regions. The amenities they seek are not merely pleasant physical environments; they include opportunities for consumption and interaction. As Castells (2001) summarizes, cities are agglomerations of economic and social life. Specifically, cities stand out in four ways:

- Cities are innovative milieux for high technology;
- Cities are key places for advanced services, including finance, insurance, legal services, accounting, advertising, marketing;
- Cities are centers of cultural industries, including media, entertainment, art, fashion, publishing, museums, and cultural creation of all kinds; and
- Cities attract knowledge creators – highly educated workers and entrepreneurs.

Camagni (2001) has put forward a similar set of roles for cities, but with emphasis on spatial roles. Camagni sees the city as 'cluster' (with increasing returns), as 'interconnection', as 'milieu of innovation and creativity', and as 'symbol'. The symbolic roles include both 'place' and 'node', as symbol of territorial control, and as a place for creation of symbols. For both Castells and Camagni, cities are clusters and milieus of innovation and creativity but, significantly, Camagni adds the symbolic and nodal roles of cities. Storper and Venables (2002) also suggest that the economies of the larger and more globally-linked metropolitan areas dominate in five areas: (a) creative and cultural functions, including industries linked to this, such as fashion, design and the arts; (b) tourism; (c) finance and business services; (d) science, technology and high technology and research; and (e) power and influence, including government, headquarters, trade associations, and international agencies.

Are these new roles being taken on by cities? No. Andersson (1985) and Hall (1998) have traced similar creative characteristics of cities throughout the past two centuries. Athens, Florence, London, Vienna, Paris, and Berlin all had their periods of cultural creativity. In the industrial era, several cities flourished (more briefly) as innovative milieux: Manchester, Glasgow, Berlin, Detroit, San Francisco/Palo Alto/Berkeley, and Tokyo/Kanagawa. Not all of these appear on lists of world cities today, a fact that suggests that creativity is part — but only part —of the new geography. Likewise, agglomeration is necessary but not sufficient for urban growth. Technological change adds to the advantages of creativity in some places more than in others, and to the benefits of agglomeration in some places more than in others.

10.3 Some Effects of New Technology

Technology has facilitated many of the activities for which agglomeration in cities remains crucial, and it enables relationships to be initiated and maintained among people and among firms and organizations spread among locations great distances apart. Couclelis (2000) paints a picture that incorporates several ways in which technology has affected people's daily lives. First, technology has *extended* human activity far beyond the local area, a point made earlier by Janelle (1973). Travel is both cheaper and more readily available to more people. Rising incomes and an expanded travel and tourism industry are causes of this extension, which affects both business travel and leisure (vacation or holiday) travel. Second, technology has *fragmented* or *disintegrated* activities among locations. Activities that used to be associated with a single location (e.g., a workplace) are now increasingly scattered among geographically distant locations (e.g., office, home, associate's home, hotel room, car, train, or plane). Third, technology has *changed accessibility* from the simple question of how easy (fast, cheap, comfortable) it is to overcome distance to a situation that substitutes telecommunications contact for physical movement. Fourth, technology has exploded the *contact set* of individuals, the number of places they interact with, from one location per activity to a potentially indefinite number of locations. Some of these contacts are carried out in virtual space; others are very much physical.

Despite these wide-ranging changes, technology is not creating a new world or re-making completely the old one. Graham (1997) debunks several widespread myths concerning telecommunications and cities:

- Myth 1: Technological determinism — technology is a force that creates changes to which society must respond. Instead, technology is socially constructed and socially and economically biased.
- Myth 2: Urban dissolution — cities will no longer be needed as telecommunications replaces physical contact. Instead, technology does not facilitate complete 'anywhere, anytime' interaction; co-presence is still needed.

- Myth 3: Universal access — the spread of technology to all will eliminate inequality. Instead, urban societies seem to be becoming more unequal.
- Myth 4: Simple substitution of transport by telecommunications. Instead, this 'is simply not happening'.
- Myth 5: Local powerlessness in the face of technological changes. Instead, policies lead to wide variations in the ways telecommunications are socially shaped.

Perhaps no myth has found more believers than Myth 4; that travel will greatly decrease because telecommunications will replace most, if not all, communications. Generally, technology has not eliminated the human need for co-presence, represented most by face-to-face contact. A great deal of research has found that telecommunications tend to complement travel, rather than substitute for it (Gaspar and Glaeser 1998; Moss 1998). Leamer and Storper (2001) have provided perhaps the clearest argument for the persistent of travel, embodied in the metaphors of the 'handshake' versus the 'conversation'. The 'handshake' represents information exchanges made while in the same physical space, whereas the 'conversation' is the interactive long-distance exchange of visual and oral information. A conversation can take place through a computer, telephone, and other forms of telecommunications, but two people cannot perform a handshake in virtual space.

Although 'conversations' are able to be done remotely and to involve the transfer of documents and other codifiable knowledge, 'handshake' interactions largely involve the exchange of tacit or uncodifiable knowledge. The exchange of tacit or ambiguous information depends on a high level of trust and shared context (Nonaka and Takeuchi 1995; Nonaka et al. 2000). Because of the complexities of tacit knowledge transfer, 'handshake' interactions are likely to continue to require a significant amount of co-presence (Leamer and Storper 2001; Boden and Molotch 1994). All data suggest that face-to-face contact continues to be important and complementary to electronic interaction. Indeed, it is central to 'buzz', the pull that large cities continue to exert despite the undeniable costs of congestion (Storper and Venables 2002).

In summary, technology is being incorporated into what we do and how we do it. It has made life more complex in many ways, as Couclelis points out. Not only do we do more things in more places, we also interact with many more people and organizations than was ever possible in the past. These technological changes, however, have not ended abruptly the processes and patterns behind urban and regional development, particularly the importance of large cities (Malecki 2001; Malecki and Gorman 2001). At the same time, however, we retain at least some of the face-to-face encounters that have always been a part of the human condition. Needless to say, some relationships suffer in this context. Families more rarely have meals in the same place and at the same time, for example. Leisure becomes difficult when people are expected to be 'always available' via e-mail and mobile phones. That is, technology has costs as well as benefits. The price of being able to contact others is that we must in some way also be contacted by others.

10.4 World Cities

The world economy is structured around a network of places that serve as interconnected hubs of global commerce. These world cities (or global cities) are: (1) command points in the organization of the world economy, where transnational firms place their management functions; (2) key locations and markets for leading industries, especially finance and advanced producer services; and (3) major sites of production for these sectors, including production of innovations (Sassen 1994, p. 4). The new hierarchy of cities, however, leaves most other centers (including most old industrial centers and port cities) largely without influence in the world economy (Friedmann 1986; Friedmann and Wolff 1982; Sassen 2000).

The world city phenomenon has been an object of research only since the mid-1980s, and changes in city status are already evident (Friedmann 1995). As the world city concept was developed, it was generally agreed that London, New York, and Tokyo stood alone as the pre-eminent world cities where the bulk of capital and control resides (Sassen 1991, 2000). The painful decline of the Japanese economy has taken away some of Tokyo's pre-eminence, and none of the Asian competitors (Bombay, Hong Kong, Seoul, Shanghai, Singapore) has replaced Tokyo in the hierarchy. Below the top three is a hierarchy of second-order financial and business centers, many of which have been financial centers for centuries, such as Amsterdam and Zürich, while others are gateways to major markets, as Hong Kong is to China (Table 10.1).

Table 10.1. The hierarchy of world cities

Global financial centres	London	New York	Tokyo
Multinational centres	Frankfurt	Miami	Singapore
	Amsterdam	Los Angeles	
Important national centers	Paris	Mexico City	Seoul
	Zürich	São Paulo	Sydney
	Madrid		
Regional centers	Milan	Boston	Hong Kong
	Lyon	Chicago	Osaka
	Barcelona	Houston	Kobe
	Munich	Seattle	Shanghai
	Düsseldorf- Cologne-Essen-	Toronto	
	Dortmund (Rhine-Ruhr	Montreal	
	region)	Vancouver	

Source: Based on Friedmann (1995, pp.24-27 and Table 2.1)

These centres link core economies to each other and to the leading three cities in what is, spatially, a Triad structure (Friedmann 1986; Friedmann 1995). Africa is largely excluded. Simon (1995) suggests Cairo, Johannesburg, and Nairobi are the nearest to world city status but they do not fully meet that status owing to Africa's peripheral position in the world economy. Some cities, such as Detroit, Honolulu, Miami, and Mecca, are 'limited-service global cities' that are clearly important in one, but not all, dimensions of world city status (Nijman 1996; Thompson 1995).

The global control functions that concentrate in world cities are linked by telecommunications. Physical infrastructure and amenities characterize world cities and their office-based functions, and air connections as well as IT link these cities at the highest levels of connectivity (Keeling 1995). It is in these centers that access to information networks is highest, telecommunications links are best, producer services are most available, and labour resources are most readily found (Moulaert and Tödtling 1995; Tödtling 1994). In short, world cities provide access to global networks and, therefore, are preferred locations for global firms. These locations provide 'economies of overview' with respect to the global economy (Moulaert and Gallouj 1993).

Probing the networks of global firms in four sectors of producer services, the research group on Globalization and World Cities (GaWC) Study Group at Loughborough University has done most to advance the state of empirical knowledge of world cities. A flurry of research during the past six years has clarified the new metageography defined by the relations among cities within the networks of firms in the four sectors (accounting, advertising, banking, and legal services) (Beaverstock et al. 1999, 2000; Taylor and Walker 2001). Taylor (2001) describes "an unusual form of network" with 3 levels of structure: cities as the nodes, the world economy as the supranodal network level, and advanced producer service firms forming a critical subnodal level.

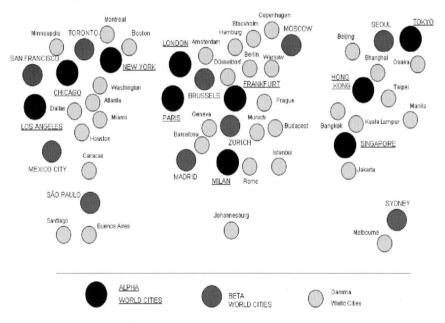

Fig.10.1. The World According to GaWC. Source: Reprinted from Beaverstock et al. (1999, p. 456), A roster of world cities, Vol 16, No 6, pp. 445-458, Copyright (1999), with permission from Elsevier

The firms create an interlocking network through their global location strategies for placing offices. Fig.10.1 shows the three tiers in the GaWC world-city hierarchy. The same pattern is reinforced by network analyses of air travel (Smith and Timberlake 2002).

The significance of the world city concept is threefold. First, it captures the notion of an urban hierarchy, long a central concept in central place theory. Second, it includes the important flows within the network of global cities — not only up and down the hierarchy, but also horizontally between functionally specialized cities (Camagni and Salone 1992). Third, it emphasizes the importance of large cities, whose essence comes from the need for face-to-face contact and their position as important nodes in global information networks (Moulaert and Djellal 1995; Parker 1995).

Essentially, world cities are groups of fragmented economic and social activities that are linked into external transport and telecommunications networks operating on continental and global scales. World cities should be seen as junctions of flows of goods, information, and people rather than as fixed locations for the production of goods and services (Rimmer 1998, pp. 437-439). In fact, world cities are 'nested' simultaneously both into their local settings and into global networks in complex ways (Hill and Fujita 2003). Both 'hard' and 'soft' networks are needed in order to form and maintain these network links (Malecki 2002a).

10.4.1 Upheaval in the Urban Hierarchy?

Separately from the GaWC Study Group, others have studied the urban hierarchy in the age of the Internet. Within the USA, for example, Moss and Townsend find that "a stable hierarchy of network hubs and spokes apparently has emerged" (Moss and Townsend 2000, p. 42). Seven urban regions have consistently placed at the top of the US urban hierarchy as 'central nodes' (San Francisco, Washington, Chicago, New York, Dallas-Fort Worth, Los Angeles, and Atlanta). However, what is striking about this group is the emergence of 'new network cities', such as Washington and San Francisco as major hubs, which have surpassed the formerly dominant cities of the industrial era — that is, the relative weakness of New York, Chicago, and Los Angeles and the prominence of Atlanta and Dallas. "Internet technology has enabled many cities to become highly specialized global information producers... Rather than a handful of regions dominating global finance and culture, a constellation of highly specialized regions now interact in a globally telemediated economy" (Townsend 2001, p. 43).

Townsend (2001) suggests that Boston and San Francisco are examples of a new breed of global city – the network city. A network city is typically a medium-sized (rather than very large) metropolitan area with excellent access to high-capacity Internet backbone networks and with "a broad-based diffusion of Internet activity throughout its educated population" (Townsend 2001, p. 54). In addition to Boston and San Francisco, network cities in the USA include Minneapolis, San Diego, Seattle, and Washington, DC. How have new network cities emerged? According to Townsend (2001, p.56), the network city "operates in an economy where the transport costs of the highest value products – information and knowledge – are fairly insensitive to distance. Furthermore, the widespread proliferation of sophisticated information technology has undermined the need to coordinate operations in a central headquarters".

Thus, the urban system is very much like that described by Camagni and Salone (1992) a decade ago — an urban system characterized by not only vertical links but also by horizontal links between functionally specialized cities. Some cities play unique roles in this system. For example, Stockholm stands out as the sole city in its cluster (of ten clusters) in an analysis of 123 world cities (Taylor et al. 2002). Overall, the global network of cities is not a hierarchy, since it reflects the corporate networks of many companies based in many places. Flows among these cities, such as air travel, however, embody some hierarchical tendencies.

A number of other changes in urban systems have been observed, including the following:

- A trend toward consolidation in a few centers, but perhaps a less hierarchically organized system than in the past (Sassen 2002).
- An "archipelago economy" in which the only "sticky" places of global capitalism are global and second-tier cities (Graham and Marvin 2001, pp304-305; Markusen 1996).
- Competition and deregulation has benefited large cities most. Finnie (1998) and Malecki (2002b) provide evidence that innovations and competition both come to the largest markets — i.e. the largest cities — first.
- The combination of enhanced competition and industry mix of knowledge-based sectors promotes the early arrival of new technologies in big cities.

Although not all of these changes in urban systems can be attributed solely to technology, taken together the changes reinforce the advantages of large cities. These advantages of city life have always existed, seen in the agglomeration of supply and demand for mutual benefit and the synergy found in planned as well as chance encounters at low cost.

10.4.2 Winners and Losers: Locational Freedom, Human Capital, and the Knowledge Economy

The phenomenon of locational freedom is a key feature of the contemporary economy. Mitchell (1999) suggests, however, that the new locational freedom will be balanced against sunk investments in particular localities. He further suggests that locational freedom does not mean locational indifference: "If you can locate anywhere, you will go where it's nice, or where it is culturally stimulating, or perhaps where you can get work done more effectively" (Mitchell 1999, p. 76). We can expect that successful localities will be those with pleasant climates, spectacular scenery, attractive residential areas, and unique architectural environments and cultural traditions.

Among the types of locational freedom witnessed in today's society is that related to human capital, particularly educated people. The skills this mobile population can bring to a regional economy surpass all other determinants of regional growth (Bradley and Taylor 1996). We have known this in a general sense and the principle is captured in endogenous growth models (Aghion and Howitt 1998; Mathur 1999). Simon and Nardinelli (2002) have tracked the role of human capital, measured by the percentage of college or university graduates, on urban growth over the twentieth century. Cities that start out with proportionately more knowledgeable people grow faster in the long run because (a) knowledge spillovers are geographically limited to the city, and (b) much knowledge is most productive in the city within which it is acquired. Simon and Nardinelli found that city-aggregates and metropolitan areas with higher average levels of human capital grew faster over the 20th century.

Whether or not they would qualify as university-educated human capital, Florida (2002a) argues that cities depend greatly on "the geography of bohemia" and the locational freedom of its constituents. Bohemians include the following artistic and cultural occupations: authors, designers, musicians and composers, actors and directors, craft-artists, painters, sculptors and artist printmakers, photographers, dancers, and artists, performers and related workers. Of 50 urban areas in the USA, the top ranked in bohemians/1000 population were Seattle, Los Angeles, New York, Nashville, and Portland. Los Angeles and New York will be expected because of their role in the "culture industries" (Scott, 2001), as is Nashville, the home of country music. Seattle and Portland are perhaps the surprises here, with their locally well-known artist communities that receive little media attention outside their region.

Although the empirical research above is based on the USA, similar agglomeration of cultural industries is found in other countries. For example, Power (2002) shows that Stockholm overwhelmingly dominates the Swedish cultural industries. In the particular case of the music industry, networks of firms in various aspects of the music industry cluster and interact intensively in Stockholm as well as with firms and artists in the industry internationally (Hallencreutz and Lundequist 2001; Power and Hallencreutz 2002).

10.4.3 The New Economy

The 'new economy' embodies two elements of technological change discussed previously: the new network phenomenon and the knowledge-based economy. Nakamura (1999) highlights the role of intangible assets such as copyrights, patents, trade secrets, brand names, trademarks, and reputation. Similarly, Teece (1998) focuses on the various forms of knowledge assets. In a series of reports, Atkinson and his colleagues at the Progressive Policy Institute have developed a "new economy index" for the 50 US states and for the 50 largest metropolitan areas. Their index is multidimensional, and includes:

- Knowledge jobs (professional, managerial, and technical jobs; workforce with some college);
- Globalization (manufactured exports/manufacturing worker);
- Economic dynamism (gazelle firm jobs, job churning, new IPOs);
- The digital economy (online population, broadband competitors, computer use in schools, .com domain names, backbone capacity);
- Innovation capacity (high-tech jobs, degrees in science and engineering, patents/1000 employment, academic R&D, venture capital) (Atkinson et al. 1999; Atkinson and Gottlieb 2001).

The recursive, mutually reinforcing relationships between the elements of the new economy are seen in an analysis of the investment patterns of Internet backbone networks (Malecki 2004). The pattern largely reflects the presence of an urban hierarchy, new network cities notwithstanding (Table 10.2).

Table 10.2. Internet backbone connections in the USA by MSA/CMSA size class

MSA size range	Number of cities	Average total bandwidth (Mbps)	Mean number of cities linked	Mean band-width/population
Over 5 million	9	373,419	25.6	40.0
2-5 million	13	165,588	17.8	53.3
1-2 million	27	67,489	9.4	49.2
500,000-1 million	30	20,704	4.5	29.7
250,000-500,000	40	12,702	2.7	33.8
Under 250,000	30	9,040	2.8	50.5

MSA Metropolitan Statistical Area *CMSA* Consolidated Metropolitan Statistical Area.
Source: Compiled from Boardwatch (2001) and firm web sites[1]

In addition to, and more significant than, a simple relationship with city size, however, the variables that significantly explain where log metro bandwidth has gone include log enrolment in doctoral-granting institutions (+), clearly a human capital indicator, and the Metro New Economy Economic dynamism score (+), which primarily reflects entrepreneurship. More than human capital, viewed simply, is at work, therefore. Evident also are knowledge production and education at research-based universities, where doctoral degrees are granted, and entrepreneurship, through which creativity and knowledge take an economic form. Cities are unevenly endowed with these features, and they compete both through their hard networks of fibre-optic bandwidth and their soft networks of human relationships (Malecki 2002a).

Relatively few cities combine what is needed to compete in this new economic environment, because of the selectivity of investment and of migration decisions, reflecting together the locational freedoms of firms and of people. The geographical preferences of creative people determine the locations of their entrepreneurial activity and influence strongly corporate location decisions (Malecki 1987). In-

---

[1] A list of the firm web sites consulted is provided in Annex 10A.1.

creasingly, despite some pull toward high-amenity environments, it is large city-regions where creative people agglomerate (Florida 2002b). "As, or perhaps because, technologies allow more locational freedom, development may become more uneven" – some places doing well, others continuing to decline (U.S. OTA 1995, p. 17). The striking unevenness of urban growth has been highlighted by Florida (2002b).

10.5 A New Urban Structure?

The influence of technology is more difficult to understand in an intra-urban context. The spatial forces set in motion by telecommunications are complex, and they sometimes tug in different directions at once (Mitchell 1999). Thus, they can produce both decentralizing and recentralising tendencies. These centripetal and centrifugal forces are a long-standing dynamic (or dialectic) of cities, identified in the 1930s by Colby (1933).

Hall (2001) maintains that the geographical structure of global city-regions today is "quintessentially polycentric." The traditional downtown centers remain, serving banking, insurance, and government, but they are now complemented by: (1) newer business centers, often developing in an old prestige residential quarter, and serving as the location of newer services, such as corporate headquarters, the media, new business services (advertising, public relations, and design), (2) "internal edge cities", resulting from pressures of space in traditional centers and speculative development in old industrial or transport land, now redundant, near to them, (3) "external" edge cities, often located on the axis of the main airport, more rarely a high-speed train station, (4) "outermost" edge city complexes for back offices and R&D, typically at major train stations twenty to forty miles distant from the main core, and (5) specialized subcentres, usually for education, entertainment and sporting complexes, exhibition and convention centers. While there is some debate about whether edge cities function as part of the larger metropolitan complex, Harris (1997, p. 19), like Hall, believes that "The periphery is not composed of completely separate edge cities; it is still a functional part of the metropolitan complex".

Although Hall's analysis stresses that polycentric urban structure is a global, rather than only a North American, phenomenon, most research on them has focused on the USA where it first emerged. Kotkin (2000) proclaims that the most obvious winners in the new geography are "the new peripheral communities, what I call nerdistans, self-contained high-end suburbs that have grown up to service the needs of both the burgeoning high-technology industries and their workers" (Kotkin 2000, p.9). He believes that communities such as these cannot be described as either suburbs in the conventional sense or even as 'edge cities' sprawling along the periphery of most major cities (Garreau 1991). They neither depend on the core city for employment, as many older suburbs did, nor seek to duplicate the traditional functions of the urban core (Kotkin 2000, p. 39). "Successful nerdistans" try to eliminate the kinds of 'distractions', such as crime, traffic, and commercial blight, that have commonly been endemic in cities and, increasingly, in older suburban areas as well.

A wide array of research in the USA and Europe has documented the fact that the monocentric city is no longer the dominant urban form. The new urban structure has been described in various ways: as polycentric, a form that includes edge cities and suburban subcentres and suburban employment centers (Groth 2000), as generalized dispersion (Gordon and Richardson 1996), as scatteration (Fujii and Hartshorn 1995), or simply as a peripheral model (Harris 1997). This urban form is much more varied than the traditional monocentric city of urban economics, and this variation reflects the fact that cities must accommodate the varied preferences and requirements of an increasingly diverse population (Champion 2001; Garrison and Ward 2000, p. 126). While decentralization has been a feature in Europe, it is different from that in the USA and it is not as uniform, because of stronger planning and because of high-speed rail transport, which favours downtown locations (Cheshire 1999).

10.6 Postmodern Urban Structure?

The new urban structure(s) that we see around us may yet supplant the long-established models of urban structure that have dominated most of the twentieth century (Pacione 2001a). The models developed by the Chicago School beginning in 1925, highlighting the monocentric city, had been waiting to be replaced by a new urban paradigm. Urban scholars in Los Angeles have now provided a new urban theory to fit new urban social, economic, and political circumstances (Dear 2002). The characteristics of postmodern urban structure, according to Dear and Flusty (1998), are: (1) ubiquitous social polarization, (2) a situation in which the hinterland organizes the centre, and (3) keno capitalism, seen in a centreless urban form with land uses unrelated to those nearby and acute fragmentation and specialization.

To many, it is unclear why any city – and maybe especially Los Angeles, also known as LaLa Land – must be the paradigmatic case, especially given the empirical variation and heterogeneity found among cities (e.g. Pollard and Storper 1996). Nijman (2000) has proposed that Miami is a much better candidate than L.A. as the city that displays more clearly than others the fundamental features and trends of the wider urban system at the start of the 21st century, more unequivocally a postindustrial and global city. Although both cities are magnets for immigrants, Miami has an absolute majority of recent immigrants, and it is more of an urban paradigm of postmodern urbanism, crammed into one fifth the space of LA.

Perhaps nothing has changed cities from old forms to new more than a single technology: the automobile or private car. Dependence on private transportation began and was, for decades, prominent only in the USA, but it has now spread to Canada, Europe, and beyond. For example, the vast majority of residents of Waterloo-Kitchener, Canada, see low density and social and functional homogeneity as desirable (Filion et al. 1999). More surprising perhaps are the trends in Europe, where public transport is available at a high standard. Even here, however, the spatial-temporal freedom provided by private cars is rapidly transforming the European urban landscape. Dutch retirees, for example, prefer to drive their own cars whenever possible (Schwanen et al. 2001).

Why has this happened? It certainly is not conscious imitation of the American lifestyle. Indeed, many resist the "Californication" of culture. Rather, it is the result of the fragmentation of activities and the dispersal of amenities discussed earlier. As more travel must be done to a greater number of destinations, public transport is less able to provide timely and efficient service than it could in a monocentric city. Finally, it also must be said that the contemporary car is a comfortable place, with high-quality audio systems and climate-controlled environments, which makes travel not only less burdensome than it once was, but actually pleasurable.

In Asia, somewhat different trends are occurring. Desakota areas emerge as the dispersal of some urban growth spills over into these cities' immediate neighbouring rural area. These former rural areas undergo rapidly urbanization and become a rural-urban transition zone while the rural residents remain (Sit 1996).

What have these changes meant for cities? Three principal changes have taken place, affecting spatial form, the economy of cities, and social interaction. The principal spatial change — in urban structure — is the phenomenon known as polynuclear urban development or edge cities, discussed to some extent above. Economically, it is not only the well-documented shift from manufacturing to services (Sassen 2000), but also the emergence of creativity and culture industries as a new economic base. Socially, there is real justification for concern about the growing gap between the haves and the have-nots, what Graham and Marvin (2001) call "splintering urbanism" — a bifurcation of urban society and space into distinct sets that have minimal interaction.

To what extent is technology a contributor to these trends? Cyberspace is not an "intrinsically unifying electronic space" (Graham 2002). Intensifying urban polarization is occurring at every scale across the globe, Graham contends. At the same time, the "disembedding" of dominant economic, social and cultural activities is occurring, both separating them from any locale and contributing to the social and technological distancing of the powerful from the less powerful. In part, it is the use of information and communication technologies (ICTs), which, as currently applied by dominant users, tend to:

- Extend the power of the powerful;
- Underpin intensified unevenness through tying together international divisions of labour;
- Allow socioeconomically affluent groups selectively to bypass the local scale; and
- Be culturally and economically biased, especially in terms of what we might term the emerging 'international information marketplace'.

Given the demographic diversity – long found in cities but newly recognized – a growing problem is that the urban space is increasingly splintered, with less interaction among the various groups. As goods and, increasingly, services are provided for customized markets, Graham and Marvin (2001) point out that most infrastructures are now divided into two (or more) levels: high-quality, high-priced service for the time-poor/cash-rich users, and lower-quality, lower-priced service for the time-rich/cash-poor users. Examples include toll roads, parking spaces, broadband connections, and energy-efficient meters. No longer is there only symbolic or implicit separation, but there is increasingly explicit separation between rich and poor (or between any one group ('us') and all others by walls and gates.

10.7 Planning in the New Context

The spatial divisions in cities have longer-term social implications as well. Urban areas could continue to bifurcate into "introverted, affluent, gated communities" interspersed with "'black holes' of disinvestment, neglect, and poverty" if the unrestrained logic of the market prevails (Mitchell 1999, p. 81). Planners and politicians have the challenge to avoid the seemingly inevitable 'dual city'. This requires policies that involve "an acceptable level of social equity". The task for architects and urban designers is to create an urban fabric that permits and encourages social groups to overlap and intersect rather than to remain isolated by distance or walls (Mitchell 1999, p. 82).

What role is there for planning in this new, unfamiliar setting? Conventional planning wisdom holds that compact rather than diffuse urban forms, mixed rather than segregated land uses, reliance on public rather than private transport — for example, European-type rather than American-type cities — help achieve higher levels of overall accessibility with lower negative socioeconomic and environmental impacts. This may no longer hold true in the information age. Planners now have even less control over the location of today's fragmented activities (and the ensuing growing transportation demands) than they did when living, working, shopping, learning, or recreating were each to be found in their own pre-assigned places (Couclelis 2000).

Can we make polynuclear urbanization efficient? Cervero (2001) has studied the influence of urban form and transportation infrastructure on economic performance. Data on 47 US metropolitan areas suggest that employment densities and urban primacy [the proportion of metro employment in the central city] are positively associated with worker productivity, suggesting the presence of agglomeration economies. More surprisingly, he also found that congested freeways are a consequence of strong economic performance. "All else being equal, bigger areas with large laborsheds, good accessibility between jobs and housing, and well-functioning transport systems appear to enjoy some economic advantages" (Cervero 2001, p.1668).

Do we understand sustainable urban development well enough to make it happen? Let me put forward one definition of sustainable urban development: meeting the needs of the present (economic, social, cultural and health needs, political) needs without compromising the ability of future generations to meet their own needs (Pacione 2001b). A related dimension of it focuses on environmental impacts, growing problems as urban populations concentrate within relatively small urban spaces. The issues include urban metabolism (cities' ecological footprints and their inputs and wastes), urban waste management (a much-neglected topic), and energy consumption (at neighbourhood, district, and metropolitan scales).

What role is there for the city centre, the 'new downtown'? Kotkin (2000) suggests that the new economic role for centre cities can best be described as that of a 'boutique.' Rather than clinging to an 'industrial-age paradigm', central business districts should rediscover their "preindustrial role as centers for the arts, entertainment, face-to-face trading, and the creation of specialized artisanal goods and services" (Kotkin 2000, p. 55). Like Florida (2002b, 2002c), Kotkin believes that a critical phenomenon in the evolution of cities has been the demographic growth of populations – gays, 'empty nesters', divorced and never-married people — traditionally attracted to the inner cores, because of the availability of a social experience uniquely to be found there.

10.8 Needed: New Ideas about Cities

Perhaps we need new ways of thinking about cities in the twenty-first century. These ideas need to be more than about urban structure, and to begin to grapple with the growing constraints not only on our space, but also on our time. In this vein, Batty (2002) proposes that we begin to think of *cities as spatial events:* events that take place in time and space, where the event is characterized by its duration, intensity, volatility, and location. Batty points out that every action that we partake in exists in time and space, and can be so classified. He believes that it is possible to represent all the spatial structures that make up the city in this way. This would require that we think of cities as schedules of events in the framework of time-budgets.

Also needed are new ways to understand accessibility to urban services. Hanson (2000) points out that traditional accessibility measures provide rather narrow interpretations of core questions such as:

- Do you know what is available at potential destinations?
- Do you value what is there?
- Is it feasible for you to get to these locations and to participate in the activities there?
- Do you have social and cultural (not to mention geographic) connections to facilitate access to those sites?

In traditional accessibility measures, if a destination is located close by, it is considered accessible. However, traditional measures of access neglect the fact that people are embedded in networks of social relations through which information is exchanged. Traditional approaches also do not consider the informational, social, and cultural dimensions of accessibility.

We also need more serious research on subcentres and the causes and effects of social splintering. Dispersed employment subcentres have not reduced average commuting time. We really do not know how important employment location is in a setting of ubiquitous, fragmented work. Moreover, we know little about the potentially negative effects of subcentres on human interaction. Finally, much more needs to be understood about the risks of splintering. There is a great risk that splintering risks changing the nature of the city as a hub of creativity, since urban creativity thrives on diversity. Social splintering risks alienating population groups who might be creative, with severe implications for economic activity.

10.9 Conclusions

Cities are a central element of human existence. They are — and also are more than — built environments, and venues for human interaction. Cities also act as hubs in networks of interaction that involve many cities. These networks, unique to each economic sector, cultural activity, and social context, coincide to a greater degree in what have become known as world cities. Peripheral places outside these networks of interaction are at risk of becoming irrelevant as competition among places for investment and for talented workers increases.

The city of the twenty-first century is not a product of the Internet or of any single technology; only the car is a candidate for that role. A dizzying combination of technological, economic, and social transformations are taking place and these, together with social changes, are changing our cities, our schedules, and the ways in which we move about in time and space. We all have various roles: as workers, as citizens, as family members, as members of several communities and social groups. In some cities, fulfilling those roles is more difficult — or more necessary — than in others, owing to the unique combination of urban structure, social cohesion, and competitiveness within interurban networks.

Technology has always created new problems as it helps solve old ones. We cannot expect cyberspace and Internet information literally at our fingertips to replace real social interactions. The long-held — and never materialized — expectation of telecommuting is an example of that in a workplace context. The urban focus is appropriate and useful, in light of the fact that so many people live in cities or their urban regions.

Acknowledgements. This research has been supported in part by US National Science Foundation grants BCS-9911222 and BCS-0296075. The comments of three anonymous reviewers were most helpful in clarifying aspects of the chapter. Thanks to Hyejin Yoon for her cartographic assistance.

References

Aghion P, Howitt P (1998) Endogenous growth theory. MIT Press, Cambridge, MA

Andersson AE (1985) Creativity and regional development. Chapters of the Regional Science Association 56: 5–20

Atkinson RD, Gottlieb PD (2001) The metropolitan new economy index: benchmarking economic transformation in the nation's metropolitan areas. Progressive Policy Institute, Washington, DC. Available at http://www.neweconomyindex.org/metro/

Atkinson RD, Court RH, Ward, JM (1999) The state new economy index: benchmarking economic transition in the states. Progressive Policy Institute, Washington, DC. Available at http://www.neweconomyindex.org/states/index.html

Batty M (2002) Thinking about cities as spatial events. Environment and Planning B: Planning and Design 29: 1–2

Beaverstock JV, Taylor PJ, Smith RG (1999) A roster of world cities. Cities 16: 445–458

Beaverstock JV, Smith RG, Taylor PJ (2000) World-city network: a new metageography? Annals of the Association of American Geographers 90: 123–134

Boardwatch (2001) Boardwatch magazine's directory of Internet service providers, 13th edn. Penton Media, Cleveland

Boden D, Molotch HL (1994) The compulsion of proximity. In: Friedland R, Boden D (eds) NowHere: space, time and modernity. University of California Press, Berkeley, CA, pp 257–286

Bradley S, Taylor J (1996) Human capital formation and local economic performance. Regional Studies 30: 1–14

Camagni R (2001) The economic role and spatial contradictions of global city-regions: the functional, cognitive, and evolutionary context. In: Scott AJ (ed) Global city-regions: trends, theory, policy. Oxford University Press, Oxford, pp 96–118

Camagni R, Salone C (1992) Network urban structure in northern Italy: elements for a theoretical framework. Urban Studies 30: 1053–1061

Castells M (2001) The Internet galaxy: reflections on the Internet, business, and society. Oxford University Press, Oxford

Cervero R (2001) Efficient urbanisation: economic performance and the shape of the metropolis. Urban Studies 38: 1651–1671

Champion AG (2001) A changing demographic regime and evolving polycentric urban regions: consequences for the size, composition and distribution of city populations. Urban Studies 38: 657–677

Cheshire PC (1999) A postscript: exurbia or Islington? In: Summers AA, Cheshire PC, Senn L (eds) Urban change in the United States and Europe: comparative analysis and policy, 2nd edn. Urban Institute Press, Washington, DC, pp 569–594

Colby CC (1933) Centripetal and centrifugal forces in urban development. Annals of the Association of American Geographers 23: 1–20

Couclelis H (2000) From sustainable transportation to sustainable accessibility: can we avoid a new tragedy of the commons? In: Janelle DG, Hodge DC (eds) Information, place, and cyberspace: issues in accessibility. Springer, Berlin Heidelberg New York, pp 341–356

Dear MJ (ed) (2002) From Chicago to L.A.: making sense of urban theory. Sage, Thousand Oaks, CA

Dear MJ, Flusty S (1998) Postmodernism urbanism. Annals of the Association of American Geographers 88: 50–72

Filion P, Bunting T, Warriner K (1999) The entrenchment of urban dispersion: residential preferences and location patterns in the dispersed city. Urban Studies 36: 1317–1347

Finnie G (1998) Wired cities. Communications Week International 18 May: 19–23

Florida R (2002a) Bohemia and economic geography. Journal of Economic Geography 2: 55–71

Florida R (2002b) The Rise of the creative class, and how it's transforming work, leisure, community and everyday life. Basic Books, New York

Florida R (2002c) The Economic geography of talent. Annals of the Association of American Geographers 92: 743–755

Friedmann J (1986) The world city hypothesis. Development and Change 17: 69–83

Friedmann J (1995) Where we stand: a decade of world city research. In: Knox P, Taylor PJ (eds) World cities in a world-system. Oxford University Press, New York, pp 21–47

Friedmann J, Wolff G (1982) World city formation: an agenda for research and action. International Journal of Urban and Regional Research 6: 309–343

Fujii T, Hartshorn TA (1995) The changing metropolitan structure of Atlanta, Georgia: locations of functions and regional structure in a multinucleated urban area. Urban Geography 16: 680–717

Garreau J (1991) Edge city: life on the new frontier. Doubleday, New York

Garrison WL, Ward JD (2000) Tomorrow's transportation: changing cities, economies, and lives. Artech House, Boston

Gaspar J, Glaeser E (1998) Information technology and the future of cities. Journal of Urban Economics 43: 136–156

Globalization and World Cities (GaWC) Study Group (2004) The world according to GaWC. Department of Geography, Loughborough University, Leicestershire, UK. Available at http://www.lboro.ac.uk/gawc//citymap.html

Gordon P, Richardson HW (1996) Beyond polycentricity: the dispersed metropolis, Los Angeles, 1970–1990. Journal of the American Planning Association 62: 289–295

Graham S (1997) Telecommunications and the future of cities: debunking the myths. Cities 14: 21–29

Graham S (2002) Bridging urban digital divides? urban polarisation and information and communications technologies (ICTs). Urban Studies 39: 33–56

Graham S, Marvin S (1996) Telecommunications and the city: electronic spaces, urban places. Routledge, London

Graham S, Marvin S (2001) Splintering urbanism: networked infrastructures, technological mobilities and the urban condition. Routledge, London

Groth NB (2000) Urban systems between policy and geography. Regional Studies 34: 571–580

Hall P (1998) Cities in civilization: culture, innovation, and urban order. Weidenfeld & Nicolson, London

Hall P (2001) Global city-regions in the twenty-first century. In: Scott AJ (ed) Global city-regions: trends, theory, policy. Oxford University Press, Oxford, pp 59–77

Hallencreutz D, Lundequist P (2001) Making knowledge funky: localized learning and competitive SMEs in the Swedish music industry. Presented at the Association of American Geographers Annual Conference, New York, 28 February

Hanson S (2000) Reconceptualizing accessibility. In: Janelle DG, Hodge DC (eds) Information, place, and cyberspace: issues in accessibility. Springer, Berlin Heidelberg New York, pp 267–278

Harris CD (1997) "The nature of cities" and urban geography in the last half century. Urban Geography 18: 15–35

Hill RC, Fujita K (2003) The Nested city: an introduction. Urban Studies 30: 207–217

Janelle DG (1973) Human extensibility in a shrinking world. Journal of Geography 72: 8–15

Keeling DJ (1995) Transport and the world city paradigm. In: Knox P, Taylor PJ (eds) World cities in a world-system. Cambridge University Press, Cambridge, pp 115–131

Kotkin J (2000) The new geography: how the digital revolution is reshaping the American landscape. Random House, New York

Leamer EE, Storper M (2001) The economic geography of the Internet age. Journal of International Business Studies 32: 641–665

Malecki EJ (1987) The R&D location decision of the firm and 'creative' regions – a survey. Technovation 6: 205–222

Malecki EJ (2001) The Internet age: not the end of geography. In: Felsenstein D, Taylor MJ (eds) Promoting local growth: process, practice and policy. Ashgate, Aldershot, pp 227–253

Malecki EJ (2002a) Hard and soft networks for urban competitiveness. Urban Studies 39: 929–945

Malecki EJ (2002b) Local competition in telecommunications in the United States: supporting conditions, policies, and impacts. Annals of Regional Science 15: 437–454

Malecki EJ (2004) Fibre tracks: explaining investment in fibre optic backbones. Entrepreneurship and Regional Development 16: 21-39

Malecki EJ, Gorman SP (2001) Maybe the death of distance, but not the end of geography: the Internet as a network. In Leinbach TR, Brunn SD (eds) Worlds of electronic commerce: economic, geographical and social dimensions. John Wiley, New York, pp 87–105

Markusen A (1996) Sticky places in slippery space: a typology of industrial districts. Economic Geography 72: 293–313

Mathur VK (1999) Human capital-based strategy for regional economic development. Economic Development Quarterly 13: 203–216

Mitchell WJ (1999) E-topia: "urban life, Jim —but not as we know it". Cambridge, MA, MIT Press

Moss M (1998) Technology and cities. Cityscape 3: 107–127. Available at: http://www.huduser.org/periodicals/cityscpe/vol3num3/article5.pdf

Moss ML, Townsend AM (2000) The Internet backbone and the American metropolis. The Information Society 16: 35–47

Moulaert F, Djellal F (1995) Information technology consulting firms: economies of agglomeration from a wide-area perspective. Urban Studies 32: 105–122

Moulaert F, Gallouj C (1993) The locational geography of advanced producer service firms: the limits of economies of agglomeration. Service Industries Journal 13: 91–106

Moulaert F, Tödtling F (eds) (1995) The geography of advanced producer services in Europe. Progress in Planning 43: 89–274

Nakamura L (1999) Intangibles: what put the new in the new economy? Business Review, Federal Reserve Bank of Philadelphia July/August, pp 3–16

Nijman J (1996) Breaking the rules? Miami in the urban hierarchy. Urban Geography 17: 5–22

Nijman J (2000) The paradigmatic city. Annals of the Association of American Geographers 90: 135–145

Nonaka I, Takeuchi H (1995) The knowledge-creating company. Oxford University Press, New York

Nonaka I, Toyama R, Nagata A (2000) A firm as a knowledge-creating entity: a new perspective on the theory of the firm. Industrial and Corporate Change 9: 1–20

Pacione M (2001a) Models of urban land use structure in cities of the developed world. Geography 86: 97–119

Pacione M (2001b) The future of the city – cities of the future. Geography 86: 275–286

Parker J (1995) Turn up the lights: a survey of cities. The Economist, 29 July: 1-18

Pollard J, Storper M (1996) A tale of twelve cities: metropolitan employment change in dynamic industries in the 1980s. Economic Geography 72: 1–22

Power D (2002) "Cultural industries" in Sweden: an assessment of their place in the Swedish economy. Economic Geography 78: 103–127

Power D, Hallencreutz D (2002) Profiting from creativity? The music industry in Stockholm, Sweden and Kingston, Jamaica. Environment and Planning A 34: 1833–1854

Rimmer PJ (1998) Transport and telecommunications among world cities. In: Lo F, Yeung Y (eds) Globalization and the world cities. Tokyo: United Nations University Press, pp 433–470

Sassen S (1991) The Global city: New York, London, Tokyo. Princeton University Press, Princeton

Sassen S (1994) Cities in a world economy. Pine Forge Press, Thousand Oaks, CA

Sassen S (2000) Cities in a world economy, 2nd edn. Pine Forge Press, Thousand Oaks, CA

Sassen S. (2002) Introduction: locating cities on global circuits. In: Sassen S (ed) Global networks, linked cities. Routledge, New York, pp 1–36

Schwanen T, Dijst M, Dieleman FM (2001) Leisure trips of senior citizens: determinants of modal choice. Journal of Economic and Social Geography (Tijdschrift voor Economische en Sociale Geografie) 92: 347–360

Scott AJ (2001) Capitalism, cities and the production of symbolic forms. Transactions. Institute of British Geographers NS 26: 11–23

Simon D (1995) The world city hypothesis: reflections from the periphery. In: Knox PL, Taylor PJ (eds) World cities in a world-system. Cambridge University Press, Cambridge, pp 132–155

Simon CJ, Nardinelli C (2002) Human capital and the rise of American cities, 1900–1990. Regional Science and Urban Economics 32: 59–96

Sit VFS (1996) Mega-City, Extended metropolitan region, Desakota, Exo-Urbanization: an introduction. Asian Geographer 15: 1–14

Smith D, Timberlake M (2002) Hierarchies of dominance among world cities: a network approach. In: Sassen S (ed) global networks, linked cities. Routledge, New York pp 117–141

Storper M, Venables AJ (2002) Buzz: the economic force of the city. Paper presented at the Danish Research Unit for Industrial Dynamics (DRUID) Summer Conference on "Industrial dynamics of the new and old economy — who is embracing whom?" Copenhagen/Elsinore 6–8 June 2002. Available at
http://www.druid.dk/conferences/summer2002/Papers/STORPER.pdf

Taylor PJ (2001) Specification of the world city network. Geographical Analysis 33: 181–194

Taylor PJ, Catalano G, Walker DRF (2002) Exploratory analysis of the world city network. Urban Studies 39: 2377–2394

Taylor PJ, Walker DRF (2001) World cities: a first multivariate analysis of their service complexes. Urban Studies 38: 23–47

Teece DJ (1998) Capturing value from knowledge assets: the new economy, markets for know-how, and intangible assets. California Management Review 40: 55–79

Thompson WR (1995) Introduction: urban economics in the global age. In: Kresl PK, Gappert G (eds) North American cities and the global economy. Sage, Thousand Oaks, CA, pp 1–17

Tödtling F (1994) The uneven landscape of innovation poles: local embeddedness and global networks. In: Amin A, Thrift N (eds) Globalization, institutions, and regional development in Europe. Oxford University Press, Oxford, pp 68–90

Townsend AM (2001) The Internet and the rise of the new network cities, 1969–1999. Environment and Planning B: Planning and Design 28: 39–58

U.S. Office of Technology Assessment (OTA) (1995) The technological reshaping of metropolitan America (OTA-ETI-643). U.S. Government Printing Office, Washington, DC

Annex

Annex 10A.1. Firm web sites consulted for the compilation of Table 10.2.

Note: The links provided in this Annex were current as of citation date. If websites are subsequently redesigned, it may happen that web links no longer work, that the information changes or that information is no longer available. These problems have their origin in the nature of the Internet; unlike printed books, the content on the Internet is dynamic and can be updated anytime.

Aleron (2001) www.aleron.com/network/topology.html, accessed November 13, 2001

AT&T (2001) www.ipservices.att.com, accessed November 13, 2001

Cable & Wireless (2001) http://www.cw.com/th_11.asp?ID=gn_index#, accessed November 15, 2001

Ardent (2001) http://ardentcomm.com/comp/network.html, accessed November 15, 2001

Cogent (2001) http://www.cogentco.com/Difference/network_map.html, accessed November 15, 2001

Epoch (2001) http://www.epoch.net/topo/index.html, accessed November 15, 2001

e.spire (2001) http://www.espire.net.service_locations/network_map.cfm, accessed November 15, 2001

Fiber Network Solutions (2001) http://www.fnsi.net/images/FNSInetworkmap.jpg, accessed November 15, 2001

Genuity (2001) (www.genuity.com/infrastructure/docs/Us_pop8-0701.pdf, accessed November 26, 2001

Globix (2001) http://www.globix.com/images/diagbig_network.jpg, accessed November 26, 2001

ICG (2001) http://www.icgcom.com/products/carrier/main.asp, accessed November 26, 2001

IDT (2001) http://www.idt.net/internet/network.htm, accessed November 26, 2001

Infonet (2001) http://www.infonet.com/services/global_internet_services/usmap.html, accessed November 26, 2001

Intermedia (2001) http://www.intermedia.com/acrobat/ibi_tir1_map9.pdf, accessed November 20, 2001

Level3 (2001) http://www.level3.com/us/products/crossroads/, accessed November 26, 2001

NetRail (2001) http://www.netrail.net/htm/network.htm#current, accessed December 2, 2001

One Call (2001) http://www.onecall.net/timages/nwmap.jpg, accessed November 20, 2001

PSINet (2001) http://www.psinet.com/network/connectivitymaps.html, accessed November 20, 2001

Qwest (2001) http://www.qwest.com/about/qwest/network/index.html, accessed November 20, 2001

SAVVIS (2001) http://www.savvis.net/network/usmap.html, accessed December 2, 2001

Teleglobe (http://www.teleglobe.com/en/our_network/default.asp, accessed November 20, 2001

Time Warner Telecom (2001a) http://www.twtelecom.com/internet.html, accessed November 20, 2001

Time Warner Telecom (2001b) http://www.twtelecom.com/natnet.html, accessed December 5, 2001

Williams Communications (2001)
http://www.williamscommunications.com/network/map/index.html, accessed November 25, 2001

WorldCom (UUNet) (2001) www.uu.net/UUNET_NA2001Oct.pdf, accessed November 13, 2001

XO (2001) http://www.xo.com/ourstory/network.html, accessed December 2, 2001

11 Regional Telecommunications Investment Impacts and Efficiency Considerations

Kingsley E. Haynes[1], Serdar Yilmaz[2], and Mustafa Dinc[3]

[1] School of Public Policy, George Mason University
[2] Social Development Department, The World Bank
[3] Development Economics Data Group, The World Bank

11.1 Introduction

The U.S. Office of Technology Assessment (1995) argues that the quality and reliability of regional information and communications infrastructure systems are likely to reshape regional economic development patterns in the future. If telecommunications infrastructure has such a major influence, it is reasonable to expect that regional policymakers to consider such investments as a force in managing economic growth as well as a regional development tool. However, little work has been done to characterize and compare the impact of telecommunications infrastructure on the economic performance of states. Studies recognize the importance of state and federal regulations on the level of telecommunications infrastructure, but fail to address its role in regional performance and interregional economic development patterns. Studies on the relationship between telecommunications infrastructure and economic growth typically focus on national estimates and ignore the role of telecommunications investment in explaining the divergent paths of regional growth patterns. Six major exceptions include Greenstein and Spiller (1995); Cronin et al. (1994); Dholakia and Harlam (1994); Nadiri and Nandi (1997); Cronin et al. (1997); and Resende (1999). There has been much speculation about the impact of the 'information revolution' on the economy as a whole, but surprisingly little is known about the actual or potential effects of improvements in communications infrastructure on the spatial distribution of jobs and output. The lack of research on the relation between local telecommunications policymaking and regional economic growth contrasts starkly with the growing interest in such an assessment. Over the last decade, many states have commissioned studies on how to use telecommunications infrastructure in economic development efforts. These policy reports include: Armstrong (1995); Howe and Gardner (1992); Wisconsin Governor's Blue Ribbon Telecommunications Infrastructure Task Force (1993); Washington Governor's Telecommunications Policy Coordination Task Force (1996); and Kansas' Telecommunications Strategic Planning Committee (1996).

This chapter is an examination of the utilization of telecommunications infrastructure on output growth in the lower states. The study first reviews the role of state level policies in telecommunications in Sect. 11.2. Then, it discusses methodological issues in Sect. 11.3 and data considerations in Sect. 11.4. Next, the results of the empirical findings are presented in Sect. 11.5. This is followed by policy considerations and conclusions in Sects. 11.6 and 11.7.

11.2 State Policy and Telecommunications

Telecommunications networks are privately owned in the United States. However, the industry has always been heavily regulated to achieve equitable and universal access to facilities. Before the break-up of AT&T in 1984, the federal government was the major regulator, and the states were "undistinguished" (Bonnett 1996, p. 21) as policy makers. Following divestiture, state governments became major players in telecommunications regulation and policymaking.

Recently states have followed a variety of telecommunications policy approaches (Teske 1995). Many governors appointed chief technology officers to coordinate and plan telecommunications investment strategies. In a report on Wisconsin's Blue Ribbon Telecommunications Infrastructure Task Force (1993), then-Governor Tommy G. Thompson described the importance of telecommunications infrastructure to the state by indicating that Wisconsin's economic future would depend on a top quality telecommunications system and all its consequences, as this would link the state to the global economy in the 21st century.

Critics argue that increasing the state regulatory role has resulted in fragmented policies that have led to significant variation in the quality of telecommunications infrastructure across states. According to Lehr and Kiessling (1999), the shift of policymaking power from the federal government to the states means that poorer states with fewer resources to devote to telecommunications are going to be less effective in protecting consumer rights against the monopoly power of local exchange carriers and in providing state-of-the-art infrastructure services to businesses. Richer states have allocated more resources and employed more people for telecommunications regulation and policymaking than have poorer states. For example, in 1994, California's utility commission had more than 50 staff members working exclusively on telecommunications, whereas in five states there was not a single person working exclusively on telecommunications (Teske 1995).

Following divestiture, state telecommunications policymakers began to experiment with different ways to set rates for local telephone services. Table 11.1 provides a summary of actions taken by state legislatures. As seen in the last column, some states took a gradual approach in setting priorities by mandating that their public utility commissions study alternative methods of regulation. Others acted quickly, giving full power to regulatory commissions to design new telecommunications policies. Variation in the states' responses has produced differential impacts on their economic performance. In the states that liberalized telecommunications quickly, gross state product rose 46.3 percent, compared to 25.2

percent in other states, and total employment increased more than two fold compared to states with no deregulation (Bottorff et al. 1993).

Most state legislatures did not limit their involvement in the telecommunications industry to regulation. They viewed telecommunications as crucial for economic development efforts and involved state economic development agencies directly in the policymaking process (Teske 1995). States like Iowa, Nebraska, and North Carolina encouraged local exchange companies "to make improvements faster than they would have on their own" (Bonnett 1996, p.37). For more on the role of state policymakers' implementation of telecommunications strategies in these three states, see General Accounting Office (1996).

Table 11.1. State telecommunications industry regulation[a] laws enacted after 1984

Deregulate Service by Service Statue	Modify Regulation on a Service by Service Statue	Enabling Statue[b]	Social Contract Legislation[c]	Study of Alternatives to Regulation[d]
Iowa	Colorado	Connecticut	Vermont	Indiana
Arizona	Minnesota	Mississippi	Idaho	Florida
South Carolina	Missouri	Ohio	North Dakota	Utah
Indiana	South Dakota	Washington	Minnesota	Colorado
Mississippi	Nevada	North Carolina	Pennsylvania	Nevada
Montana	New Jersey	Florida	Rhode Island	N. Carolina
Georgia	California	Utah		Washington
Nevada	New York	West Virginia		
Texas	Kansas			
New Mexico	Louisiana			
Wisconsin				
North Dakota				
Oregon				
Utah				
Michigan				
Washington				
Illinois				
Virginia				
Nebraska				

[a] Some state legislatures passed more than one telecommunications law
[b] Enabling statue gives authority to the Public Utility Commission to deregulate or to develop alternative rate making plans, but do not specify how or when to do so
[c] In social contract legislation, prices for basic service are held down and network modernization is ensured in return for more regulatory flexibility for the local telephone companies
[d] Laws mandate the study of alternatives to rate-of-return regulation
Source: Compiled by the authors from Teske 1995, State Telephone Regulation Report 1994, Greenstein and Spiller 1995

11.3 Methodology

In a recent study, Yilmaz et al. (2001) find that telecommunications capital stock has a statistically significant positive impact on output growth at the aggregate level[1]. They also find that the magnitude and statistical significance of this impact vary across sectors. Nationwide telecommunications infrastructure investment has the strongest positive impact on the service related sectors — wholesale trade; finance, insurance, and real estate (FIRE); retail trade; and other services. The impact was insignificant or negative, however, on agriculture, mining, construction, and manufacturing.

Here we use a three-step approach to analyse the impact of telecommunications infrastructure on the structure of output growth at the state level. First, we use shift-share to identify the sources of regional growth in each industry for each state. Shift-share decomposes economic change into three additive components: national share, industry mix, and regional share (see Annex 11A.1). The regional share component measures the change in a particular industry due to the difference between the industry's regional growth (decline) rate and the reference area growth rate. Regional share component reflects strengths (weakness) of a region coming from the region's natural endowments, entrepreneurial ability, and/or the effects of regional policy. By using the dynamic shift share analysis, for each of 48 states, we decompose the change in output, capital, and labour separately in each industry for every year from 1984 to 1997. Thus, we compile panel data for the regional share of capital, labour, and output for each industry for each state and produce 48 separate panel data sets for the second step.

In the second step, we specify a modified Cobb-Douglas production function in which telecommunications infrastructure is treated as input. Thus, we investigate the impact of telecommunications infrastructure on output growth by estimating the modified Cobb-Douglas production function for each state separately for a pooled data set of industries. Equation 11.1 represents the econometric model estimated by using pooled regressions for each state:

$$Q_{it} = \beta_1 K_{it} + \beta_2 L_{it} + \beta_3 G_t + \beta_4 TK_t + TD + \varepsilon_{it} \tag{11.1}$$

where i is industry (i= mining, construction, manufacturing, utilities, agriculture, wholesale trade; retail trade; finance, insurance and real estate; and services), t is time, and TD is a time dummy. The dependent variable, Q_{it}, and independent variables, K_{it} and L_{it}, are the regional share components of output, capital, and labour, estimated by using shift-share analysis, and TK_t and G_t are telecommunications and public capital stock, respectively.

In the third step, after determining state-specific impacts of telecommunications infrastructure on sectoral output, we identify the states where telecommunications

---

[1] In this chapter, telecommunications capital stock and telecommunications infrastructure are used interchangeably.

capital stock is used efficiently. A production function describes the technical relationship between inputs and outputs, in which the maximum output is attained from a given set of inputs. It is highly unlikely, however, that all units can achieve the maximum level of outputs. Evaluation of the comparative productive performance of state economies will help identify sources of inefficiency in the production processes.

We employ the mathematical programming approach known as Data Envelopment Analysis (DEA) to assess the (in)efficient use of input factors[2]. As in the regression model, the unit of analysis is the state, which is assumed as a decision-making unit (DMU) in the DEA model. The DEA solution procedure involves the identification of a comparison set of DMUs on the efficiency frontier that serves to evaluate the efficiency of the unit being analysed. The DEA calculates the relative efficiency of each DMU in relation to all other DMUs by using actual values of inputs and outputs.

Variable selection is a somewhat controversial issue in the DEA literature. In many cases, observation units use multiple inputs and produce multiple outputs and there is no clearly defined and agreed upon input/output relationship, and the categorization of input and output variables can become problematic. In this contribution, we focus on the production process, and there is a well-established economic theory that specifies the factors of production (capital and labour). Following the theoretical literature on economic growth, we use the production function framework in the DEA model as well. For consistency and comparison purposes, we use private, public and telecommunications capital stocks and labour variables as inputs and total value added of states private industries as output. However, the input and output variables in the DEA model are not disaggregated to sectors (unlike the econometric analysis) and they represent private sector component of the state economies. The logic behind the use of the same variables at different aggregation levels is that in the econometric model, our purpose was to investigate the impact of telecommunications infrastructure on sectoral output growth; whereas in the DEA model we focused on the efficient utilization of telecommunications infrastructure by private businesses.

11.4 The Data

Data for output (Q) and labour (L) for each industry in each state are readily available from the Bureau of Economic Analysis (BEA). Output is defined as value added of private industry i. Labour is defined as the total number of employees by place of work employed in industry i. There are no private capital stock (K) data available at the state level. BEA reports national estimates of private capital stock for each industry (BEA 2004). Following Yilmaz et al. (2002), state fixed private

---

[2] A brief discussion of the Data Envelopment Analysis is provided in Annex 11A.2. For a detailed discussion of DEA and its evolution, see Cooper et al. (2000).

capital stock in industry i, K_{si}, is estimated by apportioning the national estimates to individual states using the following formula:

$$K_{si} = \frac{(VADD_{si} - WS_{si})}{(VADD_{ni} - WS_{ni})} \times K_{ni} \qquad (11.2)$$

where s indexes state and n indexes the nation. $VADD$ is total value added (output) of industry i and WS is total wages and salaries for the same industry. In this equation, $(VADD—WS)$ represents returns to capital, which is assumed to be an indicator of the size of private capital stock in a state. Since we know national private capital value, K_{ni}, we can easily calculate state private capital stock, K_{si}. The underlying rationale to employ Eq. 11.2 is that in a perfectly competitive environment and long-term equilibrium the ratio of returns to capital at the national and state level should be identical:

$$\frac{(VADD_{si} - WS_{si})}{K_{si}} = \frac{(VADD_{ni} - WS_{ni})}{K_{si}} \qquad (11.3)$$

Actually, our hypothesis about returns to capital is further supported by a brief inspection of the ratio of $(VADD_{si} - WS_{si}) / (VADD_{ni} - WS_{ni})$, which has been steady over the study period for all industries.

Due to the relationship between input and output variables the authors explicitly controlled endogeneity by separating federally related interstate telecommunications from state related output. The results for the weighted two-stage least squares evaluation showed that state telecommunication infrastructure investment still had a positive and significant impact on output even after filtering out reverse causality impacts (Yilmaz et al. 2002, pp. 353-354).

G_t and TK_t in Eq. 11.1 are public and telecommunications capital stock. Unlike other variables, we have not decomposed these into national, industrial mix, and regional shares by using the shift-share methodology because the level of infrastructure service provision is a direct result of state policies and service provision is not limited to a specific industry. Thus, the industrial mix component of shift-share methodology does not exist for public and telecommunications capital stock. Since we have decomposed year-to-year changes into their components for other variables (output, capital, and labour), however, technically the Eq. 11.1 reduces to the first difference equation. Therefore, public capital, G_t, and telecommunications capital, TK_t, stock variables enter into the econometric analysis as the first difference form.

Similar to private capital stock, there is no readily available data set of public capital stock for individual states. This variable is estimated by apportioning the national estimates of the Bureau of Economic Analysis (BEA)[3] using the ratio of state total capital outlay to national total for each year. State expenditure patterns and the aggregate national expenditure from 1984 and 1997 followed the same trend, which confirms that each state's share in national capital outlay is a good proxy for the size of its public capital. See Yilmaz et al. (2002), and Lall and Yilmaz (2001) for discussion of a similar treatment.

The estimation of telecommunications capital stock in each state is similar to the methodology specified by Resende (1999) and Shin and Ying (1992), using the automated reporting management information system (ARMIS) of the Federal Communications Commission (FCC). The real capital stock is obtained by subtracting accumulated depreciation from gross communications plant figure for each local exchange provider[4].

11.5 Findings

In the first step of the empirical analysis, we use shift-share to identify the sources of growth in the output, capital, and labour variables. We then use the regional-share component of the shift-share in the regression analysis. The estimation results from the shift-share analysis are not discussed in this section because they are methodologically straightforward and more pertinent to policy discussions. Therefore, only the estimation results of regression analysis and DEA are discussed. In the subsequent section, we elaborate on the estimation results of all three methodologies and their policy implications.

11.5.1 Econometric Results

Table 11.2 presents the estimation results of the econometric model of Eq. 11.1[5]. The estimation results are not based on the fixed effects model. As discussed in the previous section, Eq. 11.1 is estimated in the difference form, and differencing eliminates the intercept term[6]. The downside of difference-form estimation is the inability of the model to capture industry-specific effects using variable intercepts.

---

[3] The total government fixed capital and its sub-groups from 1925 to 1997 are electronically available from BEA (BEA 2004). The state and national public capital outlay data are from the Government Finance files of the U.S. Census Bureau (2004). This data set is also available electronically.

[4] Monetary values for all variables are in constant 1996 dollars.

[5] The test results for OLS estimations suggest that heteroskedasticity is a problem therefore we used GLS estimators.

[6] A generic presentation of the difference form can be derived in the following way. For the initial year $y_{i0} = \alpha + \beta X_{i0} + \varepsilon_{i0}$, where α is the intercept term and β is a row vector coefficients for explanatory variables. By subtracting the initial year from the next year t, $y_{it} = \alpha + \beta X_{it} + \varepsilon_{it}$, one can obtain $y_{it} - y_{i0} = (\alpha - \alpha) + \beta (X_{it} - X_{it}) + (\varepsilon_{it} - \varepsilon_{it})$ which eliminates the intercept term and the specification becomes difference form: $y_{iL} = \beta X_{iL} + \varepsilon_{iL}$.

Differencing, however, mitigates the serial correlation problem. As seen in the DW column of Table 11.2, the Durbin-Watson statistics for each model fall within acceptable ranges for all states.

Time dummy variables, TD, are included in the model to capture the heterogeneity resulting from time-specific events. The last point is the reverse causal link between output and telecommunications capital stock, which we test by using vector autoregressive techniques described in Holtz-Eakin et al. (1988). The test results confirm that our estimation results do not suffer from reverse causality problems[7].

Table 11.2 reports the estimation results of the econometric specification of regional production functions. As seen in Table 11.2, signs of private capital and labour coefficients are as expected and statistically significant in all states. The magnitude of the private capital variable coefficient in each state is much higher than the labour variable coefficient.

The stable estimates of capital and labour across states and the consistency of the relationship of magnitudes of the explanatory variables suggest that the econometric model provides a robust set of results for empirical analysis. As seen in the sixth and seventh columns of Table 11.2, adjusted R^2 and F-test statistics support the argument about the robustness of the empirical estimates. Adjusted R^2 values range from 0.75 for New York to 0.97 for Delaware and Iowa[8], and F-test statistic values are significant at the one percent level for each model. These R^2's should not be surprising given the relatively high aggregated level of analysis.

The fourth column reports the coefficient estimates of public capital stock, which are statistically significant for 26 states. Among these states, the coefficient of public capital is negative for Arizona, California, Louisiana, Massachusetts, Montana, North Carolina, Nebraska, Oklahoma, South Carolina, Texas, Vermont, Washington, and Wisconsin. The negative sign of the coefficient suggests that an increase in the public capital stock has a negative impact on output in these states.

In general, appropriate and efficiently supplied public infrastructure has an inherent role in improving access to markets and reducing unit costs of production, as well as in attracting private investment. The level of public capital stock, however, influences the marginal productivity of private factors of production. Inappropriate levels of public capital stock crowd out private investments and thus decrease output (Aschauer 1989).

---

[7] Because of space limitation, we have not reported these results here, but they are available from the authors on request and were reported in Yilmaz et al. (2002). The authors, in a separate endogeneity evaluation, used the Hausman test (Hausman 1983), which was also negative. This was reported in Yilmaz et al. (2002).

[8] Adjusted R^2 values are quite reasonable for a panel data study, where much higher values are common. One may argue that since the model employed is in the difference form and does not have a constant term (intercept) so high R^2 values might be misleading. We should note that the model includes time dummies that act as time intercept.

Table 11.2. The results of the econometric model; dependent variable Q_{it}

State[a]	Private Capital	Labour	Public Capital	Telecom	Adj-R	F-Stat	D-W
AL	0.318*	0.020*	0.001*	−0.008	0.84	181.57*	1.9
AR	0.299*	0.027*	−0.000	0.254*	0.91	165.22*	2.2
AZ	0.230*	0.029*	−0.000**	−0.547*	0.85	138.39*	1.5
CA	0.425*	0.029*	−0.002*	−0.034	0.87	203.03*	2.0
CO	0.283*	0.029*	0.001*	−0.081***	0.84	155.52*	1.5
CT	0.480*	0.022*	0.000	−0.053	0.85	84.63*	1.5
DE	0.542*	0.033*	−0.000	−0.009	0.97	674.6*	2.0
FL	0.335*	0.021*	0.000**	0.037	0.82	112.95*	1.7
GA	0.333*	0.014*	0.000	−0.003	0.69	44.97*	1.5
IA	0.293*	0.023*	0.000	−0.089	0.97	711.50*	1.7
ID	0.333*	0.016*	0.002*	0.240*	0.83	85.86*	1.7
IL	0.295*	0.020*	0.000	0.073***	0.85	137.16*	1.9
IN	0.341*	0.027*	0.003*	0.263*	0.87	93.59*	1.9
KS	0.290*	0.013*	0.001*	0.209*	0.89	148.75*	2.0
KY	0.240*	0.029*	0.002*	0.079	0.88	174.61*	2.0
LA	0.182*	0.041*	−0.000***	0.156***	0.88	112.90*	1.7
MA	0.430*	0.021*	−0.001**	0.927*	0.89	101.42*	1.5
MD	0.368*	0.029*	−0.000	0.067*	0.90	266.75*	2.0
ME	0.313*	0.026*	0.002*	−0.053	0.88	108.25*	2.1
MI	0.428*	0.033*	0.000	0.121***	0.89	72.93*	2.0
MN	0.305*	0.026*	0.002	0.504	0.87	58.08*	2.0
MO	0.372*	0.019*	−0.000	−0.044	0.88	120.62*	2.0
MS	0.226*	0.032*	0.000	0.078***	0.91	262.00*	1.9
MT	0.268*	0.020*	−0.001**	0.249**	0.95	271.20*	1.6
NC	0.333*	0.028*	−0.000**	0.121***	0.87	131.40*	1.7
ND	0.280*	0.027*	−0.000	0.211**	0.96	678.52*	1.7
NE	0.295*	0.020*	−0.000***	−0.064*	0.95	513.30*	2.0
NH	0.330*	0.032*	0.000	0.550*	0.82	89.99*	1.8
NJ	0.497*	0.013*	0.001*	0.435*	0.87	117.86*	1.4
NM	0.387*	0.025*	0.000	−0.202*	0.89	255.52*	1.9
NV	0.195*	0.028*	0.001*	0.072***	0.79	78.24*	1.6
NY	0.413*	0.028*	0.000	0.114*	0.75	59.28*	1.8
OH	0.184*	0.031*	−0.000	0.020	0.85	57.32*	2.1
OK	0.239*	0.035*	0.002*	−0.062	0.88	154.43*	1.7
OR	0.435*	0.020*	0.000***	0.263*	0.96	623.35*	1.8
PA	0.289*	0.025*	−0.000	0.038**	0.81	76.15*	1.9
RI	0.407*	0.017*	0.000	0.790*	0.83	97.59*	1.9
SC	0.373*	0.025*	−0.001*	0.113*	0.87	132.16*	1.7
SD	0.369*	0.020*	−0.000	0.158***	0.93	193.16*	2.5
TN	0.357*	0.026*	−0.001	−0.176**	0.85	62.89*	1.9
TX	0.262*	0.031*	−0.001**	−0.376*	0.80	48.70*	1.4
UT	0.361*	0.022*	−0.000	0.542	0.87	68.94*	1.5
VA	0.319*	0.030*	0.000	0.151*	0.85	94.61*	1.8
VT	0.265*	0.023*	−0.000***	0.180**	0.78	104.02*	2.0
WA	0.368*	0.033*	−0.000*	0.211*	0.89	99.69*	1.5
WI	0.314*	0.023*	−0.002**	−0.420*	0.89	127.38*	1.9
WV	0.212*	0.036*	0.001*	0.080**	0.92	223.69*	1.8
WY	0.169*	0.034*	0.002*	0.289**	0.85	77.45*	2.0

* 1 percent significant, ** 5 percent significant, *** 10 percent significant, [a] The states are defined in Table 11A.1.

The impact of telecommunications infrastructure on sectoral output is reported in the fifth column of Table 11.2. The coefficient of the telecommunications infrastructure variable of the production function model is statistically significant in 34 states and positive in 22 of these states. The negative coefficient in seven states (Arizona, Colorado, Nebraska, New Mexico, Tennessee, Texas, and Wisconsin) suggests that investments in telecommunications infrastructure would have adverse effects on output growth in these states.

The estimation results of Eq. 11.1 reflect variation in the contribution of higher telecommunications infrastructure investments to sectoral output, increasing it in some states and having no significant impacts in other states. This finding has important implications for regional development patterns. A close investigation of the magnitudes of the telecommunications infrastructure variable shows significant disparity among states, suggesting that telecommunications capital stock is much less mobile than other factors. This is due partly to the immobile characteristics of infrastructure stocks but also to state regulation of return to investment. These findings suggest that telecommunications policy can be a competitive tool for attracting and retaining new businesses. At first glance, however, not all states use this power effectively. These results suggest that telecommunications policymakers are constrained by the economic and productive trends in their respective regions.

A full spatial econometric assessment was the basis of a separate paper by Yilmaz et al. (2002) on network vs. geographic neighbours. It indicated a small but significant negative spatial dependency (interstate spillover), which decreased with distance from the location of local investments. This was corrected for in the present regression analysis.

11.5.2 Data Envelopment Analysis (DEA) Results

The results from the regression analysis show that, on average, changes in output can be explained by changes in the independent variables, but they do not indicate whether it is possible to obtain the same level of output by using less input or to produce more outputs by using the same level of inputs. In order to examine how (in)efficiently resources are utilized in the production process, we employ an input-oriented, variable return to scale DEA model. Such a model provides information about the efficiency ranking of DMUs, sources of inefficiency, and targets for improvement. Since the purpose of this study is to examine the use of telecommunications infrastructure in states, we report only telecommunications related outcomes of the DEA model[9].

Table 11.3 presents the utilization level of telecommunications infrastructure. The last column shows the average utilization level during the study period: full efficiency (score of one) in eleven states and very close to full efficiency (score over 0.95) in eight states.

---

[9] Estimations results for other variables are available from the authors on request.

Table 11.3. Utilization level of telecommunications infrastructure, by State[a]

State	1984	1985	1986	1987	1988	1989	1990	1991	1992	1993	1994	1995	1996	1997	Av.
AL	0.67	0.72	0.75	0.67	0.65	0.74	0.79	0.83	0.81	0.71	0.82	0.83	0.70	0.69	0.7
AR	0.93	0.85	0.87	0.86	0.84	0.94	1.00	0.97	0.95	0.95	0.94	0.87	0.86	0.86	0.9
AZ	0.55	0.56	0.60	0.61	0.64	0.70	0.77	0.86	0.90	0.90	0.91	0.90	0.91	0.91	0.7
CA	1.00	1.00	1.00	1.00	1.00	1.00	1.00	1.00	1.00	1.00	1.00	1.00	1.00	1.00	1.0
CO	0.94	0.91	0.90	0.73	0.66	0.65	0.70	0.82	0.73	0.70	0.79	0.81	0.72	0.76	0.7
CT	1.00	1.00	1.00	1.00	1.00	0.88	0.81	1.00	1.00	0.98	0.99	1.00	1.00	1.00	0.9
DE	1.00	1.00	1.00	1.00	1.00	1.00	1.00	1.00	1.00	1.00	1.00	1.00	1.00	1.00	1.0
FL	0.55	0.57	0.58	0.54	0.67	0.69	0.73	0.75	0.68	0.66	0.66	0.67	0.67	0.67	0.6
GA	0.93	0.93	0.93	0.87	0.82	0.80	0.92	0.92	0.86	0.78	0.93	0.92	0.93	0.93	0.8
IA	0.88	0.85	0.79	0.83	0.84	0.86	0.87	0.90	0.89	0.93	0.93	0.93	0.94	0.94	0.8
ID	0.66	0.64	0.80	0.77	0.82	0.92	0.94	0.82	0.79	0.84	0.73	0.75	0.73	0.90	0.7
IL	1.00	1.00	1.00	1.00	1.00	1.00	1.00	1.00	1.00	1.00	1.00	1.00	1.00	1.00	1.0
IN	0.82	0.79	0.79	0.83	0.85	0.94	0.97	0.97	0.96	0.97	0.97	0.94	0.93	0.91	0.9
KS	1.00	1.00	1.00	1.00	1.00	0.92	0.95	0.94	0.92	0.92	0.94	0.94	0.92	0.91	0.9
KY	0.74	0.77	0.77	0.71	0.77	0.80	0.89	0.86	0.89	0.89	0.89	0.89	0.89	0.89	0.8
LA	1.00	1.00	1.00	0.78	1.00	0.78	0.83	0.81	0.90	0.89	0.92	0.94	0.95	0.95	0.9
MA	0.92	0.94	1.00	1.00	1.00	0.99	0.98	0.96	1.00	0.99	0.97	0.95	1.00	1.00	0.9
MD	0.82	0.85	0.86	0.82	0.79	0.79	0.88	1.00	1.00	1.00	0.98	1.00	1.00	1.00	0.9
ME	0.65	0.65	0.66	0.87	0.87	0.94	1.00	0.94	0.95	0.88	0.96	0.93	0.92	0.92	0.8
MI	1.00	1.00	1.00	1.00	1.00	1.00	1.00	1.00	1.00	1.00	1.00	1.00	1.00	1.00	1.0
MN	0.97	0.99	1.00	1.00	1.00	1.00	1.00	1.00	1.00	1.00	1.00	1.00	1.00	1.00	1.0
MO	0.92	0.91	0.90	0.91	0.90	0.80	0.92	0.82	0.84	0.76	0.89	0.83	0.80	0.80	0.8
MS	0.59	0.55	0.61	0.57	0.54	0.77	0.74	0.74	0.77	0.79	0.77	0.80	0.85	0.86	0.7
MT	0.77	0.73	0.95	0.94	0.92	0.94	0.95	0.93	0.85	0.81	0.95	0.91	0.96	0.93	0.9
NC	0.92	0.89	0.92	0.92	0.92	0.92	0.93	0.93	0.93	0.93	0.91	0.90	0.90	0.90	0.9
ND	0.91	0.90	1.00	1.00	1.00	1.00	1.00	1.00	1.00	1.00	1.00	1.00	1.00	1.00	0.9
NE	0.59	0.58	0.67	0.68	0.64	0.64	0.70	0.74	0.79	0.85	0.80	0.83	0.84	0.90	0.7
NH	1.00	1.00	1.00	0.70	0.79	0.93	0.94	1.00	1.00	1.00	1.00	1.00	1.00	1.00	0.9
NJ	1.00	1.00	1.00	1.00	1.00	1.00	1.00	1.00	1.00	1.00	1.00	1.00	1.00	1.00	1.0
NM	0.67	0.60	0.68	0.7	0.72	0.75	0.80	0.75	0.75	0.79	0.81	0.83	0.78	0.79	0.7
NV	0.80	0.82	0.92	0.96	0.95	0.96	0.95	0.96	0.97	0.98	0.97	0.98	0.96	0.94	0.9
NY	1.00	1.00	1.00	1.00	1.00	1.00	1.00	1.00	1.00	1.00	1.00	1.00	1.00	1.00	1.0
OH	0.97	0.99	0.99	0.99	1.00	0.99	1.00	0.99	0.99	1.00	1.00	0.99	0.98	0.97	0.9
OK	0.78	0.73	0.62	0.65	0.66	0.82	0.90	0.86	0.89	0.89	0.92	0.91	0.87	0.88	0.8
OR	0.67	0.69	0.75	0.80	0.84	0.91	0.90	0.91	0.90	0.90	0.90	0.90	0.89	0.89	0.8
PA	0.99	1.00	1.00	1.00	1.00	0.99	1.00	0.99	0.95	0.95	0.95	0.92	0.93	0.91	0.9
RI	1.00	1.00	1.00	1.00	1.00	1.00	1.00	1.00	1.00	1.00	1.00	1.00	1.00	1.00	1.0
SC	0.91	0.92	0.92	0.93	0.95	0.90	0.99	0.96	0.97	0.94	0.96	0.93	0.94	0.93	0.9
SD	0.88	0.91	0.97	0.97	0.98	0.97	1.00	0.97	0.95	0.98	1.00	1.00	1.00	1.00	0.9
TN	0.89	0.89	0.90	0.89	0.92	0.89	0.92	0.91	0.90	0.90	0.92	0.91	0.90	0.89	0.9
TX	0.95	0.89	0.79	0.67	0.74	0.73	0.77	0.76	0.90	1.00	1.00	1.00	1.00	1.00	0.8
UT	0.67	0.65	0.74	0.73	0.82	1.00	1.00	0.99	1.00	0.87	0.96	0.96	0.85	0.91	0.8
VA	1.00	1.00	1.00	1.00	1.00	1.00	1.00	1.00	1.00	1.00	1.00	1.00	1.00	1.00	1.0
VT	1.00	1.00	1.00	1.00	1.00	1.00	1.00	1.00	1.00	1.00	1.00	1.00	1.00	1.00	1.0
WA	0.78	0.78	0.78	0.77	0.76	0.82	0.86	0.94	0.93	0.86	0.85	0.88	0.91	0.95	0.8
WI	0.92	0.92	0.90	0.93	0.96	0.95	0.97	0.97	0.97	1.00	0.99	1.00	1.00	0.96	0.9
WV	0.59	0.57	0.61	0.61	0.56	1.00	1.00	0.77	0.82	0.77	0.83	0.83	0.83	0.93	0.7
WY	1.00	1.00	1.00	1.00	1.00	1.00	1.00	1.00	1.00	1.00	1.00	1.00	1.00	1.00	1.0
Av.	0.86	0.85	0.87	0.86	0.87	0.90	0.92	0.92	0.92	0.92	0.93	0.93	0.92	0.93	

Av.= average, [a] A list with the full name of the states is given in Table 11.A1.

A close examination of this table reveals that almost all states have had a significant and steady improvement in the efficient utilization of telecommunications infrastructure, particularly after 1989. The annual average utilization level for all states (bottom row of the table) confirms this observation, increasing from 0.86 in 1984 to 0.93 in 1997. This is good news for state and local policymakers as well as firms' decision-makers because it shows the outcome of their decisions[10].

A comparison of the findings from DEA and regression analysis reveals that, in general, the estimation results are consistent with each other. In most states where the coefficient of telecommunications variable of the econometric model is positive and statistically significant, telecommunications infrastructure utilization is also highly efficient, with an efficiency score close to one. At the other end of the spectrum, most states with low average efficiency scores in Table 11.3 have insignificant or negative telecommunications capital stock coefficients in Table 11.2. For example, the states with the least efficient utilization are Florida, Nebraska, New Mexico, Alabama, and Colorado, and their telecommunications variable coefficients are either statistically insignificant or negative. This consistency indicates the robustness of estimation results of different methods employed in this analysis. Only in Idaho, West Virginia, and Wisconsin are the estimation results of the regression analysis not supported by the DEA results. In Idaho and West Virginia, the coefficients of the telecommunications variable are positive and statistically significant, but the DEA results show that utilization was much less efficient than in other states. On the other hand, in Wisconsin, the coefficient of the telecommunication variable is negative and statistically significant, but the DEA results show that utilization was much more efficient than in other states.

11.6 Policy Considerations

Table 11.4 provides a comparison of the estimation results from the methodologies used in this study. The second column shows the estimation results of the shift-share analysis. The regional share of service-sector output growth is represented in quartiles. If a state's regional share increased over the study period, the sign is positive. A negative sign represents a decrease in the regional share over the same period. The magnitudes of changes are reported in quartiles: 0-25 percent (+, −); 25-50 percent (++, − −); 50-75 percent (+++, − − −); 75-100 percent (++++, − − − −).

---

[10] We should note that we calculated the efficiency for each year and did not pool the data; hence, time was not involved in the model. What is expected is that if the hypothesis of efficiency gains holds, efficiency scores of the inefficient states should move toward the efficiency frontier. In turn, the average efficiency score of the year should increase, hence, any increase in the average efficiency score signals efficiency gains for that year. This is, of course based on the assumption that the frontier is not shrinking. To test this assumption a Malmquist index based model can be performed, which was not done in this chapter.

Table 11.4. Comparison of results

	Shift-share	DEA	Regression Analysis
AL	+	0.74	0
AR	+	0.91	+
AZ	++	0.77	−
CA	−	1.00	0
CO	+	0.77	−
CT	+	0.98	0
DE	++	1.00	0
FL	+	0.65	0
GA	++	0.89	0
IA	−	0.88	0
ID	+	0.79	+
IL	−	1.00	+
IN	+	0.90	+
KS	−	0.95	+
KY	+	0.83	0
LA		0.91	+
MA	−	0.98	+
MD	+	0.91	+
ME	−	0.87	0
MI	−	1.00	+
MN	+	1.00	0
MO	−	0.86	+
MS	−	0.71	+
MT	−	0.90	+
NC	+	0.92	+
ND	− −	0.99	+
NE	−	0.73	−
NH	++	0.95	+
NJ	−	1.00	+
NM	+	0.74	−
NV	+++	0.94	+
NY	−	1.00	+
OH	−	0.99	0
OK	− −	0.81	0
OR	++	0.85	+
PA	−	0.97	+
RI	−	1.00	+
SC	+	0.94	+
SD	+	0.97	+
TN	+	0.90	−
TX	+	0.87	−
UT	++	0.87	0
VA	+	1.00	+
VT	−	1.00	+
WA	+	0.85	+
WI	+	0.96	−
WV	−	0.76	+
WY	−	1.00	+

Table 11.4. (Legend)

Shift-Share Column	DEA Column	Regression Analysis Column
+ / − = 0-25 percent increase/decrease in output	1 - 0.9: Efficient	0 = Statistically insignificant telecommunications variable
++ / − − = 25-50 percent increase/decrease output	0.9 -0: Inefficient	+ = Statistically significant positive telecommunications variable
+++ / − − − = 50-75 percent increase/decrease in output		− = Statistically significant negative telecommunications variable
++++ / − − − − = 75-100 percent increase/decrease in output		

Detailed results are available from the authors

The third column of Table 11.4 presents average utilization level of telecommunications infrastructure over 13 years (the last column in Table 11.3) from the DEA model. A value of one represents fully efficient utilization of telecommunications input. A value less than one indicates less than full efficiency. In other words, the same output could have been produced with less telecommunications infrastructure, or the economy could have produced higher output by utilizing the same level of telecommunications infrastructure. For example, if Alabama used its existing telecommunications infrastructure efficiently, 74 percent would have been enough to produce the same level of output.

The forth column in Table 11.4 reports the sign of the coefficient of telecommunications variable in the regression analysis. If the coefficient is statistically insignificant, it is reported as 0. Positive significant and negative significant signs are represented with + and - respectively.

Since the focus of this chapter is on telecommunications infrastructure, in order to analyse the estimation results further and make policy recommendations, states are divided into two groups based on their telecommunications utilization level: efficient and inefficient states. For this purpose, a state is classified as relatively efficient if its score is between 0.9 and 1.

As seen in Table 11.4, a state can be in one of several positions. The most desirable position is, of course, the one in which output of the service sectors is growing (+ sign for shift-share), telecommunications infrastructure has a significant positive impact on this growth (+ sign for regression column) and telecommunications infrastructure is being utilized efficiently (a score of 0.9 to 1 for DEA). Based on its position, it is possible to make policy recommendations for a state. It is also possible to compare a state's position with the existing state regulatory system and to reach a better understanding about the effectiveness of (de)regulation.

11.6.1 Efficient States

The comparison of efficient states where telecommunications infrastructure has been utilized relatively more efficiently, with scores between 0.9 and 1, presented in Table 11.4 with regard to each model's results as well as the regulatory structure of these states. In this table, regulation column represents changes in traditional rate-of-return regulation. Each state's regulatory policy is placed in one of the three categories based on the extent of deregulation of the telecommunications industry: 'deregulation' lists states that eliminated the regulation; 'some' denotes that states have taken a gradual approach; and 'no plan' implies no initiative to eliminate regulation.

A close examination of Table 11.4 reveals a clear pattern; in 22 states out of 27 where telecommunications infrastructure was utilized efficiently, the signs of the regression results were positive and statistically significant. The estimation results from regression analysis provide insights about margins. These results suggest that in these 22 states, additional investment in telecommunications infrastructure would increase output.

Another way of looking at Table 11.4 is to group these efficient states based on their shift-share and regression results. The shift-share column of the table shows that 12 states, Arkansas, Connecticut, Delaware, Indiana, Maryland, Minnesota, Nevada, New Hampshire, North Carolina, South Carolina, South Dakota and Virginia, had positive values suggesting these states increased their output due to some regional advantages. In three of these states, Connecticut, Delaware and Minnesota, telecommunications infrastructure had a statistically insignificant impact on output growth. This implies that the industrial mix of these three states is not heavily dependent on telecommunication infrastructure; hence, its contribution to output growth is insignificant.

In 15 states, the shift-share sign is negative which indicates a decline in output due partly to some regional disadvantages. In thirteen of these states, telecommunications infrastructure had a statistically significant impact on output growth, suggesting investment in telecommunications infrastructure can increase output growth. In general, these states are better positioned to benefit from investments in telecommunications infrastructure. The good news for these 15 states is that their existing telecommunications infrastructure has been utilized highly efficiently. If these states spend more effort in increasing their output, they might benefit more from investment in telecommunications infrastructure.

In term of regulation, five states, Arkansas, Nevada, New Hampshire, Wyoming and Delaware had no plan implying there has been no initiative to eliminate regulation. Most states in this group initiated deregulatory policies much earlier than the others, suggesting that progressive telecommunications policies can be linked to successful economic performance.

The preceding analysis has important implications for policymaking. As policymakers have long recognized, it is critical to address issues, such as the types of investment programs that would influence the economy most favourably. Since the telecommunications variable has a positive sign in the regression analysis column for 22 states, carefully designed and targeted policies may have placed their industries at a competitive advantage.

Table 11.5. Comparison of efficient states

	Shift-Share	DEA	Regression Analysis	Regulation[a]
Arkansas	+	0.91	+	No plan
Indiana	+	0.90	+	Some
Maryland	+	0.91	+	No plan
Nevada	+++	0.94	+	Some
New Hampshire	++	0.95	+	No plan
North Carolina	+	0.92	+	Some
South Carolina	+	0.94	+	Deregulation
South Dakota	+	0.97	+	Deregulation
Virginia	+	1.00	+	Deregulation
Illinois	−	1.00	+	Deregulation
Kansas	−	0.95	+	Deregulation
Louisiana	−	0.91	+	Deregulation
Massachusetts	−	0.98	+	Some
Michigan	−	1.00	+	Deregulation
Montana	−	0.90	+	Some
New Jersey	−	1.00	+	Deregulation
New York	−	1.00	+	Some
North Dakota	− −	0.99	+	Deregulation
Pennsylvania	−	0.97	+	Some
Rhode Island	−	1.00	+	Deregulation
Vermont	−	1.00	+	Deregulation
Wyoming	−	1.00	+	No plan
California	−	1.00	0	Deregulation
Connecticut	+	0.98	0	Some
Delaware	++	1.00	0	No plan
Minnesota	+	1.00	0	Deregulation
Ohio	−	0.99	0	Deregulation

Legend

Shift-Share Column	DEA	Regression Analysis Column
+ / − = 0-25 percent increase/decrease in output	Column 1 - 0.9: Efficient 0.9 -0: Inefficient	0 = Statistically insignificant telecommunications variable
++ / − − = 25-50 percent increase/decrease output		+ = Statistically significant positive telecommunications variable
+++ / − − − = 50-75 percent increase/decrease in output		− = Statistically significant negative telecommunications variable
++++ / − − − − = 75-100 percent increase/decrease in output		

[a] Based on Regularity Research Association ratings from Bottorff et al. (1993). Detailed results are available from authors

11.6.2 Inefficient States

Table 11.6 shows the states where telecommunications infrastructure has been utilized inefficiently.

Table 11.6. Comparison of inefficient states

	Shift-Share	DEA	Regression Analysis	Regulation[a]
Alabama	+	0.74	0	Some
Arizona	++	0.77	–	No plan
Colorado	+	0.77	–	Deregulation
Florida	+	0.65	0	Some
Georgia	++	0.89	0	Deregulation
Kentucky	+	0.83	0	Some
New Mexico	+	0.74	–	Some
Tennessee	+	0.90	–	Some
Texas	+	0.87	–	Some
Utah	++	0.87	0	Deregulation
Iowa	–	0.88	0	No plan
Maine	–	0.87	0	Some
Missouri	–	0.86	0	Some
Nebraska	–	0.73	–	Deregulation
Oklahoma	– –	0.81	0	No plan
Idaho	+	0.79	+	Some
Mississippi	+	0.71	+	Some
Oregon	++	0.85	+	Deregulation
Washington	+	0.85	+	Some
West Virginia	–	0.76	+	Some

Legend		
Shift-Share Column	DEA	Regression Analysis Column
+ / – = 0-25 percent	Column	0 = Statistically insignificant
increase/decrease in output	1 - 0.9:	telecommunications variable
++ / – – = 25-50 percent	Efficient	+ = Statistically significant positive
increase/decrease output	0.9 -0:	telecommunications variable
+++ / – – – = 50-75 percent	Inefficient	– = Statistically significant negative
increase/decrease in output		telecommunications variable
++++ / – – – – = 75-100 percent		
increase/decrease in output		

[a] Based on Regularity Research Association ratings from Bottorff et al. (1993). Detailed results are available from authors

In five of these states, telecommunications infrastructure had a statistically significant impact on output growth, of these; four states increased their outputs. In the remaining 15 states, the marginal contribution of telecommunications infrastructure to output growth is either insignificant or negative. Ten out of these 15 states increased their outputs. In terms of regulatory structure, in only five states was deregulation in place. Most of the remaining states took a gradual approach to deregulation, and only one state had no plan for change during the study period.

The inefficient utilization of telecommunications infrastructure in these states, combined with the above findings, suggests that there might be over-investments in telecommunications infrastructure relative to existing demand. More efficient utilization of telecommunications infrastructure in these states may potentially improve its impact on output growth.

11.7 Conclusions

The role of infrastructure in economic growth has been the centre of interest in planning and policy research to identify ways to improve the economic perform-ance of regions. The research in this chapter focused on telecommunications infra-structure and its impact on output growth of the U.S. states. We tested the hy-pothesis that investment in telecommunications infrastructure could contribute to this output growth, and that this contribution would be higher in the states that utilize telecommunications infrastructure efficiently. The first part of the analysis is based on aggregate production function estimates. Results from the econometric model support the hypothesis that telecommunications infrastructure played an important role in output growth during this period (1984-1997).

In the second part of the analysis, we employed an input-oriented DEA model to identify states where the telecommunications infrastructure was utilized effi-ciently. DEA results revealed full efficiency (score of one) in eleven states, and close to full efficiency in another eight states. An important finding is that the es-timation results of both models are generally consistent with each other, and both support the hypothesis of the study. In most states where the coefficient for the telecommunications variable in the econometric model is positive and statistically significant, the telecommunications infrastructure utilization level also was high. Most states with low efficiency scores have either statistically insignificant or negative telecommunications capital stock coefficients in the regression analyses.

Another important finding is that almost all states have made significant and steady improvements in efficient utilization of telecommunications infrastructure, particularly since 1989. The increase in the annual average utilization levels from 0.86 in 1984 to 0.93 in 1997 supports this observation.

This study suggests that a less than optimal level of telecommunications in-vestments may be a problem within the current regulatory structure in the United States. It is important to note that determination of what the 'optimal' level of out-put might be, as well as the exact nature of the relation between the marginal products of physical capital, labour, and telecommunications investments are em-pirical questions and require further investigation.

Acknowledgements. The finings, interpretations, and conclusions are entirely those of au-thors, and do not represent the views of the World Bank, its executive directors, or the countries they represent.

References

Armstrong R (1995) Creating climate for the information age: The Nebraska statewide tele-communications infrastructure plan. Nebraska Information Technology Commission, Lincoln, NE

Aschauer DA (1989) Does public capital crowd out private capital? Journal of Monetary Economics 24: 171–88

Banker RD, Charnes A, Cooper WW (1984) Some models for estimating technical and scale inefficiencies in Data Envelopment Analysis. Management Science 30: 1078–1092

Bonnett TW (1996) Telewars in the states- telecommunications issues in a new era of competition. Council of Governors' Policy Advisors, Washington DC

Bottorff P, Latham W, Stapleford J (1993) The regulation of telecommunications and state economic growth. Working Paper No. 93–34, Alfred Lerner College of Business and Economics, University of Delaware, Newark, DE

Cronin FJ, Gold MA, Mace BB, Sigalos, JL (1994) Telecommunications and cost savings in educational services. Information Economics and Policy 6: 53–75

Cronin FJ, Colleran EB, Gold MA (1997) Telecommunications, factor substitution and economic growth. Contemporary Economic Policy 15: 21–31

Cooper WW, Seiford LM, Tone K (2000) Data Envelopment Analysis. Kluwer Academic Publishers, Boston

Dholakia RR, Harlam B (1994) Telecommunications and economic development: econometric analysis of the U.S. experience. Telecommunications Policy 18: 470–477

Dinc M, Haynes KE, Qiangsheng L (1998) A comparative evaluation of shift-share models and their extensions. Australasian Journal of Regional Studies 4: 275–302

Dinc M, Haynes KE, Stough RR, Yilmaz, S (1998) Regional universal telecommunication service provisions in the U.S. Telecommunications Policy 22: 541–553

Greenstein S, Spiller PT (1995) Modern telecommunications infrastructure and economic activity: an empirical investigation. Industrial and Corporate Change 4: 647–665

Greenwood MJ, Hunt GL (1986) Migration and employment change: empirical evidence on the spatial and temporal dimensions of the linkage. Journal of Regional Science 26: 223–234

Haynes K, Dinc M (2001) Substitution and complementarity between transportation and telecommunication: a demand side approach. Paper presented at the Regional Science Association International Workshop, Port Elizabeth, South Africa

Hausman, J.A. (1983) Specification and estimation of simultaneous equation models. In: Zvi Griliches and M.D. Intriligator (eds) Handbook of econometrics, vol 1. Elsevier Amsterdam, North Holland, pp 391-448

Holtz-Eakin D, Newey W, Rosen HS (1988) Estimating Vector Autoregression with panel data. Econometrica 56: 1371–1395

Howe L, Gardner H (1992) Telecom'92: connecting Idaho to the future. Idaho Department of Administration, Boise, ID

Kansas Telecommunications Strategic Planning Committee (1996) Connections to the future: A telecommunications strategic plan for Kansas. Topeka, KS

Lall S, Yilmaz S (2001) Regional economic convergence: do policy instruments make a difference. Annals of Regional Science 35: 153–166

Lehr W, Kiessling T (1999) Telecommunication regulation in the United States and Europe: The case for centralized authority. In: Gillett SE, Vogelsang I (eds) Competition, regulation, and convergence- current trends in telecommunications policy research. Lawrence Erlbaum Associates, New Jersey, pp 97-121

Loveridge S, Selting AC (1998) A review and comparison of shift-share identities. International Regional Science Review 21: 37–58

Nadiri MI, Nandi B (1997) The changing structure of cost and demand for the U.S. telecommunications industry. Information Economics and Policy 9: 319–347

Resende M (1999) Productivity growth and regulation in U.S. local telephony. Information Economics and Policy 11: 23–44

Shin RT, Ying JS (1992) Unnatural monopolies in local telephone. Rand Journal of Economics 23: 171–183

State Telephone Regulation Report (1994) Capitol Publications. Arlington, VA

Teske P (1995) Introduction and overview. In: Teske P (ed) American regulatory federalism and telecommunications infrastructure. Lawrence Erlbaum Associates, New Jersey, pp 1-25

Yilmaz S, Haynes KE, Dinc, M (2002) Geographic and network neighbours: spillover effects of telecommunications infrastructure. Journal of Regional Science 42: 339–360

Yilmaz S, Haynes KE, Dinc, M (2001) The impact of telecommunications infrastructure investment on sectoral growth. Australasian Journal of Regional Studies 7 (3): 383-397

U.S. Bureau of Economic Analysis (2004) Regional economic accounts. U.S. Bureau of Economic Analysis, December. Available at http://bea.gov/bea/regional/data.htm

U.S. Census Bureau (2004) Federal, State and local governments- State and local government finances. U.S. Census Bureau, October. Available at http://www.census.gov/govs/www/estimate.html

U. S. Congress General Accounting Office (1996) Telecommunications initiatives taken by three states to promote increased access and investment. GAO/RCED 96–68, Washington DC

U. S. Congress Office of Technology Assessment (1995) The technological reshaping of Metropolitan America. OTA-ETI-6, Washington, DC

Washington Governor's Telecommunications Policy Coordination Task Force (1996) Building the road ahead: telecommunications infrastructure in Washington. Washington Department of Revenue, Olympia, WA

Wisconsin Governor's Blue Ribbon Telecommunications Task Force (1993) Convergence, competition, cooperation. Wisconsin Department of Administration, Madison, WI

Annex

Table 11.A1 The names of the 48 US states considered in the study

Abbreviation	Full Name
AL	Alabama
AR	Arkansas
AZ	Arizona
CA	California
CO	Colorado
CT	Connecticut
DE	Delaware
FL	Florida
GA	Georgia
IA	Iowa
ID	Idaho
IL	Illinois
IN	Indiana
KS	Kansas
KY	Kentucky
LA	Louisiana
MA	Massachusetts
MD	Maryland
ME	Maine
MI	Michigan
MN	Minnesota
MO	Missouri
MS	Mississippi
MT	Montana
NC	North Carolina
ND	North Dakota
NE	Nebraska
NH	New Hampshire
NJ	New Jersey
NM	New Mexico
NV	Nevada
NY	New York
OH	Ohio
OK	Oklahoma
OR	Oregon
PA	Pennsylvania
RI	Rhode Island
SC	South Carolina
SD	South Dakota
TN	Tennessee
TX	Texas
UT	Utah
VA	Virginia
VT	Vermont
WA	Washington
WI	Wisconsin

Table 11.A1 (cont.)

WV	West Virginia
WY	Wyoming

Annex 11A.1. Shift-Share Analysis

Traditional shift-share analysis is a well-known technique for examining sources of regional growth. It is a sectoral decomposition procedure widely used by regional economists, geographers, urban and regional planners, regional scientists, and economic development analysts. Since its introduction in 1960, it has been used in the regional science literature in analysing a variety of issues. See for details Dinc et al. (1998) and Loveridge and Selting (1998).

The traditional shift-share model decomposes economic change in a region into three additive components: reference area, industry mix, and regional share. The decomposed variable may be income, employment, output, number of establishments, or a variety of other metric data. The reference component refers to the national economy and is called the national share (for smaller regions such as counties it may refer to the state economy).

The national share (NS) component measures the regional employment change that could have occurred if regional employment had grown at the same rate as the national rate.

$$NS \equiv Q_{ir} \, g_n \qquad (11.\text{A}1)$$

The industrial mix (IM) component measures the industrial composition of the region and reflects the degree to which the local area specializes in industries that are fast or slow growing nationally. Thus, if a region contains a relatively large share of industries that are slow (fast) growing nationally, it will have a negative (positive) industry mix shift.

$$IM \equiv Q_{ir} \, (g_{in} - g_n) \qquad (11.\text{A}2)$$

The regional share (RS) component measures the change in a particular industry in the region due to the difference between the industry's regional growth (decline) rate and the industry's reference area growth rate. It may result from natural endowments, other comparative advantages or disadvantages, the entrepreneurial ability of the region, and/or the effects of regional policy.

$$RS \equiv Q_{ir} \, (g_{ir} - g_{in}) \qquad (11.\text{A}3)$$

where the subscript i indexes the industrial sector in region r. Q_{ir}, is output in sector i of region, r. The change in total output in sector i of region r is g_{ir}. The change in industry i in the reference area n is g_{in}.

Annex 11A.2 Data Envelopment Analysis (DEA)

Data envelopment analysis is concerned with understanding how each decision-making unit (DMU) is performing relative to others, the causes of inefficiency, and how a DMU can improve its performance to become efficient. To do so, the Banker et al. (1984) model requires that the reference point on the production function for DMU_k will be a convex combination of the observed efficient DMUs. The BCC model, known as variable returns to scale model, gives the technical efficiency of DMUs under investigation without any scale effect.

We use the Warwick Windows DEA software to solve the BCC model. Under input minimization and variable returns to scale conditions, Warwick Windows DEA software solves the problem in two stages. First, the intermediate point is obtained by using the following models:

BCC First Stage

$$\text{Max } q = \sum_r u_r y_{rj_0} + \Omega_1 - \Omega_2 \tag{11.A4}$$

$$\text{s.t.} \quad \sum_r u_r y_{rj} - \sum_i v_i x_{ij} + \Omega_1 - \Omega_2 \le 0 \tag{11.A5}$$

$$\sum_i v_i x_{ij_0} = 1 \tag{11.A6}$$

$$u_r, v_i, \Omega_1, \Omega_2 \ge 0 \tag{11.A7}$$

$$\lambda_i \ge 0$$
$$j = 1,...,48$$
$$q \ge 0$$
$$i = 1,...,4$$
$$r = 1$$

where x_{ij} are inputs (public capital, private capital, labour and telecommunications capital) for DMU_j and y_{rj} is the output level $(Q_{ij}$, value added) for DMU_j. λ_j is the weight of DMU in the facet for the evaluated DMU. w_i and w_r are priorities. s_i and s_r are slacks corresponding to input and output respectively (≥ 0). j_0 is the DMU being assessed. For input minimization model w_i is set equal to 100 percent, while w_r is set equal to 0, implying that the input reduction is targeted while keeping output unchanged. For output maximization models, the reverse is true. By letting q^* be the optimal value of q in the above model, the minimum and maximum limit of the Ω range is obtained by solving the second stage.

Then, the subsequent projection point is found by solving the second stage.

BCC Second Stage

$$\text{Min/Max } \Omega_1 - \Omega_2 \qquad (11.A8)$$

$$\text{s.t.} \qquad q^* = \sum_r u_r y_{rj_0} + \Omega_1 - \Omega_2 \qquad (11.A9)$$

$$\sum_r u_r y_{rj} - \sum_i v_i x_{ij} + \Omega_1 - \Omega_2 \leq 0 \qquad (11.A10)$$

$$\sum_i v_i x_{ij_0} = 1 \qquad (11.A11)$$

$$u_r, v_i, \Omega_1, \Omega_2 \geq 0 \qquad (11.A12)$$

where u_r is the weight of the rth output and v_i is the weight of ith input for DMUj. Ω_1 and Ω_2 are the distance from frontier facet.

12 Investment and Household Adoption of Communication and Information Services

Peter L. Stenberg

Economic Research Service, the United States Department of Agriculture

12.1 Introduction

What is the digital divide? The phrase, basically, describes a line separating the communication and information technology 'haves' from the 'have-nots'. Like the term 'poverty line' the concept is a bit amorphous. Both concepts are also ever evolving along with the implicit basket of household goods for the poverty line and the digital divide's set of communication and information services. Unlike the expression poverty line, however, Digital divide has never had a concise definition. Digital divide has also been used to describe situations within countries, across countries, and across hemispheres. A further discussion of the phenomenon can be found in Chap. 14.

The concept behind the expression digital divide, however, has been well known in the research community for the last half century. Digital divide, in the simplest form, is a special case within the body of knowledge known as technology diffusion. In addition, it is implicitly a political concept, given the subjective determination of what are the necessary components for modern day communication and information services.

While the research covers a number of major policy issues with respect to the on-going diffusion of new communication and information services and technology, the focus here is solely on providing an overview on the what and why in regard to the rural household. A number of major long-term trends for rural households have become apparent, including the fact that communication and information service delivery, such as the telephone and Internet, have become an increasingly significant factor in the growth of the economy. The only argument has been over the degree of its economic significance. As in technology diffusion for other service developments, however, the diffusion of communication and information services varies in time and place.

12.2 Telephone Adoption and Use Across Income Groups and Geographic Space

The main economic principles underlying the diffusion and adoption of communication services are two-fold: companies invest where they earn the highest returns
and households adopt if they can afford it and either need it or desire it (Davies
1979; Rogers 1995). Given how locational factors affect a telecommunication
company's return to investment as well as the variance in household income
across space, the adoption and use of communication and information services are
neither uniform across the country or by income group.

To understand the current process of telecommunication service diffusion it is
useful to go back over the adoption and use of basic household telephone service.
Despite new technologies in the delivery of voice communication, basic telephone
service has reached a stable equilibrium.

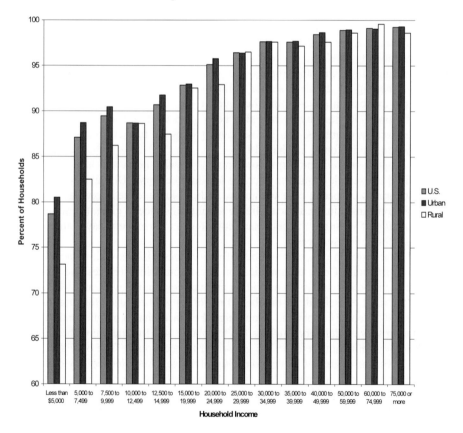

Fig.12.1. Percent of U.S. households with a telephone by income and rural-urban status,
2001. Source: Data from the U.S. Department of Commerce 2001, 2002a

The processes, and policies applied in reaching the equilibrium are of the same structure as is being experienced by the newer set of the communication and information services. Only the parameters of the processes are different.

It took nearly 100 years to reach the current household penetration rate for household telephone use. Arguably, this penetration rate is the market saturation rate, given the policy set and cost structure. From the onset there was a debate over whether telephones were a necessity or a luxury, a debate still on-going and, in addition, mirrored in the on-going debate over the Internet (Dyson 1999; Stenberg 2003). The earliest adopters were the wealthier households in urban places. The first adopters in rural areas were doctors and rich farm households (Dyson 1999; Stenberg 2000).

The household telephone penetration rate has remained stable for the last 20 years; roughly 95 percent of all households have a telephone (U.S. Dept. of Commerce 2001, 2002a, and Federal Communications Commission 2001). Penetration rates, however, do vary across regions (See Fig. 12.2) and income groups (See Fig. 12.1). The rate for rural areas is comparable to urban areas. Urban households we define here as households in communities of population 2,500 or greater.

Before one reads too much into what is shown on the map here, however, it should be noted that the data sample size does not lend itself to make a precise ranking of the states (the unit of observation shown here). Nevertheless, the data is robust enough to conclude that income is a strong indicator of the household penetration rate for a state. The regional patterns seen in the map have remained stable over the last decade (Stenberg 2003; Stenberg and Dicken 2002).

The demand for telephones in the household is highly inelastic, though it is still true that the lower the household income, the less likely the household is to have telephone service (Fig. 12.1). What may be perceptible in the Fig. 12.1, however, is an inflection point at the USD 30,000 household income level. A simple test for the inflection point using dummy variables and a least square procedure finds it to be significant at the 99 percent level. At the inflection point the cost of telephone service becomes, increasingly, an affordability issue for lower income households. The rural-urban variance within income groups is not significant.

12.3 Policy Reason for Observed Spatial Variance

The low household income location of the inflection point and the non-variance within income groups are the result of U.S. universal service programs. In the United States, universal service programs are designed to bring affordable telephone service to all households. Universal policy in the United States is multifaceted (Crandall and Waverman 2000; General Accounting Office 2002; Garcia and Gorenflo 1999; Stenberg 2003). The universal service program is the reason penetration rates are comparable between rural and urban households. The federal government role has been to apply a tax on long distance phone service providers. The proceeds are turned over to rural local phone service providers. In return the rural local phone service providers offer their services at rates less than the cost that service provision would dictate. Essentially, it is a subsidy program.

The federal government, however, is not the sole player in setting policy for promoting the universality in telephone use. State governments also set very significant telephone policy. State policy varies considerably across the states, but basically they also use an income transfer mechanism as well as a regulatory mechanism. The main regulatory mechanism has been in setting telephone rates. The result has been a reduction in the cost for having basic telephone service in the household at the expense of having a higher cost for special telephone services for households and for businesses to have telephone service. The states have also, often, required major telephone companies to provide service in underserved, often rural, communities for the right of having a monopoly on service provision in communities where their profits would be greater. This is one reason for the variance in telephone penetration rates that are seen in Fig. 12.2.

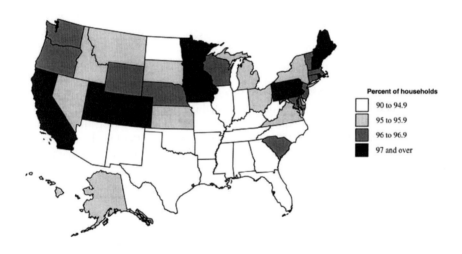

Fig.12.2. Households with a telephone, 2001. Source: Data from the U.S. Department of Commerce 2001, 2002a

If, as some propose, these universal service programs were to end, our preliminary analysis, given costs of the traditional phone and wireless services, suggests the inflection point could move above the USD 35,000 household income level. The slope of the curve up to that point also would be steeper than it is now. For rural households the change would be greater due to higher costs of service delivery and price elasticity variance over distance (Ouwersloot and Rietveld 2001).

Wireless telephone service, a.k.a. cell phones, has been touted as a more cost effective means to deliver local phone service in rural areas. Wireless, however, is not yet a perfect substitute for the traditional telephone service. The average purchase price for wireless services is still greater than the traditional telephone service. Two things may change this. First, the current programs to keep local phone service price affordable may be eliminated. Second, the current programs may be adjusted to include wireless service. Some advocate the former, but only the latter, so far, is actually taking place. At least four states now include wireless service in their universal service programs.

Wireless services are starting to make inroads into the demand for traditional phone services. Analysis of the Federal Communications Commission (May 2004) data on communication and information service use shows some middle-income households dropping traditional phone services in favour of cell phones. In high-income households they are largely using both. In low-income households, where the cost difference between traditional and wireless services is critical, they remain with the traditional telephone services. This is true for both rural and urban households. Wireless services are, thus, not affecting telephone penetration rates for households.

12.4 Internet Adoption and Use Across Income Groups and Geographic Space

Internet use by rural and urban households has also increased significantly during the 1990s, so significantly that it is one of fastest rates of adoption for any kind of service for the household (Greenstein 2000; Leamer and Storper 2001; Stenberg 2003; U.S. Department of Commerce 2000 and 2002b). Proponents of the Internet say it has been faster than telephones, television, television, and VCRs (video cassette recorders), though in actuality this is open to some debate because of one necessary determination, the choice of what the first year was for the critical technological development. No matter how history may finally determine the Internet's place there has been a remarkably fast diffusion and adoption of these services.

At least 92 percent of American households can readily access the Internet (Greenstein 2000). Household Internet use has increased for all regions and income groups regardless of the rurality. Analysis of the 2001 current population survey indicates half of all American households now subscribe to some Internet service. Over forty percent of rural households subscribe (US Department of Commerce 2001). The penetration rate varies considerably across the country (See Fig.12.3).

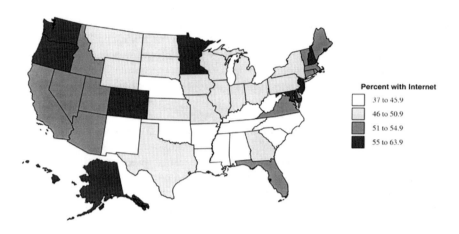

Fig. 12.3. Households with Internet connection, 2001. Source: Data from the U.S. Department of Commerce 2001, 2002a

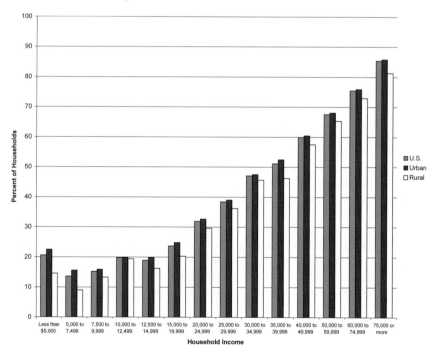

Fig. 12.4. Percent of U.S. households with Internet access by income and rural-urban status, 2001. Source: Data from the U.S. Department of Commerce 2001, 2002a

The higher the household income, the more likely the household will use the Internet (See Fig.12.4). Income is a much more critical element for Internet use than it is for telephone use. In Fig. 12.4 there is a hook at the low end of incomes levels (less than USD 5,000). It appears in each survey year and is due to the college student population. The blip appearing at the USD 10,000 to USD 12,499 is a random fluctuation due to sample size within the income group.

The concavity of the slopes in Figs. 12.1 and 12.4 is very different. Fig. 12.4 is telling evidence of the non-interventionist policy currently in place for household Internet service; the demand curve for a normal good.

Rural households lag in Internet use in the aggregate and across all income groups. Nonetheless, rural areas have been catching up in the last few years according to Bureau of the Census Current Population Survey data (U.S. Department of Commerce 2001, 2002a). The same data shows rural households had higher rates of growth than urban households for Internet adoption between 1999 and 2001, across and within income groups. The degree of rurality, however, continues to play a more critical role in the diffusion and adoption of household Internet use. The less densely populated rural areas do have rates lower than rural areas in more densely populated states (Stenberg 1993).

The adoption and use of the Internet is following the classic S-Curve, first slow adoption, followed by rapid adoption, and finally slowing adoption as the market becomes saturated. While the use and adoption of the Internet has been very fast, 2001 the Current Population Survey data for the years 1998, 2000, and 2001 indicates that this is beginning to slow down.

Higher income households, the earliest adopters of the income groups, may have already reached a saturation point. Households in this income group that do not have the Internet, and this only a small subset (Fig. 12.4), have largely indicated that they do not want it (Fig. 12.5).

The size of the 'do not want' group will largely remain unchanged unless new applications, such as video-on-demand, become compelling for the nonadopters (Madden 2003). Penetration rates will increase more rapidly for lower income households, though the lower the household income the more likely Internet service is just too expensive (Fig. 12.5). The 'too expensive' factor is greater for rural households than urban households. Other factors such as were unable to get it, did not know how to use, had it at work, did not have a home computer, and other factors were all very low.

With the slowing growth in adoption, the penetration rate for urban households has more closely reached its peak than for rural households. As a consequence, the difference between rural and urban rates will close further. The economics of Internet service provision, however, means the penetration will remain lower for rural households than urban households.

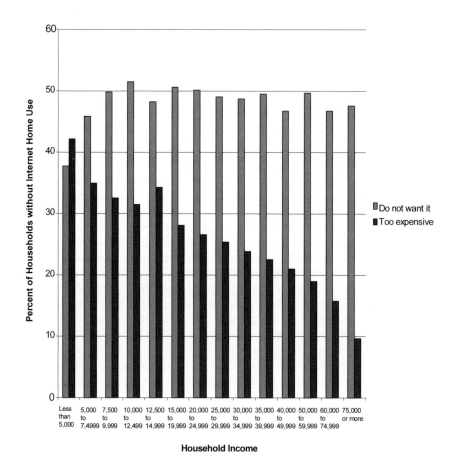

Fig. 12.5. The two most common reasons a household does not have Internet service, 2001.
Source: Data from the U.S. Department of Commerce 2001, 2002a

12.5 The Economics of Rural Telecommunication Service Delivery

The cost incurred by local exchange carriers, as local phone companies are called, in providing rural households with telecommunication services has always been higher than for urban households (Rural Task Force). For the foreseeable future, the higher cost will remain a fact of economic life. The technology changes have not altered this equation (Leamer and Storper 2001; Stenberg 1999). Economies-to-scale are at the core of why they face higher costs.

All rural areas, by definition, are characterized by low population density. The fewer people in any relevant geographic space, the fewer costs are shared for telecommunication services; fewer share in the cost of the central office switches, loop maintenance, and other common components of the local telecommunication system. In addition, rural telephone service providers must spend more per customer for maintenance and repair than urban providers. The cost function is such that as population density decreases the price of delivering phone service increases exponentially.

The economies are true whether the delivery mechanism is the traditional phone service through copper wire or wireless services. In addition, small telecommunication companies have a hard time purchasing equipment scaled for their operations (Grant and Meadows 2002). Equipment manufacturers have been focusing on the more profitable large-scale telecommunication companies (Egan 1996).

Industry structure also continues to be a major economic factor in the delivery of telephone and Internet service in rural areas. Usually when the United States telecommunication service delivery industry is discussed, people often think only of the remaining four Baby Bells (SBC, Verizon, BellSouth, and Qwest). In actuality, there are more than 1,000 providers. Most of the providers are small in scale, concentrated in rural areas, and serve as sole providers in their communities. Many of them are cooperatives. The providers range from mom- and pop-operations with as few as ten households as their customers to the Baby Bells with millions of customers. The quality of service varies considerably across these providers as well as within the largest providers.

Despite this, however, competition has been coming into rural areas. The number of high-speed Internet service providers has been growing for many localities, including rural communities. In a few rural communities, there are at least four high-speed Internet service providers, though in far more rural communities there are none (See Fig.12.6).

The reason why many rural communities have no high-speed Internet service provider, like other telecommunication services, has to do with technology, economics, and population density. DSL (digital subscriber line) is the world's most common form of delivery for high-speed (broadband) Internet service. The technology allows broadband service through copper telephone lines. A limiting factor in the delivery of DSL is the distance from the telephone provider's central office switch. In many counties less than twenty percent of the population reside within the distance that DSL service can be provided (See Fig.12.7).

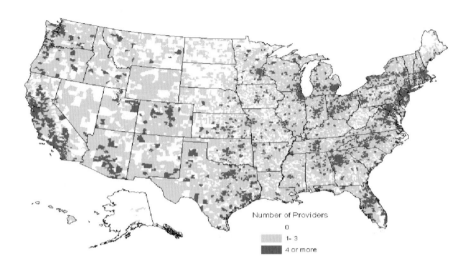

Fig. 12.6. Number of high-speed providers identified offering service by zip code, June 2001. Source: Data from the Federal Communications Commission 2001

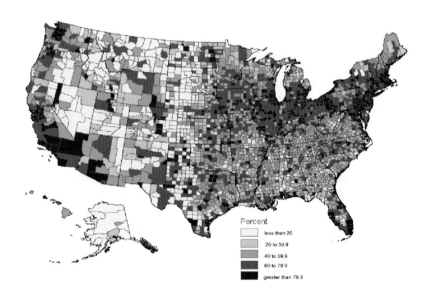

Fig. 12.7. Percent of county population within 18,000 feet of a central office switch, 2001. Source: Data from Telcordia Technologies 2001, U.S. Department of Commerce 2002a

Cable modems, for high-speed Internet connections through cable TV systems, have, unlike the rest of the world, been the most popular broadband Internet service in the United States. Their limits are based on potential customer base density, the fewer customers on a line the less economically viable they have been for the cable companies. As a consequence, they are concentrated in urban core areas, including small rural towns of less the 2,500. The effect of the variation in in-place equipment partially explains the difference in the types of Internet connection used in rural versus urban communities. Urban households are more likely to use DSL or cable modems to connect to the Internet than rural households (Table 12.1)

Table 12.1. Percent of each major type of Internet connection for home use, 2001

	Regular Dial-Up	DSL Line	Cable Modem
Metropolitan	79.2	6.9	13.0
Non-Metropolitan	89.9	2.5	6.8
Total	80.9	6.2	12.1

Numbers may not add to 100 percent because of other types of connections. Source: U.S. Department of Commerce 2001, 2002a

12.6 Future Trends in Information and Communication Technologies in Rural Areas

Two major developments, wireless and satellite telephony, have often been cited by their promoters as overcoming the economic disadvantages rural areas have in the use of traditional telephone service (Grant and Meadows 2002). Unfortunately, this is not quite accurate. First, wireless services have some cost advantages at covering the "last mile" from a phone company's switch to the household. The limitations, though, are in the technology and the terrain it is being used in; overcoming dead zones in low population density areas quickly reduces any cost advantages (Grant and Meadows 2002; Egan 1996).

Satellites have been touted as the one way that more remote rural households will be able to have broadband Internet service. So far the quality of the service has not lived up to some of the promise (Grant and Meadows 2002). In the first place the transmission speed of the service may never match broadband services obtained through the telephone or cable systems. Additional drawbacks for satellite services include the time it takes for a signal to reach a destination and the need for an unobstructed view of the southern sky (there can be no obstructions, such as trees or a hill, between the satellite and the customer's dish). Satellites will serve a niche, but they may never be fully competitive with land-based systems (Grant and Meadows 2002; National Telecommunication and Information Administration and Rural Utility Services 2000).

12.7 Conclusions

The diffusion of telecommunication service innovations has never been uniform or continuous. Innovations have gone to rich households that were more likely to adopt them sooner than less wealthy households or otherwise less likely to adopt. The rollout of Internet service has been no different. Urban areas were the first to receive new services, while rural areas lagged. High-income households adopted the new services before low-income households. The Washington, DC area led most other regions of the country. Rural areas are higher cost areas than urban areas. They also have fewer households and businesses to share in the cost of the service. Nevertheless, many rural communities are receiving these new communication and information services.

Does this mean that the Digital Divide is either an illusionary or only transitory? The answer is both yes and no. In a sense they are illusionary and transitory because, as in most technological and service diffusions, the divide is much greater at first than it is later. In another sense the Digital Divide is not. First, the availability, and affordability, of new services will be determined by four main mechanisms: governmental policy, economic feasibility, technical limits, and market incentives. While the fallout from the bust of the dot-com boom has led to excessive decline for investment in telecommunications and can only slow down the diffusion of new services, government policy will still be a critical factor in determining what degree of divide there will be. Second, technology has not changed and will not change enough to make the delivery of telecommunications to make the cost structure the same across space. Third, technology will not change enough to lower service delivery costs so that income will not be a factor in their adoption.

The federal government has played a major role in reducing the divide. The federal government operates a number of relatively small grant and loan programs that encourage private investment for rural Internet service provision, such as the U.S. Department of Agriculture's rural telecommunication service providers. The major policy mechanism, the universal program has not been tapped so far to increase Internet access for the household. The program, however, was used to bring Internet service to schools, public libraries, and medical clinics. These programs are under review by the Federal Communications Commission and Congress. The Federal Communications Commission review itself is mandated by the Telecommunications Act of 1996.

Acknowledgements. The views expressed are those of the author and do not necessarily reflect the views of the U.S. Department of Agriculture.

References

Crandall RW, Waverman L (2000) Who pays for universal service? When telephone subsidies become transparent. Brookings Institution Press, Washington, DC

Davies S (1979) The diffusion of process innovations. Cambridge University Press, Cambridge, MA

Dyson L (1999) A history of rural telecommunications. In: Stenberg PL (ed) Telecommunications in rural economic development. Workshop Proceedings sponsored by the Economic Research Service, USDA, TVA Rural Studies and the Western Rural Development Center. Western Rural Development Center, Oregon State University, Corvallis, December 1999, pp 3–6

Egan BL (1996) Information superhighways revisited: the economics of multimedia. Artech House, Boston, MA

Federal Communications Commission (2001) High-Speed Services for Internet Access. Industry Analysis and Technology Division, Washington, DC, June

Federal Communications Commission (2004). Trends in Telephone Service, Industry Analysis and Technology Division, Washington, DC, May

Garcia DL, Gorenflo NR (1999) Best practices for rural Internet deployment: implications for universal service policy. In: Stenberg PL (ed) Telecommunications in rural economic development. Workshop Proceedings sponsored by the Economic Research Service, USDA, TVA Rural Studies and the Western Rural Development Center. Western Rural Development Center, Oregon State University, Corvallis, December 1999, pp 15–28

General Accounting Office (2002) Federal and State universal service programs and challenges to funding. General Accounting Office Paper 02-187. U.S. Government Printing Office, Washington, DC

Grant AE, Meadows JH (eds) (2002) Communication technology update, 8th edition. Elsevier Science, Woburn, MA

Greenstein S (2000) Building and delivering the virtual world: commercialising services for Internet access. National Bureau of Economic Research, Working Paper 7690, Cambridge, MA

Leamer EE, Storper M (2001) The Economic geography of the Internet age. National Bureau of Economic Research, Working Paper 8450, Cambridge, MA

Madden M (2003) America's online pursuits. PEW Internet & American Life Project, Washington, DC

National Telecommunication and Information Administration and Rural Utility Services (2000) Advanced telecommunications in rural America. U.S. Department of Commerce and U.S. Department of Agriculture, Washington, DC

Ouwersloot H, Rietveld P (2001) On the distance dependence of the price elasticity of telecommunications demand; review, analysis, and alternative theoretical backgrounds. The Annals of Regional Science 35: 577–594

Rogers EM (1995) Diffusion of innovations. The Free Press, New York

Rural Task Force (2000) The rural difference. Federal Communications Commission Federal-State Joint Board, Washington, DC

Stenberg PL (ed) (1999) Telecommunications in rural economic development. Workshop sponsored by the Economic Research Service, USDA, TVA Rural Studies and the Western Rural Development Center. Western Rural Development Center, Oregon State University, Corvallis, December 1999

Stenberg PL (2000) The new economy, rural economic development and the farm sector. In: Tichá I (ed) Agrarian perspectives IX: globalization and competitiveness. Czech University of Agriculture, Prague, Czech Republic

Stenberg PL (2003) Telecommunication rural policy in the U.S.: issues and economic consequences. In: Graham D, Bryden J, Shucksmith M, Thomson K (eds) European rural policy at the crossroads. The Arkleton Centre for Rural Development Research, University of Aberdeen, Aberdeen, pp 149–65

Stenberg PL, and C Dicken (2002) Communication and information technology diffusion in the U.S. Paper presented at the International Telecommunication Society Biennial Conference, Seoul, South Korea, August 18-21

Telcordia Technologies (2001) Local Exchange Routing Guide (LERG). Traffic Routing Administration, Piscataway, NJ

U.S. Department of Commerce (2000) Falling through the Net: toward digital inclusion. Economics and Statistics Administration, National Telecommunications and Information Administration, U.S. Dept. of Commerce, Washington, DC

U.S. Department of Commerce (2001) Current population survey. Bureau of the Census, U.S. Dept. of Commerce, Washington, DC

U.S. Department of Commerce (2002a) Census of population 2000. Bureau of the Census, U.S. Dept. of Commerce, Washington, DC

U.S. Department of Commerce (2002b) A nation online: how Americans are expanding their use of the Internet. Economics and Statistics Administration, National Telecommunications and Information Administration, U.S. Dept. of Commerce, Washington, DC

U.S. Government (1996) Telecommunications Act of 1996. United States of America, Public Law No.104–104, February 8, 1996

13 The Swedish 3G Beauty Contest: A Beauty or a Beast?

Per-Olof Bjuggren

Jönköping International Business School, Jönköping University

13.1 Introduction

With system-wide changes, as described in Chaps. 2, 10 and 14, market forms and institutional arrangements become vital issues in relation to Information and Communication Technologies' (ICTs) development. As in many other countries, Sweden has recently allocated licenses to the third generation (3G) of wireless telecommunication technology. However, in contrast to Britain, Germany, and Denmark, for example, a so-called beauty contest was used to earmark the rights. The motivation was that using criteria other than price in the portioning of rights would be to the advantage of both consumers and producers and speed up the infrastructure investments (National Post and Telecom Agency (PTS) 2000a). It remains to be seen if the objectives of the contest will be met. The decision to choose such a competition was subject to some political controversy, as representatives of especially bourgeoisie parties preferred a conventional auction (the Committee of Finance 2000).

What is remarkable is that there was not much of economic analysis behind the decision to choose a beauty contest. Considering that the choice was between two ways of allocating rights to a scarce resource, the use of the radio spectrum, economists should have something to contribute. But surprisingly, they have not offered much. Theoretical underpinnings for the use of beauty contests seem to be lacking and the economic literature has very little to say. About the alternative, auctions, it has a lot to offer (see e.g. Klemperer 1999, 2002a).

An evaluation of a beauty contest is thus a little of a green field exercise. This is both disturbing and challenging. The degrees of freedom in the choice of approach are large. A strand of the literature that could serve as a theory of beauty contests is that of competition for the field. This approach has inspired the institutional economic analysis adopted in this paper.

The purpose of the chapter is to evaluate a beauty contest like the one staged in Sweden for the allocation of 3G rights. A comparative analysis is made with auction as an alternative means of allocation. Is a beauty contest like the Swedish one rewarding beauty? Might it be the case that it is better to be a beast than a beauty if a firm wants to get a 3G license? These two are examples of the questions addressed in the present study.

The chapter starts, in Sect. 13.2, with a general discussion about the nature of beauty contests and auctions as allocation means. The theory of competition for the field is put forward as a theoretical framework to be used in the analysis of beauty contests. In Sect. 13.3, the Swedish 3G beauty contest is presented. Section 13.4 is devoted to a description of two auction alternatives to the Swedish beauty contest.

The comparative analysis is done in Sects. 13.5, 13.6, and 13.7. The importance of sunk cost and to make a distinction between ex ante and ex post are highlighted in Sect. 13.5. Transaction properties of beauty contests fostering opportunistic behaviour are the subject matter of Sect. 13.6. A comparison between a beauty contest and an auction along dimensions such as selection of efficient firms, low consumer prices, and impact on public financing is made in Sect. 13.7. Section 13.8 offers a summary and concluding remarks.

13.2 Beauty Contests and Auctions as Allocation Means

The telecommunication sector is rapidly developing. A third generation of wireless communications named 3G is to be installed with the advent of this millennium. The installation cannot be done unless radio frequencies are made available to communication service providers. This is a scarce resource. A finite number of frequencies is available and demand at a zero price exceeds supply. As in all cases of scarcity, a mechanism for allocating rights to use a scant resource is needed. Seen from the viewpoint of efficiency, the allocation mechanism should reward the rights to highest valuing use and user[1].

The two ways of allocating rights to radio frequencies are beauty contests and auctions. A distinction between them is that in case of an auction the price mechanism decides who is to acquire the rights to radio frequencies. The highest bidders are those who attain the rights. In this sense, an auction is the most market-like of the two means. In a beauty contest other criteria play a role in allocating rights as they may be given to those who guarantee the lowest price for services in the future, or those promising to invest most in infrastructure, using the most technically advanced equipment etc.

The literature is rich in theories regarding auctions (see e.g. McAfee and MacMcmillan 1987 and Klemperer 1999, 2002a), but offer almost nothing regarding beauty contests. However, a close look at the way a beauty contest is conducted suggests that the theory for the competition for the field can be used. The notion of competition for the field is found already in an article by Chadwick (1859). But it was Demsetz (1968) who revived and developed the notion. He used it to demonstrate that also in the case of a so-called natural monopoly there is

---

[1] At least if a Pareto criterion of efficiency is used.

a market process through which a price level close to the price in perfect competition can be established. It was not necessary to regulate price.

Demsetz says it is possible to achieve the same or almost the same result in terms of efficiency through competition for the right to serve as via competition between a large number of firms within the boundaries of the market. If the number of firms contesting for the right to serve is large enough, and the selection mechanism is structured in an appropriate way, the winner of a bidding contest like the beauty contest will be the firm that most efficiently meets consumers' demand. Such a proper selection mechanism may rely on the lowest price on offer.

Williamson (1976, 1985) has a more critical view of the possibilities to achieve efficiency through competition for the market. He is primarily concerned about the contractual difficulties ex post (after the bidding has taken place). These most likely occur when there are investments with large sunk costs and market and technology uncertainties. Williamson's treatment of bidding for the right to a market is also interesting because of his choice of case study. He uses the bidding for a community-antenna television (CATV) franchise in 1969 in Oakland, California, as an empirical illustration of the ex post contractual problems. The CATV case has many similarities with the 3G cases in terms of characteristics of the investment (antennas in both cases), heavy sunk cost and high degree of market and technology uncertainty. Williamson's study has much bearing on studies of 3G beauty contests.

Another aspect of a beauty contest is the necessity to rely on "governments bureaucrats to assess the merits of competing firms' business plans" (Binmore and Klemperer 2002, p.6). In an auction, however, the price mechanism (in form of pecuniary bids for the right) takes over most of the work of the bureaucrats in deciding who is to get the limited number of rights[2]. The price offered for the right to the market has all the necessary details to determine the winner in the auction. In a beauty contest, however, there is a need for a central information gathering entity to evaluate the credibility of the promises (bids) of the contestants and detailed contracts have to be prepared in order to make winners bound by their promises. In that sense, a beauty contest is more like central planning.

It is difficult to tell which method ex post generates prices that are closer to those in perfect competition. This is partly a question of collusion in the pre- and post-bidding stages and how successful a strategy like a beauty contest is as a selection criterion. A beauty contest that awards the license to those providers promising to offer the lowest price can be successful in establishing a rate equal or close to the competitive zero-profit price. However, there is a post contractual problem that has to be dealt with, and Williamson (1976) has shown that the outcome of such a bidding contest can ex post be rather disappointing.

---

[2] This was also pointed out long ago by Coase (1959).

13.3 The Swedish Beauty Contest

Sweden chose the beauty contest as allocation means for distributing UMTS-licenses (UMTS is the system that will be used in the 3G network). There was some debate in the parliament preceding the decision to choose this method. Representatives from the bourgeoisie parties argued against it, favouring auction (the Committee of Finance 2000). In short, the arguments for choosing the beauty contest were its ability to promote consumer and producer interest and boost the sector (PTS 2000a). By giving away the licenses, it was maintained that the operators would not be burdened by heavy fixed costs to the same extent as in auctions. The lower costs would, according to this line of reasoning, favour consumers in the sense of lower prices and providing more funds for the companies to spend on development. Participants in the bidding game had to pay an entry fee of EUR 11, 765 (SEK 100,000)[3]. In addition, a yearly charge of 0.15 percent of revenue was to be obtained from each license (PTS 2000b).

The National Post and Telecom Agency (PTS) was in charge of the allocation of UMTS-licenses. PTS established a number of criteria for the evaluation of applications (PTS 2000b). The purpose was to encourage a good coverage of population and geography and as fast development of the network as possible. It was prescribed that a license holder was to provide a network capacity of more than 99 percent of the Swedish population or 8 860 000 people out of Sweden's 8,883 million people in 1990 (see License Conditions for UMTS issued by PTS 2000b). In the invitation for applicants, a two-step selection procedure was presented (see PTS 2000b). In the first step, an initial consideration of the applications was made. It concerned financial capacity, technical feasibility, commercial feasibility and appropriate expertise and experience. An applicant, who under PTS evaluation fulfilled all the four criteria, was allowed to enter the second step of detailed consideration. In the second step, the applicants were ranked according to commitment concerning coverage and development rate.

The number of licenses to be granted was first planned to be five but was later reduced to just four. Two of them contained an opportunity to build an infrastructure for GSM as well[4]. They were to be given to new entrants. A total number of ten applications were received (3G Newsroom 2001).

The first step, initial consideration, appeared to be insurmountable for many of the applicants. PTS rejected several applicants due to deficiencies especially in technical feasibility (3G Newsroom 2001). The planned network architecture submitted was deemed inappropriate for the prescribed coverage. As many as four applications were turned down; among them Telia, the largest and oldest of the established Swedish mobile phone operators. Telia had a different view from that of PTS about the number of base stations necessary to provide the prescribed coverage for 8 860 000 people. Telia was of the opinion that a lower number of base stations than what PTS deemed necessary was sufficient (Carlbom 2000).

---

[3] The exchange rate used is SEK 8.5 = EUR 1, the exchange rate at the time of the bidding process.

[4] GSM is the system used currently, 2G, network.

The five applicants who made it to the second phase were apprised on the basis of their description of planned development and its speed. The description included information about how much of infrastructure was to be completed by the end of 2003, 2006, and 2009. Four applicants —Europolitan, HI3G, Orange and Tele2— got the highest points for coverage and speed of network development. They all promised to provide a network that covered at least 8 860 000 persons at the end of 2003. (At the time of the beauty contest it corresponded to 99.98 per cent of the entire Swedish population.) The fifth, Telenordia Mobil, ranked lower and dropped out. Two of the winners, HI3G and Orange, were newcomers, and under their licenses, they could build a GSM network. The awarded licenses are valid from 16 December 2000 to 31 December 2015 (approximately 15 years).

There will be four competing providers of UMTS network services in all. A certain amount of co-operation is however allowed amongst license winners as well as between them and other firms in the construction of the network. Each license holder is required to do about 30 percent of the network investment assigned to it. The rest can be done through joint ventures with other firms (PTS 2001).

There is also a national roaming condition that obliges license holder to offer excess capacity to new providers on a cost basis (Jonasson 2001). As mentioned, two of the licenses gave opportunity to GSM investment. The number of competitors in GSM services could thereby be increased from three to five.

All the license holders have taken advantage of the opportunity to cooperate in infrastructure building. The first one to enter into an agreement with another company on sharing infrastructure cost was Tele 2 (Called Netcom at the time of the agreement). Within less than one month, January 16, 2001, after the four licenses had been awarded, Tele 2 reached an agreement in principle with Telia on founding a joint venture company that would own the UMTS license it originally had. The agreement was very important to Telia, as it is felt an urgent need to take part in the establishment of the UMTS technology in Sweden. Tele 2, in turn, needed someone to share the cost of the infrastructure with. The agreement was signed on 15 March 2001 (Telia 2001). A new separate company, Swedish UMTS Network Ltd., owned fifty-fifty by Telia and Tele 2 was founded. It will construct and maintain the UMTS network and own the UMTS license too. The Swedish Competition Authorities and PTS approved the agreement.

The other three license holders, Hi3G, Europolitan and Orange, were also to enter into agreements to lower the costs of infrastructure investment. Hi3G and Europolitan (now Vodafone) announced, also in January 2001, that they were to establish a joint venture company, 3G Infrastructure Services AB, to construct and operate an UMTS infrastructure covering 70 percent of the Swedish population. For the remaining 30 percent, in Stockholm, Gothenburg, and Malmö, each of the two companies would build their own networks. Five months later, on 16 May 2001, Orange also signed a contract to acquire an ownership share in 3G Infrastructure Services AB (Hi3G 2001). Then there were three firms each with one-third ownership —Hi3G, Vodafone (Europolitan) and Orange. This situation is about to change as Orange on 20 December 2002 announced that it would withdraw from the Swedish market (Orange 2002). The companies will build separate network only in the Stockholm, Gothenburg, and Malmö for 30 percent of the Swedish population.

As it stands, there will competition between three separate networks in the metropolitan areas of Stockholm, Gothenburg and Malmö, the most densely populated regions of Sweden. For the rest of the country there will be only two competing network companies.

13.4 What Would an Auction Alternative Have Looked Like?

As stated above an important aim of the allocation is to promote efficiency. Efficiency is achieved if the licenses are awarded to actors who can make most profitable use of the limited number of available radio waves. A means to achieve this is competition. It was important to have several bidders as well as several companies offering 3G services. It is therefore crucial that auctions and beauty contests are designed in a way that stimulates competition both ex ante and ex post. In an auction, it is also of interest to get high proceeds. Two issues that matter for competition and the size of the proceeds (in auctions) are attracting entry and preventing collusion (Klemperer 2002a).

In order to make a comparative analysis of the merits and faults of the Swedish beauty contest, the auction alternative has to be specified. What would a carefully designed Swedish auction have looked like?

Regarding design there are two main types of auctions to choose from. They are the ascending auction (or English auction) and the sealed-bid auction (or Dutch auction). McAfee and McMillan (1987) provide a description of both. In the ascending or English auction, the price is progressively raised until the number of bidders exactly matches the number of licenses. Its essential feature is that each bidder at any point of time knows the level of the other bids. Thus, every one of them has the opportunity to continue bidding in order to win. In the sealed-bid auction, there is no such opportunity. Each bidder submits one tender and the ones with highest offers declared winners. In a first-price sealed-bid auction, the winners have to pay exactly the prices tendered. In 3G auctions, a variant of sealed-bid auction called uniform-price is used (see Klemperer 2002a), where the price paid by each winner is equal to the lowest winning bid.

Klemperer (2002a) offers a description of the advantages and disadvantages of the two types. Collusion amongst the bidders is easier in an ascending auction than in a sealed-bid one. The opportunity to observe other bids and adjust one's own facilitates collusion. An ascending auction also has the disadvantage of not attracting bidders others than the incumbent ones (incumbent bidders are companies that already have 2G licenses). To attract new bidders is important for the ex post competition as well. This type of auction can repel especially less experienced firms. One reason is that the new firms assess a higher probability to be outbidden in an ascending auction. Another reason is that if a new less experienced firm wins in an ascending auction it is more likely than in a sealed-bid auction to suffer from a winner's curse (i.e. that they have been far too optimistic in predictions of future net cash flows). One advantage of an ascending auction, if it functions properly, is that the highest valuing firm is more likely to win and that the proceeds sometimes can be really impressive as was the case in Britain and Germany.

A critical factor in the choice between the ascending and the sealed-bid auction is the relation between the number of incumbents and the number of licenses offered. If the number of licenses offered in the auction is larger than the number of incumbents, using the English auction will be more profitable. But if the number of licenses is equal to or less than the number of incumbents, the sealed bid type is likely to be better (see more about this in Klemperer 2002a).

The auction in UK can be used as an example of a case where the ascending type of auction functioned well (see Binmore and Klemperer 2002). The number of licenses offered was five and the incumbents only four. It was, in other words, inevitable that there would be at least one entrant. The auction was concluded on 27 April 2000. The four incumbents and on entrant were awarded licenses. A staggering sum of EUR 4.17 billion was raised (two and a half percent of GNP or more than 600 euros per person).

The Danish auction, which took place in September 2001, almost a year later, can serve as an example of a well functioning sealed-bid auction (see Klemperer 2002b). The number of licenses offered was equal to the number of incumbents (four licenses and four incumbents). It was therefore possible that no entry would take place. A sealed bid offer helps in such a case to encourage entrants to participate as collusion amongst incumbents is made more difficult and the probability for a new firm to suffer from the winner's curs is lower. The Danes chose the uniform-price variant of a sealed-bid auction. The telecom bubble had burst and interest in 3G was much cooler than before. Nonetheless, the Danes succeeded to attract 95 euros per capita (EUR 560 million), a quite impressive result given the climate for telecom. Out of the four licenses on offer, one went to an entrant. The Danes were successful in efforts to encourage entry.

In the Swedish case, an appropriate form seems to have been the English ascending type of auction as the number of licenses exceeded the number incumbents (four licenses at stake and only three incumbents).

13.5 Sunk Cost and the Distinction between Ex Ante and Ex Post

Building 3G infrastructure involves heavy investment that is of a sunk cost character. There is hardly any use of equipment other than wireless mobile telecommunication with 3G technology. In an analysis of the sunk cost, a distinction between ex ante and ex post is important.

Ex ante, before the investing, a venture will be considered worth undertaking only if an assessment of cash flows indicates a positive net present value. Every local investment must show a positive net present value. A positive net present value implies that average total cost (investment costs included) is lower than expected price (expected average revenue). The assessment has to be made separately for each geographical area that can be covered through a mast and a base station. Investments in the most potentially profitable regional areas are likely to be made first. In Sweden, the most profitable regions are those of Stockholm, Gothenburg, and Malmö. Investments in less densely populated areas of Sweden will be next in priority.

It is necessary to be very careful when calculating the net present value of each local investment because ex post, once the investment is made, there is no escape. Ex post it will more or less only be the costs of operating the equipment that matters for the production. Irrespective of eventual accounting losses, the production of telecom services will continue as long as revenues are high enough to cover operating costs. Telecom companies might go bankrupt because of the heavy fixed cost of the infrastructure, but the equipment will be used by someone as long as operating costs are covered.

Let us to start with the assumption that there are no special costs associated with financial distress and bankruptcy. The interesting point is then that, in principle, it does not matter for the assessment of investment opportunities whether firms have acquired the right to invest in an auction or in a beauty contest. The same net present value assessment has to be made for every local investment. The fact that the company might have obtained its license via an auction and paid a large sum of money for it does not change the assessment of investment opportunities. The huge license fee is in itself a sunk cost with the ex ante and ex post characteristics accounted for above. Before bidding, the company must or at least should have made a calculation of the sum of the net present values from the different regional investments and made sure that the license fee paid in the auction did not exceed that sum. But ex post the license fee paid in the auction is of no interest in the subsequent investment decisions. In the same way, as described above, every investment must show a positive net present value, demonstrating that average total cost (investment cost included) is lower than the expected price (expected average revenue). The ex ante criterion for the investment is the same for both auction and beauty contest companies. The ex post situation is also the same.

If we let costs and incentive effects of financial distress and bankruptcy into the picture, the choice of allocation mechanism might matter. Financial distress in the sense that the bankruptcy risk has been substantially increased affect operating and financing costs and distorts the incentives for investment. A seminal article that deals with this problem from a principal agent perspective is Jensen and Meckling (1976). A standard textbook like Brealey and Myers (1991) has also a section about financial distress and bankruptcy. The simple result derived above that the ex ante criterion for investment and the ex post situation are the same does no longer hold. But it is difficult to say in what direction the analysis has to be changed. A company that in beauty contest has promised too much investment can end up in a financial distress as easily as a company that has paid a high price in an auction.

One difference between the auction and the beauty contest is the possibility of paying a fine or other kind of penalty if contractual stipulations signed by winners of the beauty contest are not met. Not to make the promised local investment is a breach of contract that may entail payment of damages. In its investment decision, a firm ought to take the payment of these damages into consideration when calculating the net present value. If the fine is heavy, it may spur companies to embark on investment, which otherwise might be unprofitable.

The question is whether it is economically efficient to have clauses forcing companies to make local investments that would otherwise show a negative net present value. According to the law and economics literature, it is efficient with contractual breach if the promisor's cost of performing is larger than the promisee's benefit from performing (Cooter and Ulen 2000, p.190). The promisor is in this case the telecompanies that have signed the Swedish beauty contest contract and the promisee is the Swedish population represented by PTS. It is reasonable to assume that the benefits lost by not building in a certain region will be expressed through the price system. The upshot is that from the society's viewpoint the cost-benefit analysis made by the private telecompanies is expected to generate an efficient scale of investment. It is difficult to find any market imperfections that justify public enforcing of investments. There are no reasons why the price system for teleservices should function less well than other goods and services.

13.6 Opportunism

Beauty contests have in a legal sense an ex post dimension that cannot be found in auctions. In a beauty contest, licenses will be awarded to companies making the most 'attractive' promises about investment, price policy, quality etc. In an auction, however, the licenses go to highest paying companies for the right to use a certain spectrum. Promises of future conduct are likely to invite to opportunistic behaviour, especially since it is the companies that promise the most get the licenses. Opportunistic behaviour in this context implies that a contestant, in a beauty contest, gives false statements or self-disbelieved promises of future investment (c.f. Williamson 1985). In an auction, there is upfront payment with no leeway for opportunism.

According to Williamson (1975, 1985, 1996), the human being, besides an inclination for opportunistic behaviour when profitable, is also characterized by bounded rationality. Bounded rationality refers to limited capacity of the human mind to conceive and evaluate all alternatives pertinent to a decision. In an environment clouded with uncertainty, the bounded rationality makes it almost impossible to take all future changes in transactional conditions into account when a contract is concluded. Complete contingent claims contracts are not feasible.

The emerging 3G market is characterized by uncertainty about both demand and technology. It is also characterized by large investment of a sunk cost type. The sunk cost and the problems of redoing the beauty contest create a situation of mutual dependence between the license giver and the license holders (especially in a small country like Sweden). In line with Williamson (1975, 1985, 1996), the compounding of bounded rationality, uncertainty, and mutual dependence feature a contractual situation in which opportunistic behaviour is likely to pay off.

The heavy long-lived investments of sunk cost character make it important to use long-term contracts. Consequently, 15 years-long contracts were chosen in Sweden and other countries. With short-term contracts, there would have been very difficult and costly transition problems to face in a transfer of a license to a new company. To decide the terms a new company can take over the infrastructure would be tricky. It is likely that the interest in the contest would have been much lower with shorter-term contracts.

A long-term contract in a business like 3G has to be adaptable to circumstances unforeseen at the time the contract was signed. Bounded rationality coupled with uncertainty about future demand and technology make long-term contracts incomplete. Trying to get everything set in the original contract and then enforcing the contract rigorously is not efficient. There is a need for gaps and loopholes that provide for contractual adaptability to changes in demand and technology.

But gaps can be taken advantage of ex post in an opportunistic manner. Even if there are no gaps, it might not always be in the interest of a public authority like PTS to always force a company to live up to the letter of the contract. It is costly to redo the bidding process and punishment in the form of a fine can result in financial distress and bankruptcy. Taking all these factors into consideration, it is likely that both PTS and the license holders are stuck into a bilateral relation. Mutual dependence of this sort is one of the prerequisites for viability of opportunistic behaviour.

The scope and the incentives for opportunistic behaviour make it questionable if a beauty contest like the Swedish one really is a contest for beauties. It might very well be the case that the opportunistic company (opportunistic in the sense of making promises that even the company believes that are extremely difficult to honour) has a better chance of winning. In other words, it might be better to be a disguised beast than a beauty.

The Swedish beauty contest might very well have awarded the licenses to the companies that were most unrealistic in their promises of future investment (Carlbom 2000)[5].

---

[5] During the year 2002 applications for amendments of the conditions were sent in to PTS. Orange started with a request for a three-year postponement and a decreased coverage from 8 860 000 to 8 300 000 inhabitants. PTS decided to reject Orange's application (PTS 2002). On the 20 December the same year Orange as a response announced that it plans to withdraw from the Swedish market. The pressure placed on it by the UMTS requirements was stated as the cause for its decision (Orange 2002). Also, Orange is not planning to give back its license in Denmark, which it got through an auction. Furthermore, in March 2004, three months after the deadline the end of 2003, the geographical coverage was far from promised for all license holders. More exactly, Hi3G had 67 percent, Tele 2 had 74 percent and Vodafone had 66 percent of promised geographical coverage (PTS 2004).

13.7 Are There Any Advantages of a Beauty Contest?

An evaluation of the beauty of a beauty contest has to consider more than the number of base stations and masts. Other dimensions along which beauty contests and auctions can be compared are selection of efficient telecom firms, low consumer prices and public financing. Let us consider these dimensions.

13.7.1 Selection of Efficient Firms

The information processing properties of an allocation mechanism are important for its ability to select efficient firms. Coase (1959) has already highlighted this fact. In a beauty contest, the bidding firms are requested to supply an administrative agency with information about important facts concerning plans and firms. Winners are selected on the basis of the information received. In an auction, information gathering is decentralized. The bidding companies themselves make a judgment of how valuable a license is. The information is condensed in prices offered for licenses. This way, a market allocates rights where the price serves as sufficient statistics of available information.

An evaluation of the two means of allocating rights has to consider the ability of administrators to know more of the market than the companies do. A beauty contest has an informational advantage if administrators, like a visible hand, locate the most efficient producer better than the invisible hand represented by the price in auction.

Assume now that the bidders have perfect foresight enabling them to rightly estimate future quasi-rents (i.e. can forecast the net cash flows from a license). In an auction, it is then likely that the company with the lowest service cost and the most innovative potential will be willing to pay the highest price for a license. The most efficient producers will thus be the ones who obtain a license. With this in mind, there is no reason to believe that a beauty contest results in more beautiful outcomes than an auction. On the contrary, an auction is more likely to award beauty.

If the assumption of perfect foresight is dropped, the existence of a winner's curse could change this result. A winner's curse is the denomination for the phenomenon in which the rival with the most overoptimistic view of net revenues tends to be the winner (see e.g. Bulow and Klemperer 2002). Bearing in mind that the most overoptimistic bidder is not necessarily the most efficient firm, it is no longer certain that an auction always rewards rights to the most efficient producer.

Winner's curse is however most likely to pester inexperienced companies. For example, most of those winning the European 3G auctions have been large and experienced companies. The knowledge of the risk to be affected by a winner's curse can serve to make the curse less likely to occur. There might also be a winner's curse in beauty contests as well. In the Swedish contest, licenses were awarded to the companies that offered more infrastructure. The most generous offers might be a result of over optimism as well as an outbreak of opportunism[6].

13.7.2 Low Consumer Prices

From the point of view of consumers, a beauty contest would be beautiful if it ex post resulted in lower prices for telecom services. It has been argued that by not having to pay large sums for licenses, the companies selected in a beauty contest will charge less than the winners of an auction would. The logic is that paying of large sums of money for the rights in an auction makes it necessary for the firms to ex post charge high consumer prices in order to break even. In the Swedish beauty contest all that the companies had to pay was EUR 11, 765 (SEK 100,000), which expressed per capita, is trifle, when compared, for example, to the costs of obtaining a license in Great Britain, which on average was more than 600 euros per person.

But claiming that a low cost license means lower price charged ex post for services is a misconception. The amount of money paid for the right to airwaves does not influence the rate charged for services (see also Binmore and Klemperer 2002). The amount paid for a license is a sunk cost as are the costs of investments in masts and base stations. What matters for the prices charged is competition (rival behaviour of suppliers) and demand conditions not sunk costs.

There is no reason to expect that an auction would result in a less competitive market than a beauty contest. As Klemperer (2002a) explains, a properly designed auction will generate a competitive market structure. It is not easy to produce a competitive market structure with a beauty contest like the Swedish one with infrastructure investment as selection criterion. A comparison of the outcomes of the Danish auction and the Swedish beauty contest can serve as an illustration. In both cases, four licenses were awarded and in both cases, there was entry. The outcome of the allocation was, in other words, rather similar in terms of competitive market structure. (This can change as Orange plans to give back its Swedish but keep its Danish license)[7].

In conclusion, it is ex post competition, operating costs and capacity constraints that determine charges. There is no reason to expect that these factors will lead to lower prices if airwave rights are allocated through a beauty contest. The only beneficiaries of a beauty contest are the companies that acquire a scarce resource, access to radio wave space, almost for free.

---

[6] It is very difficult to test which of these two incentives for exaggerated bids has been operating. A distinction has to be made if the optimistic bid is due to self-disbelieved promises (opportunism) or simply self-believed but overoptimistic promises (winner's curse).

[7] Beside the number of firms, size distribution and cost differences are other factors that can have an impact on market behaviour and performance. But there is no obvious reason why these factors would be different in an auction than in a beauty contest.

13.7.3 Implications for Public Financing

The sale of spectrum rights through auctions has raised staggering amounts of money to the government treasury. The British auction raised over EUR 33 billion (USD 35 billion), the German auction over EUR 43 billion (USD 46 billion) while the Danish auction half a billion of euros[8]. Over EUR 95 billion (USD 100 billion) have been funnelled into European government coffers totally. Considering the heavy governments debts of most of the European countries, these auctions have been an important source of finance.

An attractive feature of this sort of public financing is that the money paid for spectrum rights has the character of a lump sum tax. As has been demonstrated, the amount paid for the rights is not likely to have any implications for investment and pricing decisions. Though hard to find, lump sum tax opportunities are very attractive from an efficiency point of view. If the same amount was raised in another way, it could be difficult to avoid distorting effects. To this can be added that the need to reduce government debt in most European countries and Sweden is no exception. Since Sweden has the highest taxes (expressed as a portion of GNP) of all OECD countries, alternative sources of financing should be welcome.

While the rights have been allocated in principle with almost no charge there is in the Swedish case a royalty fee amounting to 0.15 percent of revenue to be paid as soon as the companies have started to operate their nets. This is of course a very small proportion of revenues, but nevertheless its effects on allocation are like a sales tax on separate items. Like a sales tax, there will be an incidence effect and a deadweight loss (allocation distortion). Part of the royalty fee can be expected to result in price increases and the quantity, demanded and supplied, might be marginally affected.

To sum up, it is hard to find any advantages of a beauty contest compared to an auction in terms of investment, efficiency, and consumer prices. In addition, one should consider the effects on wealth distribution of giving away rights, and the contribution to public funding that an auction has. On balance, it seems that an auction has more of a beauty character than a beauty contest like the Swedish one.

13.8 Summary and Concluding Remarks

The term 'beauty contest' has acquired a new meaning recently. It is used to refer to an administrative way of allocating rights to scarce resources. The right to spectrum for the new third generation (3G) telecommunication technology is such a scarce resource. Beauty contests and auctions are the alternative means to allocate this right. The paper has looked at the pros and cons of using a beauty contest instead of an auction in the allocation of 3G spectrum rights.

---

[8] To be noted that the Danish auction was late. The IT boom was over and quotations on the stock exchanges for telecom firms were much lower than before.

In contrast to auction, there is no established theory for a beauty contest. In this chapter, the theory of competition for the field has been introduced as a candidate for a theory for beauty contests. The theory of competition for the field has a contractual character with Demsetz and Williamson as seminal contributors to its development. A contractual approach does not find that a beauty stands a better chance to win in a beauty contest like the Swedish one than in an auction.

There is no reason to believe that the Swedish beauty contest will result in an infrastructure of masts and base stations that, from welfare point of view, is superior to what an auction would generate. There is a risk of selecting companies with the most opportunistic promises about future investments as winners. It is also hard to see why the administrators in a beauty contest would be better positioned to select efficient firms as license holder than the price mechanism in an auction. A beauty contest cannot be expected to result in lower consumer prices for telecommunication services. The price paid for a license in an auction is like a lump sum tax. The alternative ways to raise the same sum to cover public expenditures are likely to have an adverse impact on efficiency.

Acknowledgements. A grant from Jenz och Carl-Olof Hamrins stiftelse is gratefully acknowledged. Comments by lecturer Leon Barkho are gratefully acknowledged

References

Binmore K, Klemperer PD (2002) The biggest auction ever: the sale of the British 3G telecom licenses. Economic Journal 112: 74-96. Available at
http://www.paulklemperer.org
Brealey RA, Myers SC (1991) Principles of corporate finance, 4th edn, McGraw-Hill, New York
Bulow JI, Klemperer PD (2002) Prices and the winner's curse. Rand Journal of Economics 33: 1-21. Available at http://www.paulklemperer.org
Carlbom, T (2000) Telecom – unrealistic, gigantic and wishful calculations (in Swedish). Business of the Week 8: 36-43
Chadwick E (1859) Results of different principles of regulation in Europe. Journal of Royal Statistical Society Series A 22: 381–420
Coase RH (1959) The Federal Communications Commission. Journal of Law and Economics 2: 1–40
Cooter R, Ulen T (2000) Law and economics, 3rd edn, Addison-Wesley, New York
The Committee of Finance (2000) The report of the Committee of Finance 1999/2000: FiU 27. Addition to the 2000 Budget (Law 1999/2000: 100). Diverse Opinions (in Swedish). The Committee of Finance, Stockholm. Available at
http://www.riksdagen.se/debattt/9900/fiu/fiu27/fiu27044.asp
Demsetz H (1968) Why regulate utilities? Journal of Law and Economics 11: 55–65
Hi3G (2001) Orange signs a contract in the form of a letter of intent to cooperate with Hi3G and Europolitan Vodafone in building the UMTS-infrastructure (in Swedish). Hi3G May 16. Available at http://www.hi3gaccess.se/items.asp?id=66

Jensen MC, Meckling W (1976) Agency costs and the theory of the firm. Journal of Financial Economics 3: 305–60

Jonasson E (2001) Service providers on the mobile telephone market – an analysis of the changes of the telecommunication act in 2000 (in Swedish). PhD Thesis, Jönköping International Business School

Klemperer PD (1999) Auction theory: A guide to the literature. Journal of Economic Surveys 13: 227-286

Klemperer PD (2002a) What really matters in auction design. Journal of Economic Perspectives 16: 169–189

Klemperer PD (2002b) How (not) to run auctions: the European 3G telecom auctions. European Economic Review 46: 829- 845

McAfee PR, McMillan J (1987) Auctions and bidding. Journal of Economic Literature 25: 699–738

National Post and Telecom Agency (PTS) (2000a) Rapid and large investments in infrastructure are important for the mobile phone network of the future (in Swedish). PTS press release February 9. Available at
http://www.pts.se/dokument/getFile.asp?FileID=150

National Post and Telecom Agency (PTS) (2000b) Invitation for applications for license to provide network capacity for mobile telecommunications services in Sweden in accordance with UMTS/IMT-2000 Standards and GSM Standards. Guidance for applicants, May 12. Available at http://www.pts.se/Nyheter/pressmeddelande.asp?ItemID=733

National Post and Telecom Agency (PTS) (2001) Fact Sheet- Information on UMTS (in Swedish). PTS, August 13. Available at http://www.pts.se

National Post and Telecom Agency (PTS) (2002) No change of Orange's 3G bid conditions (in Swedish). PTS, September 30. Available at
http://www.pts.se/Nyheter/prinptressmeddelande.asp?ItemId=610

National Post and Telecom Agency (PTS) (2004) So many have 3G coverage in the municipalities (in Swedish). PTS, March 17. Available at
http://www.pts.se/Nyheter/printpressmeddelande.asp?ItemId=3094

3G Newsroom (2001) Country Information- Sweden. 3G Newsroom, 2 December. Available at http://3gnewsroom.com/country/sweden.shtml

Orange (2002) Orange SA announces plans to withdraw from Sweden (in Swedish). Orange press release 20 December

Telia (2001) Telia and Tele2 have made an agreement to cooperate in developing UMTS (in Swedish). Telia press release 15 March. Available at http://www.telia.se

Williamson OE (1975) Markets and hierarchies: analysis and antitrust implications. The Free Press, New York

Williamson OE (1976) Franchise bidding for natural monopolies – In general and with respect to CATV. Bell Journal of Economics 7: 73–104

Williamson OE (1985) The economic institutions of capitalism. The Free Press, New York

Williamson OE (1996) The mechanisms of governance. Oxford University Press, New York

14 The Digital Divide: A Review of Socioeconomic and Spatial Distributional Issues in ICTs

Robert J. Stimson

Center for Research into Sustainable Urban and Regional Futures, University of Queensland

14.1 Introduction

We live in a rapidly changing, uncertain and increasingly competitive world in which the processes of economic, social and technological change are forging dramatic and sometimes unexpected impacts on the fortunes of both people and places. Innovations in information and communications technologies (ICTs) are creating differential opportunities and outcomes for people, firms, and places at different levels of spatial scale. The degree to which those outcomes are concentrating or dispersing activity and benefits derived from innovation in ICTs—what is popularly referred to as the 'digital divide'—is an issue of importance for policy in regional development.

Graham (2002, p.35) proposes four questions relevant for regional analysts to address to understand the "interaction of ICTs and human settlements":

1. How do digitally-mediated economic flows articulate with city [regional] economies and urban systems in different places and sectors within developed, developing, newly industrializing and post-communist economies?
2. What are the relationships between the application of ICTs and broader processes of social and geographical polarization that have recently been observed within and between cities and regions?
3. How can urban and regional analysis and policymaking grapple meaningfully with invisible and intangible domains of electronic flow and real-time international exchanges at multiple geographic scales?
4. How can the policy worlds of cities and regions be brought together with those of cyberspace and ICTs to foster creative policy initiatives that harness the power of new technologies for positive urban and regional social and economic development?

These represent a comprehensive research agenda, which Graham makes an admirable attempt to consider in his recent review paper in *Urban Studies*, which, along with the other literature reviewed and referenced in this chapter, has been a useful guide in structuring the discussion here[1].

This chapter begins by referring to the implications of the shift from the Fordist (or industrial) to the post-Fordist (or post-industrial) era. The implications of ICTs for regional development, particularly from the perspective of endogenous growth, are then considered. The chapter proceeds to look at the extent to which ICTs are enhancing the concentration or dispersal of activity in the context of urban systems, paying particular attention to equity issues resulting from the differential impacts of ICTs for both people and places. Consideration is given to public policy issues and regulatory frameworks for ICTs in the contexts of equitable access and regional development. Finally, some tentative conclusions are proposed about the role of ICTs with respect to convergence and divergence in regional development.

14.2 The Changing Context for Regional Development

Atkinson (1999) argues that national and regional economic systems increasingly are of two forms:

1. One is the 'old economy' which is an artefact of the old industrial or Fordist era, with its vertical and hierarchical forms of organization; while
2. The other is the 'new economy' typified by more horizontal form and flexible production and an increasing reliance on knowledge and technology.

In regional economic development analysis, a limitation of neoclassical economic theory is that technology and human resources are treated as given and homogenous. That assumption coincides with the Fordist mode of production, where products and processes were largely standardized, and where semi-skilled labour dominated. The Keynesian focus on impacts of fiscal and monetary policy on trade balances and exchange rates also relates to the Fordist regime of accumulation. However the decline of the Fordist mode of production has changed the nature of international and regional competition. In post-Fordist regimes the focus on continuous improvement of products and processes through effective organizational learning and knowledge creation gave rise to the notions of competitive advantage (Porter 1990) and innovative regional milieu (Saxenian 1994). The concepts of 'earning capacity' and 'knowledge creation' (Nonaka and Takeuchi 1995; Senge 1992) are also being used to integrate those factors influencing the competitive advantage of firms, industries, regions and nations, with the learning organization (both firms and institutions) promoting the capacity of regions to be innovative and flexible utilizing knowledge networks and value chains (as proposed by Porter in his diamond model).

Productivity gains are an important component in both national and regional economic growth and development, as well as for the competitive performance of

---

[1] See also Chaps. 2, 10, and 12.

firms. But a crucial issue is the degree to which productivity gains may be attributable to 'capital deepening', and in turn the way the process of capital deepening may be attributable to spending on ICTs or on other capital items. The element of productivity growth attributable to investment in ICTs has been rising rapidly and steadily since the mid 1970s, whereas that attributable to increased investment spending other than on ICTs often has been in a general decline. Access Economics (2001) refers to evidence from Australia that suggests most of the ICT related lift in productivity growth in that country has been from spending on computer hardware, although spending on software has also increased. This is consistent with comments by Alan Greenspan, US Federal Reserve Chairman, that "there are grounds to believe that new technologies will be helping out the world for sometime to come" (as quoted in Access Economics 2001, p. 22). Indeed, it is feasible to argue that globalization would not have become the pervasive force it is without the innovations and diffusions that have occurred in ICTs.

The growing interest in regional development theory in learning organizations focuses attention on the creation, acquisition, and transfer of knowledge. Activities are highly reliant on innovation, technology, and network interactions. In the context of regional economic development (as discussed by authors such as Malecki 1990), this is seen in the contemporary focus on the importance of geographical clusters of industries, and increasingly there is recognition of the role of trust and reciprocity as proposed in theories on social capital. Hansen (1992) suggests that the geographic concentration of an industry acts to attract talented people and other factors, with proximity increasing the concentration of information and the speed of information flows. He draws the conclusion that, as a result, the learning capability of firms increases and is geographically based, thus enlarging interregional differences in competitiveness. That learning capability is derived largely from a region's learning infrastructure, which includes factors such as the education system, R&D capacity, technology transfer and promotion, R&D, business consortia, and ITC infrastructure.

The view that technology-focused economic activities are catalytic and generative is central to the proposition by Smilor and Wakelin (1990) that regional economic development increasingly is driven by a nested hierarchical system of factors called 'smart infrastructure'. They propose a model with four central elements—talent, technology, capital and know-how. This may be seen as incorporating the notions of 'innovative milieu', which has been documented as being so important in the development of technology regions such as Silicon Valley in the Bay Area of California (Saxenian 1994). It is a widely held view that the majority of new jobs are created in small and medium size businesses and start-up ventures (Stough 2002, p. 5). Armington and Acs (2002) show how the highest rates of entrepreneurship are occurring in the more technically intensive industry sectors, suggesting that this may be a good reason for the emergence of a greater focus on venture formation policies. Stough (2002) also draws attention to two key factors that influence the successful development and implementation of entrepreneurship and firm formation development policy, namely:

1. Strategic regional economic development leadership; and

2. Better information and knowledge for planning and decision-making.

Stough (2001) refers to a model testing the notion that once exogenous factors are accounted for, leadership effort and resource endowments are important determinants of regional economic performance. In an application of the model to 35 metropolitan regions in the US, both static and a dynamic multiple regression analysis and path analysis was used to reveal how the variable leadership makes a statistically significant contribution to the explanation of economic performance, amplifying the resources effect.

Thus, building on earlier work of theorists such as Romer (1986, 1990), what we see in the recent evolution of regional economic development theory and in some of the empirical analyses is a renewed focusing on endogenous based processes and factors. This is documented in the recent volume by Johansson et al. (2001).

It is not surprising that this is occurring at a time when there has been on explosion in the rate of innovation associated with new technologies. This is demonstrated, for example, by Quinlan (2004) who notes the exponential increase in the number of patent applications from 7,095 in 1985 to 19,159 in 1990, 38,906 in 1995, and 103, 947 in 2001.

Graham (2002, p.38) points to two dominant trends that define contemporary patterns of regional development. These are:

1. The most momentous process of urbanization in human history; and
2. An extraordinarily rapid (but highly uneven) application of digital information and communications technologies (ICTs).

Graham (2002, p.33) says, "close inspection reveals that these two trends are actually closely interrelated". Three reasons are put forward as to why this is so:

1. ICTs enable specialist urban centres to extend their powers, markets and controls over more and more distant regional, national and international hinterlands (Wheeler et al. 2000);
2. The complexity and riskiness of information in a volatile global economy demands concentration in those urban centres with the ICT assets and an 'innovative milieu' to sustain their on-going competitiveness (Castells 1999a); and
3. Demand for ICTs overwhelmingly is driven by the growth metropolitan markets, with large global cities being disproportionately important as drivers of ICT investment and innovation (Graham and Marvin 1996).

Thus, we are seeing a resurgence of interest in the nature of locational growth in the spatial economy, an issue that is considered further later in this chapter.

But the above discussion needs to be placed in a broader perspective of global processes of change. Cutler (2002a) provides a neat summary of the structures and processes that are shaping contemporary economies. He sees the following eight factors as constituting the complex worldwide web of forces as shaping the 21st century landscape:

1. *Globalization* with the intensity and detail embedded in interdependency between new trades in skills and knowledge, services and people, and the emergence of global electronic commerce;
2. *The collapse of the second world*, representing a huge shift towards integration and internationalisation of the global economy to the extent not seen before;
3. *Digital technology* and the emerging digital economy, where ICTs continue to develop and its impact will be more pervasive;
4. *Industrial restructuring*, with transactions fundamentally affected by communications networking and information processing power at the heart of the digital revolution changing the nature of the firm;
5. *Labour market restructuring*, with the growing divergence between location specific employment and globally mobile and footloose knowledge workers;
6. *21st century corporate governance*, with the cultural shift associated with the democratisation of stock markets, the new primacy of intellectual capital, and the emergence of stock options and employee participation in firm ownership, changing the fundamentals about careers, employment and the nature of labour in organized economic activity;
7. *Internationalisation of business regulation*, with the proliferation of international inter-government and supra-government global organizations defining key parameters to business functions, leading to increasingly complex poorsharing arrangements and questioning the levers of influence national governments can exercise; and
8. *New value motivators* making it difficult to quantify and calibrate new drivers as we move increasingly from tangible to intangible assets and grapple to understand the inter-connections and links that make the difference in understanding the context of innovation.

14.3 Information and Communication Technologies, Spatial Concentration and Dispersal

Townsend (2001) has reminded us how almost forty years ago Webber (1964) advocated that telecommunications would bring to non-metropolitan regional locales the services available in the big metropolitan cities, and how later Toffler (1980) predicted a future where advanced electronic goods and services would result in a decentralization of population and of production. It was even suggested that cities would decline in importance or even become redundant as artefacts of the industrial age. Negroponte (1995) went as far as suggesting that 'digital living' would include less and less dependence upon being in a specific place at a specific time, and the transmission of 'place' itself would start to become possible.

Cyberspace has thus been cast as transcending social and geographic barriers, as heralding the 'death of distance' (Cairncross 1997), and representing the 'end of geography'. But as Graham (1998, p.35) points out, the reality is "both very different and a good deal more worrying, for there is now a great deal of evidence that the dominant trends surrounding the application of ICTs are serving to under-pin and support processes and practices of intensifying urban polarization".

This finding should not be surprising, as the regional science literature abounds with both theory and empirical observations of agglomeration of economic activi-ties at a variety of levels of spatial scale and about the relationship between the in-cidence of innovation and the degree of industry diversification or specialization across national urban systems. However, Townsend (2001, p.39) does demonstrate how the rapid diffusion of ICTs challenges the "traditional dichotomy of centrali-zation or decentralization, pointing to the existence of a complex new network of networked cities". Aspects of these issues are discussed in the following sections.

14.3.1 The Power of Urban Scale Agglomeration

In his seminal book on *World Cities*, Hall (1966) began by stating how there are certain great cities in which a quite disproportionate part of the world's most im-portant business is conducted. In fact it was 1915 when the pioneer thinker and writer on city and regional planning, Patrick Geddes christened such places 'world cities'. Since then a large research agenda has been developed investigating the 'world city' phenomenon. This includes contributions by Friedman (1986), Sassen (1991, 1994), Knox and Taylor (1995), Leyshon and Thrift (1997), and more re-cently the Internet publication *GaWC Research Bulletin*, established by The Glob-alization and World Cities Study Group and Network (GaWC 2001). Contempo-rary work on 'world cities' is placing more emphasis on the one hand on analysis of their participation within actor networks investigating aspects of connectivity and interdependency, and on the other hand on the rise of globalization. It is ad-dressing issues such as those raised by Castells (1996, 2001) in his work on 'space of flows' ideas, and by Smith (2001) in his "agency-oriented theory of urbanism".

However, Townsend (2001, p.41) argues that the "global city concept is far too rigid to account for the potentially dramatic shifts in economic and cultural geog-raphies made possible by telecommunications systems". In the US there are at least a dozen large metropolitan areas that outpace the traditional global cities in the adoption of Internet technology. Townsend (2001, p.41) also argues that "technological innovation is no longer the hallmark of global cities", pointing out how the Internet has "emerged in a far different geography of innovation" com-pared with many earlier innovations in ICTs. Townsend notes how the US land-scape is "characterized by a dispersed system of university-based research net-works and 'technopoles', such as Silicon Valley and the Boston 128 corridor in Massachusetts" (2001, p. 42), as demonstrated in earlier research by Saxenian (1994).

Townsend (2001) has proposed a new framework for analysing the centralizing and decentralizing impacts of ICTs. He refers to the emergence of a new network of networked metropolitan cities is emerging, "capitalizing upon the continued importance of face-to-face contact in business and social life, yet increasingly us-ing telecommunications systems to overcome traditional geographic barriers" (2001, p.42).

But empirical analyses do reveal the continuing strength of big cities as concentrations of ICTs activities and of the businesses that make intensive use of those technologies. For example, Taylor et al. (2002, p.4) show how "advanced producer services have become more concentrated in leading world cities". And Stough (2000) demonstrates how the geographic concentration of technology employment among U.S. metropolitan areas illustrates not only the scale and scope of technology driven transformation experienced by regional economies over the last decade or so, but also the strength of its spatial concentrations. Stough tells how technology intensive sectors accounted for 10.1 percent of the labour force in 1988, with employment in those sectors increasing by over 3.6 million by 1998. However, this in fact represented an actual decrease of 0.5 percent points to 9.6 percent of the labour force in 1998, due in part to some change in the classification system, but more likely due to a net substitution of technology and capital for labour resulting in increased productivity. Over the decade 1988–1998 there was only a minute decrease (from 90.3 percent to 89.2 percent) in technology intensive employment concentrated in metropolitan areas, with the non-metropolitan areas gaining only a one percent increase. By 1998, just 50 of the 321 U.S. metropolitan areas accounted for almost 70 percent of all technology employment in the US. The largest technology concentrations of employment at over 200,000 jobs were (from east to west coast) in Boston, New York, Philadelphia, Washington DC, Chicago, Los Angeles, and San Jose (Silicon Valley). Stough (2000, p. 7) points out that, in aggregate, there is a "modest relative decentralization of technology employment away from large metro areas and from metro areas to non-metro areas, most probably to non-metro areas adjacent to metro areas", but he concludes, "metropolitan size appears to be a more important factor than geographic location".

Studies investigating the provision of ICT specific services mainly tend to focus on the spatial distribution of the physical properties of services such as the Internet (Gorman 1998) and its providers (Greenstein 1998), as well as on the proliferation of 'dot.coms' (Zook 2000). Early work by Gillespie and Williams (1988, p. 1317) suggested the Internet would allow for "time-space convergence ... at a fairly profound scale"; and more recently Cairncross (1997) has argued that space will be rendered virtually useless through instantaneous communication and frictionless markets. There is evidence of such time-space convergence, as seen in Internet banking where some firms can provide from one location a 24 hour call centre with no physical outlets for clients. However, Wheeler and O'Kelly (1999) and Gorman and Malecki (2000) demonstrate how relative location does play a more than even pivotal role in access to ICTs. Research in the U.S. shows how the most accessible cities on the Internet are located at major network access points, which favours concentration of ICT activity in places like New York and San Francisco.

Zook (2000) expands on work by Moss and Townsend (1997a, 1997b, 1998) to show how global cities (like New York and Los Angeles) have the largest agglomerations of businesses using the Internet. But in the U.S. it is the university towns and corporate research and development clusters found widely across smaller size cities that have the highest density of domain registrations. Townsend

(2001, p.43) claims such findings "suggest that, although Internet use has diffused most widely in the locales where it was first adopted, commercial applications have moved the largest clusters of activity to major business centres". Moss and Townsend (1998) show that over the period 1994–1997 in the US it is the major urban areas that drove the overall growth of Internet activity. Townsend's (2001) analysis of regions ranked by density of Internet activity, rather than by magnitude, puts San Francisco/San Jose at the top, but many medium size metropolitan cities rank highly, including Seattle, San Diego, Miami, Denver, Phoenix, Minneapolis, Portland and Atlanta. And the larger metropolitan areas of Washington DC, Los Angeles, Boston, Dallas and Houston all rank in the top 20. However, Los Angeles is the only global city in the top 20 on this density of Internet activity measure.

Moss and Townsend (1998) identify just seven metropolitan areas in the US that serve as regional hubs for the interurban Internet backbone networks. And Gorman (1998) shows how the coastal cities of the US are more tightly linked to each other than is the case for interior cities. Townsend (2001) claims that it is the medium-sized metropolitan areas that dominate as centres for large and dense clusters of Internet activity. But the smaller metropolitan areas (many being remote or isolated), which could benefit greatly from the use of Internet technologies to overcome geographic limitations to economic growth, which are experiencing low levels of Internet activity. He goes on to say how "this pattern coincides with the geographic distribution development of backbone networks ... which largely bypassed the smaller metropolitan areas" (p. 51). Townsend provides a series of maps to illustrate the uneven pattern of domain density by both metropolitan area and by postal code across the US.

A problem for those regions that cannot achieve what Townsend (2001, p.56) refers to as "the critical mass necessary for development to 'take-off' " is that the networked cities are pulling away from both the smaller cities and the interior regions in the US. This is also evident in the UK.

Pelletiere and Rodrigo (2001) have used spatial modelling to develop two indices to measure Internet use and on-line information production in the US. They use a simple linear model with independent variables—including income per capita, education levels, and the level of urbanization in states—to explain Internet use and dot.com concentration across the 48 contiguous states. The concentration of dot.com domains in a state is shown to be highly dependent on urbanization and to a lesser degree on the proportion of the population with a college education. But the only significant predictor of Internet use is the proportion of the population with a college education. However, when those two Internet variables are made the dependent variable, urbanization becomes the most important predictor of both variables, being a positive predictor of growth in dot.com concentrations but a negative predictor of growth in Internet use. Pelletiere and Rodrigo (2001) tentatively conclude that while Internet use continues to disperse across states, when one moves away from urbanized areas Internet business location definitely does not disperse. Pelletiere and Rodrigo (2001) conclude that the preliminary evidence suggests the extension and expansion of the Internet will not necessarily lead to the dispersion of the production of Internet information goods and services. They also say their findings suggest that education is an important explanatory factor in the distribution of Internet use at home. The authors claim that their analyses indicate support for the hypothesis that lowering information costs will not diminish and may actually cement the advantages of location and spatial proximity.

Despite the weight of evidence referred to above, nonetheless broadband technology is being touted by some commentators as providing further potential to enable activities to be more locationally footloose and to create job opportunities in localities which have been suffering population and economic decline. For example, Wilkinson, a CSIRO IT scientist in Australia, recently is reported (in Lynch 2002, p.7) as claiming the use of broadband telecom pathways means "an opportunity exists for Australia to site new technology export industries in rural areas, thus creating the needed jobs" because "the new technology is location-neutral". But such hopes depend on the location decisions of the appropriately skilled workers, and the overwhelming evidence in Australia to date is that the new knowledge-based information-intensive jobs are highly concentrated in selective locations in the big cities, and especially in Sydney (O'Connor et al. 2001). Improving broadband pathways to non-metropolitan Australia may provide the technological facilitation for what Wilkinson refers to as 'expert business services' to diffuse across the towns of rural and regional Australia; but this alone may not be a sufficient catalyst to change the firm location and residential location preferences of businesses and information economy workers, particularly for the development of business services clusters incorporating finance, education, building and design industries.

Thus, there seems to be a consensus that the Internet favours large cities, and especially those where high-tech information technology R&D and industries are concentrated.

However, at an international scale, when considering the production of ICT goods, there is evidence of considerable dispersal associated with the international division of labour and the globalization of production sources. For example, research by Ernst (1997) demonstrates how the semiconductor industry in Southeast Asia displays a pattern of widely dispersed activity across many regions that are networked in complex chains. Townsend (2001, p.43) says this demonstrates how, "rather than a handful of regions dominating global finance and culture, a concentration of highly specialized regions now interact in a globally telemediated economy".

14.3.2 Localized Spatial Growth and Clustering

The centralizing effect of ICTs is enhanced if we look more specifically at recent developments in the theory of localized industrial growth and clustering. Firms and industrial activity generally tend to concentrate in urban locations, with different mixes of activities tending to cluster together in different places (Gordon and McCann 2000, p. 513).

Krugman (1991a) has observed the coincidence between spatial industrial clustering and regional specialization as being fundamental to the wide adoption of the principle of increasing returns to scale in urban and regional economic analysis as firms and labour congregate to take account of increased factor rewards. Krugman (1993) and Fujita and Mori (1997) have further developed such arguments, demonstrating how increased factor rewards are evident over limited spatial domains at locations where clustering/agglomeration occurs. As Gordon and McCann (2000, p.513) say, "the resulting balance between localized increasing returns to scale and transaction costs can provide an explanation of the development of the types of hierarchical spatial industrial patterns typically observed".

The contemporary interest in localized spatial growth and on spatial clustering comes from a variety of disciplines, as outlined by Gordon and McCann (2000) in their review article in *Urban Studies*. They refer to these four disciplinary approaches:

1. From *neoclassical economics*, modern trade theory that has shown explicit interest in geographical issues (Helpman and Krugman 1985). But as well, there have been investigations into spatial allocation problems (Krugman 1991b), and a focus on increasing returns to scale and market structure in determining patterns of spatial investment (Romer 1986, 1987; Arthur 1994).
2. From *business and management*, location is seen as part of the broader question of optimal relationships between the firm and its customers and suppliers (Piore and Sabel 1984; Porter 1990), the nature of the firm and of transaction costs over space (Williamson and Winter 1993; Pitelis 1993), and the communication possibilities—especially for the services sector—through new information technologies.
3. From *geography and planning* comes an interest in the 'new industrial districts' from observation of the spatial organization of production in key industries (Scott 1988, 1993; Saxenian 1994), and as well a renewed interest in spatial clustering and its implications for a public-private role in local economic development (Castells and Hall 1994).
4. From *sociology and geography* comes the notion of innovative milieu (Aydalot and Keeble 1988; Camagni 1995), which relates issues of spatial clustering to the process of innovation.

Gordon and McCann (2000) suggest there are three basic forms of clustering. Two have developed from the neo-classical traditions of economics: the *classic model of pure agglomeration* and the *industrial complex model*. The third form of clustering is the *network model*, developed outside mainstream economics, which incorporates sociological perspectives.

The *pure form of agglomeration*—as it relates to the importance of businesses being able to exploit internal economies of scale as well as being able to avail external economies, and in which space is fundamental to the business the advantages of co-location increasing the probability of business linkages and employment matches—fundamentally underlies modern urban theory, as proposed by Fujita (1989). As Townsend (2001, p.42) expresses it, advance in ICTs actually "increases the need for institutions, people, and districts that can extract meaningful knowledge from the rapidly increasing glut of undifferentiated information". Thus, close proximity provides an effective way of interpreting information, enhancing agglomeration effects. While the notion of the 'electronic cottage' might "obviate the need to travel to a central area for shopping, work and entertainment" (Townsend 2001, p. 42), nonetheless as Glaeser and Gaspar (1996) show, there is ample evidence of a strong complementary relationship between business travel and spending on ICTs.

The *industrial complex model* proposes that sets of identifiable and stable relations among firms are, in fact, manifest in their spatial behaviour—principally through trading links—with firms co-locating to minimize spatial transaction costs. As Gordon and McCann (2000) point out, the industrial complex might be regarded as in effect being a 'closed hub', with firms having made substantial capital investments to set up the appropriate trading links.

The *social-network model* argues that there is more order to inter-firm interactions and less order to intra-firm interactions than the economic models imply (Granovetter 1985). This is so because strong inter-personal relationships transect firm boundaries dependent on trust and informality. Social networks are seen as a form of "durable social capital, created (and maintained) through a combination of social history and ongoing collective action" (Gordon and McCann 2000, p. 520). According to Amin and Thrift (1992), network development is favoured within agglomerations offering a wide range of patterns as well as providing actors with superior access to communication and potential links with other nodes within national and international networks. Gordon and McCann (2000) suggest that much of the recent interest in 'embeddedness' and in 'social capital' as a productive asset arises from the fact that the "social network model has been viewed as largely applicable to particular observations of spatial industrial clustering" (p. 521).

This is seen, for example, in the Emilia-Romagna region of Italy (Scott 1988) and in Santa Clara County in California (Saxenian 1994). The focus on social capital is evident in much of the contemporary work on endogenous regional development when associated with a place-specific industrial cluster.

14.3.3 Specialization, Diversity, and Innovation in Urban Systems

A key issue in regional development is the degree to which there are advantages and disadvantages in specialization and diversity in local economies, and in particular in urban economies. Duranton and Puga (2000) provide a review of the literature on this issue (on which the following discussion is based). They identify the following five 'stylised facts' concerning specialization and diversity:

1. Specialized and diversified cities co-exist;
2. Larger cities tend to be more diversified and cities of similar specialization are of similar size;
3. Regarding the distribution of relative city size, individual city-size rankings and individual city specialization are stable over time;
4. Individual city growth is related to specialization and diversity, and to relative location; and

5. There is a high rate of plant turnover, most innovations taking place in particularly diversified cities and most new plants being created there, with most relocations being from diversified to specialized cities.

An important consideration with respect to the above is the degree to which innovation—in particular in ICTs and their applications—is related to specialization and diversity.

Research shows how, in most countries, a co-existence seems to exist between cities that are largely specialized with those that are more diversified. For example, Black and Henderson (1998) have use a relative specialization index for two-digit manufacturing sectors in a study of selected US centres to show that the most specialized cities are those largely dependent on natural resources or very specific industries. Using a Hirshman-Herfindahl diversity index (corrected for differences in sectoral employment shares at the national level), they show how some of the most diverse cities are also not very specialized in any particular sector. One interpretation of the co-existence of diverse and specialized cities is that the patterns are random; but Ellison and Glaeser (1997) say this is unlikely, noting how the distribution of economic activity in the U.S. is too spatially orientated (at the four digit level) to be the result of random processes. Duranton and Puga (2000, p. 536) suggest that patterns of specialization and diversity in cities might "merely mirror the spatial distribution of resources" as seen, for example, in the tourism activity of cities in the French Alps or French Riviera. But Henderson (1997a) shows how specialization in cities is, in part, the outcome of localization economies, while diversity is related to urbanization economies.

There is a widely held belief that larger cities are more diversified, a supposition which is backed by substantial empirical evidence. But, as Duranton and Puga (2000) point out, there are exceptions. For example, Henderson (1997b) shows how large cities tend to be more specialized in the producer services and less so in manufacturing than are medium size cities, while medium size cities are more specialized in mature ('old economy') manufacturing industries and less so in 'new economy' industries. Henderson (1998) also shows that cities specialized in similar activities do tend to be of similar size; but he does remind us that the evidence is not particularly strong.

As a general observation, it seems that the distribution of the relative size of cities tends to remain stable over time, this being evident in the US (Black and Henderson 1998), Europe (Eaton and Eckstein 1997), and Australia (O'Connor et al. 2001). And there is a "strong persistence of the same activities in the same cities" (Duranton and Puga 2000, p. 537), although there are exceptions, such as the decline of textiles and still in some old industrial cities (as seen, for example, in Leiden and Haarlem in the Netherlands and Pittsburgh in the US). In many cases, such cities have gone through a successful economic restructuring process, which involves the use of new technologies, including ICTs. But Kim (1995) demonstrates a high correlation (+0.64) between regional localization for two digit industries in the U.S. between 1986 and 1987, and Dumais et al. (1997) demonstrate the existence of great stability over time at the three-digit level in patterns of agglomeration in the US. Furthermore, Henderson (1997b) provides evidence of stability over time in patterns of industry specialization over time for medium size cities in the US.

However, Duranton and Puga (2000, p.533) point out that over time "some cities prosper, whereas others decay", and this is despite the overall stability in the relative city size and individual city specializations over time in the US urban system. That finding raises the question: What contributes to the economic growth or decline of cities? Glaeser et al. (1992) have looked at employment in U.S. cities, finding that diversity and local competition engender urban employment growth, whereas specialization reduces growth—a finding that is probably explained by the relative decline in 'old economy' manufacturing employment which is concentrated in medium size cities.

The importance of urban diversity as an attractor of 'new economy' activities, and in particular of innovative industry sectors, is demonstrated by Henderson et al. (1995). However, they point out that a history of past specialization does seem to matter for the more mature industry sectors. An interesting finding by Harris-Dobkins and Ioannides (1998) is that larger cities in the US tend to grow at a slower pace, while growth favours development of adjacent cities but hinders the development of cities located at a medium distance of 80 to 500 km away. This suggests that a positive effect of external market potential disappears if lagged own-city size is not considered. Duranton and Puga (2000, p.538) suggest that an interpretation of that finding might be that "cities tend to grow more when their market potential is large relative to their size, and that growth slows down as city size catches up". But they go on to say the evidence about the effects of relative location on urban growth is "very patchy" (p. 538).

Studies in the US by Dunne et al. (1989), Davis and Haltiwanger (1992), and Dumais et al. (1997) on the changing patterns of industry—including firm creations and closures—show how about one half of the employees in manufacturing in 1992 were working in firms that did not exist twenty years earlier, and about three quarters of manufacturing plants that existed in 1972 had closed by 1992. The research found that the creation of new plants does seem to be occurring in locations with below average specialization in a corresponding industry sector. Duranton and Puga (2000) cite studies in France, which show how most new plant creations take place in cities with above average diversification. They conclude that the empirical evidence suggests that "not only is the creation of new plants biased towards larger and more diverse cities, but so is the location of innovative activities that lead to new products" (p. 539). That finding confirms the proposition put forward four decades earlier by Jacobs (1960) that locational diversity favours innovation. It supports the results of research in the U.S. by Feldman and Audretsch (1999) that found that 96 percent of innovations were made in metropolitan areas in 1982, which accounted for just 30 percent of the US population. Such findings lead to the proposition that industries sharing a common scientific base tend to cluster together, as shown in the work of Fujita and Ishii (1999).

Duranton and Puga (2000, p.533) note that some cities "specialize in churning new ideas and new products" that require a diversified base. However, other cities "specialize in more standardized production, [but] this in turn is better carried out in a more specialized environment" (p. 533). Urban systems seem to have an "innate tendency to create this type of imbalance" (p. 553).

This is reflected in the well-established finding that large places with diversified regional industrial portfolios tend to have lower levels of employment uncertainty and unemployment rates (as discussed by Conroy 1975, Kort 1981, Sherwood-Call 1990, and Hunt and Sheesley 1994).

14.3.4 Concentration of Innovators Within Specific Cities

Reich (1991) has invented the term 'symbolic analysts' to refer to the knowledge workers of the 'new economy'. Some of them are described by Cutler (2001a, p.26) as the "corporate and country nomads: globally mobile and corporately footloose, frequent fliers who know the importance of networking and building an impressive address in their Palm Pilots". Growth in their numbers and their relative importance is highly concentrated in the labour force of a relatively small number of large metropolitan city regions—often 'world cities'—and this has enhanced the economic performance and competitiveness of those places. These innovators and drivers of the information economy also tend to congregate in selective spaces within those large urban centres, giving rise to increased socio-economic polarization across those urban landscapes.

Work conducted for the Brookings Institute in the US (Florida and Gates 2001) demonstrates the direct link between three socio-cultural factors that are crucial issues to consider in understanding better the link between smart people and high technology success, for both countries and cities or regions within them. These are:

1. A large gay population, which is a leading indicator and predictor of high technology success;
2. Cultural richness and a high concentration of artisans and bohemians; and
3. Cities with high concentrations of foreign-born residents.

Florida (2002) refers to a 'creative class' of people who write software, songs and stories, create new architectural designs and discover new ways to combine chemical elements. They are the new productive force driving a group of cities in the US. Bishop and Lisheron (2002) describe them as being in the business of producing ideas, congregating in 'cities of ideas' that are the new centres of growth and commercial innovation.

Cutler (2001b, p.26) also points to "the significance of the arts in scientific and technological endeavour" telling how "digital arts and electronic media—media energized by truly interactive electricity—are reshaping our culture and our industries". He suggests, however, that the role of creativity in the innovation process is not well understood. Cutler (2001c, p.32) reminds us "innovation in all its contexts, revolves around the concepts of novelty, risk and uncertainty".

Cushing (2002) has compiled three lists of U.S. cities that are labeled as 'new economy cities', 'high innovation cities', and 'old economy cities'. He differentiates between them on the basis of their ratings on the Milken Institute's city technology output and growth measure (tech-pole) as well as on their production of patents per 100,000 inhabitants. Referring to San Francisco, one of those 'high innovation cities', Graham (2002, p.38) tells how some of its downtown neighbourhoods have developed a clustering of over 2,200 small and medium size firms providing over 56,000 jobs in a digital cluster embracing design, advertising, gaming, publishing, fashion, music, multi media, computing and communications. "Major urban social and political conflicts have emerged as 'dot. comers', with their extraordinary wealth, have—along with real estate speculators—colonized selected districts" (Graham 2002, p.36).

Thus, the concentration of innovators and creative people in particular locales within selected cities is creating new socio-economic landscapes of diversity and high enterprise that are dependent on utilizing ICTs.

14.4 Equity Issues and the Digital Divide

From the above discussion, it is clearly evident that many equity issues will arise from the production and the use of ICTs. The constraints on the acceptance of and the diffusion of technological innovation—which implies progress—need to be considered at a variety of levels of spatial scale. On the one hand the gap between the rich and the poor nations is increasing, while on the other hand within the developed nations distributional inequities are reflected through differential levels of income and purchasing power for people and in differential levels of economic development and performance for places. Those divides might be expected to widen. And we need to remember that a major inhibitor to the even spread and potential universal diffusion and acceptance of new technology is the differential abilities of some people and of some places to assimilate change.

There exist a wide range of issues relating to equity of access and use—for individuals and households, for business both large and small, for communities in cities and regions, and for nations—in the provision and diffusion of ICTs. For example, Castells (1996, 1998, 1999a,b) writes about the 'complex dialectic' between the 'space of flows' and the 'space of places' in his discussion of how the intersection of human settlements and ICTs is forging new landscapes of innovation, economic development, cultural interactions, political dynamics, and social inequalities within cities and city regions. Picon (1998) refers to 'cyborg cities', while Skeates (1997) talks of 'infinite cities' made up of transnational urban corridors. But as Graham (2002, p.34) states "societal diffusion of ICTs remains starkly uneven at all scales". He goes on to say clusters and enclaves of 'super-connected' people, firms and institutions with broadband connections giving them intense access to information services, often rest "check-by-jowl with large numbers of people with non-existent or rudimentary communications technologies and very poor access to electronic information" (p. 34).

Graham (2002, p.36) demonstrates how ICTs tend to:

1. "Extend the power of the powerful;

2. Underpin intensified unevenness through tying together international divisions of labour; and
3. Be culturally and economically biased, especially in terms of wider development of what we might term the emerging 'international information marketplace' ".

The discussion in Section 14.4.1 considers a number of the socio-economic and spatial equity issues associated with ICTs.

14.4.1 ICT Diffusion and Access at Different Levels of Scale and Across Different Socio-Economic Groups

When considering the dispersal and the diffusion of ICTs and the accessibility of both people and businesses to services—such as the Internet and broadband technology—it is important to address the issue of spatial scale, both for individuals, households and also for business.

At the global level, a UNDP (1999) report reminds us that between 60 percent and 70 percent of people in the world has never made a phone call, and that the Internet remains the preserve of a small global elite of between two percent and five percent of the world's population. Even as recently as 1998, in over 70 developing nations no Internet access existed at all (Everard 1999). The UNDP thus characterizes the Internet as a 'global ghetto', encompassing just two percent or 250 million, of the most privileged and powerful of the global population, 80 percent of whom live in OECD nations (although this 250 million was expected to rise to about 700 million by 2002). There exists also socio-economic selectivity in the use of the Internet. In the UK, 30 percent of Internet users come from income brackets exceeding EUR 55,500[2] p.a.; while in Latin American 90 percent of users come from higher income brackets. Globally, 30 percent of Internet users have at least one university degree, and this is 60 percent in China, 67 percent in Mexico and 70 percent in Ireland. Male users dominate in the U.S. at 62 percent, and they comprise 75 percent of users in Brazil, 84 percent in Russia, 93 percent in China, and 94 percent in the Middle East. The average age of Internet users is young at 30 years of age in the UK and China, and 36 years in the US. And Internet websites are dominated by English as the language used, at 80 percent globally.

Goslee (1998) cites data for 1997 in the US, which show that:

1. 24 percent of whites had on-line access in major cities while only seven percent of blacks did;
2. 50 percent of city residents earning over EUR 63,200 p.a. had Internet access, but it is only six percent of those earning under EUR 8,400; and
3. Only 50 percent of female-head households living at or below the poverty line and 43.5 percent of families dependent wholly on public assistance had access to a telephone (data from NTIA, 1999).

---

[2] Approximately USD 60,000. The exchange rate used for the amounts in dollars in this study is USD 1=EUR 0.8426, early January 1999.

Graham (2002) notes that even in the advanced industrial nations with their rapidly expanding Internet markets there are, nonetheless, large sections of the population who lack the education and/or resources to be 'online'. "This is so at precisely the time when being on-line is becoming ever more critical to access key resources, information, public services and employment opportunities" (p.37).

Thus, significant spatial disparities exist within cities in patterns of access to and use of ICTs. In the US, Goslee (1998, p.7) says it is the central city, especially where the 'ghettoization of non-connected groups' is particularly evident, giving rise to a "concentration of poverty and the deconcentration of opportunity'". Braczyk et al. (1999) demonstrate how, at the same time, certain urban spaces in 'global cities' have developed gentrifying 'cyber districts' as found in San Francisco's 'multi media gulch' and SOMA areas, as well as in special districts of New York and London. Graham (2002, p.38) describes these new economic enclaves as "driving the production of Internet services, websites and the whole digitisation of design, architecture, gaming, CD-Roms and music". The cities developing such enclaves tend to have great strengths in the arts, cultural industries, fashion, publishing and computing.

Schiller (1999, p.205) tells how potentially "digital capitalism is now free to physically transcend territorial boundaries and, more importantly, to take economic advantage of the sudden absence of geopolitical constraints on its development". He goes on also to say "not uncoincidentally, the corporate political economy is also diffusing more generally across the social field" (p. 205). ICTs are certainly offering unparalleled choice and flexibility for firms to exploit differences between people and places, adding new and elaborate dimensions to the international division of labour, enabling not only the 'unbundling' of elements within production chains to geographically dispersed locations, but also the development of 'one-stop-shop' for international corporate ICT systems (Sussman and Lent 1998). According to Graham and Marvin (2001, p.139), ICTs are being used to "tie together a seamless and instant integration of plants in global networks of specialized and very different urban places across the globe". All of this presents a challenge for urban development agencies in their attempts to 'package' spaces and zones with subsidies, labour, infrastructure, services, and security in attempts to attract investment that is instantaneously mobile geographically. As Graham (2002, p.139) puts it, a challenge is how to "configure their spaces with the right local-global (or 'glocal') infrastructure connections".

In liberalized telecommunications environments such as those existent in the big city regions of advanced nations, spatial unevenness in the provision of and access to ICTs is clearly evident. Graham (2002, p.40) discusses how ICT providers 'cherry-pick' spatial and sectoral markets to capture the most lucrative business and professional customers from across the urban landscape. Schiller (1999, p.54) cites AT&T in the US as an example to illustrate how the strategies of the ICT conglomerates are underpinning the "dualism in infrastructure provision across urban landscapes". He tells how AT&T derived 80 percent of its EUR 5.01 billion profits from just 20 percent of its customers. Where these 'power users' operate their businesses and where they live represent the 'hot spots' for the roll-out of ICT infrastructure in the internationally oriented 'global cities'. As Graham

(2002, p.46) says, "the centres of global cities like New York and London now have six or more separate optic-fibre grids, offering the most capable, reliable, competitive and cost-effective electronic connections on the planet". Finnie (1998) shows how these 'global city areas' with small high capacity networks generate and capture enormous global economic flows. He refers to the World Com/MCI fibre network in London, which by 1998 had secured 20 percent of the international telecommunications traffic in the UK with only 180 km of fibre. In contrast, internationally huge cities like Beijing, Sao Paulo and Mexico City still lack competitiveness in their global telecommunications links, their systems still being dominated by state-owned providers that are expensive and which offer limited bundling of services. Similarly, the Afro-American and blue collar neighbourhood of large US cities remain "prone to under-investment and deteriorating service quality as universal service regulations that applied to telephony fail to be translated to regulate broadband investment" (Graham 2002, p.41).

Castells (1996, 1998) shows how 'cyber spaces' are creating intensified social polarization within cities. This is occurring through the restructuring of real urban space by the elites and the corporations, through walls, ramparts, security fences, electronic fences, armed guards, and defensive urban design. This further segregates both production and living spaces into socio-economic enclaves.

We also see in many of the cities of the developing nations how high quality ICT infrastructures are "being packaged together into enclosures and industrial parks for internationally oriented firms and socio-economic elites" (Graham 2002, p.43). Examples include the following:

1. Bangkok's 'intelligent corridor' along the major outer arterial ring road;
2. The fortified enclaves around the Murumbi district in Sao Paulo (Caldeira 1996);
3. The export-oriented flagship manufacturing enclaves of Johore in Malaysia and the Riau islands of Batan and Bintan in Indonesia (Grundy-Warr et al. 1999);
4. The EUR 16.85 billion (USD 20 billion) 'multi-media super corridor' in Malaysia; and
5. The fragmented and polarized urban structure of high-tech growth in Bangalore in India (Madon 1998).

There exists as well a heavy cultural basis domination in the application of ICTs and the things that flow on from them (Everard 1999). This creates what Graham (2002) refers to as "electronic economic power" (p. 46). It raises questions about "geopolitical relationships, accountability, democracy, global citizenship, the ownership and control of digitised information and the means of cultural expression, and the relationship between global and local cultures that surround global urbanization" (Graham 2002, p.46). Anglo-Saxon content—especially from the US—dominates TV and Internet media. Ricardo Petrella (1993), a former EU Commissioner, was so pessimistic as to suggest that the concentration of then current ICT logistics and of wealth and power in key cities in the technological core of the global economy was risking the creation of a "new Hanseatic phase in the world economy" ridden by 'techno apartheid' (as cited in Graham 2002, p.47).

14.4.2 Local Geography Does Matter

It is well known that Internet activity unevenly distributed within metropolitan areas in the US. Townsend (2001, p.52) refers to social polarization which characterizes development in the past and which is reflected in the diffusion of Internet technologies. But Townsend does suggest that, in comparison, "in the medium-size metropolitan areas that have high domain density—the new network cities—variations are much smaller" (p. 53).

Grubesic and Murray (2002) point out how little empirical research has been conducted at the local (sub-metropolitan) level of scale in the analysis of patterns, provision, and access to ICTs. They present a case study of Franklin County, Ohio, within which the city Columbus is located. In an analyses of broadband xDSL network access, they contend that "local geography can have a major impact on infrastructure accessibility, connection speed and connection quality" (p. 119).

Using an integer-programming model, a maximal covering location problem, and a geographic information system, Grubesic and Murray (2002) evaluate broadband access in Columbus. Their results suggest "the presence of a more complex and multifaceted divide" (p. 219) than is documented in much of the literature or the digital divide, which tends to emphasize the importance of socio-economic status and demographic characteristics as factors determining the frequency and quality of Internet access and use (NTIA 1999; Hoffman and Novak 2000). Grubesic and Murray (2002) find that this is characterized by demographic characteristics and socio-economic status. But the 'digital divide' for broadband access is somewhat counterintuitive. "Instead of challenged inner-city populations lacking adequate infrastructure, many of the more affluent suburban locations in Franklin County are likely to be without xDSL coverage" (p. 219). They also find that the most significant aspect of physical limitations of the infrastructure is the proximity of a household to a central office/exchange, with service providers rarely generating high quality service at the 18,000 feet current geographic limits of xDSL transmission technology. Grubesic and Murray (2002) contend that 12,000 feet is a more realistic geographic estimate of high-quality, low interruption service. In their study region, it was the most rapidly growing affluent outer suburbs that were most likely to suffer the infrastructure challenges of the xDSL service. Some of the most distressed parts of Columbus do need network upgrades, but as per the findings of other studies, the residents lack financial resources to derive benefit from the service availability.

In their Columbus study, Grubesic and Murray (2002, p.219) suggest that the "geographic distribution of xDSL service is likely to be a function of profit seeking by firms", with the combination of DSLAM costs, co-location fees, and line leasing making xDSL set-up costly for competitive local exchange carriers. Thus, "although many central office locations are available for DSLAM installation, one might suggest that only those COs with a potential for immediate return on investment will be selected for hardware upgrades" (p. 219). That finding raises a significant policy issue for many metropolitan areas, posing the question: "how can equitable broadband access be achieved/provided for all groups, regardless of race, income or location?" The authors also say "the answers to this question are elusive" (p. 219), particularly given the prohibitive access costs to broadband for single family households which make equitable access to privatised Internet markets difficult to achieve.

14.4.3 A Dualization of Communications

In view of the discussion so far, it is not surprising the UK think-tank Demos (1997, p.6) talks of the "poverty of communications", which it argues is as important as traditional poverty, placing some people, groups and localities in a subordinate position *vis-à-vis* controlling information and adding value to it. As Graham (2002, p.37) says, "urban societies become separated into the 'on-line' and the 'off-line' in complex tapestries of inclusion and exclusion which work simultaneously at multiple geographical scale".

Evidence is emerging that could be turning the social capital thesis on its head. In the US, Cushing (2002) has expanded Putnam's (2000) study of 40 different regions to the 50 states and the 100 largest cities. Cushing comes up with the discovery that cities generally high on most traditional measures of social capital are lower in technology development, lower in income and population growth, and lower in the production of patents. Places strong in faith-based institutions are also weaker in the development of technology and patents. He finds that high technology cities are the exact opposite. What Florida (2002) calls the 'cities of idea'—which produce most of the patents in the US, a primary measure of innovation and economic vitality—are poor performers on some of Putnam's measures of social capital (such as strong ties to family, churches and civic organizations), but they are high performers with respect to diversity of networks and engagement in 'interest politics'. Cushing (2002) says the following of these 'cities of ideas': "there is something dynamic about the individualistic and polarized types of communities—cities of ideas are marked by many weak connections, momentary alliances, limited commitment, shifting applications ... people want diversity, low entry barriers and the ability to be themselves" (as reported in Bishop and Lisheron 2002, p.4).

Perhaps these footloose ties are akin to Putnam's (2000) "bridging social ties", which he identifies as the drivers of economic growth, rather than the traditional "bonding social ties" between which the social capital literature differentiates.

At the individual household level, the accumulation of ICT goods and services by some segments of society represents a new wave of consumerism. For example, Gibbs (2000) refers to market research survey results in Australia which indicates that about 50 percent of households have at least one computer, compared to 22 percent five years earlier; subscribers to pay TV has grown from two percent to 18 percent; Internet use has soared from two percent to 35 percent; and by 2001 78 percent of households have CD/stereo players, 70 percent electronic tools, 45 percent have TV with stereo sound, 39 had 35mm cameras, and 21 percent have a large screen TV/home theatre and video camera/camcorders. Such statistics give rise to what some social commentators are calling 'caving', which refers to stay-at-home individuals and households who are "bunkering down in their high-tech dens, where they control their own environment in security protected residential bliss" (Gibbs 2000, p.48).

Pringle (2002) links the phenomena of the 'symbolic analyst' in the 'creative city' addicted to ICTs as 'bowling alone' [to use Putnam's (2000) phrase]. Pringle tells how "dating has become a casualty of the overworked age, with more women facing the reality that few have the lifestyle of Carlie Bradshaw—instead, for many, life is sexless and the city" (p. 12). He cites a case in Britain where one business woman has given up dating and opted to auction herself to the highest bidder, with one man offering on the Internet the equivalent of EUR 316,000 (USD 375,000) to marry her. In big cities around the world, dating agencies specialize in seeking to match rich professional clients. According to Pringle, in one U.S. city they are charging EUR 3,000 (USD 3,500) to EUR 7,200 (USD 8,500) just to register!

14.5 The Limitations of ICTs

While there is plenty of evidence that ICTs are important drivers underlying the rapid economic development of many cities and regions and that harnessing ICTs is an important factor underpinning productivity growth, nonetheless questions have arisen about the limitations of ICTs. For example, U.S. economist Paul Krugman suggests that, despite the significant contribution of services such as the Internet to the recent prosperity and growth of the economy, there are doubts about the extent to which that contribution can be maintained, with some economists thinking that the productivity surge being experienced has nothing to do with the Internet, and that the Internet is running into diminishing returns.

Data compiled by the Australian Bureau of Statistics (ABS) (2001) and the National Office of the Information Economy (2002) shows how computer use, Internet access rates, and the website presence of businesses in Australia continues to increase, with 68 percent of businesses having Internet access and using it for email, information searching, banking, government services and e-commerce. But the report notes how a website presence is a low priority for most business, with almost 77 percent of business saying they have no intentions of setting up a website. However, over 80 percent of larger companies (with 100 plus employees) have an appropriate website. Denton (2002, p.31) tells how these findings "echo sentiments expressed in [the February 2002] Dun & Bradstreet poll of 400 Australian executives [where] half the executives said their companies had a website, but 34 percent—more than previously—said websites were not important". The ABS data show how that 3 percent of businesses integrated their back end applications with web technology to enable online transactions. The report identifies the UK, Finland, Denmark, Sweden, and Norway as being ahead of Australia on Internet access and web presence measures, while Canada and Australia are on a par.

Evidence is emerging of a growing frustration among corporate users of ICTs (Chong 2002). The ICT industry is very capital intensive and the benefits of investment are uncertain. Denton (2002, p.31) tells how the Managing Director of the Commonwealth Bank, in an address to the 2002 World Congress on Information Technology in Adelaide, Australia, went as far as branding ICT to be a "costly failure". Industry leaders cite product failures, failure of systems to deliver promised outcomes, inflexibility in being locked into a particular supplier's platform, and the high cost of consistent upgrades. There exists as well a sense that benefits from ICT investments are a long time in coming. And MacKenzie (2002a) tells of the lack of security in business wireless networks, referring to a study, which claims that 80 percent of such networks in Sydney's Central Business District (CBD) in Australia had no security at all.

It is not always the case that the take-up and dispersed of new ICT services will actually occur at the rate and scale envisaged in the industry's marketing hype. For example, in Australia, despite the obvious known and potential benefits of broadband, user take-up is slow even though ADSL was available to 74 percent of homes nationally by early 2002 (MacKenzie 2002b, p.1). Together with cable, this should allow most Australians to access broadband. However, MacKenzie (2002b, p.2) reports that "many outside the major metropolitan areas will still be out in the digital cold, as they are either too far away from a telephone exchange to use ADSL, or have no access to cable".

In Australia, as elsewhere, the banks have been 'upbeat' about the potential of online banking. But with more than four million Australians registered as online banking customers, fewer than half are regular users of Internet banking services. The banks are reported to be disappointed with the rate of progress in online services, with few getting the savings from e-commerce that they had projected (Kavanagh 2002a, p.68). There is also a widespread and perhaps growing negative sentiment by consumers towards the banks as they withdraw face-to-face services through branch closures across the suburbs of the cities and the towns of regional Australia. Similar failures are being experienced in Asia, Europe and the U.S. in shifting customers from other distribution channels to online services.

Furthermore, call centre technology and on-line customer service systems are creating frustrations for users, and the skills of staff in dealing with customers are crucial. According to a Perth (Australia) Management Consultant, Jillian Mercer "the bottom line is no matter what technology you have got between the customer and you, there is a human at the end of the mouse" (quoted in Hannen 2001, p.93). Consumers are becoming less tolerant of what they consider to be poor service. "They will not tolerate long periods in telephone or retail queues, and they will not give you their business unless service delivery is equal to perceived product quality" (Lloyd 2001, p.95).

Much of the rapid growth in the number, and sometimes size, of firms in ICT has been related not only to innovation-led new business starts, but also to corporate and public agency strategies of outsourcing and downsizing, as companies restrict their operations to concentrate on core business and core competencies. This has led to a dramatic rise in business process outsourcing (BPO) (Gartner 2001) that is estimated in the US to have grown from about EUR 90.16 billion (USD 107 billion) in 1999 to EUR 235.6 billion (USD 301 billion) in 2004. Howarth (2001a) tells us how the U.S. research company Gartner has identified information technology, administrative services, finance and accounting, human resources, payment services, logistics and distribution, along with sales, marketing, and customer care, as being the most popular business functions for outsourcing. Howard notes how advances in web-browser technology fuelling that trend. That can have profound implications for concentration of market share as seen, for example, in Australia where 14 of the largest companies (including the Fosters Group, ANZ Bank and Coles Myer) have set up CorProcure—similar to the US car industry exchange Covisinet, set up by the Ford Motor Company, General Motors and Daimler Chrysler in February 2000—to connect buyers and sellers (Howarth 2001a).

But in addition to the creation of new ICT and other technology-related business through outsourcing and downsizing, occurring in parallel has been an increasing amount of business activity involving mergers and acquisitions (M&A). Referring to Australian businesses, Kavanagh (2002b) relates some of this to the shedding of none-core assets to focus on profitable lines of business. He tells how most of the EUR 32.9 billion (USD 39 billion) per annum activity is evident in the ICT, health care, retail and manufacturing sectors.

However, the ICT 'bull-run' can collapse, as seen in the crash in technology stocks from April 2000. Following that bust of the dot.com bubble, it seems that the global information technology sector is in some degree of turmoil. For example, in 2001 the information technology industry in Australia shed between 6,000 and 10,000 jobs out of a total industry workforce of about 200,000, with revenues and profits will down after a period of double-digit growth in the second half of the 1990s, a period when over-investment profitability occurred (Howard 2001, p.66). Globally, losses among ICT providers have been very high. For example, in the US in 2001, the Cisco corporation reported a net loss of EUR 255.8 million (USD 268 million), with its share price collapsing from EUR 48 (USD 57) in November 2000 to EUR 19 (USD 20) in October 2001; Nortel reported a net loss of EUR 2.95 billion (USD 3.5 billion) for just three months to September 30, 2001, compared to a loss of EUR 494 million (USD 586 million) in the corresponding period in 2000; and Lucent Technologies lost revenue of EUR 2.52 billion (USD 3 billion) over the year to September 30, 2001, recording an operating loss of EUR 766 million (USD 909 million), with its workforce world-wide being reduced from 123,000 to 60,000.

While the technology stock market did burst in April 2000, the technology sector is not actually finished, as continued technology breakthroughs will guarantee. Rennie (2002, p.32) explains how technology does not just mean ICTs—rather, it embraces network services and equipment, computer hardware and software, semi conductors, industrial technology, voice recognition technology, bio-medical sciences, earth sciences, etc. The convergence of ICTs with other technologies—such as life-sciences solutions (bio-technology), nanotechnology, new energy technologies and smart micro computers—will likely accelerate innovation and new product development in the years ahead. Haywood (2001) suggests there will be a considerable challenge in how that convergence is managed in terms of both business strategy and public policy. Undoubtedly some businesses, some people and some places will benefit more than others, while others may not benefit at all.

14.6 Policy Issues for ICTs and Implications of the Digital Divide

Policy issues arising from innovation and growth in ICT activities are manifold, ranging from:

1. Concerns over strategies for planning and market intervention to harness ICTs in both a national and a city and regional development context; to
2. Developing regulatory frameworks for competition in the provision of, and consumer access to ICT services.

Policy concerns inevitably include addressing socio-economic and spatial disparities manifest in the 'digital divide'. A number of such issues are discussed in what follows.

14.6.1 Coverage and Access: Market Behaviour and Equity

The 'digital divide' has been referred to by Pelletiere and Rodrigo (2000a, p.160) as "one of the most interesting and pressing policy issues of recent years". As discussed earlier in this chapter, inequalities of access to ICTs—for both people and places—assumes many and complex dimensions, of which one is space.

Take a country like Australia, which the eminent historian Geoffrey Blainey (1968) convincingly argues was shaped largely by what he called the 'tyranny of distance'. In the contemporary context of innovation in ICTs, Cutler (2002b) tells how many of that nation's telecommunications challenges might be summed up with the phrase 'the tyranny of density'. Australia is a stand-alone large continent with 70 percent of its population concentrated in just five big metro city regions; the market is small, it is a long way from the rest of the world; and it is never likely to be a hot spot of competition. Cutler (2002b, p.26) suggests that to enhance coverage and access across such a vast and unevenly populated space, "a primary reliance on competition policy is not likely to work, particularly outside the big central business districts". The economic logic is basic. Even if small regional markets could offer a reasonable return on investment, those areas need to compete with markets which provide a high return or which have greater growth potential. With competition for capital investment, Cutler (2002b, p.26) notes, "low-density, lower-growth market segments will lose out regardless of their attractiveness on a stand-alone basis".

Typically government intervention takes a universal minimum standard approach to address inequities in coverage and access to ICT services. But Cutler (2002b, p.26) questions whether a standard approach to standard services is appropriate, suggesting rather that "telecommunications infrastructure needs the same customized solutions that have evolved in broadcasting, personalized web services, water and electricity". He makes the point that services geared to higher-density city markets are not likely to be appropriate for low-density rural and regional markets.

Graham (2002, p.48) refers to campaigns in both the UK and Australia involving non-profit organizations and lobbyists who have successfully argued for universal or community service obligations (CSOs) to be expanded to multiple private providers of ICTs. He also cites initiatives in the U.S. at the municipal level in both big city and regional communities in California, Oregon and Florida to develop partnerships with utility and telecom firms to install trunk optic fibre networks. Mansell and Wehn (1998) refer to initiatives involving public-private partnerships to develop information infrastructure in both developed and developing nations to enhance socio-economic development. And widespread across the world we see public subsidies directed to providing ICT connections to marginalized groups and rural and remote communities. Examples of the diversity of such initiatives include: public Internet booths in Amsterdam; Internet access points across the entire nation of Estonia (UNDP 1999); and the program of Rural Transactions Centres for small towns in Australia. However, Jones (1995, p.12) urges caution saying "connection to the Internet does not inherently make a community, nor does it lead to any necessary exchanges of information, meaning and sense-making at all". And Steyaert (2000) warns that far too often initiatives to connect disadvantaged groups and localities to the Internet are not backed up by community development and training, and that they often lack the means necessary for developing institutional capacity.

Access is also an issue for business—and not just in the sense of locational disparities in provision of ICT services. An enduring outcome of the 'dot.com bubble' has been the rapid growth of business-to-business (B2B) electronic hubs, arrangements in which companies combine in hubs for group buying and selling, offering substantial price, sales and other advantages for participants wanting to operate at the technological cutting edge. There can be exclusionary effects, as Allan Fels (2001, p.24), Chairman of the Australian Competition and Consumer Commission (ACCC), warns: "B2Bs can be used as a market bottleneck. The Internet can make it easier for competitors to collude ... Regulators around the world have been seriously considering the effect of B2B exchanges".

Thus, monopolistic and other exclusionary market behaviour is a fertile and necessary field for regulators to consider. It can have surprising effects, as Cutler (2001c, p.32) suggests: "monopolies and quasi-monopolies have mastered [the] art of anti-innovation" just as much as public agencies tend to stifle innovation using techniques such as "discrediting the evidence or the innovator, and commissioning further work to delay decision-making".

14.6.2 Rules Governing Digital Technology

Around the world, an often controversial debate is occurring over the rules that will govern digital technology. This is seen, for example, regarding the types of services that can or cannot be delivered on the next generation of digital television sets that allow users to see interactive TV (iTV) services. Most countries seem to only offer those enhanced iTV services through pay TV.

However, we see in Australia, for example, how free-to-air networks are hoping also to deliver similar services through digital TV. There the big issues engulfing the public policy debate concern the kinds of services that companies other than the TV networks can provide on the excess digital TV spectrum. Schultze (2002) discusses how it has been argued that digital TV could help ease the 'digital divide', as people with digital decoders may get access to some services currently available only through PCs. These include education and training providers. And it has already been shown that digital TV permits diversification of service offerings through TV products being supplemented by multimedia content. Additionally, access could be provided to a wide range of other services including booking tickets, sports, on-line shopping, etc. The umbrella term 'datacasting' is used for new services able to be provided on the excess digital TV spectrum. An unresolved issue is what will be the restrictions for the free-to-air networks *vis-à-vis* the pay TV networks. Not surprisingly, there is little consensus on what the restrictions will be and how they will be applied (Schultze 2002, p.2). However, because datacasting regulation is essentially a product of broadcasting regulation, as Schultze (2002) points out, discussion on reform cannot be separated from a discussion reviewing the broadcasting regulatory regime. This gets into the complex and politically sensitive issue of cross-media ownership between television broadcasters, the print media, and the interface with digital service providers.

While some ICT services—such as the Internet—potentially are essentially egalitarian in nature, Graham (2002, p.53) says it is "being replaced by 'smart' corporately controlled systems which sift users precisely according to their profitability and allocate them different functionalities accordingly". This raises the need for "new models of social innovation within which transnational media and knowledge industries are made accountable for their actions" (p. 53). Addressing such concerns involves complex regulatory mechanisms including taxation, cross-subsidies, and ownership of ICTs.

14.6.3 Interventions for ICT-Led Regional Development

Governments certainly approach things in vastly different ways in addressing how public policy might embrace ICTs and foster innovation, to enhance national and regional development. An interesting question concerns whether public policy interventions have made, or can make, a difference in the degree to which there is concentration or diffusion of innovation and new economic development derived from ICTs, or whether regions experiencing technology-led endogenous growth do so due to non-public institutional and market factors.

Gordon and McCann (2000, p.55) discuss how, during the 1980s and 1990s, there have been concerted attempts in many parts of the world for regional economic development policy and strategies to stimulate endogenous growth in redundant or marginal areas. They refer to strategies resplendent in the use of terms such as 'globalization', 'clusters', 'new industrial areas', 'embeddedness', 'milieu', and 'complex'. Strategies often focus on small and medium size business development to serve growth and innovation, relying heavily on social network models as described by Camagni (1995) in an analysis of the Emilia-Romagna region of Italy.

Bartik (1996) provides a review of specific models of industrial organization and industrial targeting, evident in local or regional attempts at strategy, which strive to use the Third Italy or Silicon Valley experiences as an ideal approach. While Duranton and Puga (2000, p.533) say, "not all of these interventions are necessarily misguided, many seem to lack a clear rationale or even to be based on common misconceptions". Sometimes narrow specialization focusing on ICTs has been proposed as a means to foster innovation, especially through strategies seeking to develop clusters of small and medium size businesses to secure growth and innovation in lagging regions as well as in smaller urban centres in developed regions. But such propositions do not seem to be supported by the bulk of the empirical evidence. As discussed earlier, generally narrow specialization tends to hinder innovation, while diversity across a range of related activities promotes it. It is important that we remember Cutler's (2001b, p.26) contention that "people in technology business are drawn to places known for diversity of thought and open-mindedness". Thus, policies addressing issues such as immigration and multiculturalism, urban renewal, transport, and cultural diversity, which give thought to "the contemporary meanings of citizenship and democracy" (Cutler, 2001b, p.26) become important considerations.

It is neither realistic nor feasible to expect that every community can create the next third Italy or Silicon Valley. However there is plenty of evidence to suggest that the link between innovation and industrial diversity is robust. Duranton and Puga (2000, p.553) go as far as to suggest, "highly innovative clusters cannot be bred in previously highly specialized environments". This reaffirms the earlier work of Reich (1991) whose analysis of the restructuring of labour markets highlights the growing divergence between location-specific employment and globally mobile and footloose knowledge workers. That has implications for labour market policies and practices, which have tended to be poorly thought out in much regional development strategy.

Perhaps one of the most explicit—and possibly successful—attempts at policy based on the pursuit of information technology strategy is the case of Singapore, a city and a nation. IT has been a core component of its national development planning from the late 1980s. Savage and Pow (2001) tell how that involves strategies embracing the new knowledge-based economy. It includes:

1. The 'Industry 21' program to attract investments in high growth, high value-added industries focusing on electronics, chemicals, life sciences and engineering clients;
2. 'Trade 21' which seeks to make Singapore a global city of international trade and services;
3. 'Tourism 21' which provides a blueprint for the development of a world-class tourism industry;
4. 'ICT 21', an information and telecommunications technology plan to harness ICT for national competitiveness;
5. Building a world class financial centre; and

6. 'Technopreneurship 21' initiative involving public officials and private business leaders to development entrepreneurial high-tech businesses in Singapore.

There is a strategy to link all of Singapore's residents into the new type information era through integrating 800,000 households centrally into two service providers—Singapore Telecommunications and Singapore Cable Vision—the objective being a "seamless integrated system of cyber space in which just about every activity can be performed from the workplace, school and home" (Savage and Pow 2001, p.111). Singapore ranks very high in IT usage and management, with about three in five houses having a computer—higher than in the US (54 percent), Australia (47 percent), and Japan (42 percent) (The Straits Times 2000, p.74). However, Townsend (2001, p.57) alludes to the underutilisation of Singapore's new data networks, which indicate, "the real challenge to information development is not physical or financial capital, but human capital".

The differences between national governments in their investments in high-tech strategies are well-illustrated comparing Singapore and Australia. The Economic Development Board in Singapore has invested the equivalent of EUR 3.71 billion (USD 4.4 billion) in a 40 percent share of ES Cell International to commercialise stem cell research. Over EUR 0.51 billion (USD 0.6 billion) is provided in an investment pool to chase bio-technology development opportunities globally, and the Singapore government has committed EUR 2.28 billion (USD 2.7 billion) over five years to bio-technology initiatives with over 50 investments having been made in companies outside Singapore. That level of strategic funding initiatives dwarfs the figure of just EUR134 million (USD 159 million) of total Commonwealth Government funding for biotechnology in 2000–2001 in Australia (Quinlan 2001, p.47).

The proactive, comprehensive and committed approach taken in Singapore contrasts with what is a more constrained, reactive approach by government in Australia to develop public policy for ICTs and to address the 'digital divide'. There has been a proliferation of reports and launching of strategies on developing the 'information economy' (such as the South Australian Government's *Information Economy 2002 Strategy* and the Queensland Government's *Smart State Strategy*), including creating centres of excellence and taking new initiatives in biotechnology and information technology. In addition, there has been a focus from time-to-time by both the Commonwealth Government and the New South Wales Government on attracting regional headquarters. But as seen in a report for the Australian Business Foundation by Thornburn et al. (2001), it is common for doubts to be cast on the long-term national economic benefits of hi-tech and other multinational companies locating regional headquarters in Australia (about 2,500 foreign businesses and 800 regional headquarters operate there). Thornburn et al. (2001) suggest that there could be a freezing out of local firms, with regional headquarters tended often to focus on sales and marketing operations, with no valuable links to local industries, and resulting in exclusion from the global knowledge loop. It is thus not surprising that, at the level of the national government, there exists scepticism about the desirability and feasibility of taking public policy intervention initiatives to help create local production of ICT products. That view is based on the supposition that economic development benefits at a national level occur through the productivity gains from capital and labour in the adoption by firms of innovations in ICT.

In view of the policy significance currently being invested in many nations and in many regions across the world in the promotion of industry clusters and in stimulating an innovative milieu and associated economies (see, for example Cooke 1998), Gordon and McCann (2000, p.527) warn that considerable care needs to be exercised, even though "intellectually respectable cases can be made for selective interventions to promote growth paths which it is hoped will lead to high local real incomes". As Krugman (1996) points out, there is reasonable suspicion that in most instances such approaches prove to be unwarranted cases of special pleading on behalf of specific interest groups. And Simmie (1998) reminds us that a well-defined relationship does not exist between the location of innovative activities and regional spatial structure that is applicable widely across industry sectors.

Townsend (2001) provides a stern warning about the feasibility for most regions of looking towards ICTs as the panacea for regional economic development. He says "regions attempting to bootstrap their economy into a growth cycle [through ICT development] will not be able to attract the necessary labour force ... [as] ... places that already have a large skilled labour force will become even more special and attractive to footloose firms" (p. 57). Townsend reminds us that "quick fix policies that try to use physical infrastructure as an incentive often fail without substantial commitments to develop the skilled labour force which is necessary to make those facilities a valuable asset" (p. 57).

14.7 Conclusions

What general conclusions can be drawn from the discussion based on the review of literature undertaken in this chapter?

There certainly seems to be plenty of evidence demonstrating how ICTs are being shaped and mobilized to extend the powers of many large corporations and of certain socio-economically powerful groups in society. ICTs are "inherently flexible technologies" (Graham 2002, p.47), possessing the potential capacity to democratise societies and empower people across the globe and across the socio-economic spectrum. Castells (1999a, p. 301) talks of a "creative cacophony" through initiatives and experiments with ICTs at the grass-roots level that might work to reduce the polarization so evident both socio-economically and spatially. Costs of hardware and access are going down as markets mature; with the "club effect" of network externalities meaning network diffusion tends to work cumulatively (Graham 2002, p.53).

But it is difficult to disagree with Graham's (2002, p.52) contention that "the dominant trends surrounding the current extension of ICTs are far from being socially, geographically and culturally neutral". The digital divide exists and might be developing new dimensions, extending the "powers of the powerful over space, time and people" (p. 52). Graham (2002, p.54) calls for new policy models that "tie together local, urban, national and international scales in ways that explicitly seek to match the dominant development logistics of our time". That will require incorporating ICTs into the core thinking about planning and regulating urban and regional environments and our urban systems.

The evidence is overwhelming that addressing the unequal direct and indirect outcomes of the impacts of ICTs will be particularly difficult in the context of strategies for regional development. This is because of the undoubted strong link between innovation, urban scale, and diversification. There exists already a strong and probably an increasing concentration of innovation and employment in sectors such as ICTs in those industries that are strongly dependent on those technologies being in relatively few large cities, particularly 'world cities' with the attributes that attract the 'creative class' that Florida (2002) refers to. Thus Cutler (2001a, p.26) proposes a focus of public policy on the "need to develop strategies for attracting smart people".

But, as Duranton and Puga (2000, p.553) remind us, urban systems have an innate tendency to create an imbalance between relatively few diverse cities with innovative milieu which actually specialize in churning new ideas with more specialized, more numerous and often smaller places with more specialized industrial environments. Agglomeration, through both localization and urbanization economies, remains strong despite the potential diffusion propensities of ICTs. The findings in research such as that conducted by Pelletiere and Rodrigo (2001) casts doubt on whether the expansion of ICT services, such as the Internet, will result in dispersal of production of information goods and services.

According to Graham (2002, p.33), "all the evidence suggests that the processes of urbanization and agglomeration and the rapid application of ICTs are mutually supporting each other". But as Townsend (2001, p.57) says "it is increasingly clear that a new type of global city, the network city, is emerging in the US and possibly elsewhere in the world". These highly prosperous regions attract the skilled workers and investment in infrastructure needed to sustain growth. Often that is at the expense of other regions. Those networked cities are "being organized into an exclusive a highly co-dependent economic system" (p. 57).

The ICT revolution in the context of globalization does seem to be a driving force in the refocusing of emphasis on endogenous factors in regional economic development that emphasizes entrepreneurship and firm formation (Stough 2002). Townsend (2001, p.57) emphasizes how the transformations associated with ICTs are "favouring those regions with firms and individuals that are most able to create and shape these new technologies. Without the capacity to use these new tools, struggling regions will always fall behind". Thus, the evidence appears to suggest that divergence rather than convergence in regional development is an outcome of the impact of ICTs; and as well, socio-economic differentiation seems to be exacerbated rather than diluted by ICTs. At least that seems to be the story thus far.

References

Access Economics (2001) Business outlook. Business Review Weekly Nov 1–7: 22

Amin A, Thrift N (1992) Neo-Markallian nodes in global networks. International Journal of Urban and Regional Research 16: 471–587

Armington C, Acs Z (2002) The determinants of regional variation in new firm formation. Regional Studies 36: 33–46

Arthur WB (1994) Increasing returns and path dependence on the economy. University of Michigan Press, Ann Arbor, MI

Atkinson R (1999) The state new economy index: benchmarking the economic transformation in the States. Democratic Progressive Policy Institute, Washington, DC

Australian Bureau of Statistics (2001) Business use of technology 2000–2001. ABS, Canberra

Aydalot P, Keeble D (1988) High technology industry and innovative environments. Routledge, London

Bartik T (1996) Strategies for economic development. In Aronson R, Schwartz E (eds) Management policies in local government finance. International City/County Management Association for the ICMA University, Washington, DC, pp 287–311

Bishop B, Lisheron M (2002) Rise of the creative cities. Austin American Statesman April 28 (Special): 1–6

Black D, Henderson JV (1998) Urban evolution in the US. Mimeograph, Department of Economics, London School of Economics

Blainey G (1968) The tyranny of distance: how distance shaped Australia's history. Macmillan, Melbourne

Braczyk HJ, Fuchs G, Wolf HG (eds) (1999) Multimedia and regional economic restructuring. Routledge, London

Cairncross F (1997) The death of distance: how the communications revolution will change our lives. Harvard Business School Press, Boston

Caldeira T (1996) Fortified enclaves: the new urban segregation. Public Culture 8: 303–328

Camagni RP (1995) The concept of 'innovative milieux' and its relevance for public policies in European lagging regions. Papers in Regional Science 74: 317–340

Castells M (1996) The rise of the network society. Blackwell, Oxford

Castells M (1998) The end of millennium. Blackwell, Oxford

Castells M (1999a) Grassrooting the space of flows. Urban Geography 20: 294–302

Castells M (1999b) The culture of cities in the information age. Report to the U.S. Library of Congress, Washington, DC

Castells M (2001) The Internet galaxy: reflections on the Internet, business and society. Oxford University Press, Oxford

Castells M, Hall P (1994) Technopoles of the world: The making of 21st century industrial complexes. Routledge, New York

Chong F (2002) Corporate backlash against IT. The Australian IT April 2: 1

Conroy ME (1975) Regional Economic Growth: Diversification and Control. Praeger, New York

Cooke P (1998) The Associational Economy: Firms, Regions and Innovation. Oxford University Press, Oxford

Cushing R (2002) A look at the creative class. Austin American Statesman, April 28, (Special (Special Reports): 1-2. Available at http://www.austin360.com/aas/specialreports/citiesofideas/0428socialcapital.html

Cutler T (2001a) The art of innovation. Business Review Weekly June 29: 26

Cutler T (2001b) A clear country connection. Business Review Weekly Aug 23–29: 26

Cutler T (2001c) Creative tension. Business Review Weekly Nov 15–21: 32

Cutler T (2002a) A niche view of broadband. Business Review Weekly Jan 24–30: 26

Cutler T (2002b) The building blocks of a new century. Business Review Weekly Feb 21–27: 26

Davis S, Haltiwanger J (1992) Gross job creation, gross job distribution and employment relocation. Quarterly Journal of Economics 107: 819–863

Demos (1997) The Wealth and Poverty of Networks. Collection Issue 12. Demos, London

Denton T (2002) Website still not a business priority. The Australian IT, March 26: 31

Dumais G, Elliston G, Glaeser E (1997) Geographic concentration as a dynamic process. National Bureau of Economic Research, Working Paper 6270, Washington, DC

Dunne T, Roberts M, Samuelson L (1989) The growth and failure of U.S. manufacturing plants. Quarterly Journal of Economics 104: 671–698

Duranton G, Puga D (2000) Diversity and specialization in cities: why, where and when does it matter? Urban Studies 37: 533–555

Eaton J, Eckstein Z (1997) Cities and growth: theory and evidence from France and Japan. Regional Science and Urban Economics 27: 443–474

Ellison G, Glaeser E (1997) Geographic concentration of U.S. manufacturing industries: a dartboard approach. Journal of Political Economy 105: 889–927

Ernst D (1997) From partial to systematic globalization: international production networks in the electronics industry. Berkeley Roundtable on the International Economy (BRIE), Working Paper 98, Berkeley, CA. Available at http://repositories.cdlib.org/cgi/viewcontent.cgi?article=1101&context=brie

Everard J (1999) Virtual States: the Internet and the boundaries of the nation-State. Routledge, London

Feldman M, Audretsch D (1999) Innovation in cities: science-based diversity, specialization and localised competition. European Economic Review 43: 409–429

Fels A (2001) Dangers lurk in the rise of B2B. Business Review Weekly Aug 23–29: 24

Finnie G (1998) Wired cities. Communications Week International 18 May: 19–22

Florida R (2002) The rise of the creative class and how it's transforming work, leisure, community and everyday life. Basic Books, New York

Florida R, Gates G (2001) Technology and tolerance: the importance of diversity to high technology growth. Centre on Urban and Metropolitan Policy, Brookings Institute, Survey Series, Washington, DC

Friedmann J (1986) The world city hypothesis. Development and Change 17: 69–83

Fujita M (1989) Urban Economics. Cambridge University Press, Cambridge

Fujita M, Ishii R (1999) Global location behaviour and organizational dynamics of Japanese electronics firms and their impact on regional economies. In: Chandler A, Hagstrom P, Sölvell O (eds) The Dynamic firm: The role of technology, strategy, organization and regions. Oxford University Press, Oxford, pp 343–383

Fujita M, Mori T (1997) Structural stability and evolution of urban systems. Regional Science and Urban Economics 27: 399–442

Gartner (2001) The Rise of BPO. Gartner Company report, January

GaWC (Globalization and World Cities- Study Group and Network) (2001) GaWC Research Bulletin. Available at http://www.lboro.ac.uk/gawc/publicat.html#bulletin

Gibbs D (2002) Back to the cave. The Sunday Mail Jan 6: 48–49

Gillespie A, Williams H (1988) Telecommunications and the reconstruction of regional comparative advantage. Environment and Planning A 20: 1311–1321

Glaeser E, Gaspar J (1996) Information technology and the future of cities. Harvard Institute of Economic Research, Working Paper 1756, Cambridge, MA

Glaeser E, Kallal H, Scheinkman J, Schleifer A (1992) Growth in cities. Journal of Political Economy 100: 1126–1152

Gordon I, McCann P (2000) Industrial clusters, complexes, agglomeration and/or social networks. Urban Studies 37: 513–532

Gorman S (1998) The death of distance but not the end of geography: the Internet as a network. Paper presented to the 45th Annual Conference Regional Science Association International, 11 –14 November, Santa Fe, NM

Gorman S, Malecki E (2000) The networks of the Internet: an analysis of provider networks in the USA. Telecommunications Policy 24: 113–134

Goslee S (1998) Losing ground bit by bit: lower income communities in the information age. Benton Foundation and the National Urban League, Washington DC

Graham S (1998) The end of geography or the explosion of space? Conceptualising space, place and information technology. Progress in Human Geography 22: 165–185

Graham S (2002) Bridging urban digital divides? Urban polarisation and information and communications technologies (ICTs). Urban Studies 31: 33–56

Graham S, Marvin S (1996) Telecommunications and the city: electronic spaces, urban spaces. Routledge, London

Graham S, Marvin S (2001) Splintering urbanism: networked infrastructures, technological mobilities and the urban condition. Routledge, London

Granovetter M (1985) Economic action and social structure: the problem of embeddedness. American Journal of Sociology 91: 481–510

Greenstein S (1998) Universal service in the digital age: the commercialisation and the geography of U.S. Internet access. National Bureau of Economic Research, Working Paper 6453, Washington, DC

Grubesic TH, Murray AT (2002) Constructing the divide: spatial disparities in broadband access. Papers in Regional Science 18: 197–221

Grundy-Warr C, Peachey K, Perry M (1999) Fragmented integration in the Singapore-Indonesian broader zone: Southeast Asia's growth triangle against the global economy. International Journal of Urban and Regional Research 23: 304–328

Hall P (1966) The world cities. Weidenfeld and Nicholson, London

Hannen M (2001) Service lane to success. Business Review Weekly Sept 6–12: 92–97

Hansen N (1992) Competition, trust and reciprocity in the development of innovation milieu. Papers in Regional Science 71: 95–115

Harris-Dobkins L, Ioannides Y (1998) Spatial Evolution of U.S. Cities. Mimeograph, Department of Geography, London School of Economics

Haywood B (2001) Innovate. Business Review Weekly Nov 2–Dec 5: 28

Helpman E, Krugman P (1985) Market structure and foreign trade. MIT Press, Cambridge, MA

Henderson JV (1997a) Externalities and industrial development. Journal of Urban Economics 42: 449–470

Henderson JV (1997b) Medium size cities, Regional Science and Urban Economics 27: 583–612

Henderson JV (1998) Urban development: theory, fact and illusion. Oxford University Press, Oxford

Henderson JV, Kuncoro A, Turner M (1995) Industrial development in cities. Journal of Political Economy 103: 1067–1090

Hoffman DL, Novak T (2000) The evolution of the digital divide: examining the relationship of race to Internet access and use over time. Mimeograph, Owen Graduate School of Management, Vanderbilt University

Howarth B (2001a) The outside experts. Business Review Weekly July 31: 62–65

Howarth B (2001b) IT hits the wall. Business Review Weekly Nov 29–Dec 5: 66–69

Hunt GL, Sheesley TJ (1994) Specialization and econometric improvements in regional portfolio diversification analysis. Journal of Regional Science 34: 217–235

Jacobs J (1960) The economy of cities. Random House, New York

Johansson B, Karlsson C, Stough R (eds) (2001) Theories of Endogenous Growth. Springer, Berlin Heidelberg New York

Jones S (1995) Understanding community in the information age. In: Jones, S (ed) Cybersociety: computer mediated communication and community. Sage, London, pp 10–35

Kavanagh J (2002a) Internet banking still waiting for the fiz. Business Review Weekly Jan 31–Feb 6: 68

Kavanagh J (2002b) The hungry adventurers. Business Review Weekly April 4–10: 32–33

Kim S (1995) Expansion of markets and the geographic distribution of economic activities: the trend in U.S. regional manufacturing structure 1860–1987. Quarterly Journal of Economics 110: 881–908

Knox P, Taylor P (eds) (1995) World cities in a world system. Cambridge University Press, Cambridge

Kort JR (1981) Regional economic instability and industrial diversification in the US. Land Economics 57: 596–608

Krugman P (1991a) Geography and trade. MIT Press, Cambridge, MA

Krugman P (1991b) Increasing returns and economic geography. Journal of Political Economy 99: 183–199

Krugman P (1993) First nature, second nature and metropolitan location. Journal of Regional Science 34: 129–144

Krugman P (1996) Development, geography and economic theory. MIT Press, Cambridge, MA

Leyshon A, Thrift N (1997) Money/space: geographies of monetary transformation. Routledge, London

Lloyd S (2001) Up to scratch on service. Business Review Weekly Sept 6–12: 95

Lynch A (2002) Broadband to pump jobs into the bush. The Australian IT, April 16: 7

MacKenzie K (2002a) Hack heaven: wireless nets unprotected. The Australian IT, Jan 29: 19

MacKenzie K (2002b) Digital pipe dreams. The Australian IT, Technology Survey Series 2 March 26: 1–2

Madon S (1998) Information-based global economy and socioeconomic development: the case of Bangalore. The Information Society 13: 227–243

Malecki E (1990) Technology and economic development: The dynamics of local, regional and national change. Wiley, New York

Mansell R, Wehn U (1998) Knowledge societies: information technology for sustainable development. Oxford University Press, Oxford

Moss ML, Townsend AM (1997a) Manhattan leads the net nation. (Research report by the Taub Urban Research Centre, New York University, New York)

Moss ML, Townsend, AM (1997b) Tracking the 'net: using domain names to measure the growth of the Internet in U.S. cities. Journal of Urban Technology 4: 47–60

Moss ML, Townsend AM (1998) Spatial analysis of the Internet in U.S. cities and States. Paper presented at Urban Futures – Technological Futures Conference, 23-25 April, Durham, England. Available at
http://www.urban.nyu.edu/research/spatial-analysis/spatial-analysis.pdf

National Office of the Information Economy (2002) The current state of play: Australia's scorecard. Commonwealth of Australia, Canberra

Negroponte N (1995) Being digital. Knopf, New York

Nonaka J, Takeuchi H (1995) The knowledge creating company: how Japanese companies create the dynamics of innovation. Oxford University Press, New York

National Telecommunications and Information Administration (NTIA) (1999) Americans in the information age: falling through the net. NTIA, Washington, DC

O'Connor K, Stimson R, Daly M (2001) Australia's changing economic geography: a society dividing. Oxford University Press, Melbourne

Pelletiere D, Rodrigo GC (2001) An empirical investigation of the digital divide in the United States. Journal of Public Affairs Review 2: 159–174

Petrella R (1993) Towards a global 'techno-apartheid' (in French). Le Monde Diplomatique, May

Picon A (1998) The City- cyborgs' territory. (in French-La ville territoire de Cyborgs). L'Impremeur, Paris

Piore MJ, Sabel CF (1984) The Second industrial divide: possibilities for prosperity. Basic Books, New York

Pitelis C (ed) (1993) Transaction costs, markets and hierarchies. Blackwell, Oxford

Porter M (1990) The competitive advantage of nations. The Free Press, New York

Pringle G (2002) Money can bring me love. The Courier Mail Feb 5: 12

Putnam R (2000) Bowling alone: the collapse and revival of American community. Simon and Schuster, New York

Putnam R (2002) Robert Putnam's response (to Bishop and Lisheran 2002 and Cushing 2002). Austin American-Statesman April 28 (Special Report): 1-2. Available at
http://www.austin360.com/aas/specialreports/citiesofideas/0428socialcapital.html

Quinlan B (2001) Singapore goes on a biotech spree. Business Review Weekly Nov 29–Dec 5: 47

Quinlan B (2002) Battle of the biotechs. Business Review Weekly March 14–20: 56–59

Reich RB (1991) The work of nations: preparing ourselves for 21st century capitalism. Vintage Books (Random House), New York

Rennie P (2002) Stay tuned to technology. Business Review Weekly Feb 21–27: 32–34

Romer PM (1986) Increasing returns and long run growth. Journal of Political Economy 94: 1002–1037

Romer PM (1987) Growth based on increasing returns due to specialization. American Economic Review 77: 56–72

Romer PM (1990) Endogenous technological change. Journal of Political Economy 98: S71–S102

Sassen S (1991) The global city: New York, London, Tokyo. Princeton University Press, Princeton, NJ

Sassen S (1994) Cities in a world economy. Pine Forge Press, London

Savage VR, Pow CP (2001) 'Model Singapore': crossing urban boundaries. In: Williams JF, Stimson RJ (eds) International urban planning settings: lessons of success. JAI (An Imprint of Elsevier Science), Amsterdam, pp 87–121

Saxenian A (1994) Regional advantage: culture and competition in Silicon Valley and Route 128. Harvard University Press, Cambridge, MA

Schiller D (1999) Digital capitalism: networking the global market system. MIT Press, Cambridge, MA

Schultze J (2002) TV's zero hour. The Australian Media Feb 7: 2–3

Scott AJ (1988) The industrial spaces. Pion, London

Scott AJ (1993) Technopolis: high-technology industry and regional development in Southern California. University of California Press, Berkeley, CA

Senge PM (1992) The fifth discipline: the art and practice of the learning organization. Random House, Milsons Point

Sherwood-Call C (1990) Assessing regional economic stability: a portfolio approach. Economic Review Federal Reserve Bank of San Francisco, Winter: 17–26

Simmie J (1998) Reasons for the development of 'islands of innovation': evidence from Hertfordshire. Urban Studies 35: 1261–1289

Skeates R (19990 The infinite city. City 8: 6–20

Smilor RW, Wakelin M (1990) Smart infrastructure and economic development: the role of technology and global networks. The Technopolis Phenomenon, IC^2 Institute, University of Texas at Austin, Austin, pp 100–125

Smith MP (2001) Transnational urbanism. Blackwell, Oxford

Steyaert J (2000) Local governments online and the role of the resident. Social Science Computer Review 18: 3–16

Stough RR (2000) The new generation technology economy: comparative regional analysis and the case of the U.S. National Capital Region. Paper presented at the American Association for the Advancement of Science, Annual Meeting, 17-22 February, Washington, DC

Stough RR (2001) Endogenous growth theory and the role of institutions in regional economic development. In Johansson B, Karlsson C, Stough RR (eds) Theories of endogenous regional growth: lessons for regional policies. Springer, Berlin Heidelberg New York, pp 17-48

Stough RR (2002) Strategic management of places and policy. Presidential Address, Western Regional Science Association Annual Conference, 17-20 February, Monterey, CA

Sussman G, Lent J (1998) Global productions: labour in the making of the 'Information Society'. Hampton Press, Cresskill, NJ

Taylor PJ, Catalano G, Gane N (2002) A geography of global change: services and cities, 2000–01. GaWC Research Bulletin, Globalization and World Cities Study Group and Network 77: 1–9

Thornburn R, Langdale J, Houghton J (2001) Friend or foe: leveraging foreign multinationals in the Australian economy. Australian Business Foundation, Sydney

Toffler A (1980) The third wave. Bantam Books, New York

Townsend AM (2001) The Internet and the rise of the new network cities, 1969–1999. Environment and Planning B 28: 39–58

United Nations Development Program (UNDP) (1999) Human settlement report. Oxford University Press, New York

Webber M (1964) The urban place and the nonplace urban realm. In Webber M (ed) Explorations into urban structure. University of Philadelphia Press, Philadelphia, PA, pp 79–153

Wheller D, O'Kelly ME (1999) Network topology and city accessibility of the commercial Internet. Professional Geographer 41: 327–339

Wheller J, Aoyama Y, Warf B (eds) (2000) Cities in the telecommunications age: the fracturing of geographics. Routledge, London

Williamson OE, Winter SG (eds) (1993) The nature of the firm: origins, evolution and development. Oxford University Press, Oxford

Zook M (2000) The web of production: the economic geography of communication Internet contact production in the United States. Environment and Planning A 32: 411–426

15 The Emerging Digital Economy: Conclusions

Börje Johansson[1], Charlie Karlsson[1], and Roger R. Stough[2]

[1] Jönköping International Business School, Jönköping University
[2] School of Public Policy, George Mason University

15.1 Introduction

This book has been compiled with the purpose of adding to the complex picture of possible impacts of information and communication technologies (ICTs) with a special focus on spatial effects and, at the same time, hopefully, in some instances, making the picture more comprehensible. This concluding chapter creates a synthesis of the major aspects of the book and lessons for future research, and explores avenues for public policy making in the emerging digital economy.

It is appropriate to devote attention to the effects of the generation, diffusion and the use of ICTs, because they represent a new technological paradigm that belongs to the family of *general purpose technologies* (GPTs). A GPT has the potential for pervasive adoption and adaptation in a wide range or even all sectors in ways that drastically change operations and products as well as the relationships between different sectors. The characteristics of GPTs have been described by Bresnahan and Trajtenberg (1995, p. 84): "Most GPTs play the role of 'enabling technologies', opening up new opportunities rather than offering complete, final solutions." General purpose technologies also involve 'innovational complementarities', i.e. "the productivity of R&D in a downstream sector increases as a consequence of innovation in the GPT technology".

Thus, GPTs have two major characteristics: generality of application; and, innovational complementarities. However, other characteristics of GPTs are also important (Lipsey et al. 1998): (i) much scope for improvement initially, (ii) many varied uses, (iii) applicability across large parts of the economy, and (iv) strong complementarities with other technologies.

Luc Soete, in Chap. 2 in this book, does not use the GPT concept when he characterizes ICT but instead he characterizes ICT as 'a break-trough technology'. However, there is not a major distinction between the two concepts. The characterization of ICT as 'a break-trough technology' is supported by the following arguments:

- There is a dramatic and seemingly continuous technological improvement in the capacity of semi-conductors (e.g. Moore's Law) that has led to a gigantic increase in the capacities and speed of computers to store and process data.

- There is the tendency to miniaturise ICT components, (e.g. wearable electronics).
- There are the almost equally radical and significant technological improvements in the area of telecommunications.
- There are specific developments in the area of mobile communication.
- There are developments in the field of supporting technology, such as software and other communication standards, in particular Internet protocols (for example WWW), mobile communication standards (such as GSM, WAP and UTMS), and location based systems that it supports (e.g. GPS).

When these factors are particularly strong, as in the case of ICT, they lead to fundamental changes in the way economies and societies are organised, in how production is performed and which products are produced. In other words, they impact not only the superstructures but also the infrastructures of existing economies. They reshape the macro-economic conditions of economies, the conditions for R&D and innovation and the structure of markets by changing conditions for competition and entrepreneurship including the introduction of new industries. Further, they impact the demand for knowledge and skills and the functioning of labour markets, the internal organisation of firms as well as the structure of the relationships between firms. Finally, the factors determining the location of firms and households as well as the territorial competition between functional regions are transformed by the conditions for public policy at all levels from the local to the international.

The fundamental changes of economies and societies initiated and stimulated by the developments within ICT and the diffusion of ICT have led to the emergence of a digital economy. The contributions presented in this book highlight three important aspects of this emerging digital economy:

- Clusters, innovation and entrepreneurship
- Location and dynamics of ICT industries
- Telecommunications and policy

By bringing these essays together, we hope to encourage further exploration of these aspects of the emerging digital economy. The purpose with this final chapter is to summarize some of the findings in these essays and to point out important areas for future research.

15.2 Clusters, Innovation and Entrepreneurship

A basic observation is that economic activities are clustered in space. Krugman (1991) finds the geographic concentration of production to provide evidence for the pervasive influence of some kind of increasing returns. When many firms in one sector cluster together geographically, an industrial or sectoral cluster is said to exist. Inside such a cluster one or several forms of direct and/or indirect interaction is assumed to take place. This interaction generates positive externalities for firms belonging to the cluster.

In what way does the emerging digital economy affect the tendencies of firms and industries to cluster, i.e. to agglomerate or de-agglomerate? In Chap. 3 *Karen Polenske* analyses this issue using a concept of 'dispersion economies'. This is intended to 'catch' the economies from dispersing economic activities, which is an important factor affecting regional development. Information and communication technologies certainly play an important role in promoting the dispersion of firms and activities over space, partly because they may allow firms to reduce costs. Regional, national and global supply chains are strongly affected by dispersion economies/diseconomies. Firms are adopting supply-chain management techniques, enabling them to push risks and costs along the supply-chain by demanding just-in-time deliveries and to find the suppliers offering the lowest costs. Information and communication technologies have provided firms with radically new tools to manage supply chains. Interestingly, little research has been conducted on how ICTs via their effects on supply chains impacts the development in different types of regions in rich as well as poor countries.

General purpose technologies are radical innovations that create innumerable opportunities for incremental innovations. Even if it is possible and perhaps even probable that the forces that drive incremental innovations are different from those driving drastic innovations it seems to be generally true that innovations are dependent upon proximity among the relevant knowledge handlers. Innovations within ICTs are no exception. This implies that central elements of innovation processes are regional rather than national or international. Despite much focus in recent years on national systems of innovation the critical issue for success in innovation is the functioning of regional innovation systems. *Martin Andersson and Charlie Karlsson* in Chap. 4 show how a better understanding of regional innovation systems demands stronger analytical frameworks based upon clearly defined concepts. The literature on regional innovation systems unfortunately offers few insights that help us to understand how ICTs innovations emerge and how ICTs stimulate innovations in other sectors. We see regional innovation systems as a major research focus for future research.

As GPT, ICTs offer countless opportunities for innovations, and thus countless opportunities for entrepreneurs. A critical question is of course how entrepreneurs discover these opportunities and what determines their willingness to act on these opportunities and transform them to real business ventures. A still more critical question is the relationship between ICTs-induced entrepreneurship and economic growth. In Chap. 5 *Christian Friis, Thomas Paulsson and Charlie Karlsson* show that the relationship between entrepreneurship and economic growth is not firmly established in the literature. The role of the entrepreneur for economic growth is theoretically not well understood and must be dealt with more thoroughly. Casual inspection of ICTs-induced entrepreneurship in different countries and regions seems to indicate that the importance of ICTs-induced entrepreneurship for economic growth has varied substantially. Further empirical studies across countries and regions concerning the role of ICTs-induced entrepreneurship for economic growth are much needed to begin to better understand the role of entrepreneurship in the digital economy.

Most countries and major sub-national governments such as states and provinces have established science and technology agencies or authorities to help develop and guide policy in support of economic development. These efforts have had differential success and have increasingly come under public budgetary scrutiny and in some cases have even been disbanded. In this context there is a further question of how these science and technology oriented programs can guide substate and sub-province level efforts to create a more effective strategy in support of economic development. In Chap. 6, *Roger Stough* creates and uses a methodology to uncover or define such clusters and then employs a focus group technique to elicit science and technology strategies in support of sub-state regional economic development. This chapter offers new methodological contributions for conducting industrial cluster analyses and for identifying policy and strategy relevant concepts from informed public and private sector officials in pursuit of economic development objectives. Case studies of two regions in the Commonwealth of Virginia are presented to illustrate the techniques and show how they can be used to identify realistic but creative strategy elements for science and technology driven economic development.

15.3 Location and Dynamics of ICT Industries

The location of ICT industries has been an important and pressing research issue during recent decades. 'Silicon Valley' has been the role model and numerous regions have tried to create their own 'Silicon Valley' but most have failed. One fundamental reason for the numerous failures is of course that it is very difficult to imitate success, because 'nothing breeds success like success'. Another reason for these failures is that surprisingly little is known about the location behaviour of ICT industries and the dynamics of the life-cycles of ICT industries.

Börje Johansson in Chap. 7 provides several important inputs for at better understanding of the location behaviour and location dynamics of ICT industries. He outlines two models that can help us understand input-based and output-based localisation and urbanisation economies. These models also contain a representation of intra-industry spillover and scale effects. Secondly, using regression analysis he examines the clustering of employment in the ICT sector as a whole and in different ICT sub-industries, and of ICT establishments themselves. A major result of this is that localisation economies dominate urbanisation economies. This chapter indicates a research avenue that can substantially increase our understanding of the location behaviour and location dynamics of ICT industries. Of course, there is a need to deepen the analysis into the issues and also to extend to cover more countries.

Chapter 8 by *Johan Klaesson* and *Lars Pettersson* contains an empirical analysis of ten service industries within the ICT sector in Sweden. The industries chosen are assumed to be dependent on local market demand and are at the same time important characteristics of the supply of ICT services in the local economic milieu. The basic theoretical assumption behind the study is that the presence locally of service industries can be explained by the size of local and regional markets. To test their theoretical assumptions the authors use an approach, where the probability of the existence of a particular ICT service industry is explained by the accessibility to local demand, demand in the rest of the functional region and demand from other regions. Resulting estimations show a limited geographical reach of ICT service industries. Local demand is significant in all ten cases; regional demand is significant in five cases while demand from other regions is significant in only one case. This study has strong policy implications. Access to local demand is of high importance implying that local and regional development can be assumed to be self-reinforcing and cumulative. In a dynamic perspective development can be promoted by investment in transport infrastructure, which reduces travel times and thus increases accessibility. The methodological approach presented in this chapter has strong qualities and should be used for analysing not only the location of ICT service industries but could be applied more broadly in the analysis of all types of service industries.

Johan Klaesson and *Martin Andersson* in Chap. 9 also apply an accessibility approach in a study that can be seen as a complement to the study presented in Chap. 8. Their intent is to examine the existence of systematic patterns of growth of ICT service industries across municipalities in Sweden. Local employment growth in different ICT service sectors is explained by different types of market accessibility. It was found that local employment growth in ICT service industries coincided with overall local private sector employment growth. During the 1990s, the vast majority of the ICT service industries displayed rapid diffusion tendencies. However, spatial diffusion was coupled with increased employment in metropolitan and large urban areas. ICT employment growth differed substantially across categories of municipalities. It turns out that ICT employment in municipalities with larger initial market-accessibility grew fastest. This chapter is another example of a creative methodological approach that can be used for analysing employment growth at the local level not only for ICT service industries, but for service industries in general. It also provides an example of how the effects of investments in infrastructure for employment growth in various service industries can be analysed.

The three chapters in this section provide new information on the location and dynamics of ICT industries in general and ICT service industries in particular in Sweden. However, more important is that they give excellent examples of new empirical methods for analysing the location and dynamics of industries.

15.4 Telecommunications and Policy

In recent decades we have witnessed a digitalisation of the telecommunication sector, i.e. the successful marriage of computers and telecommunications, and the proliferation of new modes of telecommunications based on both (Helpman and

Trajtenberg 1998). These developments constitute one of the utmost expressions of the power of microelectronics, its extremely wide reach, and of its potential for bringing forth deep and pervasive changes in the economy and in the society at large. However, adoption of digital technology was extremely slow in the early days of microelectronics and had little impact on the telecommunications sector as a whole until much later. The reasons for the slow adoption is that telecommunication is not a single thing but a huge, intricate and delicate system that poses strict demands on the technologies from which it feeds in terms of compatibility, reliability, durability, etc. Moreover, telecommunication technology is embedded in a massive stock of capital, and hence any major change in technology requires large capital outlays and concomitant adjustment costs. The sheer magnitude of these capital outlays, coupled with the rapid change in microelectronics and difficulties in forecasting future developments made it extremely difficult to take decisions about future adoption. Furthermore, the telecommunication sector was heavily regulated in most countries, thus, giving negative incentives for rapid adoption of new technology. These general observations are strong motivations for thorough investigations of the telecommunications sector in the digital economy and for analysing the role of public policy.

In Chap. 10 *Edward Malecki* shows how the emergence and growth of the Internet influence urbanisation, urban hierarchies and the form of urban regions with special emphasis on the largest urban regions. In particular, he discusses the winners and losers among urban regions in the new digital economy but he also assesses the challenges posed for urban planning in the Internet age. The particular strength of this chapter is that it provides a much needed synthesis of the research in the field during the last two decades. Malecki efficiently destroys many of the myths concerning the effects of telecommunications on cities and urban regions. He observes the emergence of new network cities as major hubs in the urban hierarchy that might transform the urban hierarchy and produce winners and losers. The digital economy gives rise to a new network phenomenon that may generate new types of synergies when integrated into the knowledge economy. This contributes to the emergence of a new urban structure – the polycentric city. However, the trends may differ between macro-regions in the world. But the risks for the emergence of 'dual cities' should not be neglected. Thus, new challenges may emerge for urban planners. This may also generate a need for new theories and new ideas about cities. This chapter offers an excellent starting point for the generation of new theories and ideas about cities in the Internet age.

Kingsley Haynes, Serdar Yilmaz and *Mustafa Dinc* in Chap. 11 take as their starting point the explosion of telecommunications and its apparent integration into the production activities of many firms, in particular service firms, which implies that this industry not only deserves attention in its own right but also deserves attention as a central element in an increasingly information oriented economy, i.e. the digital economy. Given that telecommunications infrastructure has public good characteristics and that deregulation implies the introduction of a new policy regime, questions of the measurable impacts of telecommunications investments gain increased importance. Concerns also arise about the relationships between older networks of interaction represented by the traditional systems for passenger transportation and the quantitatively and qualitatively improved tele-communications networks. The current chapter is focused on the issue of utiliza-tion of telecommunications infrastructure and its impact on state economic output levels in the U.S. during the period 1984-1997 applying a production function ap-proach as well as data envelopment analysis (DEA). Their results show that tele-communications infrastructure played an important role for output growth during the period. It also shows that there are significant differences between states of the U.S. in terms of how efficient the telecommunications infrastructure was utilised. However, almost all states had made significant improvements in the degree of utilization. In the literature much has been written about the importance of tele-communications infrastructure in the digital economy. This study is unusual in the sense that it tries to estimate the economic importance of such infrastructure. We certainly need more of this kind of work, among more economies and for different time periods to be able to better understand the importance of telecommunications infrastructure for economic development in the digital economy.

In Chap. 12 *Peter Stenberg* analyses an issue that has become known as the digital divide. This issue plays an important role on the political agenda in the digital economy in most countries. The digital divide is difficult to work with be-cause it is a political concept. It relates to the fact that the adoption of any innova-tion follows an S-shaped curve over time. At any given moment of time there are adopters and non-adopters. For most innovations we can observe that the adoption rate never reaches 100 percent. During the last century we had a telephone divide, a radio divide, a TV divide, etc. So is the digital divide different? This chapter does not answer this question, but it provides an overview of investment and household adoption of communication and information services in rural areas in the U.S. The analysis clearly shows that rural households lag behind urban house-holds in terms of Internet access. Certainly, the costs of Internet access play an important role for non-adoption. High-income households adopt Internet to a higher extent than low-income households. But for any innovation the pattern would be similar. So, why is the digital divide more important than so-called other divides? This chapter gives several answers. Availability and affordability will be determined by government policy, economic feasibility, technical limits, and mar-ket incentives. Technology is not changing enough to make the cost structure of telecommunications the same across space. Moreover, it will not change enough to lower service delivery costs. This analysis is welcome, since it places the issue of the digital divide in an economic analytical framework, thus making it possible to understand the limits of market forces as a factor driving adoption. In this sense this analysis could serve as a guideline for other researchers studying digital di-vide issues.

Per-Olof Bjuggren in Chap. 13 evaluates the Swedish 3G beauty contest. Like many other countries Sweden has recently allocated licenses to the third genera-tion (3G) of wireless telecommunication technology. But in contrast to Britain, Germany and Denmark, for example, a so-called 'beauty contest' was used to earmark the rights. The motivation given in Sweden was that using other criteria than price in the apportionment of rights would be to the advantage of both con-sumers and producers and would speed up infrastructure investments. Considering that the authorities in Sweden had two major alternatives to choose between in allocating a scarce resource – the use of the radio spectrum – Bjuggren finds it natural that economists should have something to contribute to the understanding of the two alternatives and their effects. However, although there exists a rich literature on auctions as a means to allocate rights, the economic literature has little to contribute when it comes to understanding 'beauty contests'. In this respect this chapter contributes to an increase in our knowledge about the effects of beauty contests. It suggests that the theory of competition for the field could be tested as a candidate for a theory for beauty contests. A major conclusion from this chapter is that there is no reason to believe that the Swedish beauty contest will result in an infrastructure of mast and base stations that, from a welfare point of view is superior to what an auction would have generated.

Chapter 14 by *Robert Stimson* provides a broad review of socioeconomic and spatial distributional issues in ICTs. It begins by referring to the implications of the shift from the Fordist (or industrial) to the post-Fordist (or post-industrial) era. The implications of ICTs for regional development, particularly from the perspective of endogenous growth, are then considered. It proceeds to look at the extent to which ICTs are enhancing the concentration or dispersal of activity in the context of urban systems, paying particular attention to equity issues resulting from the differential impacts of ICTs for both people and places. Consideration is given to public policy issues and regulatory frameworks for ICTs in the contexts of equitable access and regional development. At the end some tentative conclusions are proposed about the role of ICTs with respect to convergence and divergence in regional development. The scope of this chapter is much broader than in earlier chapters in this book. As such it provides an integration of several themes. Even if the scope of this chapter is broad, it generates a number of important general conclusions as regards the effects of ICTs and the implications of these effects for policy. It contends that the dominant trends surrounding the current extension of ICTs are far from being socially, geographically and culturally neutral. Most of the evidence seems to suggest that the processes of agglomeration and urbanisation and the rapid application of ICTs are mutually supporting each other. Further, it seems that urban systems have an innate tendency to create an imbalance between a relatively few diverse cities with innovative milieu, which actually specialise in churning new ideas and more specialised, more numerous and often smaller places with more specialised industrial environments. Thus, the evidence appears to suggest that divergence rather than convergence in regional development should be the expected outcome of the impacts of ICTs, and that socioeconomic differentiation seems to be exacerbated rather than diluted by ICTs, at least over the intermediate future. This implies that it is necessary to incorporate ICTs into the core thinking about planning and regulating urban and regional environments and urban systems. These conclusions are of great interest not least since the political thinking on ICTs often is based on the too simple assumption that general access to computers, broadband and mobile phone connections would make lagging regions more competitive. Obviously, much more is needed from public policy than measures to create equal access to ICTs if regional convergence is to be achieved!

The five chapters in this discussion on telecommunications and policy offer important contributions to our understanding of the digital economy. At the same time they highlight the limits of our understanding. Telecommunications policy, regional policies, urban policies and public policy in general need to be reformulated to fit the new framework generated by the penetration of a new general purpose technology. Unfortunately, we do not yet fully know what a reformulated policy should look like. This is a major challenge for future research on the emerging digital economy.

References

Bresnahan T, Trajtenberg M (1995) General purpose technologies: "engines of growth". Journal of Econometrics 65: 83-108

Helpman E, Trajtenberg M (1998) Diffusion of general purpose technologies. In Helpman E (ed) General purpose technologies and economic growth. MIT Press, Cambridge, MA, pp. 85-119

Krugman P (1991) Geography and trade. MIT Press, Cambridge, MA

Lipsey RG, Becar C, Carlaw K (1998) What requires explanation? In Helpman E (ed) General purpose technologies and economic growth. MIT Press, Cambridge, MA, pp. 15-54

List of Contributors

Andersson, Martin
  Jönköping International Business School, Jönköping University
  P.O. Box 1026, SE-551 11, Jönköping
  Sweden

Bjuggren, Per Olof
  Jönköping International Business School, Jönköping University
  P.O. Box 1026, SE-551 11, Jönköping
  Sweden

Dinc, Mustafa
  Development Economics Data Group, The World Bank
  1818 H Street NW, Washington DC 20433
  USA

Friis, Christian
  LänsTeknikCentrum AB (LTC)
  Elmiavagen 9, SE-554 54, Jönköping
  Sweden

Haynes, Kingsley E.
  School of Public Policy, George Mason University
  4400 University Dr., Fairfax, VA 22030
  USA

Johansson, Börje
  Jönköping International Business School, Jönköping University
  P.O. Box 1026, SE-551 11, Jönköping
  Sweden

Karlsson, Charlie
  Jönköping International Business School, Jönköping University
  P.O. Box 1026, SE-551 11, Jönköping
  Sweden

Klaesson, Johan
  Jönköping International Business School, Jönköping University

P.O. Box 1026, SE-551 11, Jönköping
Sweden

Malecki, Edward J
Department of Geography, The Ohio State University
1036 Derby Hall, 154 N. Oval Mall, Columbus, OH 43210
USA

Paulsson, Thomas
AstraZeneca Sweden AB
Se-151 85, Södertälje
Sweden

Pettersson, Lars
Jönköping International Business School, Jönköping University
P.O. Box 1026, SE-551 11, Jönköping
Sweden

Polenske, Karen R.
Department of Urban Studies and Planning, Massachusetts Institute of
Technology (MIT)
77 Massachusetts Avenue, 9-535, Cambridge, MA 02139
USA

Soete, Luc
Maastricht Economic Research Institute on Innovation and Technology,
Maastricht University
Tongersestraat 49, NL-6211 LM Maastricht
The Netherlands

Stenberg, Peter L.
Economic Research Service, U.S. Department of Agriculture
1800 M Street NW, Washington DC 20036-5802
USA

Stimson, Robert J.
Center for Research into Sustainable Urban and Regional Futures, University of
Queensland
Level 8, Building 69, Room 814, St Lucia, Queensland 4069
Australia

Stough, Roger R
School of Public Policy, George Mason University
4400 University Dr., Fairfax, VA 22030
USA

Yilmaz, Serdar
Social Development Department, The World Bank
1818 H Street NW, Washington DC 20433
USA

Figures

Tables

Index

Printing: Krips bv, Meppel
Binding: Stürtz, Würzburg